West of the Blindman
Observations of a Half Century

By
Fred Schutz

Edited by William Baergen and David C. Jones

With a Foreword by
Myrna Pearman

National Library of Canada Cataloguing in Publication Data

Schutz, Fred (Frederick George), 1920-
West of the Blindman: observations of a half century / Fred
Schutz;
William Baegen, David C. Jones, eds.; Myrna Pearlman, fore-
word.

Includes index.
ISBN 1-55056-957-0

1. Schutz, Fred (Frederick George), 1920- 2.
Pioneers—Alberta—Blindman River Valley—Biography. 3.
Blindman River
Valley (Alta.)—Biography. 4. Blindman River Valley (Alta.)—
History.
I. Jones, David C., 1943- II. Baegen, William. III. Central Alberta
Regional Museums Network. IV. Central Alberta Historical
Society. V.
Title.
FC3695.B55S35 2003 971.23'3 C2003-911101-6

This book is published with the financial assistance of the Alberta
Historical Resources Foundation.

1st printing 2003
Printed and bound in Canada

Published by
The Joint Publications Committee,
Central Alberta Historical Society &
Central Alberta Regional Museums Network
4525-47A Avenue
Red Deer, AB., Canada
T4N 6Z6

TABLE OF CONTENTS

FAUNA

LAND AND SKY

FOREWORD

The Rimbey Record was delivered to our rural route mailbox each Wednesday afternoon. For our family, the highlight of reading this fine weekly was Fred Schutz's column, "West of the Blindman." We perused it without fail, partly because it was always so interesting, and partly because Fred was such a close personal friend.

My earliest recollection of Fred is of him, newly acquainted with our family, standing beside an open window of our old barn. He was patiently trying to have a conversation with our father, who was milking cows at the time. We children soon discovered that Fred was of the perfect height and temperament to act as a solid and accommodating landing pad, so for the entire duration of that milking, we would launch ourselves out the window and onto his shoulders. He caught us safely and accepted the torment with grace and humour.

Grace and a sense of humour are two of the many characteristics that describe Fred Schutz. A sharp intelligence, a keen sense of observation, a quick wit, a remarkable memory, and a deep respect for the earth are a few of his other attributes. Add to this impressive list his sense of adventure, his natural ability with words, and his insatiable appetite for all things related to history, archaeology, antiques, astronomy, photography, travel and natural history.

It was Fred's keen interest in nature, archaeology and antiques that first brought him to the acquaintance of our family. These were passions he shared with our father, and the two of them, over a span of some twenty years, shared many an interesting hour poking around abandoned homesteads, scouring local fields for Indian artifacts or going to antique auctions. As we children grew, we came to form our own friendships with Fred. During our school years, he helped us choose interesting topics for 4-H speeches, he listened to our many stories with interest, and he always knew the answers to puzzling questions. He took us on rambles into the west country and showed us unnamed lakes, calcified springs, loon nests, delicate orchids and feather moss. He taught us that the night was not to be feared, but was instead an ethereal world full of sounds to recognize and constellations to identify. He taught us how to draw on artist's fungi, chew spruce gum, stare down a porcupine, and to tell an aspen poplar from a balsam. He first identified for me the boisterous call of the ruby-crowned kinglet and the haunting boom of a bittern. Fred and I tracked down great gray owlets one afternoon, following their raucous shrieks deep into the forest. A bolt of lightning suddenly struck a tree just metres from where we stood. The magnitude of that bolt, the mess of shattered splinters that were once a massive tree, and the purity of the ozone that filled the air, provided for both of us a sobering sense of vulnerability, insignificance and relief.

On drives through the countryside, Fred would provide fascinating chronicles of the triumphs, eccentricities and hardships of long-deceased pioneers. He showed us spots where, as a youngster, he harvested bounties of wild blueberries or strawberries, and he once pointed out the spot where he helped extricate a petrified elk antler (thereafter used as a hat rack) from a peat bog. He also told us stories of his high school years at Monte Vista, a one-room school located on the quarter section purchased by our parents when they first settled in that district in the early 1950s. He impressed upon us that shank's mare was an authentic mode of transportation.

The Schutz family home, which we visited frequently, was like a mini-museum and library—jammed floor to ceiling with books, rocks, Indian artifacts, memorabilia, plants, antiques and photographs. Visits, which were adventures in themselves for us children, always ended with a lavish lunch that Gertie set out for us beside the soul-warming heat of their old Home Comfort stove. Last winter I accompanied Fred to check on the now-empty Schutz house. As I stepped inside, the smell of fires past swept me back to a warm wood stove, a gurgling kettle, wild strawberry jam on fresh bread, and Charlie sitting quietly in his favourite chair, smiling.

Although time and space have often separated us, I have many times called upon Fred for sage advice, and have relied on both his memory and his records for input on a wide range of issues and topics. And in the decades that have passed so swiftly since our childhood rambles, Fred has always been considered an honorary member of the Pearman family.

I was delighted when, before leaving on one of his many overseas trips in the early 1980s, Fred asked if I might pen a few guest "West of the Blindman" columns. I feel similarly privileged to have been asked by the publishers of this book to write a foreword. As preparation for the assignment, I was asked to offer input into the selection process. The reading was as delightful as the choosing was difficult. However, I feel that the editors and their helpers have done an admirable job in making the final selection of these 222 columns, a mere sampling of the more than 2,200 columns that he wrote. It is my hope that the means can soon be found to publish the remainder of these important works.

West of the Blindman is a gift of priceless value, a gift bequeathed by Fred Schutz to the people of central Alberta. By setting pen to paper, week after week, month after month, year after year, he has captured four decades' worth of events, observations, characters, experiences, details, mysteries and phenomena that would otherwise have been long lost and forgotten. His columns are unique because they are both a chronicle of his life as well as an engaging and eloquent series of vignettes on a wide and eclectic variety of topics related to natural and cultural history. They tell of wild places and wild creatures. They tell of the original peoples who once called these lands home, and they tell of both pioneers who moved into and settled the area—the Schutz family among them—and of subsequent generations. They recount bits and bites of life and death that have rarely, if ever, appeared in more traditional literature. Where but in *West of the Blindman* would we have the opportunity to read lively and interesting accounts of such items as the slop pail and the stone boat? How would we know that hemp was once a valued garden plant, or that what many believe to be pemmican is really the sclerotia of a fungus called tuckahoe? Where else would we hear about the mysterious burial, long ago, of a little girl, or learn that some pioneers lived in dugout houses, that bedbugs and houseflies caused endless grief, that jackrabbits dance under the light of a full moon for the pure joy of it, that there exists a stone with *Holy Water* etched upon it, or that Drayton Valley, at the onset of its boom period, was dusty and chaotic? Where else would we be apprised of the fine art of hilltop sitting, learn that Fred's farm is at the eastern edge of the alpine fir, be reminded that tamaracks look "bewitchingly feminine" in the spring, when they are a "wistful shade of light, ferny green," or find out that, following the incredible snowstorm of 1951, folks drove their vehicles atop snowdrifts *over* the telephone lines? Fred, ever the diligent record-keeper, was able in later years to go back to his own records—dating back to 1943—and recount the dates and severity of major weather events, and to state with some authority that there have been many brown Christmases in years past, and that white-tailed deer were once absent, and ravens once rare, in central Alberta.

History is often considered to comprise only major events that transpire elsewhere, that nature occurs in some far-off wilderness, or that habitat loss affects only the tropical rainforest. But through *West of the Blindman*, Fred has documented the vitality and importance of local cultural and natural history. He has validated the notable contributions of those who came before us, and has endeavoured to instill in his readers a respect for the beauty and diversity of nature found in our own backyards and our own "back 40s." He has helped ensure that future generations—descendants of First Peoples, Bluffton-area pioneers and newcomers alike—will have a link to their past and to their land, and know that both are worth preserving.

Unlike columnists of large daily newspapers who address masses of nameless readers, Fred wrote to share his stories and his knowledge with his audience, many of whom he counted among his neighbours, friends and acquaintances. He didn't preach or admonish but he was not afraid to express his concern or opinions—the poisoning of wolves, the use of DDT, elk farming, and the destructive practice of forest clear-cutting, to name a few.

Fred's life and his writings have spanned interesting times—from the era when only those with sufficient fortitude survived, to the present, where much of the landscape he loved has been radically altered, and technology has brought dizzying changes to all aspects of modern life. As we find ourselves rushing ever faster in a society where speed and consumerism are the reigning mantras, it will do our souls good to peruse and savour this collection. Not only will we be richer for the reading, but we might also be encouraged to embrace some of the tenets by which Fred approached each day…tenets that have guided his long and productive life, a life that has been rich and interesting and full of in-the-moment adventures. From his column "September Gold," September 9, 1986, "…for goodness' sake don't go straight there. Dawdle a bit; stray from the pavement, meander down side roads and really see the country. Use shank's mare and hike the mountain trails or walk the railroad ties to new vistas. Get sidetracked into the little places…."

Myrna Pearman
Ellis Bird Farm
Lacombe, Alberta

ACKNOWLEDGMENTS

We are greatly indebted to the following friends and colleagues for their help in the preparation of this book: Morris Flewwelling, Annette Gray, Don Hepburn, Wendy Martindale (chair), Maxine O'Riordan and Lantry Vaughan of the Joint Publications Committee of The Central Alberta Historical Society & The Central Alberta Regional Museums Network; and Lorie Anderson, Joan O'Riordan, and Myrna Pearman. For the maps, we commend Dwight Arthur of Photek, Red Deer, and for the layout and printing we thank Sandy Beckel of Sage Creek Books and Jim Beckel of Friesens Printers. The photos are from Fred Schutz's personal collection, except for the small sunset picture on the cover, taken by Jon Paine, and the certificate on page 277.

William Baergen and David C. Jones, editors

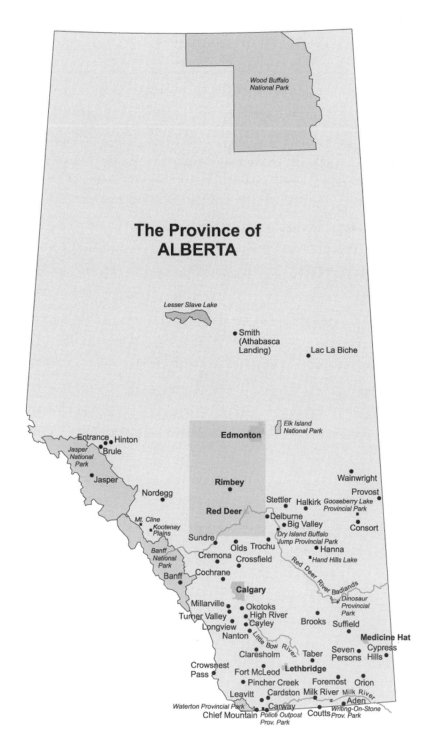

The Province of
ALBERTA

Wood Buffalo
National Park

Lesser Slave Lake

Smith
(Athabasca
Landing)

Lac La Biche

Elk Island
National Park

Edmonton

Entrance • Hinton
Jasper   Brule
National
Park
• Jasper

Rimbey

Wainwright

Provost

Nordegg

Stettler   Halkirk   Gooseberry Lake
Provincial Park

Red Deer

Delburne
Big Valley
Consort

Mt. Cline
• Kootenay
Plains

Dry Island Buffalo
Jump Provincial Park

Sundre
Hanna

Banff
National
Park

Olds   Trochu
Cremona   Crossfield

Hand Hills Lake

Red Deer River Badlands

Banff

Cochrane

Calgary

Dinosaur
Provincial
Park

Millarville
Turner Valley
Longview

Okotoks
High River
Cayley

Brooks
Suffield

Nanton

Medicine Hat

Little Bow River

Seven   Cypress
Persons   Hills

Claresholm

Taber

Crowsnest
Pass

Fort McLeod

Lethbridge

Pincher Creek   Foremost   Orion

Leavitt   Cardston   Milk River   Milk River

Aden

Waterton Provincial Park   Carway   Coutts   Writing-On-Stone
Prov. Park

Chief Mountain   Police Outpost
Prov. Park

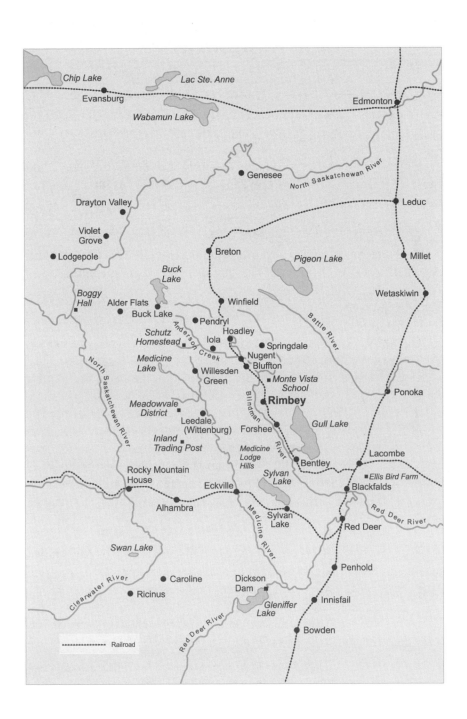

INTRODUCTION

Frederick George Schutz was born "in a prairie shack six miles west of Trochu, Alberta, at midnight on October 14, 1920."[1] The friend assisting his mother at his birth—in the absence of a medical doctor—was a young school teacher named Mamie Simpson, who was to become the well-known and well-loved dean of women at the University of Alberta. When his family moved to Iola, two years later, he found himself on the edge of settlement, with a freedom known to very few children today. This freedom in a natural environment undoubtedly contributed to his easy-going style, along with the love of nature and a desire to preserve it.

Fred's father, Charles, a multi-talented man, had been born and raised in London, England. His mother, Gertrude, a devoted and capable farm wife and mother, was born in Goulais Bay, Ontario. Fred has a brother, Allan, born at Iola in 1923, and a sister, Dorothy, also born at Iola, in 1926.[2]

The family farm at Iola was located on NW Section 2, Township 44, Range 4, West of the 5th Meridian, seventeen miles northwest of Rimbey, and nine miles west of Bluffton. Schooling was a problem for the Schutz family. The Blindman River District #4244 had a school three miles distant at SW 16-44-4-W5, but it operated only part-time between 1925 and 1935. The parents were determined, however, that their children should receive an education, and had been at the forefront of those organizing the Blindman River School District in 1925. For a few years, starting when Fred was in grade two, the Schutz children were driven to the Iola school by horse and buggy in summer, and horse and cutter in winter. The Department of Education paid the family seventy-five cents a day to drive the children the four and one half miles to and from school. Most often Father drove the eighteen miles, but sometimes it was Fred's grandfather or his mother. And some years the Schutz children took correspondence lessons.[3]

---

[1] Interview with Fred Schutz. Much of the information in this introduction comes from Fred's interviews with Ken Larsen in 1983 and Rod Trentham and Bill Baergen in 2002.

[2] Fred Schutz, *The Life and Times of Charlie Schutz* (Rimbey: The Printed Form, 2000), 1. See also Fred's columns "Gertrude" and "Charles Herbert Ernest Schutz" in *The Rimbey Record*, February 12, 1991, and March 27, 1974, respectively.

[3] Schutz, *Life and Times*, 55-56.

In 1935, when Blindman River school opened again, Fred took grade eight there. He took grade nine at Iola, and high school, from 1937 to 1941, at Monte Vista High School, northeast of Rimbey. Here he boarded five days a week with local families. His father paid sixty cents a day for his board, but Fred had to work each fall in the harvest fields to earn money for books and clothes for school.

To cover the seventeen miles home on weekends and back again, Fred writes, "I rode a bicycle, or walked to Bluffton where one of the family would meet me with team and buggy or sleigh. Sometimes I caught the train at the water tank and rode in or atop a boxcar from the water tank to Bluffton, and occasionally I walked the whole distance."[4]

Fred's habit of reading began early, and eventually led to a life of writing. He never took journalism, as such, but studied books on writing, and remembers being encouraged by one of his high school teachers, Pearl Zaharchuk.

His interest in writing about nature dates back to Sunday walks that the Schutz family enjoyed on section 11, the school section, immediately north of the Schutz homestead. It was a mix of open, park-like area, dense woods, spruce and tamarack swamp, hillside springs and a tiny creek that drained into the swamp. With its numerous berries—saskatoons, chokecherries, blueberries, raspberries, and hazelnuts; and wildlife—coyotes, Canada lynx, great horned owls, red-tailed hawks, saw-whet owls, pileated woodpeckers, ruffed grouse, rabbits, squirrels, deer and sometimes moose, red-breasted grosbeaks, warblers, vireos, and marsh-marigolds, "it was a square mile of wonder," said Fred, "a place of enchantment, a place to take visitors...."[5]

After high school, Fred helped his father on the farm, gradually taking over management of a mixed farm that had been developed out of a raw bush homestead. It became a grain farm in the 1940s and 1950s, and eventually a cattle ranch. By the late 1960s, grain had given way to hay crops and pasture for some fifty beef cows and their progeny.

As early as the 1940s and 1950s when eco-preservation was viewed with incredulity by many, Fred applied his conservation ethos to his ranching practices by preserving large tracts of natural habitat.

---

[4] Ibid, 56.

[5] Ibid, 31.

Fred ranched in the area until his retirement, which began in 1974. He moved off the farm to Rimbey in 1993 when vision loss brought on by macular degeneration prevented him from driving. Fred can still enjoy travel, however, and the summer of 2002 saw him take a trip to Russia. He reads with difficulty, and is no longer able to enjoy bird watching or canoeing. But he still writes. In January 2003, he published a biography of a former Bluffton pioneer and neighbour, John Christian Hinrichsen, a Nebraska transplant who settled in the area in 1921.

As children, Fred and his siblings had to create their own amusement. They were never bored, and the freedom to explore and experiment led to interests such as photography, astronomy, reading, archaeology, weather, cross-country skiing, hiking, canoeing, travel, bird-watching, rock hounding, even wild mushrooms. This variety of pursuits has given Fred a life both rich and satisfying. In an interview in September 2002, he said, "I am content with my life as I have lived it, not always as I once dreamed, but in some ways far beyond early expectations."

Fred remembers well the day in November 1954, when he hesitantly climbed the steps to the *The Rimbey Record* with three or

Fred's brother Allan at age nineteen.

Fred's sister Dorothy at age twenty-one

four articles he had written on outdoor topics to show the editor and ask if he were interested in publishing them. Editor Charlie Worton was not at the counter that day so Jack Parry, the assistant editor, read them. In a moment, he said, "Yes, we'll publish them for you." Fred was somewhat taken aback when he was told the paper would need a column once a week, but the die was cast. He determined to live with the deadlines, even though that meant sacrificing "Lux Theatre" and "Lucille Ball."

Fred's column, "West of the Blindman," appeared in *The Rimbey Record* from 1954 to 1997—a span of forty-three years. The column also ran in the *Eckville Examiner* and the *Innisfail Province* for a few years, with occasional appearances in the *Rocky Mountaineer*. "West of the Blindman" started out with an emphasis on the natural history of Rimbey and west central Alberta, but soon it seamlessly incorporated all kinds of human history and local flavour. Fred is a great storyteller. In fact, he won many awards and citations over the years, including the prestigious Cadogan Award for Outstanding Columnist in a Canadian Weekly Newspaper in 1989.

In one of his 1962 columns Fred suggested that Rimbey needed a museum to preserve its history. He was concerned that the Rimbey Anglican Church, built in 1907, was to be demolished and that the first school house in the area, built in 1902, was also in jeopardy. He worried about American oilmen in the 1960s who attended farm sales and auctions and bought up all manner of artifacts like coal oil lamps, furniture, and antique dolls. These they would purchase at fire-sale prices, and local residents tended to undervalue them. Fred was convinced that the only way to preserve these artifacts was in a museum.

In 1962 Fred wrote a history book entitled *Pas-ka-poo: An Early History of Rimbey and the Upper Blindman Valley*—before government funds were made available for such projects. That year he was elected president of the Rimbey Historical Society, a position he held for seven years. During his term the town applied for a centennial grant and purchased five acres of land for a museum. Lieutenant Governor Grant MacEwan attended the official opening of the new Pas-ka-poo Park and Museum in 1967—fully six years before the much larger community of Red Deer opened its museum.

Serving as honorary director for many years, Fred remained active in the Rimbey Historical Society into the mid-1990s. He also joined the Alberta Natural History Society (ANHS) in 1969, after making a presentation to the group on "The Snowshoe Hare or Bush Rabbit"—one of many presentations he made over the years. Though the ANHS had over a half-century of history, having been formed in 1906 under the presidency of Dr. Henry George, it was slipping in the late 1960s when Fred joined. Membership had dwindled to a small group of bird watchers with nine to twelve members attending monthly meetings. The year's financial transactions, Fred recalls, totalled $71.41. Fred was one of a handful of people who revitalized the ANHS around a broad range of environmental concerns.

But the name, Alberta Natural History Society, was often confused with the newly established Federation of Alberta Naturalists (1970), so the society changed its name. Fred's suggestion—Red Deer River Naturalists (RDRN)—was accepted in 1976, and he served as president for the 1976-1977 term.

With the naturalists, Fred made several monthly presentations and led many field trips where he shared his knowledge of natural and human history. He rode with a group on horseback to the Howse Pass in 1974, and returned on foot in 1976. He did the research and wrote the letters to have a large tract of land near Bluffton designated a Natural Area in the 1970s just after the Province initiated the Natural Areas Program.

Later, with the RDRN, Fred submitted many briefs on the Eastern Slopes hearing, Dickson Dam (Site 6 Hearings), and the Odyssey proposal at the Kootenay Plains (near Nordegg)—all of which aimed to preserve the natural environment on the eastern side of the Rockies in the face of economic development. The RDRN was recognized with an Emerald Award (2000), the Canadian Federation of Naturalists-Affiliate Award (2001), and from the Province's Voluntary Steward Program with the Steward Excellence Award (2001). And Fred was recognized with the second Owl Award from the RDRN in 1999 for his significant contributions to that organization over three decades.

In the early 1980s, as the petrochemical industry started to surround the Ellis farm, the RDRN entered into a year and a half of legal negotiations with Union Carbide to honour and uphold the years of work that Charlie ("Mr. Bluebird") and Winnie Ellis had put into the protection and preservation of the mountain bluebird. Fred worked on that committee and was a founding director of Ellis Bird Farm Ltd., and served on that board for ten years. The Ellis Bird Farm welcomes thousands of visitors each year, including many school groups. Its director, Myrna Pearman—who grew up in Rimbey and cites Fred as an important mentor—travels rural Alberta, teaching young people about rural conservation. Ellis Bird Farm Ltd. received an Emerald Award in 1997, and Myrna Pearman received the Roger Tory Peterson Education Award in the early 1990s. In 1983, Fred received the Loran L. Goulden Memorial Award from the Federation of Alberta Naturalists for his contribution to the preservation of natural history.[6]

In his spare time, Fred was a director of The Rimbey Rockhounds and of The Bluffton Agricultural Society.

Besides the columns in *The Rimbey Record*, and his *Pas-ka-poo* book, Fred wrote *Hog Pool: A History of the Blindman Valley Shipping Association Co-operative* [c. 1982]; *The Life and Times of Charlie Schutz* [2000]; "Irene Wright, Rimbey's Confidante" in *Aspenland: Local Knowledge and a Sense of Place* [1998]; "History of Buildings in Pas-ka-poo Park" in *The Rimbey Review* [2001], and *John Christian Hinrichsen—A little Ahead of His Time* [2002]. He contributed articles to *Tributaries of the Blindman* [1972]; *Remember When: The History of Trochu and District* [1976]; *Over the Years* [1982], a history of the Rimbey district; and to the *Alberta Bird Atlas* (n.d.), a five-year project of the Federation of Alberta Naturalists.

In 2002 The Historical Society of Alberta recognized Fred for his outstanding contribution to Alberta history for half a century.

William Baergen
Rod Trentham
Michael Dawe

---

[6] Ken Larsen nominated Fred for this award.

PEOPLE

GERTRUDE
February 12, 1991

Goulais Bay, Ontario, where my mother was born, was a small centre in the late 1890s, with a school, a post office, and sometimes a store. Although it was four miles from the water, it was named for the bay on Lake Superior situated just above Sault Ste. Marie. "We could hear the sound of the ships' horns when there was a fog," my mother used to tell us. "I missed that sound when I left the Bay," she said. She didn't get down to the shore very often as a child, but once or twice a year a group of school children, usually including Gertie's older brother and the teacher, would climb Slate Mountain behind their one room school, and from there they would have a broad sweeping view of the lake. "It was just like looking out over the ocean," she said, "you couldn't see the other side."

Gertie was second in a family of five. Her mother died when she was ten, and since she was the oldest girl, she became housekeeper and mother to three younger children. Her father owned a farm which did not allow him to make ends meet, and so he worked in the lumber camps during the winter months, until he came west to Alberta before World War I. Our mother did not come west until 1915, when she was twenty-one. She came first to Saskatchewan, where she had uncles, aunts and cousins, and where she lived for a time in a sod house, then to Trochu, Alberta, where her father had a farm. When she came, she did not plan to stay for the rest of her life, but then she met my father, who lived two miles down the road from the Coates farm. They were married in Calgary on December 3, 1919, and farmed at Trochu until 1922, when they moved to a raw homestead which my father had filed on the year before. I still reside on that homestead.

My mother was a full partner on that homestead, as over the years it gradually became a farm. Here for the next fifty-eight years

1

she would live, raise a family, help develop the land and take part in community affairs.

She was not, at first, a willing resident of the Auxiliary Hospital, and always wanted to go home. "I'm practically as good as I ever was," she would say to me, but as she entered her tenth decade and her mind receded more and more into the past, she became more content with the life in an institution. For ten years she received the nursing care and constant attention which she needed and to which Albertans are extremely fortunate to have access.

In those first years in the hospital she was fairly mobile, getting outdoors on sunny days with the aid of a stroller or walker. Later she was confined to a wheelchair, and almost wore one out, so many miles she put on it, paddling with her feet. In January 1986 some kind and thoughtful person presented several of the Auxiliary residents with Cabbage Patch dolls. Our mother was one of the recipients and it was the best Christmas present she had that year, for her, for her family, and, I am sure, for the hospital staff, because that doll became her almost constant companion. It made her less restless, and a generally happier person. She held it, talked to it, even sang to it, and showed it off to her visitors.

Gertie did not have an easy childhood. Her education was cut short at age fourteen because her father thought her too young to go away to high school, and he perhaps felt also that it would be a financial hardship. So she went to live with her aunts, Aunt Mary MacDonald and later Aunt Mary Healy. She loved and remembered and often talked of these two aunts for the rest of her life. They taught her everything she would need to know to be a good and efficient twentieth-century housewife. She learned to cook and sew, to churn butter and make vinegar, to card wool and to quilt, to make good bread and to make soap from beef fat and candles from tallow. They developed her green thumb in the vegetable garden and flower garden and in raising house plants.

It seemed to me that the loss of her mother made Gertie an adult at ten and a teenager (a term not in use at that time) at about seventeen, or eighteen, after she left the households of her Aunt Marys. Life would be no bed of roses after she came west, either. Her introduction to life on a prairie homestead included walking miles on spring days putting out gopher poison, and helping with the haying in summer and harvest in the fall. There were some good times, as some pictures in her photograph album attest, but unfortunately it was wartime, and many commodities, including sugar, were scarce.

2

Any extravagance was frowned upon, including desserts, fancy parties, big weddings or any social functions unless they were in aid of the war effort. Worse than all this, however, was the epidemic of influenza that swept the continent, taking many lives, including that of Gertie's younger brother, Clarence, who died on a troop ship on his way to England in 1918. Although the official cause of death was given as pneumonia, his family seemed to know that it was the flu. During World War II she had a son in the forces, my brother Allan, to worry about.

The homestead and the Depression were struggles of another sort. The first fall in the Iola district, my father left with the team and bundle rack to go back to Trochu for the threshing, leaving my mother alone with me, not yet two years old, for about six weeks. He left her with less than a dollar in cash, and she spent it on potatoes, bought from a neighbour. We had arrived on the homestead July 22, too late to plant a garden that year. She had, however, picked and canned many quarts of wild fruit during the summer, mostly saskatoons, raspberries and black currants. She had some canned meat, a milk cow named Spot, and some laying hens. That was probably one of the most difficult periods on the homestead.

For the rest of her active life, Gertie's favourite summer pastime was picking wild fruit. Then she would have to stay up until midnight cleaning and canning it. Her girlhood training forbade her to put off until the morrow anything she could do today. It stood her in good stead during the Great Depression, too. She used every trick in the book to feed and clothe a growing family of three kids. In those years there was usually one and sometimes two extra men to cook for, as well as my grandfather, making eight in all. Nothing was ever wasted and a dollar went a long way. When the time came that money was more plentiful, she was still very careful with it.

She knew one way to spend her money though. Like my father, she loved to travel. They went to England to visit relatives there. They went with my sister to California to visit her sister Stella. They went nearly every summer to Vancouver or Victoria or Prince Rupert and to many other places in British Columbia where Allan and Grace have lived during Allan's career with the B. C. Forest Service. She loved her six grandchildren and liked to spend as much time with them as possible. And her grandchildren all loved her.

We are extremely fortunate here in Alberta to be able to provide the care for our elderly citizens that has been exemplified by the Auxiliary Hospital in Rimbey. Speaking for all of Gertie's family,

Gertrude Schutz, c. 1970.

we are very, very grateful to the staff there for the care they have given for more than ten years. The Auxiliary enabled our mother to wring the last bit from a long and useful life.

People have told me that they dread having to go to the Auxiliary, even as a visitor. They say they find it too depressing. Depressing it may be for some, but I take a different view. I see these people as the fortunate ones. They have lived a full life—usually a longer than average life. If most of them are over the hill and some are out to lunch to use twentieth century idioms, is that not a small price to pay at the end?

Gertie Schutz, despite some arthritic pain, and despite what amounted to banishment from the rural home where she had spent a major part of her life, never lost her cheerful mien or her sense of humour. What more could we ask?

CHARLES HERBERT ERNEST SCHUTZ
March 27, 1974

My father said, not long ago, "I have no kick coming. I've had a pretty good life."

I know that life was not exactly a bed of roses for him as a young man, but I know from the stories I've heard him tell from the time I was old enough to listen, that he managed to get the most out of life, both in times of prosperity and in times of adversity.

He was born in 1889, in London, England, number five in a family of ten, five boys and five girls. At the age of sixteen years he left his home and family to come to Canada, to his brother Bill's prairie homestead near Rapid City, Manitoba, about twenty miles from Brandon. His most vivid memories of his first Canadian winter were of himself and his brother hauling hay into Brandon for sale to the livery barns, and the long trip home in the sub-zero night, and getting a fire going in the cast iron heater to warm the shack,

Charles Ernest Schutz at age twenty-three, 1913.

then making their supper of bread and jam, the bread frozen so hard they would have to chop it into chunks with an axe on the kindling block.

My father must have decided that life on a prairie homestead was perhaps not as glamorous as he had pictured it back in London, because he headed for Vancouver in the spring, and the following year, 1908, found him in Victoria, where he got a job in a bakery. Jobs were very scarce in those years and pay was barely adequate, but having a trade proved a help, and over the next several years his wanderlust led him to such places as Seattle, San Francisco, St. Paul, Minnesota, and back to Alberta to look at homestead land around Athabasca Landing and Flat Lake. Then he rented his brother's farm at Trochu for a few years before finally homesteading this quarter, NW 2-44-4-W5, in the month of June 1921.

Because I have spent almost as many days on this homestead as my father, I know something of his joys and his sorrows here, his work and his fun. I know about the achievements of which he is proud and the dreams that never were realized; the gains and the times that were forever tempered by things like Depressions and hailstorms and unseasonal snowstorms.

This homestead was the place he settled down and decided to stay for a while; where he and my mother worked together to raise a family and help and build a community, and to make a farm out of a ten-dollar piece of real estate. I know he felt he had succeeded in his goals, not beyond his wildest dreams, exactly, but in sufficient measure to be able to rest content at the end of his days; to be able to say, "I have no kick coming."

My father loved to travel, and in 1972, at the age of 82, he and my mother went to England to visit his three remaining sisters. It was his third trip back since he first left home. Then in the summer of 1973 he enjoyed in full measure a motor trip to Los Angeles and back, with no ill effects of any kind. That was to be his last extended trip.

He will be missed as much as most men by those he leaves behind. He will be greatly missed by members of the younger generation, for there was a great friendship between himself and his six grandchildren, and, in fact, he had many friends in the school-age and teenage groups.

But none of us is indispensable, no matter how much we may be missed when we go, and we all know this, so the world goes on, and we go on....

TALES MY FATHER TOLD ME
October 27, 1992

When my father was sixteen years old, his life took a radical turn. His parents bought him a steamer trunk, a twenty-pound ($100) life insurance policy with London Life, and a ticket to Montreal on the *Empress of Ireland*. The year was 1906 and Charlie was bound for the Manitoba homestead of his brother Bill, who was twenty-two and had been in Canada for two years. Bill lived near Rapid City, twenty miles north of Brandon. The main crop on his land seems to have been hay, and my father arrived on that homestead in plenty of time for the haying season. Charlie seemed to have good memories of helping with the haying that first summer, although it must not have been easy for a 130-pound boy who had never before been out of the city of London, at that time the world's largest.

There were some diversions for a city kid. One evening after work, Bill handed Charlie a double-barreled shotgun and told him to go down to the slough and see if he could bag a duck for supper. It was probably the first gun my father ever had his hands on. "I crept through the tall grass close to the slough's edge," he related. "I loaded both barrels, squatted on my heels and waited until some ducks came over. I pulled back the hammers, got some ducks in the sights and pulled both triggers! The next thing I remember was being flat on my back in the grass with a mighty sore shoulder." I don't remember whether or not they had roast duck for supper.

Winter on the homestead was not so much fun. Charlie remembered the long trips to Brandon to sell the hay at the stockyards or at the livery stables. They would load up the load the day before, then leave at daylight on the twenty-mile trip into town, arriving about noon. They would unload the hay, eat their lunch of partly frozen baloney sandwiches, buy a few groceries and head home.

6

The horses would make better time in this direction, with only an empty rack to pull, but it was a much colder, less comfortable trip for Bill and Charlie. On the way in they would be reclining in the hay, out of the wind and fairly snug. Going home they would be standing on the bare floor of the empty rack. They would usually arrive well after dark, with the temperature often at twenty below, Fahrenheit. Sometimes the roads would be drifted, making them really late. They would put the horses in the barn, unharness and feed them, and head for the shack. "We usually found it just as cold inside as out," said my father. "We'd get a fire going and thaw out a bit, but we would be so hungry we couldn't wait to cook a proper meal. We would set the butter dish and the jam can close to the stove. We'd take a loaf of frozen bread to the kindling block and chop off pieces with an axe and put these on the stove to thaw. We would chip out some jam with the butcher knife and have our first grub since noon. Soon the shack would be warm and life would be back to normal."

THE COPPER STICK
February 5, 1991

Beside me on my desk is a short length of broomstick, but it is no ordinary piece of broomstick. For one thing, it dates back at least seventy-eight years to 1913. For another thing, one side is carved the full length, and third, I know the story behind it.

In 1913 my father was living in Victoria where he had a job with a bakery. His brother Bill was in the Yukon where he had been stationed for three years with the Royal North West Mounted Police. Bill's five-year stint with the Force expired in May that year. He would rejoin in 1914, but in the meantime he had plans to take a trip back to London, England, to visit his father and mother, two brothers and five sisters, whom he had not seen in nine years. He wrote his brother, Charlie, my father, suggesting that he go along.

Charlie was just able to scrape up the funds for his train fare and steamship passage, but he, too, longed to see his family again. He had been gone from them for seven years. He was twenty-three. He met Bill in Grand Central Station in New York, and they sailed for Southhampton. I believe they spent some weeks in London, and by all accounts had a very enjoyable time. My father often talked about that trip.

My grandmother was a hard-working woman with a large family to care for. The washing was done in what was known as a copper, a

7

built-in wash boiler beneath which was a fireplace. To lift the clothes from this hot boiler into a rinsing tub, one used a copper stick, in this case a short length of broom handle. My father picked up this copper stick one day, and with his pocket knife, began to carve. Coming from Victoria, he was quite familiar with west coast totem poles, and, from memory, he proceeded to carve ten totem faces on that eighteen-inch stick. Had I been his mother, I might have put that copper stick aside then and there, and found another one for the wash. She did no such thing ... she continued to use it for the purpose at hand.

We now skip half a century, to 1963, when my father went back for a second time to the city of his birth. He found London vastly changed, even in this city where change comes slowly and reluctantly. But one of the things that had changed only a little was the old copper stick. It was still in use, passed down from my grandmother to my Aunt Elsie and the carved faces that decorated all one side of it were still plain to see, although the end ones, top and bottom, were almost worn away. My father couldn't believe his eyes and his sister kindly gave it to him to bring home to Canada.

Under more favourable circumstances my father might have been a sculptor, a painter, an astronomer, a mathematician or an architect, even a great photographer; for these were his hobbies and his dreams, and he had beautiful handwriting. So much potential subjugated to an Alberta homestead, but he never complained about that.

THE BAREFOOT BOY
May 15, 1957

Where is the barefoot boy who used to wade the roadside ditches on the way to school, searching for frogs and frightening millions of tadpoles? He could once be found on any sunny morning in early summer, sauntering along, hands in pockets, picking dandelions with his toes, and flipping them this way and that. Shoeless and carefree, he loved the cool, moist feel of the fresh-tilled fields of spring, but found September's stubble less to his liking.

Today he is a rare sight, even on a quiet country road, and if he is seen occasionally, he is usually found to be in the pre-school-age group. Twenty to twenty-five years ago, a large proportion of all youngsters under the age of fourteen who attended country schools went barefoot all summer long, indoors or out, at work or at play, at school or at home, and quite often away from home as well.

Not only boys but many girls, too, enjoyed this freedom from foot attire, although they were by no means so keen on it as were the boys. They had to don shoes when the going got rough; their soles wouldn't callous like the boys'. Boys climbed trees, walked rails, stole second, ran backwards, pole vaulted and waded many miles in the course of a day, and when they had to put on their shoes they found their activities much hampered and restricted.

Many kids came barefoot to school before all the snow was gone from the roadsides and with the water ice cold in the ditches; and for all anyone can tell, it didn't hurt them a bit. In our house there was a rule. On the quarter section across the road there was a hillside spring where the ice piled up all winter long and made a wonderful place for winter play. The rule was that we could go barefoot when the ice had all melted in the spring, or by the 24th of May, whichever came first. This made for some excitement if the weather was warm and it seemed we would see the last of the ice before the King's birthday. We watched it very closely, I can tell you.

Today that rule wouldn't work the same. The spring does not flow at anything like its former volume, and we would be going shoeless along about the first week of May.

There are some disadvantages to unshod feet as I remember. First, the rose bushes. In the woods you had to watch every step, although some boys developed such thick, tough soles before midsummer that rose briars never bothered them. Another disadvantage was having to wash your feet every night before bedtime. If it was raining, or had been raining, this was easy. You just went out and ran around in some wet grass somewhere.

Then there were always stubbed toes. Many an adult who grew up in this part of the country can point to blunted digits to this day. Other hazards were rusty nails in grass-covered boards, and bits of broken glass. Looking back, it almost seems that many benefits were pretty well balanced by the drawbacks. Today's kids, if they are wise, will continue to go about with shoes on. Still, if they do, they will be missing one of childhood's more pleasurable sensations.

LEARNING TO SKATE
February 18, 1986

I learned to skate on a pair of blades that today would be found only in a museum, and, in fact, were museum material even then. They had been my father's, and he probably skated on them at the St. Paul-Minneapolis Winter Carnival in 1910. They clamped onto leather-soled boots and were tightened with a key like a clock key. I haven't seen them for a while, but I am sure they are still around somewhere. They were too big for my younger brother, Allan, but he needed skates too. One fall he took the money he had earned as his half of our gopher tail and magpie egg bounty, which at one cent per tail and two cents per egg didn't amount to a whole lot, and he bought himself a pair of brand new skates. He had found just what he needed at a price he could afford in Eaton's catalogue, that wish book of every kid that came up through the Great Depression. For one dollar even he got a pair of steel blades and twenty-four screws for attaching them to the soles of his summer boots. Leather boots were not worn in winter anyway and he would be able to leave the skates on until the snow went in the spring.

Our skating rink was on the creek about a quarter of a mile from the house, on the Peabody side of the road. Here the creek flooded naturally each winter at a small open meadow, making us a rink thirty or forty metres long by twenty metres wide. In addition to that we could follow the course of the creek among the willows, upstream to the foot of the hill where we skied, downstream a shorter distance to the road. An axe borrowed from the wood pile was used to extend and widen the way and make some side runs. A scoop shovel borrowed from the chop bin was used to clear snow and twigs from the ice. On the main rink we could use a hand-pushed ice scraper, made from a three-foot length of eight-inch board with a four-foot willow handle nailed to it, trimmed at the bottom edge with old wagon-box iron for a smoother job of ice clearing.

Five kids spent hours down there on that rink after school: my brother Allan, sister Dorothy, who didn't yet have skates, Wilfred and Marion Connett, who lived on the other side of the creek, and myself. We groomed that patch of ice amongst the willows daily. It was incredible how much work five kids can do in the name of fun. Had our parents worked us like that, they would have risked censure if not arrest for child abuse or whatever the term may have been in those days.

If the ice got rough or cracks began to erode enough to trip a skater, we attempted to improve it by flooding. If we could find a place where creek water was backing up into the snow at a few inches' higher elevation than the ice, we would try to utilize it by careful and devious channelling. Failing that, we would chop a hole with an axe in what seemed a sure place to find water and wet the rink down using the old three-gallon-bucket method. Sometimes we came home to supper without having put on our skates, and sometimes all our work went for nothing as snow or wind or other weather phenomena ruined the surface. Or perhaps a pair of snow-shoe rabbits would decide to play a game of tag on our rink just when the new ice was in the slush stage.

And that, kiddies, is how we learned to skate back in the Great Depression.

I ALMOST MISS THE TRAIN
March 16, 1960

I was running alongside a boxcar, about to haul myself aboard the northbound train before it picked up speed, when I stumbled over a stake that stuck up several inches above the shoulder of the grade and that seemed to have been driven there for the express purpose of sending me sprawling.

I can still remember those heavy wheels clanking by at face level before I was on my feet and running again to catch the second car back from the one I had missed.

The place: the water tower beside the Blindman. The time: a good many years ago.

Possibly a present day resident of Hoadley who watched my ungraceful performance from a window of the nearby Alfred Schrader home will also remember that day.

This was long before school buses were seen in the Blindman Valley, and I often caught the *Peanut* here at the water tank on my way home from Monte Vista High School for the weekend. By leaving school thirty minutes early on Friday afternoon, and if the train was not too close to its schedule, I could pretty well depend on catching my ride, because the old steam locomotive always stopped here to take on water.

The Peanut, *1948.*

11

Once or twice I missed it, owing to the fact that its schedule was so unreliable that you couldn't even rely on its being late. Then I had two alternatives. I could follow it down the track on shank's mare, or I could take to the road in hopes of catching a ride. Even more annoying was to wait for a good while, then start out walking, thinking it must have gone early, only to hear the whistle behind me after I had walked a mile down the track—and in a few minutes to see it go rolling by.

If I caught it and the day was fine, I rode to Bluffton atop a boxcar. If the weather was unpleasant, I rode in an empty, or sometimes I simply stood between two cars. Rarely did I spend a quarter to ride in the coach. That was not only a waste of good money but much less fun.

Often I had the company of other travellers: men who asked about the prospects of a job in the harvest fields, or, later in the fall, were heading for Winfield to seek work in the lumber camps. And a motley bunch they were, I can assure you. Once or twice I even rode with a genuine hobo who was not looking for work of any sort.

I WALK THE LINE
March 26, 1985

I am driving along Highway 12 between Rimbey and Bluffton. It is early winter. A dirty east wind is blowing, but I am warm and comfortable; have been since I left Calgary two and a half hours ago. The highway is bare of snow, traffic is not heavy and my cruise speed is set at one hundred. In a few short minutes I shall turn off the pavement and follow a gravelled surface the twelve kilometres to my house. That will take me ten more minutes.

Just before I cross the Blindman six kilometres north of Rimbey, I come alongside the right of way of the old Lacombe Northwestern, which also crosses the river at this spot and follows a line surveyed about 1920 on level land between the hills to the west and the river to the east. My mind goes back, and as I pass the entrance to the picnic site in a loop of the river, I suddenly see myself, thirty metres and forty-five years away....

The year is 1939, early winter, little snow. A dirty east wind is blowing. I stand on the railroad crossing, disappointed and somewhat out of breath, for I have been running. I am disappointed because I have missed the *Peanut*, also called the *Muskeg Express*, the *Blueberry Special*, the *Toonerville Trolley*, and some other names. I am on my way to Bluffton where I am hoping that my father will be waiting for me with a team and sleigh to give me a ride the nine miles home. That nine miles, over rough, rutted and frozen roads will take more than an hour behind King and Star, the driving team I have known all my life. It will take nearly three hours if I have to use shank's mare.

I left Monte Vista High School half an hour early this Friday afternoon to go home for the weekend. It is two miles to the water tank where the train almost always stops for the engine to take on water. This gives me a chance, if I am there at the right time, to swing aboard an empty boxcar as the train starts up. It could never be said you could set your watch by the *Peanut*. It has a schedule, published in *Waghorn's Guide*, but it never keeps the hours, only the days. It runs north on Mondays, Wednesdays and Fridays; south on Tuesdays, Thursdays and Saturdays. I always know if it has or hasn't gone on Fridays, because from my desk near the school's south window I can see it leave Rimbey, four miles away, but I rely more on the whistle to let me know of its whereabouts.

This is not my lucky day. I was just nicely on my way when I heard the whistle north of Rimbey station. I started to run, knowing that it was a futile effort unless the train stayed longer than usual at the water tank. Sure enough, they hauled up the spout and got underway with me still four minutes from the crossing.

The dirty grey coal smoke is still blowing in against the hillside as I stand there making a decision. It is five and a half miles to Bluffton by road, as I follow the route in my mind, west up a long hill, across the canyon, north at Wagner's corner, past the cemetery, down Hansen's hill, and finally past the General Sherman Shultz farm into Bluffton. The hill looks formidable, chances of a ride are slim, and it is getting late, not long until dark.

I turn and head up the track, turning my face to the left, away from the biting wind. It is a long hour's hard walking to Bluffton.

I FALL THROUGH THE ICE AND GET WET
December 14, 1982

My friend Dennis has just lost a bet.

He and I were hiking in the back country the other day. We were more than three miles from our vehicle when we came out into a shallow valley and a white expanse of snow-covered ice that was the southern end of Chain o' Lakes, named by 1930s homesteader, Jack Brady, whose ruin of a log cabin sits beside Brady's Branch (of the Medicine River system) about two miles away.

13

There are about six little lakes in a mile-long chain. I use the term lake quite loosely here, as some of them are little more than glorified beaver ponds, and, indeed, the beaver have enlarged most of them since Brady's time. There were no beaver in the area when they were named. I have seen them only a few times, as they are rather hard to get to.

It had turned into a beautiful day for hiking. The morning's overcast had cleared away to the east and the low midday sun elongated the spruce shadows around the shore as we walked the length of this smallest of lakes. Then, near the north end we heard the scary sound of dead ice beneath our steps. Dead ice has air beneath it, not water, although the water may be only an inch away. It occurs when the water level of a body of water is lowered after ice has covered it at freeze-up time. Something, perhaps just a slight pressure ridge, keeps some of the ice up off the water. Not only does that ice not thicken with the advance of winter and become quite safe, it now has no water to support it. Hikers beware!

We began moving cautiously toward the lake margin where an old beaver dam extended out into the lake. Dennis and I were several paces apart, luckily for him. Without further warning a patch of ice gave way under my feet and dropped me hip deep into icy water. Instinctively I fell forward, spreading myself as wide as possible over the shelf of ice in front of me. It held, and I crawled out onto safer territory.

I was lucky in many ways. There was probably nothing but ooze on the pond bottom. I didn't actually feel the bottom, but there was thin grey mud on one boot when I got out. I had my 35-mm camera over my shoulder, my binoculars in my hand and my lunch on my back. None of them got wet. My upper body was dry and so were my mitts. And it was the warmest part of the day, with the temperature just below freezing. I was annoyed nonetheless. Our further exploration of Chain o' Lakes was cut short. We were too far from the truck to head straight back. My boots were full of cold water and I had to get them off. I was not really uncomfortable as we walked down the trail to where we had seen a patch of bare ground under a spreading pine tree on a sunny slope. Dennis quickly had a fire going while I removed boots, socks and pants, wrung the water out of them and hung them on the pine tree to dry, while I stood as close to the fire as I dared in my underwear until it was steaming like mad and I had to turn every few seconds.

We ate some lunch, Dennis kept the fire fueled and in less than

14

an hour I was able to dress and we got on our way, but not before Dennis added insult to injury by taking some snapshots—with my camera.

In thirty-six winters of roaming that back country and walking or skiing on hundreds of lakes and beaver ponds, this was the first time I had ever so much as gotten my feet wet. It was a sobering experience.

"I'll bet," said Dennis, as we were walking out, "that you don't write about this little episode in your column, like you did about the time I got dunked trying to canoe over a beaver dam."

Pay up, Dennis.

RETIREMENT PARTY - A. C. SCHUTZ
March 16, 1982

I went eight hundred miles to a party last weekend.

It is spring in Vancouver—just barely. Mauve and yellow crocuses are poking up in clumps and clusters through green grass. The ornamental fruit trees are showing pink, and some lawns are getting their first mowing of the year. Although there may still be frost on the grass in the mornings, and the sea breezes can be cool, even cold despite the sunshine, and robins are still in flocks, some of the waterfowl are pairing and there is an air of expectancy that doesn't develop on the Prairies until some weeks later. I made the remark that Albertans who come out to Vancouver in early March should stay at least until April to lessen the shock of return.

Weather was nice in Alberta when we boarded Air Canada Flight 113 to Vancouver from Calgary on March 5, but we were not too sure what to expect out there, since they had just experienced the second-wettest January in their history. Much to our delight, the weekend, Friday through Monday, turned out sunny and dry.

I boarded the plane in company with my sister and brother-in-law, Dorothy and Percy Barker, and George and Edith Rogers, all of Calgary. The occasion was a huge retirement banquet and party on Friday evening in the ballroom of the Georgia Hotel. It was sponsored by the British Columbia Forest Service in honour of my brother Allan, and an associate, Bill Smith, on their retirement from the British Columbia Forest Service. The program was a merry combination of roast and testimonial that lasted until late. Guests numbered 175, mostly Forest Service people, plus family and friends of the retirees. My brother had not been informed that the group from

15

Alberta was coming, so it was a fun surprise when he walked in during the happy hour.

The Friday night festivities were followed by smaller gatherings at home and at the home of Loa and Jim VandenBurg in Delta. Maureen Ott, Allan and Grace's elder daughter, was not able to make it from Ottawa.

Allan began his career with the B. C. Forest Service even before he had graduated from the University of British Columbia. For two summers he was engaged in what I considered at the time to be one of the world's best jobs. It was called Lookout Photography. He and a young fellow named Rory Flannigan, who is now Superintendent of Jasper National Park, travelled all over B. C. taking infra-red photographs from mountain tops, which were thus assessed as possible locations for fire lookouts. They travelled the

Brother Allan, on left, with Fred, at Capilano Lake.

back country by foot and canoe, sometimes with Indian guides, climbed remote mountains where grizzlies roamed, had adventures with wildlife, and got paid for doing it.

After graduation Allan started out as Assistant Ranger at Merritt, went to Kamloops, Blue River, Vancouver, Prince Ru-pert, Victoria and Vancouver again, working his way up the ranks as he went along. Since 1979 he has been Timber, Range and Recreation Manager in the Vancouver Forest District. At retirement he was honoured for thirty-two years of service.

Retirement, for him, will mean active retirement. He has so many interests he wants to pursue that the days and the seasons will not be long enough. He will garden, travel, paint, ski, bird watch, photograph and do a hundred and one other things that there has never been quite enough time for. He is a prime example of a person who should retire as early as possible, while there is still time to do all these things and any more that may come to his attention.

FIRE IN THE HOUSE
April 3, 1990

When I saw a dense grey mushroom cloud of smoke burst laterally from my shattered bathroom window and reach out ten metres before beginning to disintegrate, I thought it was the end of my home. Incredibly, two minutes later, the Rimbey Fire Department had the fire under control. While my memory of those minutes is somewhat distorted, I know I was mentally saying goodbye to the house in which I had lived since I was twelve years old.

My family moved into this house on March 9, 1933, leaving the twenty-year-old homestead shack to be occupied by the flock of chickens. The chickens had lived in a corner of the barn before that. We all thought it was a pretty fine house when it was new, and we were proud of it. We considered ourselves fortunate in comparison with many of the people who were flooding into the district at the time from the dried out areas of the prairies. They were starting from scratch; we were almost old-timers, having been here eleven years. My father took out insurance on the house right at the start, valuing it at $500. That was the approximate cost of the lumber, shingles, doors and windows and some kegs of nails.

Over the years we kept adding to it, making improvements inside and out. We put in cement chimneys, added a porch and two other rooms, extra insulation, then wiring and plumbing, and new

Fire in the house, December 22, 1989.

17

windows. While the original shingles have been replaced with asphalt, the original drop siding, wearing several coats of paint of different colours, still covers the outside walls.

When the smoke had cleared enough for me to go in, last December 22, I was appalled at the mess. The bathroom was gutted, the stairs destroyed and there was debris and wet ashes inside and out, all mixed with broken glass. "I'll never live here again," I thought, as I inspected the damage. Everything, upstairs and down, even where the fire hadn't reached, was blackened with smoke. Most of my clothes, hanging in a closet adjacent to the bathroom, were destroyed. Hundred-year-old jars and bottles, in an open bookcase upstairs, cracked in the heat and fell apart. Twentieth-century glass fared much better. There was also water damage to books and paper.

The day following the fire, a moving van drove into my yard, and all my belongings were packed into boxes, and along with furniture and appliances, were carted off to a shop in Camrose for cleaning and de-smoking. The next day a second van headed east, leaving my house empty for the first time in six decades.

The de-smoking process is accomplished with the use of more smoke. An apparatus shaped like a miniature cannon equipped with a gasoline motor spews from its nozzle a white fog that is actually a neutral smoke, the molecules of which combine with the smelly smoke molecules and render them neutral also. It works.

While all this was going on, I had moved, with my typewriter, which I cleaned myself, into Charlie Plank's house in Rimbey. Charlie had gone to Kelowna for Christmas and on Christmas Eve I left for three more relaxed days in Calgary, but before I could leave, I had to visit the men's store for a complete re-outfitting.

By the end of the first week after the fire, a cleaning crew had gone over the house from top to bottom. The carpenters came in at the end of the second week and built new stairs and reconstructed the bathroom. They and I hauled away several loads of garbage.

The next weeks saw new carpet laid and a paint job upstairs and down. My furniture and other belongings were returned, most of the latter in approximately two hundred cardboard boxes which were piled in the rooms and left for me to unpack. That job is still not done, but the house I had never expected to occupy again is once more back to its former state of comfort and usefulness. It is good to be back with familiar things around me, the ones I can find, that is.

MY HAUNTED FIELD
June 16, 1971

One of my fields is haunted. The ghosts are not the eerie, wraith-like apparitions of a moonless night, but ghosts of pioneer days, conjured up in broad daylight by tangible evidence of someone's existence on this piece of land over half a century ago.

The field in question is on the quarter which, as far back as I can remember, has been called by us "the Cole Place," because it was homesteaded and occupied for a few years by an English couple, Mr. and Mrs. Joshua Cole. Josh Cole was a veteran of the First World War, and following the armistice he came to this country and took up land under the watchful eye of the Soldier Settlement Board. He was one of the "greenhorn Englishmen" who were the subject matter for many a story being told in those days, and, in fact, one of the stories concerned Josh Cole himself. A horned owl came out of the woods one night, and, as horned owls sometimes do, perched for an hour or so on the chimney jack that sat on top of the Cole's log shack and hooted away at frequent intervals. The occupants were terrified and stayed awake until daylight in case the beast came back, for, as Josh related the incident to a neighbour next morning, he was sure a blood-thirsty coyote had climbed up on the roof and was trying to get in through the stovepipe hole.

Josh Cole was perhaps not the best farmer in the district, and hardly a conservationist. He believed that the easiest way to clear the land was to burn it off every spring, and if the fire got into adjacent property he likely reasoned that he was doing someone a favour. The couple were both handicapped by poor health and they must have reaped small reward for their efforts, for they died within a short time of one another of consumption, as tuberculosis was called in those days. About 1925 the log house, still containing the furniture, dishes and personal possessions of the couple who had resided there, was razed; the outbuildings, corrals and pigpens piled and burned also, and the farmyard became part of a field. This area still produces a rank, green growth of grain or hay, and, when it is ploughed and harrowed, a crop of rusty nails and staples and harness buckles and odds and ends of iron.

It is almost as easy to see where the house stood. About a tenth of an acre is strewn with reminders that folks once dwelt here: a porcelain door knob; hundreds of fragments of thick, heavy pottery and fine English china; fire-melded glass in colours of deep olive green and dark brown and amber, and shades of purple and rose

19

and amethyst; glass that once was dishes on a table or panes in a window; and bottles of an age and colour and design to make a bottle collector weep. I have picked up bent spoons and three-tine table forks and corroded or broken knives, and even what once had been a pair of scissors. Battered pewter I have found, and tin rusted almost to nothing, and a lot of metal that was once a cookstove. I have recently seen a furniture caster, a length of bucksaw blade, the barrel of a .22 rifle, the remains of an alarm clock, and once I found an English penny dated 1874.

Every time I look at one of these fragments from the past, a kind of nostalgia for that other way of life seems to radiate from it, even though I never knew the people who owned it.

The Coles are gone from this land but their ghosts remain.

CHILD'S GRAVE DISCOVERED
May 19, 1971

The mystery of a child's grave, discovered thirty-six years ago near the forks of the Medicine River in Township 44, may be slightly less of a mystery today, but only slightly.

The first part of the story was told to me about eighteen years ago by John Balan, who, in 1935, was living on his homestead NE 1-44-5-W5, not far from the forks. One day he and his neighbours, one of whom was George Spruham, were clearing land for breaking. They hooked the horses to a large poplar tree, and in pulling it down a large amount of sod and dirt was displaced. Exposed at the base of the tree was a box made of shiplap, and within, when the well-rotted boards were pulled back, was the skeleton of a child, identifiable as a white girl by the strands of long, blonde hair and a row of blue buttons that were all that remained of a dress.

The remains were re-buried nearby and inquiries were made of old-timers in the neighbourhood or anyone who might have a clue as to the child's identity, but although the Willesden Green area had been settled for less than thirty years at that time, nobody had even the slightest idea.

Thirty-six years pass.

In May of 1971, I met an early resident of the Willesden Green district, Dwight Sawyer, and he told me he had a trapline up the river half a century ago and knew the country well. He remembers the signs of habitation that early settlers thought must have been a trading post not far from the forks and not far from the grave site described by John Balan.

Years later Mr. Sawyer met and compared notes with a man who had known the area even earlier. This man was a government surveyor who said he had cruised alone through the region ahead of the preliminary survey; and according to official maps the first survey in that area is dated July 21, 1900.

At that time, to this man's surprise, he found people living near the forks, almost on the township line, which would be right in his path. They were two couples, one of which had a child. Their two cabins were built a short distance apart, and between them and connecting them was a horse corral. There were quite a number of horses about, not mustangs, but quality stock—riding and saddle horses that showed good breeding.

The people themselves were friendly and hospitable and the surveyor visited with them and ate with them on occasion during his stay in the area. The men wore guns, he said, and wore them unconsciously, as a part of their clothing, as though they had been born with them. When he returned with the survey party, in May of 1904, according to the map, the people and the horses were gone and the place abandoned.

Had they left the little girl behind, in a shiplap casket, beneath a lofty poplar?

One part of John Balan's story doesn't fit. He says that on that poplar was a plainly legible date—1927. But since there were many people in the area by 1927 hunting game, or [looking for] strayed horses or cattle, or picking berries, anyone might have carved that date, quite unaware of the grave beneath their feet.

JOHN ILLE'S TRAGIC END
July 24, 1963

This is the tragic tale of a man's last days and something of the weeks and months preceding them. The man was John Ille (rhymes with Riley), early homesteader in the Pendryl district between Winfield and Buck Lake, part-time trapper and mill hand.

I first became interested in Ille's story in 1949, when I was hunting in the country where he had lived and run a trapline, south and east of Buck Lake. A small lake near the base line in Township 44, Range 5, is still called Ille's Lake, and there, on the north shore, you may still find the site of the cabin where John Ille lived years ago.

Ille was an American by birth, but other than that, little seems to be known of his background. Those who knew him say he was

21

always a bit unconventional and very uncommunicative. His homesteading efforts never bore much fruit. He never became a farmer, although he appears to have homesteaded on two different quarter sections. Sometimes he worked in the lumber camps, but he preferred to make his living on the trapline, and this, together with hunting and fishing, provided for all his needs.

Sometime in the 1930s, Ille developed a disfiguring illness which might be diagnosed today as an eroding ulcer or cancer that spread from his mouth over the rest of his face. He refused to see a doctor or have any medical attention, and continued to live alone, becoming more and more of a recluse as the disease progressed. Whenever he chanced to meet someone, he would pull the corner of his shirt collar or his coat collar in front of his mouth and keep his head averted while talking to the person.

After a time, he took to tying a handkerchief around his face in the manner of a masked bandit and persons who saw him at that time noted the sores were creeping into his eyes.

Still later he resorted to wearing a cotton sack over his head. He had cut two small holes for his eyes and was never seen without this Klux-like hood once he took to wearing it. About the same time he began to answer his door with a gun in his hand. It can be readily imagined that from this point on he would be left pretty much to himself and his last days would not be brightened by many visitors.

One day toward the end, an Indian looking for strayed horses knocked on Ille's door. He heard sounds of movement within the cabin, and then the unmistakable clatter of a shell being levered into the breech of a rifle. He waited no longer, but left with all possible haste, and at the first opportunity took steps to have the RCMP at Wetaskiwin notified of the situation.

A few days later, the police arrived on what they may well have supposed to be a routine investigation. They found John Ille quite dead.

An epilogue to the story, which may or may not be true, or only half true, says that when the police removed John Ille's body, they burned the shack to the ground as the only means of leaving the place in a safe and sanitary condition. In doing so, the story continues, they may have burned a sizable bundle of cash, as it was thought that the trapper's income for some years past had far exceeded the amount he spent for his few necessities, and he had never had a bank account.

TRAPPER OLAF OLSEN
November 25, 1954

Every November it's the same. I, like a great many other fellows I know, start looking westward and thinking of the deep woods, camping out, and game tracks in the snow. It is a wonderful time of the year to be in the outdoors—no mosquitoes, blackflies or no-see-ums. No rain, or hardly ever. And you can walk almost anywhere without getting your feet wet.

I would enjoy going hunting even if I never saw any game. For me there is a wealth of enjoyment in exploring country that I have not seen before. I have run into some unexpected things in the wilderness, and I am going to tell you about one of these. This is not a hunting story, even if it starts off like one.

A friend named Sam and I were hunting elk west of the North Saskatchewan River, which we always called the NSR. We were camped about half a mile from the Atlas lumber road, some miles north of the Baptiste River, and about six miles from the NSR. Up and down the Atlas road, within six miles or so, there were about thirty other hunters, very few of whom ever got more than two or three miles from the road, so the first thing Sam and I did each morning was to head for the river. We never felt safe until we were near enough to hear the water, usually when we were about a mile away. And besides, that was where all the elk were.

Sometimes we would separate for the whole day, sometimes we would meet on the river for lunch, and sometimes we hunted more or less together. One day, just after lunch, we spotted some old log buildings not far from the river's edge, and as we always did, went to investigate. We found an old cabin and a couple of smaller buildings, all carefully and expertly constructed of smooth, straight logs, and now falling to ruin. There seemed to be no sawn lumber anywhere.

Floors, doors, sills, as well as remnants of furniture were hand hewn. The door, as in most of the old trapper's cabins I have seen in that country, was the size of a small window, perhaps two feet wide by four feet high and eighteen inches off the floor—just large enough for a man to crawl through. It was heavily barred from the inside and contained a one-inch peep hole with a cover that swung aside. We concluded that the old boy who had lived there was probably quite a character.

Then just as we were leaving, I saw something else—a wooden cross about three feet high, just behind the cabin. Carved on the cross-piece was the inscription: Olaf Olsen, Dead July 1936. Then we really began to wonder. How did he die? Why was he buried here and by whom? Someone had taken some pains to carve so plainly and so lastingly on that hewn tamarack cross. We made up our minds to do some enquiring.

On our way home we stopped at Rocky Mountain House to see Mrs. Freeda Fleming, writer and historian of that part of Alberta. Mrs. Fleming was much interested by our story. She remembered something of the trapper's death and said she would look up the details. This she did, both in the files of the Rocky Mountain House *Mountaineer* and the RCMP records. Olsen had starved to death and had kept a diary of his privation. His last entry was July 16, and he had ticked off his calendar for another ten days. A fellow trapper discovered his death and brought word into Rocky. The investigation and burial were made by Constable Leyland, RCMP.

Still unexplained were some of the whys and wherefores. Olsen was an experienced trapper and had lived in the wilds since 1929. Why had he starved to death with meat and fish for the taking? He was about sixty years old. Had illness or rheumatism confined him to his cabin?

This summer I heard the rest of the story. We had a picnic lunch near the mouth of the Baptiste River one day last July. There that afternoon I met a lady who had known Olaf Olsen well. While she waited for her husband to return from fishing, we talked, and this is what she told me.

Olsen travelled to and from Rocky in a beautiful Indian-made birch-bark canoe, transporting himself and several hundred pounds of supplies in the fragile craft. He often stopped off at her farm home on the banks of the river. In the winter he travelled by dog team and ran a productive trapline. During his early years in the country he never locked his door. The Indians who passed his cabin from time to time were his friends, and behaved as such. Then, in the 1930s, the government moved some Indians from Saskatchewan to the reserve northwest of Rocky, and amongst these was an undesirable element. No longer was his cabin safe, but was broken into and his supplies pilfered. Once, he claimed, some drunken Indians had demanded from him food and other items far in excess of what he could afford to part with, and when he refused to be victimized, they threatened his life.

Olsen never felt entirely safe again, but he felt a concern for these Indians and their erring ways, and resolved to do all he could for them. He became deeply religious and tried to get the Indians to change their ways and follow his example. So concerned did he become that he neglected his trapping and acquired a reputation for being eccentric. Finally, when nothing he could do seemed to have any effect, he turned to fasting, and that is how he ended his days.

THE POCHA STORY
January 22, 1964

The first people to carry on farming operations in the upper Blindman Valley were, so far as can be learned, a family named Pocha who were known the whole length of the river, from Buck Lake to Blackfalds.

I have been interested in learning more about these earliest pioneers on the Blindman, and for most of the information below I am indebted to Mr. Jim Reynolds of Ponoka, also an early pioneer (though not so early as the Pochas). He was well acquainted with Mr. and Mrs. Pocha, their two sons and four daughters. I myself can say I knew one of the daughters. Her name was Mrs. Reber, and she etched herself permanently in my memory by making me a gingerbread boy one day when I was two. Mrs. Pocha was of Scottish and Indian descent.

William Pocha was born some 120 years ago, of a French father and Indian mother. As a young man he lived in what is now Manitoba, and during the Riel Rebellion was one of a small but famous group of mounted men known as Boulton's Scouts. Major Boulton served in the North West Field Force under General Middleton, and played an important role in establishing peace and order during the 1885 uprising in the West. It may well have been his time served under Major Boulton that gave Pocha his first look at Alberta and led him to return later with his family.

The first frame buildings in Fort Garry had just been erected when the Pochas took the trail to the west. They lived for an indeterminate period at Prince Albert and may also have stopped for a time at Batoche before coming to Blackfalds in the 1890s.

One day Pocha met some Indians who had a number of large whitefish, and when he enquired of them where these exceptionally fine fish had been caught he was given directions to a lake of plenty. And those directions led the Pochas through the upper Blindman country, right to the river's source, then across the bush to Buck Lake. They made their own trail much of the way, taking twenty-one days for the trip.

25

The first thing William did on arrival at the lake was set his fish net and the family had boiled whitefish and bannock for supper. Long years later, William Pocha declared that this was one of the most enjoyable meals he had ever eaten.

They made several trips up and down the river from Blackfalds to Buck Lake, then decided to locate nearer the lake. Son Henry homesteaded about a mile southeast of the present site of Bluffton, and son Edward (Ted) chose a spot near where Hoadley would some day rise.

"I remember passing their place on our way to Buck Lake up the old Pocha Trail," writes Mr. Reynolds. It may be that portions of that trail could still be traced northwest of Hoadley.

While the Pochas raised pigs and cattle and cultivated a small acreage, they did not pretend to make all of their living farming. Hunting and fishing always provided a large measure of their livelihood. They built a small house near the south end of Buck Lake, where the hotel now stands, and made it their home during their fishing expeditions.

Trapping also helped to increase their earnings. They tanned buckskin and small hides, and one of the products of this line of their endeavours that Mr. Reynolds remembers well were the buckskin-faced, coyote skin driving mitts Mrs. Pocha made. They were well adapted to keeping hands from freezing while hanging onto leather lines in cold weather.

One of William Pocha's sayings was "... never leave home in winter without feed for men and horses. Always be prepared for sixty below."

"And he was right," agrees Mr. Reynolds. It was very good advice in those pioneering days.

Grandpa Pocha, as he came to be known, died at Buck Lake about 1930. His son Edward passed away a short time later.

"To tell the whole story [of the Pocha family] would take a lot more pencil and paper," writes Mr. Reynolds. "I knew the family well. It just seems like yesterday they were driving down the old trail."

ROUSE, THE MUSKRAT FARMER
February 1, 1967

One of the most engaging nonconformists in all the Blindman Valley lived about five miles east of Bluffton during the era of the Great Depression. His name was Rouse; I don't know his

26

given name, but he is usually remembered today as The Muskrat Farmer.

I never knew the man, nor saw him as far as I know, but had heard of him for many years, and some of the information about him stirred my curiosity, so I began to make inquiries.

The following material was obtained from people who knew Mr. Rouse, but I am sure there must be others who would have stories about him. Stories about such people should be preserved, for they lend colour to our history and sometimes become a part of our folklore.

Rouse's homestead took in a good portion of a wide, steep-walled canyon or coulee that is almost steep enough and deep enough to be called a gorge, and which, from aerial photos, seems to be a glacial-era phase of the Blindman's course.

Near the foot of one of these brush-covered walls, Rouse built his home—a dugout. This bachelor's abode boasted a unique fireplace. The chimney was constructed of round culvert tile. His fuel was the poplar that grew profusely just about anywhere around, but Rouse saw no reason to waste time and effort cutting it into stove or even fireplace lengths. He used full length poles and shoved them down the chimney about three at a time, creating, in effect, an automatic stoker, with the poles lowering as they burned.

The dugout faced southeast, right into the mid-morning sun. It had wide, swinging double doors, and when the day was fine, Rouse would throw them both open. In less clement weather only one might be open, or they might be closed tight to keep out the cold. His air-conditioning, it appears, was only semi-automatic.

Rouse's appellation of Muskrat Farmer derived from his venture to raise muskrats in captivity. He constructed a dam across the flat, marshy floor of his canyon to create the necessary depth of water, and enclosed a considerable area with wire mesh. But the project was not a success. The rats did not take well to confinement, and poachers from up the river took much of the profit.

Some of his neighbours remember him best at threshing time. He was always one of the crew. They tell about the wagon and rack he built for hauling bundles, the like of which was never seen before or since. A basket rack was mounted between two high, wide, steel wheels from some long outmoded piece of machinery, with two smaller wheels set closer together out in front. It took a good team of horses to haul it when loaded with bundles. The floor of the

27

rack was at stubble level for easy loading, but the work began when he got the load in to the machine.

Rouse was by no means a recluse, but has been described as a good mixer. He was a big, round-faced man with a somewhat roly-poly appearance. Well-educated and well-read, he loved to discuss the political issues of the day, and defended with some zeal views and theories that were slightly unorthodox in the 1930s. This, I gather, detracted somewhat from his social popularity in some quarters.

Little seems to be known about the man's background, which I believe I had been told was British. He had no known relatives in this area, probably none this side of the Atlantic. One day he pulled stakes and left, to be seen no more by his friends in the Blindman Valley. His dam, flattened and eroded by the years, and a depression where his dugout intruded into the slope, are all that remain as reminders of Rouse, the Muskrat Farmer.

HAPPY BIRTHDAY! "J. C."
February 23, 1972

Jack Hinrichsen, who was born in a sod house in Nebraska, woke up on the morning of April 1, 1905, to find himself in Canada. He was just past twenty-one, and had just come with his brother from St. Paul, Nebraska, on a seventy-car immigrant train, two cars of which were loaded with the settlers' effects of the Hinrichsen brothers, including farm machinery, livestock and a well-drilling outfit. The train was stopped on a siding near the immigration office of North Portal, and somehow Canada was not quite what they had expected. Let Jack tell it.

"Like most Americans from as far south as Nebraska, we expected to find the whole country still covered with snow. Instead, the prairie was covered with crocus blooms—a beautiful sight.

"Several of the attendants of the cars had gathered near the immigration office, and here I had the pleasure of a look at my first Mountie. We had been told that shooting irons were not favored in Canada, so I had unstrapped mine and hung it on a nail (in the car) before leaving Nebraska. The Mountie came toward us, and with a pleasant 'Good morning' and a 'Welcome to Canada,' he looked us all over. A middle-aged but well-built six-footer had evidently decided to be on the safe side and had strapped on a pair of Colts. As the young Mountie, also six foot plus, walked among us, he came to the man we all called Buffalo Bill. He tapped the guns lightly with one finger and said, 'The Canadian government does not approve of side arms, and so as not to get into trouble with the law, you would be well-advised to take them off and put them in your trunk. You will not need them here.'

"The muscles in Bill's jaw tightened, his eyes narrowed to slits and his right hand twitched. We all tensed, expecting something to happen. It was likely the first time anyone had ever told that cowboy what he could do with his guns. But the Mountie looked him right in the eye for a minute and then walked off, quite unconcerned, to talk to the next man. We started kidding Bill, 'Why did you back down?' Bill said, 'I play a lot of poker and I know when a man is bluffing. That Mountie was not bluffing.'

"We were eleven days before reaching Calgary from Nebraska, and eventually arrived at High River, our destination. I was one of the first homesteaders in what is now the Vulcan district. I came looking over the country west of Lacombe in 1910 and decided this Blindman Valley was the best and that I would be in ahead of the railroad. So in 1921 I located in the Bluffton district, and the Blindman Valley has been my home ever since."

Every year around this time I say a few words about this early Alberta pioneer who will have a birthday this year for the first time since 1968. He will be 88, and it's many the story he can tell you of his years in the West, and for this one I have used Jack's own words.

Happy Birthday, Jack.

STORIES BY DAVE ADAMS
February 21, 1973

While researching material for *Tributaries to the Blindman*, a detailed regional history of the area presently served by the Bluffton school that is being compiled by a large committee of interested people, I came across a box of odds and ends of information that had been gathered as far back as 1952 and 1955. In those years, *The Rimbey Record* published special editions to mark the golden jubilees of the Town of Rimbey and the Province of Alberta, respectively. Among these items were some that have not, as far as I can find out, ever been published in their entirety, and one of them is a narrative of more than usual interest written by the late Dave Adams. It is much too good to be hidden away any longer.

Dave Adams' parents, Mr. and Mrs. Peat Adams, came to the Lacombe area from Michigan in 1895, although Peat had been in central Alberta as early as 1890. They raised a family of ten children,

29

and today the descendants of this pioneer couple are known far and wide, and much has already been written by them and about them. Peat Adams was known to many of his neighbours as "Uncle Sam," because he was an American who, except for tall hat and starred-and-striped vest, looked the part of the cartoon character of that name. He was tall and slim and wore long chin whiskers. He died in 1935 at the age of 82, having built a reputation as one of the province's most energetic and industrious pioneers. He has been described as "a hustler from the boots up" who would seek out and take on any job for fifty miles around.

Here are the opening paragraphs of Dave Adams' narrative:

"We landed in Lacombe in June 1895 and called on an acquaintance of my father's and remained there until the first of July when we went to a celebration in Lacombe.

"There were about three Indians to every white person at this celebration. The night we arrived in Lacombe the livery stable burned, killing one horse, and the squaws came down and cut the steaks off the horse, already roasted. It wasn't long until the horse was gone and they didn't have to haul him out to the dump. They ran horse races from the Royal Bank north up the street and a horse fell on a corner hole and broke his leg and they had to shoot him. It wasn't more than fifteen minutes before the squaws had him all cut up so they fared very well that day.

"There was a hardware store where Morrison and Johnson's store is now. There was a small hotel about the size of a big farmhouse. There were two grocery stores, and a butcher shop run by W. F. Puffer; the size would be about ten feet by twelve feet.

"There were very few dwelling places. In a few days we moved into a log house with a sod roof. When it rained we didn't get wet but it leaked for two days afterward. We lived there for two weeks until we got our house built on the homestead.

"Our next celebration was on the 12th of July at Gull Lake. We went there with a team and wagon, about fifteen of us altogether. We had a big tent and put that up, then went out and speared a few fish. The next day I was walking up the creek when I heard a noise and splashing in the water and I took off, not knowing what it was. It was the creek full of suckers. I jumped in the creek and threw out about thirty of them and dragged them down to camp. They asked me where I got them and I told them, so we all went fishing up the creek."

PETE ANDERSON
January 10, 1973

"If I ever move," Pete Anderson told me more than once, "it will be farther west." He lived, at the time, at the end of the road; only trails went beyond—and I'm sure he had no intention of moving at all. He was, I think, merely expressing his love for the wilderness, the wide-open spaces and a way of life that had to provide the ultimate in peace and quiet and contentment and do this within the confines of an agricultural community.

That was many years ago and circumstances were to dictate to Pete and his wife Emma that they and their family would move from their well-established farm that they had literally carved from the wilderness, and that move would be eastward rather than to the west, closer to the amenities of the day—telephone, school bus, all-weather roads and snowploughs. I don't remember now whether I knew or merely suspected that the move was really a form of health insurance for their youngest daughter, Lorraine, known then to one and all as "Poppy." Lorraine was every bit as happy but not quite so robust as the other four children. I'm sure it must have caused a wrench to leave the farm into which they had put so much of themselves, but if either of them ever complained I was not around to hear.

I was just a boy when I first remember Pete. He had come to this district from the Lacombe area and taken up a homestead back on Section 23 in the next township west, well up along the north branch of the Medicine River, some seven or eight miles from where I lived, and it was to be some years before I got around to visiting him there. Right from the first I looked on Pete as a true frontiersman, and in the decades since I have never changed my mind. I never knew a man who was more resourceful with an axe, a posthole digger and a team of horses. Though never a hunter, he always wore a heavy steel hunting knife that he used any number of times in an average day as a tool for any purpose. It was a crowbar, hammer, axe or scalpel, whatever the occasion required. Pete's natural affinity for the land, combined with a remarkable inventiveness which enabled him to design and construct (in a single process) scores of items for which a use arose, helped him turn his homestead into a farm, and do it in the face of obstacles that would have frightened away other men. With Emma's green thumbs (her vegetable gardens were annual cornucopiae), and the willingness of the whole family to pitch in and help, they came as close to being

31

self-sufficient as anyone could be in that time and place. Yet despite so busy a life they always took time to be good neighbours. They enjoyed a way of life inside the edge of wilderness but in no way apart from the community, and that would be the envy of thousands today. And it is my impression that it suited the whole family.

The last three miles of road in to the Anderson farm in those early years was a wagon trail that followed ridges, skirted muskegs and crossed creeks on beaver dams, and while I am sure there must have been places where it ran straight and level for more than forty feet at a stretch, I cannot now remember any. It took a certain amount of time and work each summer for a team of horses just to keep that road in shape, but if anyone suggested to either Pete or Emma that they lived in some sort of isolation, they were apt to be given a few words of wisdom. Gradually, and eventually, as road construction and the age of the automobile advanced through our district, the trail became a road, but no one ever did describe it as either straight or level.

Pete was one of those men blessed with an amazing ability to adapt to his environment. He always made the best possible use of whatever raw material was at hand. At the same time he had an eye to see great beauty in a root or a knot of wood and the talent to bring out that beauty that others might see it also. He and I had much in common in our outdoor interest, our regard for old things and our fascination with the past.

In the years since he retired from farming, I have enjoyed perhaps two or three visits a year with him. I was fortunate enough to have had two such visits very recently, one in late fall just after he had returned from a long, lonely summer at a forestry lookout near Fort Vermillion in northern Alberta. Then, a few days before Christmas, he and Emma spent most of an afternoon with us, and we talked of all the usual things. And he gave me a small pioneer antique he had brought, in which I had once expressed a keen interest.

There will be no more visits with Pete. Nineteen seventy-three and the years to follow will be poorer without him. Ask anyone who knew him.

POPPY
November 21, 1973

Back in July 1961, I used this column to do a character sketch of a very remarkable cat. His name was Sylvester, usually shortened to Syllie, and he was an intelligent animal, as are most cats. Unlike most of his kind, however, he was willing to demonstrate—not hide—his intelligence, but only as part of a team. The other half of that team was a lively and engaging teenager named Lorraine, who went, at that time, by the name of "Poppy." There was a rapport between Poppy and Syllie the like of which you don't often see between a person and a non-person, although I have an idea that Syllie believed himself to be a person. I used to marvel at his ability to recognize the sound of the school bus which he knew Lorraine would step out of at the gate. To other traffic he paid not the slightest attention. What was between them could not be explained; only accepted.

Lorraine was the youngest daughter of Pete and Emma Anderson, and I knew her from the cradle. She was a diabetic and as a small child she learned to administer her daily dose of insulin and to successfully cope with a disease that was especially constraining for one so young. One never thought of this active, happy girl as frail, yet one always knew that she was vulnerable where her health was concerned.

I was a guest at Lorraine's wedding, the day she married Gordon Ferguson, and they were such a happy couple, and the bride was so radiant that any unspoken doubts for her future were forgotten as everyone wished them all the best in the years to come.

I only saw Lorraine occasionally after this, but the Schutz and Anderson families kept in touch and we always knew how she was faring and it wasn't always well. A highway accident three years ago proved a severe setback, and failing eyesight in recent years further curtailed her activities. Yet whenever I met Lorraine she was always bright and cheerful and I was filled with admiration for the stuff of which she was made, and the way in which she accepted, without complaint, the hand that fate had dealt her. I often thought, when talking to Lorraine, about her old friend, Sylvester, of how they seemed to read each other's mind. I wondered about it anew when she told me about her cat named McGee who repeatedly demonstrated that he was aware of her loss of sight.

I have never been good at uttering words of comfort to bereaved people. I am more likely to sit and wonder to myself why it is that some chronic grouch whose only purpose on earth seems to be to make miserable his own life and the lives of everyone around him, will live to be a hundred, while someone like Lorraine, who could brighten your day just with a few minutes of casual conversation, should be cut off at twenty-seven years. If I, who only saw her once or twice a year of late, will miss, her, and I know I shall, what can

I say to those who were with her daily? And why can't I dismiss the notion that a cat named Sylvester, a dozen years ago, knew something that the rest of us didn't?

LOU WILL MAKE AGRICULTURAL HALL OF FAME
April 6, 1977

Lou Hendrigan is a cowman with half a century of experience behind him and some revolutionary ideas about how to make the business pay. He doesn't claim to have all the answers. "I'll be too old too soon for that," he says, but there seems no doubt that he has found some of the answers to some of the beef cattlemen's most pressing problems.

His best answer to one no central Alberta cattleman can argue: "When I started farming here," says Mr. Hendrigan, "we grazed cattle for four months and fed them for eight. Now I graze them eight months and feed them for four." He does it with fescue.

Lou Hendrigan came to his homestead west of Winfield in 1922, some years before the Lacombe Northwestern Railroad got that far north, and before very many other settlers had come either. It wasn't any easier to get started in those days than it is today; only different. For seven years he worked away from his land for a good part of each year, but from 1930 he lived on it permanently.

Mr. Hendrigan was always looking for better ways to farm, and for many years his land was the location for a government Illustration Station where experimental work was carried out with cereal crops. However, he had recognized sooner than some that this grey-wooded-soil country was better suited to growing grass than to growing grain, yet it was hard to convince the experts. He once had nine hundred different plots of grain being grown experimentally, yet he had difficulty getting any experimental work done on forage or grazing.

Mr. Hendrigan once kept weather records for over a twenty-year period, and these, he says, indicated to him that he ought to be practicing dry land farming, for summer rainfall was often inadequate. One summer, I can't give you a year, rainfall was a scant three inches. However, there were other extremes; one summer it was thirty-eight inches!

After years of experimenting with grasses, legumes, and fertilizer, he concluded that creeping red fescue, with red clover to supply nitrogen, and some phosphate fertilizer, provided the cover he was looking for. Fescue is high in protein, and remains nutritious even when frozen. Fescue, says Mr. Hendrigan, is much like prairie wool, and cattle grow slaughter-fat on it, even when it is covered by several inches of snow. Further, an established stand of fescue can be grazed on in the early spring without damage to the field.

So Lou Hendrigan manages his fifty-cow beef operation with basically but one range of machinery—for putting up loose hay. And he only has to put up half as much per cow as he used to. If you would like some good practical ideas on cutting beef production costs, stop and talk to Lou some day. I think you'll come away convinced.

PHIL PEARMAN
November 18, 1980

Phil Pearman and I had a number of things in common. The one that brought us together about twenty years ago was a deep-rooted interest in Alberta archaeology. Phil, even at that time, had amassed an impressive collection of prehistoric Indian artifacts, nearly all of which he recovered from his own farm. Over the years the hobby gave him many happy hours, not only in the enjoyment and thrills of the hunt, but in displaying these treasures of the past for others to enjoy, in learning all he could about them and imparting that knowledge to others: to annual classes of school children down through the years and to everyone who showed an interest. Ranking archaeologists from afar have been visitors to the Pearman home to photograph and document his collection.

Phil and I were both afflicted with collectomania, specializing in pioneer antiques. We both loved the outdoors, and while he went hunting each fall for years after I had given up the sport, he truly appreciated the beauty and wonder of nature. He was a creative artist of some talent and ingenuity, whether painting in oils, playing a musical instrument, building with wood, or sculpting in metal. Phil was born an entertainer. He could do sleight of hand, tell an ethnic joke with malice to none, and devise on the spot a practical joke that would prove hilarious yet harmless to any or all concerned.

He was a barrel of fun, but he had the time to be serious, too, and took part in various community activities, including many years of involvement with the Rimbey Historical Society, serving for a term as president. In addition to all this, he gave more time than most to his family and to his church. Finally, Phil's full-time occupation was farming, and he put in the long hours at his work that any farmer must to be efficient.

Ill health had plagued Phil in recent years, curtailing some of his activities, stalking him more destructively than he or any of us knew. Now he and I will no longer prowl the likely field together, along the Battle or Blindman or Medicine Rivers, searching for tools or projectile points of stone. We will not stand together at an auction sale, deciding which of us will bid on what.

Let me quote something I said in this column fifteen years ago, on August 25, 1965: "Phil Pearman, like all good farmers, puts in a full day at his business, but he has found the time to pursue his various hobbies, giving his surroundings that extra touch that helps to make a farm a home and not merely a place of business. The Pearman youngsters, now and in many years to come, will be the richer for it."

I played and romped with those Pearman youngsters as small children. Later I went snowmobiling and horseback riding and cross-country skiing and canoeing with them, on the back forty and in the back country. Over the years I watched their young minds expand until they sometimes spoke a language I did not understand. My loss is small, compared to theirs, but their parents, Phil and Norma, have equipped them to cope successfully with the eventualities of life. Knowing them as I do, I know they will cope with this one.

Phil had a deep-seated interest in Pas-ka-poo Park. He came to the directors' meetings many times in recent years when he would rather have stayed home and gone to bed. He made a valuable contribution to this worthwhile cause, and a memorial fund has been set up in Philip's name for Pas-ka-poo Historical Park and Museum. Sue White, at the park, is in charge.

AUGUST BELTER
August 9, 1983

I had been away from home for several days in mid-July, taking in a Federation of Alberta Naturalists meeting in the Crowsnest Pass, then wandering into B. C. for a few days. As I drove past the Iola-Fairview Cemetery, just four miles from my house, I noticed a newly dug grave with a rough box beside it, and I knew that a funeral was imminent, although I had no idea whose. Only the following day did I learn the identity of the deceased. It was August Belter, age ninety, whom I had known since I was a boy at Blindman River School.

The four acres on which the school was built had been a part of August's homestead and donated by him. That building is much

36

used to this day as the Blindman River Community Center and it was filled to capacity following the funeral as relatives and friends gathered with the family.

When I first knew Mr. Belter in the 1930s, he lived in a dugout on the side of a hill on his homestead about a quarter of a mile from the school. "Never live in a dugout," he once said to me, "Too many mice, too many spiders! And they always leak for three days after the rain has stopped." Otherwise, he told me, a dugout wasn't bad, warm in winter, cool in summer.

There was no well at the school when it first opened, but arrangements had been made to carry water from Belter's well and the task fell to the older students. We took turns bringing the cold water back in a galvanized metal pail to fill the keg-shaped stone crock that kept it cool. Belter's well was dug by hand, wooden-cribbed; the water not pumped, but hauled up hand-over-hand with a bucket on a rope. Sometimes when it was my turn to go for water, I would find Mr. Belter at lunch in his dugout and if I had an excuse to speak to him I might get a peek inside his meagerly furnished home. It would take a moment or two for my eyes to become adjusted to the poorly-lit interior and to this day I only remember the lack of clarity about Mr. Belter's quarters. My visits were usually short, not only because I hadn't much time to get back with my pail of water, but because I had great difficulty in understanding Mr. Belter. His German accent was very pronounced at that time, and he was afflicted with a stutter which hampered his English even further.

August and Karoline Belter on August's 80th birthday.

August Belter was a benevolent figure in this community for almost half a century. I was honoured to be asked to act as master of ceremonies at Mr. and Mrs. Belter's fiftieth wedding anniversary in June 1966. I pointed out to the many people assembled that evening in the Blindman River Community Center, that while August and Karoline had been fifty years married, they had enjoyed only thirty-one years of married life together. August had come to Canada in 1929, lured by promises of free land, rich soil and bountiful crops. He fully expected to earn enough money in a short time to send for Karoline and their seven children, but of course he ran headlong into the Great Depression. That was followed immediately by World War II, when for many years there was not a hope of even communicating with anyone in Poland, let alone getting them out and into Canada. It was not until the children were all grown that August was reunited with his family in 1948.

August and Karoline lived on the homestead until 1977, when they moved to Edmonton. Two summers ago, when he was 88, I was pleased to have a visit from my old neighbour and friend. We talked of many things—the old days and the new, and I found him much easier to talk to than on those first occasions nearly half a century before.

August will be remembered in the Blindman River district for a long time to come. For more information on his life and times see *Tributaries to the Blindman*, pages 420, 431 and 452.

PURE NOSTALGIA
February 17, 1987

I still remember with some nostalgia the day I learned the meaning of the word. I was eighteen, working for Charlie Smith on his threshing outfit, where one of the other bundle haulers was Rudolph Dentman. The four high school boys, including myself, who were on the crew, somewhat disrespectfully it seems in retrospect, called Rudolph by his last name—Dentman; no Mr. He didn't seem to mind and he and I would become good friends, even though he was about a generation and a half ahead of me on this planet. We had some things in common. We both liked to argue, and we both needed a little less sleep than other members of the crew, with the possible exception of Charlie. So, long after the lantern was out in the bunk house, and all the others had been lulled to sleep by our conversation, Dentman and I would discuss politics, agricultural economics, religion, war, and the effect on the world of advancing technology. Anyone who knew Dentman will know I am telling the truth. We often continued our discussion next morning in the field, or over coffee in the afternoon. It was in a grain field somewhere not far from Rimbey that Dentman explained to me what nostalgia was. I was barely old enough to understand, for it was not much a part of my experience.

Today I understand. I get frequent bouts of the affliction; have done so for years. A few days ago I was caught in a whirl of memories that revolved around the winters of my childhood. I just happened to walk onto an ice surface that was the exact spot where five kids of two families once had a skating pond, and the setting was so much the same as it was on a winter's day in the 1930s that an unexpected wave of nostalgia almost bowled me over. All that was missing were the banks of snow along the sides of the pond, the ice scraper hanging in a willow tree, and the sounds of our skates scraping and chattering over the less-than-perfect ice. There are willows above and below this open area along the creek. Why they never grew along this short stretch in my lifetime, I can't say.

The pond was the first link in a series of three play areas. Just up the creek, along a skating trail through the willows, you came to an open, south-facing slope where a calcareous spring emerged higher up and fed a half-acre hillside bog, in winter covered with rippling ice to a depth of several feet. Our fun here was to slide down this rough but slippery surface on low wooden sleds made from the ends of a packing crate. Sometimes we used an old scoop shovel. The iron-runner hand sleigh was not rugged enough for this sport.

I found the hill still open and treeless, but with only a thin, skimpy patch of ice no bigger than my kitchen floor. The dead seed stalks of shooting stars and little elephants stuck up from the rough frozen ground that in the thirties was seldom free of ice before the 24th of May. That patch of ice could be seen from the house and we watched it carefully, for we were allowed to go barefoot when it was gone or on the 24th of May, whichever came first.

Just beyond the spring to the northwest is a cultivated field, larger now than in the thirties. That is where our ski hill was located. It would be poor skiing this winter. In the first place the hill is nearly bare of snow. In the second place there is a gas well where the ski slope used to be. It is gouged into the hillside to make a level site. The wellhead installations, the flare pit, the excavation into the side of the hill, the gravelled access road all mean that this hill will not likely be skied again.

It is equally unlikely that the hillside spring will ever provide a play area for five kids, nor the open stretch of creek a skating rink.

And the day will come when they will not even produce a waft of nostalgia.

ENTREPRENEUR ED MONTALBETTI
December 6, 1994

When the Lacombe Northwestern Railway pushed northward up the Blindman Valley to Bluff Center in 1922, Ed Montalbetti came with it. Ed's father, Felix Montalbetti, railroad builder in Canada for many years, was general foreman on the line. When the steel went on to Haverigg in the fall, Ed stayed behind, together with his parents, Felix and Irene, and his two brothers, Charlie and Ambrose. It was the Bluffton Store that changed his destiny. The Montalbetti family opened the store in the fall of 1923, having finished and furnished and stocked a building begun by a committee of local citizens earlier in the year. Ed Montalbetti would be a part of Bluff Center, soon to become Bluffton, for the next forty-six years.

I first remember Ed about 1924, when I was scarcely able to look over the counter. I remember that in those years when Ed or his brothers were behind the counter, there was always a gumdrop forthcoming for a little kid. More than that, there was very often a bag of gumdrops or hard candy tucked into the bottom of the grocery box when you unpacked it at home. I think this was generally Felix's doing. Later, when clerks stood behind the counter, the dispensing of gumdrops ceased, but an even more generous practice took its place.

At the back of the store stood the ice cream freezer, containing three flavours in three different tubs. It was a self-serve operation. A dispenser of cones hung on the wall; the scoop reposed in a jar of water. I seldom went into the store in those years without availing myself of this wonderful opportunity that could be found nowhere else that I knew. This is how it was done: take a cone, put in a scoop of vanilla and push it well down with the back of the scoop; put in a scoop of maple walnut to level it off, then add a scoop of chocolate or strawberry to make it look like an ice cream cone. Then you tossed a nickel on the counter as you walked out.

When I was a teenager, I wanted a bicycle in the worst way. In fact I needed one. I was going to school at Monte Vista, seventeen miles from home, and I was tired of walking that distance or even part of it on weekends. I had been studying the CCM catalogue, and I knew the bike I wanted, the CCM Rambler, all chrome and maroon, with stripes on the fenders, one speed, $46.60. I bypassed the manager of the hardware department and went straight to the owner. I had ten dollars in my pocket. Would he sell me the bike for ten dollars down, the rest as I could manage it? He didn't even hesitate. He wrote down my order and in about three days I was riding a brand new bike. It took me almost a year to pay for it, five dollars at a time, no service charges. I have never bought a vehicle on credit since, but I certainly did appreciate owning the CCM that first year.

It was with feelings of sorrow and nostalgia that I learned that Ed Montalbetti died in Penticton on November 19, 1994, at the age of ninety.

KEN LIDDELL—HILLTOP SITTER
November 24, 1987

I thought of Ken Liddell this morning as I sat on the highest point on this farm and gazed out over its acres and beyond.

I haven't written about hilltop sitting for some time, mostly because I have not indulged very often of late in that outdoor pursuit made famous in southern Alberta by the father and practitioner of the sport, the late Ken Liddell. Ken was for many years, in the 1950s and 1960s, outdoor columnist for the *Calgary Herald*.

I used the word "indulged" a moment ago because hilltop sitting is something you do best when there is absolutely nothing else to do. You must be free from closing deadlines and undone chores nagging at the back of your mind, or you cannot do it justice. Hilltop sitting is really a lazy man's diversion, as Ken Liddell would have been the first to admit. You would never find him atop a hill that he had to climb on foot. If he couldn't get there in his car, he found a hill where he could. That is where Ken and I differed fundamentally. I often had an urge and sometimes fulfilled it, to climb any elevation, be it a mere knoll or a forestry tower or sometimes a mountain, under my own steam. Ken admitted to an admiration of those who possessed this trait, but he hated exercise, and shunned it almost religiously, so I was saddened but not surprised when he died at too early an age from a lack thereof. Although I had only met Ken a few times, I have missed him, for he had a mild wit and easy style to his writing that I much admired.

It is hunting season in this area, and I am out this morning monitoring my fields, for my NO HUNTING signs are often ignored. It is a beautiful, crisp, frosty Indian summer morning. It is 8:30 and the sun is already ten degrees above the horizon. The temperature is about -5 degrees, and the air is dead calm. There is fog in the river valley two miles away. I can see over it to the northeastern horizon about eight miles distant, but that horizon, on the high land north and east of Bluffton, is quite indistinct with blue haze and frost and a trace of smoke. To the north the horizon is hidden by the top of the fog layer in the valley. Above that is a brownish streak that may be smoke from brush windrows burning in the Buck Lake or Alder Flats or Drayton Valley areas.

Even in the half-mile-wide valley of the creek below me, the restful, flat, faded colours of late fall are still further muted by haze in the air and frost on the grass. There is less contrast than usual between field and woods. The line of beaver-thinned trees along the creek blends easily into the field behind. The colour tones before my eyes are all duns and tans and pale browns and dull greens, many of them further greyed by clinging frost and atmospheric haze. It is a scene that will be found on this farm at no other time of the year and not every year at this time.

It would have been interesting to have shown Ken Liddell this view from this hilltop, and to see how he might have described it. The visual aspect he would have relayed richly and professionally, but he might have heard the quiet conversational tones of the gray jays in the pine woods at the foot of the hill and would not have known what made the sounds. Nor could he have named the rough-legged hawk that came sailing over the windbreak and dropped low over the brow of the hill right before my eyes.

Ken was a writer and historian, and a chronicler of local and regional history and of the people who made it, but he was not a naturalist and not a bird watcher. However, as I sit here in the sharpness of a beautiful November morning, I am glad that he had been a hilltop sitter.

SHOT FOR A MOOSE
December 10, 1996

Carl Berg lies in an unmarked grave on the west side of the Rimbey Cemetery.

At eleven o'clock on the morning of Sunday, December 11, 1932, Carl Alfred Berg died from a 6.5-mm bullet which severed the arteries above his heart and lodged against his shoulder blade. The shot was fired by a hunter named Henry Powell who said he thought he was shooting a moose. Two other men were present at the scene. One was a man named Keith Anderson of Calgary, a friend of

Powell's. The other was Powell's son-in-law, Clyde Wilson, who died this fall at the age of 96.

Berg's body lay unattended until 4 p.m. the following day, when Constable R. James of the RCMP, and Dr. Sam Byers, coroner, arrived at the scene. During the interval the snowshoe rabbits had chewed away the outer edge of the lining of his fur cap, relishing the salt.

A coroner's jury sat on Tuesday and Wednesday in Cliff Hewitt's Funeral Home. Thorpe Braithwaite, a longtime friend of Berg's, identified the body. The jury: W. A. Saunders, foreman; Dr. H. E. Halpin, W. Cotton, R. Simonsen, Lloyd Newsom and J. Adamson. Miss Bertha Adamson was court stenographer. Dr. John Byers performed the autopsy. The gun and the bullet were included in the exhibits. The jury rendered an open verdict. No charges were laid.

Carl Berg had lived on his homestead two miles east of Medicine Lake as the crow flies. He had been there since about 1920 when a small settlement was formed in this remote spot, mostly of veterans returned from World War I. Berg was a veteran of the Spanish-American War, although he would have been very young at the time of that conflict. He was forty-seven when he died. His address was Willesden Green.

Berg was well-liked by the many who knew him. His small cabin was a popular stopping place for many as they came and went from Medicine and Island Lakes, fishing or hunting. He did some farming, even raised sheep, and operated a sawmill for a time. He did some trapping in winter and partially lived off the land. In addition, he was said to receive a pension from the United States Government, and this just may have been why he was one of the few to survive on a homestead that far west. Most of his neighbours had gone by 1932.

I was just twelve years old at the time of the incident, but I remember the buzz in the community. It was about 1955 that I decided to do some investigative reporting, and I interviewed anyone I could find who had first-hand knowledge, or who had been at the scene. These included Victor Owen, municipal councillor at the time and purveyor of hunting licenses; Bob Fox of Bluffton; Thorpe Braithwaite of Rimbey, who had homesteaded not far from Berg; Alton Snyder, who lived a few miles east of Berg; Harold Saunders, Reinhard Vetsch and Phil Foss.

The accounts of Berg's death that these men related were often at some variance with one another after twenty-three years, and I

43

found that investigating was one thing; reporting quite another. So I sat on it. It was not until January 1991 that I talked to Clyde Wilson about the event. He and Carl Berg were standing in a moose bed, estimating the minutes or hours since the moose had been in it, when Powell appeared, riding horseback, on the other side of a small draw. They watched him dismount, then Berg hollered, "Get down! He's going to shoot!" and he gave Clyde a shove, pushing him out of harm's way, but taking the bullet himself in doing so. The distance from Powell to Berg was fifty-seven paces, as measured the following day—an extremely short distance for distinguishing a man from a moose. The lighting was good, by all accounts, and the only cover was small poplar and willow, four to five feet high.

And that is how Carl Berg died in 1932, and why Clyde Wilson lived to 1996.

FRIEND AND NEIGHBOUR HARRY STRAIN
September 10, 1996

Almost half a century has passed since Harry Strain moved onto the farm across the road from me. The half section had been homesteaded in 1911 by Father and Son James and Cliff Hewett. It was later owned by the notorious Bill Sherman and still later by Frank Peabody. It had been unoccupied and neglected for some years when Harry bought it through the VLA (Veterans' Land Act).

In the summer of 1947, Harry and his father set up bachelor quarters in the old house and went to work cleaning up the place, razing the old barn, piling and burning old pens and corrals, hauling away loads of junk and old machinery, building new fences and otherwise transforming a farmstead that had become an eyesore. After they had been at work for a few days, my father and I went over to visit them, and I remember that Harry made us coffee and served us bread and butter and cranberry sauce made from wild cranberries that he had just picked.

Harry decided to move the two-story, 1920s frame house up the hill onto the south quarter. He prepared the new site, and one day in the summer of 1948 he and I hooked our two John Deere Model D tractors onto it and hauled it off like a breeze. In the early winter of 1948, Harry and Marge Littman were married, and lived in that refurbished house for many years, and raised their family of three girls there.

I first knew Harry at Iola School in 1928, but he was in grade four, and one of the big kids, so I did not get to know him well at that time, but I remember even then that he was a pretty good ball player. I saw him on the ball diamond many times in the following years, and it was a sport he enjoyed and excelled at, but the sports at which he really excelled were hunting and fishing. On rainy days he and I would put on our rain gear and our gum boots and strike out on foot for the Blindman or the Medicine River. We carried fourteen-foot-long saskatoon poles, with heavy green line attached, and a tin box of spoons and plugs. Harry usually caught the first fish. It was a new sport to me, but he had been perfecting his skills for many years, having lived beside the Blindman as a boy. We soon graduated to rod and reel, but that is where he left me. Harry went on to become one of the most proficient fly fisherman I have ever known. I am sure he would have ranked with the greats. He also became one of the most innovative experts in the art of tying flies, a craft he learned from another expert in the field, the late B. W. MacGillivray of Rimbey.

I frequently went hunting with Harry, too, but, once in the back country, he usually saw to it that we took off in different directions. He much preferred to hunt alone. In late November 1949, before his prowess in this field had become so widely known and his services as an unofficial guide had become so much in demand, he and I went with team and wagon on a memorable four-day outing into the wilderness to the northwest. There was no snow, and it was sunny and warm, hardly ideal hunting weather, but we didn't mind that at all. It was great for exploring new country and having new experiences. It was one of the few times in his hunting career that Harry came home without meat. I, of course, fared no better in that department, but I learned a great deal on that and subsequent forays into wild places with Harry, about the ways and habits of wild animals.

Harry was keenly interested in Alberta's prehistoric past. He and I spent many an hour, many an afternoon, hunting stone-age artifacts together. For this pursuit we both had infinite patience, and our collections grew. We both had fertile sites on our own farms, but Harry's site produced the older pieces, projectile points dating back eight thousand years. For decades we always compared our finds, whether hunting in the same or separate fields. Our finds never failed to stir our imaginations.

Harry had many other hobbies. His vegetable garden was always to be admired. His outdoor photography deserved far more public exposure than it got. His woodworking skills in the form of picture frames, made from everything from diamond willow to seasoned tamarack, are displayed on walls for miles around. He was much too modest about his skills and talents.

Above all, Harry loved the outdoors, was at home in it, revelled in it even, and understood it better than most. He had a unique sense of humour which enabled him to tell a story well. He was my friend and close neighbour for nearly half a century. I shall certainly miss him.

Harry Strain, the outdoorsman, died on August 31, 1996.

HARRY IN 1955
September 17, 1996

Rarely do I recycle a column, but this is a worthy occasion. The following was published in *The Rimbey Record* on April 21, 1955. It was column number 22, and the fifth to deal with human history, whereas the other seventeen had focused on natural history.

"The longer I've known Harry, my friend across the road, the more I've come to realize that he is a true outdoorsman, one of the old school, so to speak. He likes to hunt and fish, this I have known for a long time, but he also has a curious interest in all things wild— fish, flesh or fowl. He has, to state it simply, a strong attachment for the deep woods and the wide-open spaces.

"When he leaves home on an outing, he will almost always rather go west than east, whatever the means of travel. A crowded resort beach is not at all his idea of a good place to spend a Sunday afternoon. He much prefers a wilderness stream, or a quiet inaccessible lake where loons are hollering and beaver swim about in broad daylight.

"His approach to things of the wild is, in general, one of inquiry and investigation, and he thinks of ways to test animal behavior that would never occur to most of us. Let me tell you of some of the instances.

"He was walking down the road one day when he noticed a coyote trotting along in his direction, but some distance away. He was in a dip in the road and the coyote had not seen him. The wind, too, was in his favour, so he quickly lay down in his tracks and waited for Mr. Coyote, who thought the road was his. When the coyote was just three or four rods away, he caught sight of Harry lying there motionless, and he stopped to reconnoitre. Then he came forward a few feet, weaving from one side of the grade to the other, hesitated, then came on again, more slowly and more cautiously still. He was about thirty feet away and still advancing when he began to growl—a deep, throaty growl, like a pup who is about to bark, but wants to know what he is barking at. At this point Harry had his curiosity sufficiently satisfied. He leaped to his feet with an Indian war-whoop and watched Mr. Coyote leave without saying good-bye.

"On another occasion, Harry happened to uncover a litter of very young weasels, and sat by the nest while the mother carried them off, one by one, to a new location. He said they looked like tiny lions, complete with mane and tail.

"Once he was sitting on a stump, rolling a cigarette and listening for his cowbells, when he heard an animal walking toward him through the dry autumn leaves. Being in an inconspicuous place, he just sat still, his cigarette unlighted. Soon the animal came into view, taking a course that would bring it three or four rods in front of Harry's position. It was a lynx, and when Harry saw that the cat was oblivious to him, and about to leave the area as leisurely as it had come, he did the first thing that came into his mind. He lit out on all fours, barking like a dog, in the hope that the animal would be sufficiently fooled to take to a tree. Not that lynx! He merely put on a burst of speed, leaving the vicinity in a few long, swift, ground-covering leaps, never letting on it even saw a tree.

"Harry's garden is just chock-full of those wonderful little soil conditioners, the earthworms. Some of them not so little, either, and when he finds an extra-long one in the potato patch, he is apt to give it to his small daughter, Cheryl, to take in to her mother, who is not as fond of them as Harry is.

"Once he mentioned his garden pets to a visiting neighbour, who proved to be very sceptical, asserting that there were no earthworms in this part of Alberta, nor for a long way around. The climate wasn't right, or something.

"'Come on,' said Harry, rising and heading for the garden. 'I can show you scads of them. Follow me.' Out they went, Harry grabbing a spade and heading for the richest, wormiest part of the garden. He shoved down full-depth, lifted the mellow earth and shook it out. Not a worm. He tried again with the same result. Then he dug deeper, and in different parts of the garden, while his guest stood by, trying not to look smug. Harry couldn't find one earthworm that evening. A short time later, the fellow moved back to B. C., where they also have earthworms in quantity, and so far as Harry or I know, he still thinks there are none in Alberta."

Harry took a bit of a ribbing from some of his friends when this appeared in the paper, and I hadn't given him any warning.

THE WATKINS MAN
May 26, 1996

My friend Peter was honoured one day by a visit from Ivor Johnson, the Watkins Man. The two were good friends and Ivor never departed Peter's place without a sale. This day he had a special offer on Watkins pepper. "Pepper is half peas," Peter told him.

"Not Watkins pepper!" exclaimed Ivor.

"Oh, yes!" reiterated Peter.

"Prove it and I'll give you a pound."

"Three PPPs, two EEs and one R," rejoined Peter, illustrating with pencil and paper. Johnson gave him the pepper.

Watkins Black Pepper was excellent quality, as I myself can testify. All Watkins products were noted for high quality, although they were not always the lowest-priced.

When I was a boy, the Watkins Man was a familiar visitor to the farm kitchen. I can still see him, seated on a chair, bending over to reach for a bottle or a tin from a well-packed case on the floor. Those cases were heavy. He must have wondered if he had missed his calling when the house was situated on a rise at the end of a long path. One case might be full of condiments, spices and flavourings to make a housewife's mouth water. Another might contain soap, shampoo, household cleaners, giving her the urge to get at the spring cleaning. Still another might contain medicinal items—liniment, cough syrup, ointments and a variety of pills and tablets—necessities in any household. He was sure to have a good supply of the most popular items, like pure vanilla extract, coconut oil shampoo, rubbing liniment and gall cure for horses and louse powder for cattle. Each of his customers had their favourites from among the hundreds of items offered.

As a boy, I remembered the Watkins Man arriving with a horse drawn rig. I think it was a light wagon or buck board on which had been built a covered, weather-proof box, with doors on the sides as well as front and back. Later, of course, he became motorized. I cannot say if he went door to door in the towns, where he might expect to incur the displeasure of local merchants. In the rural areas, the Watkins Man was welcome pretty well wherever he stopped, and we never worried or asked if he had a peddler's license.

Joseph Ray Watkins began mixing his own liniment and selling it door to door in a Minnesota town in 1869. From that humble beginning there sprang a continent-wide business which extended into Canada early in this century.

I had a visit from the Watkins Man earlier this winter, only it wasn't the Watkins *Man*, but the Watkins *Lady* who rang my doorbell. She couldn't have come at a more opportune time, not because I had a large order for her, but because I needed not vanilla or gall cure, but some information. And she was most helpful. I had just searched some thirty regional histories, from Hinton to Cochrane and from Rocky Mountain House to Brooks, plus the local library, without finding a single reference to the Watkins Man, yet that conglomerate personality, of various names and manners over the years, was a familiar and universally accepted constituent of life in our rural areas for many decades of this century. Why have the hundreds of writers of regional history, including myself up to this point, failed to remember and acknowledge him? Was it because we thought of him as an ongoing institution, not yet a part of our history? I don't know. What I do know is that the Watkins Man has not been accorded his due in our written accounts of pioneer living.

THE GREAT BLINDMAN RIVER REUNION
July 10, 1984

It was a memorable weekend. The two-day Blindman River Reunion was a total success: one long round of old memories, great good humour, hearty laughter, good food and unbeatable old-time music. Halfway through the first afternoon one of the good old boys said to me, "I've shaken a lot of hands, I've hugged a lot of women, I've kissed a lot of my old girl friends, and I'm ready to go around again."

That night we had a dance that was right out of the 1930s, with Margaret Connett on accordion, Wilfred Connett on banjo, and Christy Killian on the fiddle. These three played for many a dance at Blindman River away back then.

The gathering was held at Iola Hall, but on the second morning we all went up to the Blindman River School, four and half miles west, to reminisce, to have our pictures taken and to give a brief history of our lives over the past forty-odd years. It was the people who went to school here in the 1930s who were best represented. A school photo taken on teacher Douglas Sargent's little Brownie

49

camera shows thirty-seven kids standing in the snow on the east side of the school. Doug had that photo enlarged and mounted, one copy for each family represented. An even larger copy was hung at the reunion. Twenty-one of those people were present last weekend, each one of them forty-eight and a half years older. Their names, in 1935: Eva Mahood, Stan Mahood, Joyce Mahood, Martha Graham, Audrey Aldrich, Lee Aldrich, Elton Aldrich, Ila Steeves, Fred Schutz, Allan Schutz, Dorothy Schutz, Wilfred Connett, Marion Connett, Reuben Odenbach, Laddie Dersch, Virginia Pittman, Elaine Pittman, Charlie Hank, Dan Hank, Frances McVittie, Violet Dersch. It was the most enjoyable party I'd been to in years.

I will tell you just one of the many stories that came out of the weekend. It concerns two men who met forty-one years ago under very bizarre circumstances.

During World War II, Carl Knutson was a member of the First Special Force, a select group, half Canadian, half American, better known at the time as the Devil's Brigade. One night in August 1943, twenty-five hundred men of this force were put ashore at Kiska, in the Aleutian Islands. Their task: to rout an estimated ten thousand Japanese soldiers thought to be digging in there. They were landed without food, without tents, just small arms and ammunition. The reputation of that group as one of the roughest, toughest outfits on the Allied side must have gone before them, because the Jap soldiers left in a great hurry, without contest, and Carl and his men found the soup still warm in the Japanese kitchens.

Albert Odenbach's outfit, the 24th Field Regiment, was landed at Kiska some hours after the Devil's Brigade, as a back-up or mop-up force. By then the soup was cold. But because Carl and his men had no place to sleep and were getting mighty tired and hungry, that night they shared the tents and rations with the 24th. Carl happened to share a two-man pup tent with Albert and his mate. In the sack, in the crowded tent, the two men learned that the log houses where they had lived as boys in the Blindman River district were only half a mile apart. Carl had lived there in the 1920s, Albert in the 1930s, but they both knew many of the same people. Both, for example, knew the Schutz family. So they went to sleep thinking it was a small world, but never expecting to see each other again.

Then, in the rounds of handshaking in the earlier stages of the reunion last weekend, Albert read Carl's name tag and the name struck a chord in his memory. "Were you at Kiska in August 1943?" he asked.

"I was there," said Carl. The excited reunion that followed was contagious, as we gathered 'round to hear their story.

It is a small world.

TEACHER WM. FERGUSON
January 24, 1989

When I was a young fellow in my twenties, I would often stop in at the teacherage for a visit with the teacher of the Blindman River School. I would just happen to be walking home that way as winter twilight approached, and since I was still three miles from home and a bit tired, the warmth of the little log building and the conversation that would ensue, were temptations not to be easily passed up, and well-worth walking the remaining three miles in the dark. I can't remember now what we talked about: the war, I'm sure, and politics, and all current events. The teacherage was always untidy, with piles of books, magazines and clippings overflowing the shelves, and stacks of *Edmonton Journals*, which came by mail subscription, piled up on the floor. I fell heir to boxes of these clippings, which I have to this day. I'm sure I learned much from this well-educated, well-read, loquacious and eloquent person, but for the life of me, I can't put my finger on a single item. I just have a good memory of those visits.

The teacher's name was William Ferguson, and he was more than forty years my senior, being born 110 years ago this year. I

Log teacherage where William Ferguson lived. This teacherage was so comfortable that the last teacher to stay in it asked the school board for permission to remain there after she retired. The request was not granted.

don't know if there are many people left in the district who re-member him. Even in the 1940s—and he lived in that teacherage for several years—those who knew him hereabouts likely did not know much about the man. It was only recently that I learned enough about William Ferguson to make me wish I could go back to talk to him again.

On my recent bus tour of the Maritimes, I met a lady named Toddy Ferguson, who lives in Lacombe. I have met her a couple of times since our return from that trip, and on the first of those en-counters she heard me mention Iola, my erstwhile post office, and the name rang a bell for Toddy. "My husband's uncle once taught out there," she told me. "His name was William Ferguson. Do you remember him?"

I remembered. Iola was his address, but his school was Blindman River, and he also taught for a time at Willesden Green. To me and his students he was Mr. Ferguson; to some he was Bill, and to oth-ers he was Fergie. I quizzed this lady who had known him so well, and who had also been a teacher. From her I learned more about Fergie than I'm sure anyone in the district would have known in the years he lived here.

This man had degrees from Queen's and from McGill, and had been ordained as a Presbyterian minister, a fact he had never wanted known during his teaching career. In 1924 he decided to come to Alberta. He got off the train at Halkirk, and walked the fifteen miles out to his brother's farm. He soon en-rolled in the Camrose Normal School and began his teaching career in the Cornucopia district, (near Big Valley, I believe). He taught at the Big Valley Mines, which was separate from the village school in Big Valley. Later, he taught near Hanna, in the little country schoolhouse which years later was used in the movie, *Why Shoot the Teacher?* I believe Blindman River was his last school. He didn't need to teach in his later years, for he was wealthy by the standards of the time. He cashed his paycheques only once a year.

William Ferguson died in Calgary in 1963, at eighty-four years of age. He lies buried in either the Union or Burnsland Cemetery beside the MacLeod Trail, just south of the Stampede Grounds, along with other members of the Ferguson family.

I hope there will be some who read this will remember this man, or who were among his pupils at Blindman River. I feel a bit sad that I knew so little about him when he lived here, but pleased to learn so many fascinating things about him a quarter of a century after his death, thanks to Toddy Ferguson.

GRIEVING FOR LORRAINE
September 27, 1994

Lorraine and I were friends from day one—or perhaps day four. I photographed her, played with her, laughed at her antics, vied for her attention with all the other people in her life. She was the firstborn of my sister Dorothy and her husband Percy, and to say that she did not lack for attention and affection would be an understatement.

We all realized very early that Lorraine was a precocious child. She loved to be read to, and one of her favourite books was filled with pictures of real animals—not the Disney kind. One day when she was just a few months old, she heard her mother say, "There's a draft coming in under the door." Lorraine became terrified and it took hours to find the cause of her terror and calm her down. She thought a giraffe was going to come in under the door.

Charlie and Lorraine Barker, c. 1962.   *Lorraine died in September 1994.*

At eighteen months Lorraine was talking a blue streak, but long before that she was extremely articulate in a language of her own invention, and she would become quite exasperated, sometimes frustrated, when we adults failed to understand the words, phrases, sentences, and chapters of her stories.

In school Lorraine did so well that she was accelerated two years in succession. That was good news and bad news. It kept her from being bored in her grade but by skipping two grades she found herself at fourteen in a class of sixteen-year-olds, and she did not exactly fit in.

At this time (1960s), it was not cool for anyone over the age of ten to be seen riding a bicycle, so Lorraine and her friend Janet would take their bikes or their siblings' bikes and ride around the streets of Calgary after midnight on Friday and Saturday nights. Those were the days when it was safe to do so. It was about this time, too, that a group called the Monkeys came to Calgary. One of their number, named Davey Jones, seemed to have about the same status with Calgary teens as Ringo Starr of Beatle fame. The night of the concert, Lorraine won Davey Jones' shirt and she was on Cloud Nine. I suggested she cut the shirt into two-inch squares and sell them for five dollars a piece and make herself a small fortune. I'm sure she could have done just that, but the very suggestion lost me a lot of points. That was one of the few times that we were both aware of any generation gap.

Lorraine loved to write and some of her stories from her school years were published in this column. Points restored. After high school she took a course in journalism and eventually writing became her career and source of income. That career was cut short in ascendancy when on September 10, 1994, Lorraine died of cancer. She was forty-two.

Of all the scores of funerals I have been to in my time, often as pallbearer, sometimes as mourner, this one, for me, was by far the saddest. She was wife, mother, sister, daughter, aunt, cousin, niece, friend. For me she was niece and friend. We often lived a year between visits of late, except on the telephone. Our calls between Rimbey and Victoria often ran to forty minutes. I shall miss her greatly; beyond all words.

JUST A GIRL BY THE RIVER
October 4, 1978

I found her sitting alone by the river's edge, gazing with a dreamy expression out into the fast-moving, glacially-silted waters forty feet below. Her feet hung over the bank, her hands on the turf behind her so that she leaned back a bit like a photographer's model posing, only hers was an unconscious natural pose, and a pretty picture she would have made.

How, I wondered, could I, a camera buff, get caught like this without my camera, and with photography in mind into the bargain, for I was looking for a spot to take a group photo. I had a strong wish, before I broke the girl's reverie, that the instrument was in my hand and not back in the car.

I also wondered why this slim, attractive girl, with her hair cut short, should be here, so pensive and apart from the rest of the group who were so active and polyphonic, back around the buses at the parking site a hundred yards behind us. About fifty other people there were of her age group, noisy with talk and laughter and teenage banter, and here she sat, quietly daydreaming, with no hint of loneliness, but with an appealing little-girl look about her, so that I could almost feel a nostalgia in my own mind for the days of her childhood.

I did not really know her. I knew the names of only a few of the girls and boys that formed the group she was part of, and I had not spoken to her previously. Yet because I had been travelling with this group for two days now, she was not a stranger.

"Watching the water rush down to the sea?" I asked as I lowered myself onto one heel and followed her gaze out over the broad river.

"Mm-humm," she answered, "how fast is it moving?"

"If we had a stick, we could throw it in and see." I looked around for a stick. "I guess all the sticks have been thrown in long ago," I said.

I had spoken to her for only a few seconds, but already I felt a rapport between us, and her presence there on the river's edge seemed so natural and right and normal that the scene would have been incomplete without her. We both watched the milky, muddy water below us for a minute or two.

"I like to sit by myself in a spot like this," she said, looking at me, "and just think about things."

"Sometimes," I told her, not at all facetiously, "you can learn more that way than by listening to someone lecture for double the time." She nodded gravely and we watched the river some more. I felt completely at ease with this youngster, despite a wide generation gap—a kind of ease I find now and then with people her age. "I have often sat right here on this spot, and watched the water roll by, thinking about its long journey from away back there to away out there," I said. "I first came here about twenty years ago, before you were born."

"A long time before I was born."

"Not so long," I answered. "How old are you? Fifteen?"

"Fifteen," she confirmed, and smiled at me. She found it good to be fifteen. How much better it was, or could be and should be, I thought, than when I was fifteen. I felt I could have explored fifteen with her and compared a little with fifteen in my day, for we were talking easily, honestly, forgetful of the others, until someone called to me. My time just then was not my own.

I left her reluctantly, saddened that I might never see or talk to her again. And I did not even know her name.

That was the summer of 1970. That fifteen-year-old will be a woman of twenty-three. I wonder if she still finds time to daydream by the river.

PROCESS

FARMING BEGINS IN MY AREA
November 15, 1972

Not long ago, a young friend and neighbour of mine who has not lived in this district many years asked me for information for an essay he had to write, titled "How Agriculture Began In My Community." I gave him some facts and what I considered some reliable information about the district and its homesteaders and settlers; and I hope he gets an "A."

Then I took a look at what I had collected for him, and I said to myself, "The makings of a column."

The beginnings of agriculture were undoubtedly different in my home district from some nearby areas, due, I think, to a difference in soils. The soil is lighter and more clayed here and was considered next to worthless compared to the deep black soils found farther down the Blindman. Interspersed with the grey wooded soils, as they came to be called, were areas of lowland peat soils. These were referred to as swamp and muskeg and were considered of even less value than the grey soils. Both the grey and peat soils took many years to prove their worth. I think, therefore, that the soil was the main reason that our district was settled one to two decades after land farther down the valley was all taken up. Had it been level and black, distance from roads and railroad would not have been much deterrent to settlement.

Although this township was surveyed during the first six years of the century, it was not until just prior to World War I that settlers took any interest in the area, and that war, when it came, set the district back on its heels before it had even been properly established. Many of this first group, a large percentage of whom were bachelors, left for the services or to take jobs outside. Many, having no real roots here, never returned, and their homesteads were given up, some to be filed on several times before they were finally proved up, i.e. before someone obtained patent or title.

After the war, the district settled gradually. My own father came in 1921 to file on the quarter where he still lives, and neighbours were pretty well spaced in those days.

Most early settlers came here behind horses. Horses were their power for clearing and working the land and for building roads and doing all things that must be done but were beyond the capabilities of a man's two hands.

In 1924 there were enough children in the district to motivate their parents into forming a school district, with considerable opposition from the bachelor element and others who feared a school would raise their taxes. But the district was formed and named Blindman River, in 1925. Within three or four years, however, the school was closed for lack of pupils.

About 1933 a new wave of settlement hit the district. It stemmed from the dried-out prairie areas and from the cities where many were jobless, and this influx of homesteaders is again reflected in the history of the school district. In 1934 a new log school was erected and furnished mainly with volunteer labour, donated material and homemade furnishings, including desks. It opened for business in 1935 with thirty-five pupils in attendance, right in the depth of the Great Depression.

Times were hard. A few cows and pigs and chickens, together with wild game, wild fruit and a meagre relief allowance, kept many a family on their homestead until the end of the Depression. Some stayed on. Those who left when times got better sold or rented their land instead of leaving it vacant. Agriculture was at last on solid footing on 44-4-W5.

Mechanization, delayed by World War II, became a reality here by the late 1940s, and soon thereafter the potential of the grey wooded areas for livestock production became evident. You need not drive many miles today to see more cattle than the whole township was worth in 1935.

MEDICINE RIVER LOG DRIVE
January 2, 1963

It isn't every day that a hammer is turned up by the plough, even along the banks of a river like the Medicine. And it must be mighty seldom that anybody anywhere ploughs up a hammer like the one I have before me at the moment. Yet George Jensen turned up not one, but two such hammers while breaking land on his farm in the Meadowvale district, about seventeen miles west of Rimbey.

First, let me try to describe this hammer. It is made of cast iron and weighs six pounds. It is six inches in length, two inches wide by two and one-half inches deep at the centre, tapering toward the ends. The hole for the handle is oval-shaped and small—too small for the weight of the hammer, it seems to me.

It is the ends of this hammer that make it different. They consist of the letters "NN," raised and cleanly cut, so that when the hammer is swung against the end of a log, not only does it leave an imprint of those letters, but the grain of the wood is altered for several inches into the log, and the brand is visible even when a few inches are sawn off the log. I had never seen one of these hammers before, but apparently they were much used in the days of the log drives, when logs of several companies and individuals might all be rolled into the river in spring to be driven to the various mills downstream.

We usually think of these log drives as having taken place in Old Quebec or Ontario, but the fact is that a drive of no small proportions took place on the Medicine River, half a century or more ago.

The logs, consisting almost entirely of big spruce in the amount of approximately one million board feet, were cut on the hill that is now part of the Max Lawson farm, probably in the winter of 1911-12. They were hauled to the river bank close by where George Jensen now lives, and when the water rose and the river broke up in the spring, they were rolled into the current and the long drive to Bentley's mill at Eckville was begun.

Jerry Bell, an old-timer of the Meadowvale district, took part in that drive, and he says the crew were never dry during that whole six weeks. The logs had to be continually extricated from the willows, sometimes hundreds of feet from the river channel, and pushed back toward the current. It went much faster once they had worked the logs down the few miles to the forks of the river—about two miles as the crow flies.

There were few bridges over the Medicine in those days. One, near Wittenburg (Leedale), had the centre support removed to allow for the passage of the logs, and then it took two weeks to funnel them through. Another bridge did not fare so well, and was taken out completely—by the logs.

Once, during the drive, one of the men missed his footing and went down between the logs. Luckily, he came up in a bit of open water and got hold of a log, but couldn't get out of the water as the log kept rolling. Jerry Bell, who was nearby, jumped over there and got his pike pole into the log to steady it, while he worked log and man toward shallow water.

About this time Jerry noticed the fellow's hat floating merrily away downstream. "There goes your hat," shouted Jerry, pointing.

"The hell with my hat," gasped the half-drowned man, "just get *me* out!"

Putting two and two together, it would seem a safe bet that "NN" was Bentley's log brand.

1922 CATTLE DRIVE
October 4, 1994

I went on my first cattle drive in 1922, and while I don't have any memory of it, I do know something about it. It lasted ten days in July, and as with most cattle drives preceding it, the route was from south to north, with much better grass at the end. It started from a farm near the prairie town of Trochu, Alberta, and ended in the Blindman Valley, eighteen miles northwest of Rimbey, at the homestead my father had taken up fifteen months before.

There were five people on the trip: my father and mother, Charlie and Gertie Schutz; my Uncle Fred Schutz; and a six-foot-three-inch teenager named Wesley Williams. Waiting for us at the homestead was a young Yorkshire man named Allan Barnes. Two wagons—one mounted with a wagon box, the other with a hay rack—were loaded with some essential household goods and furniture, and some necessary farm tools and equipment. Wesley road horseback, and his job was to keep the cattle together and keep them moving. The pace of the trip was geared to the speed of the cows. It was always worthy of note when my parents were telling the story of that trip that the milk cows increased their output daily as they moved from the dry prairie into the lush parkland. They were milked twice a day as usual, cream was separated and butter churned en route.

While I may not remember the trip, some of those cows lived on for years into my memories of the homestead. There was Spot, a benign Ayrshire with a large black patch on one hip; Jean, also multicoloured; Bluey, a large cow with a descriptive name; Rattles, all red and smaller, likely part shorthorn, part Jersey. There were three calves, Jack and Jill and Jo (across the field they go). There were also some yearlings and two-year-olds.

60

I have chased a good many cows since that move to the homestead; chased them through willows, over creeks on pole bridges, into new pastures and along paths made by the cattle themselves. I have followed, led, headed, guided, called, turned, herded, hollered at, raced, corralled, loaded and hauled quite a few, on horseback, on a bicycle and on foot. Sometimes I had a dog to help but mostly the dog was useful just for his presence. Often I had other persons. When I went out of the cattle business after more than half a century, I did it cold turkey, and I missed them for a full year.

Now I have signed up for one more drive, but this time I have no intention of doing anything but spectate. I am not even going to ride a horse those seventeen miles to the pasture and back. I thought I might be doing a fair bit of walking, as I can't see me riding seventeen miles in a wagon, either. But then I heard that the double-decker bus may be out on the trail. Now that is more my style in 1994. In any case, I don't expect to sleep as much this time.

If you are taking part in the mini-drive, I'll see you early over pancakes on October 8.

THE GREAT DEPRESSION
November 13, 1979

Last October 29 was the fiftieth anniversary of the great stock market crash of 1929 and the beginning of the Great Depression. I didn't notice anyone calling it a golden anniversary, but the media last week did have a lot to say about that day and the days and months and years that followed.

I don't remember anything about the stock market crash. Here on the homestead the news probably wouldn't reach us for at least a week when the *Free Press Weekly* arrived in the mail. I wouldn't have been reading the newspaper in 1929 anyway except for "Little Orphan Annie." As for my parents, preoccupied with making a farm out of a homestead, the story might not have had much significance for them at the time, although they always kept up with the news of the world to the best of their ability.

The Great Depression I certainly remember. That was the decade in which I grew up and it was the origin of some of my most vivid memories. I remember the shortage of cash. For example, as kids we had a limit of thirty-five cents per gift for Christmas presents to other members of the family. Sometime in the fall, as early as was convenient, my father would stash away a five-dollar bill for buying Christmas goodies—candy, nuts and a box of Japanese oranges.

61

He did not want to risk being broke at Christmas time. Item by item—raisins, candied peel, almonds, spices—my mother would also begin early to buy the ingredients for a Christmas cake. I remember one year she couldn't swing it; I guess the hens were moulting instead of laying, and we did not have a Christmas cake.

I remember the terrible roads of the 1930s, in many cases—especially in winter—no more than trails through the bush. Municipalities were also short of cash. The portion of your taxes designated for municipal purposes was usually paid by working on the road. Anyone who has built a grade, dug a ditch or covered a culvert using a team of horses hooked to a scraper or fresno can tell you why we didn't have a grid system of good roads in those days. Road building and repairing was slow, hard work, and you were not getting any cash, but it was with a great deal of satisfaction that you saw your road to the nearest town or railway shipping point gradually improve, year by year.

I remember the influx of settlers to our area from the dried-out regions to east and south, and from the cities. For them, this was a green and fertile land but they could still find the going mighty rough, especially if they had a family of any size. I remember that many of the people in the upper Blindman Valley, particularly those who had not had time to become established, were forced to apply for relief, the 1930s term for welfare. There were no welfare bums, however. I think ten dollars per month was about maximum for a family of six. If crops and garden got hailed, or if the milk cow ate poison hemlock and died, it meant real hardship for a family on a quarter section that was mainly uncleared bush.

By comparison with some, I was pretty well off during the Great Depression. My parents had homesteaded here in 1921, and had had time to get established. With three kids, there was the eternal shortage of cash but we had never known it any other way, and even I, as the eldest, was too young to have to worry about it as I am sure my parents must have worried. But we were never hungry, and if our clothes were darned and patched and made over and eventually ragged, we never worried about that, either. I think I enjoyed the 1930s.

THE DIRTY THIRTIES—MY VIEW
November 20, 1979

We who lived in the Blindman Valley during the Great Depression were missing one of the better known ingredients of the Dirty

Thirties. We did not have drought, therefore no dust storms, and no gazing at a dirt-laden sky and wondering if it would ever rain again. We did occasionally see a brown haze blowing up out of the south-east when the wind had been blowing from that direction for a couple of days in May. While dry winds were blowing the soil away from the seed, creating great depressing dust storms in the south of the province, we were having bumper crops here in the 1930s. While the dust filtered into even the tightest of houses on the prairie, leaving a grey film on floors, furniture, house plants and bric-a-brac, we were more likely to be plagued by leaky roofs and muddy yards and muddier roads.

I remember that our gardens produced more than one family could use, and I remember some of our friends from the Iola Valley who had their gardens frozen, coming up to help us pick peas. I remember huge bins of potatoes in the cellar, and I remember going with my father and uncle with a truck load to Calgary to try to sell them. I think there were about two tons of them, an unnamed variety which we found to be excellent eating potatoes. However, every wholesaler and produce buyer in Calgary seemed to want netted gems. Finally a fish-and-chip place agreed to test them, and found that they made excellent chips. They bought the whole load. I remember being utterly fascinated by the mechanical potato peeler.

I remember the six-hundred-dollar men who came into this area from the City of Calgary. They were really battling long odds, but some of them did remarkably well considering what the game was. These men were among the unemployed in Calgary and as such they were on municipal relief. Somebody in City Hall conceived a diabolical plan to get some of these people off their hands. The City offered them six hundred dollars in cash to get out of town and stay out. There were strings attached, however. They had to use a portion of the money to purchase farm animals and machinery, and a portion would be meted out to them at their new address at the rate of ten dollars per month to buy groceries while they were getting established. In return they signed a statement that they would not take any further relief from the City of Calgary. Some of them actually managed to get through the Depression with that six-hundred-dollar start, but it wasn't easy.

I remember one family who had come to the upper Blindman from a dried out area of southern Alberta. There were six of them all told, and the father had just driven to Bluffton with the monthly ten-dollar relief voucher to stock up on necessities, including a hundred pounds of flour and two gallons of kerosene for the lamps and lanterns. Somehow, on the trip home, the stopper, probably a gumdrop, came out of the spout of the coal oil can and some of the fuel was sloshed onto the floor of the sleigh-box and from there absorbed into the bag of flour. For the next month, that family ate coal-oil-tainted bread. There was no alternative. There just was no money to buy another sack of flour.

THE "CHRISTMAS TREE" 1930s
December 19, 1962

For the children, there just isn't another day, or another season, or another event in all the years that can compare with Christmas. But in regard to the days and weeks leading up to that happy time, I can't believe today's children will ever know quite as much excitement, or quite the same thrill of anticipation, or even quite as much fun and gaiety as was enjoyed by the pupils of a one-room rural school twenty-five years or more ago.

It would be about the first of December that the teacher would announce plans for the annual Christmas concert, and as the month sped by there was progressively less and less school work done as more and more time was devoted to practicing (it was never called rehearsing) for the "Christmas Tree."

And "Christmas Tree," you will remember, is what those concerts were called.

You may remember, too, that it took a lot of practicing in order to have things go smoothly on that final night. It was a real competition, of a sort, because it was not only the parents of the district who came to see the program; everybody came, not just from that one district, but from all the districts around. Many people attended three or four School Trees, and it was inevitable that performances would be compared.

For all the work of practicing, there was an increase of freedom and relaxation of discipline that made even the avowed school-haters admit that school was fun, for a change. You could even talk out loud or move about as you wished, provided that you appeared busy with the enterprise at hand.

It wasn't all practicing, of course; there were costumes to be made, and lettered cards spelling out WELCOME or MERRY XMAS had to be cut out and coloured. There was corn to be popped and strung on yards of string to make garlands for the tree. The lower grades were put to work making red and green paper chains to decorate

64

the room, and by the time they were all put together and hung up, the room sometimes looked a little over-decorated.

So well did the teacher retain her composure through it all that her pupils took it for granted that she was enjoying it every bit as much as they were. In retrospect, it seems more likely that she may have felt embroiled in a nightmare from which there would be no awakening until about December 23.

Each child would be given a part in the program. There were recitations, monologues, dialogues and three-act plays. There were solos, duets, quartets and mixed choruses. There might be dances and drills and acrobatics. There was humour and reverence; and pervading over all was the spruce aroma of the big, busy, beautiful Tree.

With the final song by the school, a jingling of bells would be heard outside, then Old Santa himself would be seen trying to get in through the windows until someone showed him the door. Then in he would bounce, with his "Merry Christmas, boys and girls! Ho! Ho! Ho!" and if a teacher was young and pretty, Santa always got a kiss.

When the presents had all been passed out and every last little one had received a bag of treats, a box of apples, or a box of Christmas oranges would be passed among the crowd as Santa made his way back to the door amidst jokes and wisecracks from the "big boys" at the back of the room.

Then, for the next hour, the old folks visited, the young ones laughed and milled about, the little ones ran hither and thither, and the tiny ones slept through it all atop the desks along the wall.

Finally, with the room ankle-deep in coloured paper, peanut shells and orange peel, parents began rounding up their children, and hunting for lost mittens and scarves and caps to dress them for the long, cold ride home in cutter or sleigh.

I never heard of a school "Christmas Tree" that wasn't a complete success.

JOHN IN THE BARN
January 23, 1996

For the first half of this century that is rapidly winding down, rural people in Alberta—and they were the majority of the population then—got along more or less satisfactorily without the amenities of electricity and indoor plumbing. We knew we were less well off than our city cousins in those respects, but we made light of it.

"Don't forget to flush the toilet," was our admonition to anyone taking the train to the city for a few days. Along with "don't be dazzled by the bright lights."

Not until the early 1950s, when there was finally some real prospect of catching up to our friends in the city, did we become fully aware of our deprivations. A few farmers had lighting plants, and while these helped to bridge the gap, they were somewhat less than completely satisfactory. Fewer still had running water, even cold in the kitchen, and even fewer boasted indoor flush toilets. All that would change soon after mid-century, but that leaves a great many seniors and old-timers still in our midst who have vivid memories of coal oil lamps and barn lanterns and water that was hand- pumped and carried indoors in a bucket. And not at all the least of their memories will be the outhouse. Coal oil lamps we could get along with. Mantle lamps gave good light and the fuel was cheap. Keeping the house supplied with water was a chore, especially on wash day. Carry it in and carry it out. But it was an accepted chore. If you had good water and it was not too far from the kitchen door, as our farm did, you never thought of complaining, because you were luckier than many.

The same could not be said about that little building at the end of the path. It was not really such a hardship to use it in the summer months, but in winter it was well short of a pleasurable experience to spend time in that dreary, unheated structure. No problem for the young and healthy perhaps, but if you were ill with the flu, or even a bad cold, it became an ordeal when the temperature was minus thirty. I had a friend who installed a ceramic seat. How I hated that thing in winter. I threatened to rip it off and just let it drop. Wood felt much warmer to the skin in freezing weather.

I grew up in a frontier neighbourhood, although we didn't think of it as such at the time. There was a custom amongst the men and youths that may or may not have been known in other districts. I cannot really say. The barn, you see, was a whole lot warmer— above freezing, even in the coldest weather—due to all those large, warm bodies. The seat was a fork handle across the corner of a stall right beside the horses.

One of my friends of those pre-plumbing days got married, to a girl from far away, as they would say down east. The bride was puzzled by the absence of any footsteps but her own in the direction of the outhouse on snowy days. Then she noticed that hubby made what seemed extra trips barnward. Putting two and two together, she chided him and teased him, even when he explained about the warmth and comfort, but she didn't change his ways. One bitterly cold morning he saw her don her parka and casually head toward the barn. As soon as she was out of sight, he slipped on his parka and ran down to the barn and threw open the door. There was his bride, quite comfy on the fork handle beside the cows.

THE SILK TRAINS
December 12, 1995

I was never lucky enough to see a silk train go by, but as a boy I knew all about them, both from people who had seen them and from stories I had read about them, very probably in the magazine section of the *Alberta Farm Journal*, a weekly that my parents subscribed to, published by the *Edmonton Journal* during the 1920s and 1930s.

The silk trains were to the railroads what the *Concorde* is to air travel. They were the fastest trains in North America. They crossed the continent west to east almost nonstop, halting only for two minutes at designated points along the route to change locomotives and inspect the wheels. The freight they carried was not really silk, although it was called raw silk. What it was, was silk worms in the cocoon stage. Live worms, packed in bales. And that was the reason for all the hurry. Those bales had to reach the silk factories in the east, mostly in New York, before the caterpillars matured and burst their way out of the cocoons, making it impossible to spin it into thread or fabric.

The CPR, using its own steamships, could deliver the bales from Japan to New York in just thirteen days. The minute the ship docked in Vancouver the bales would be transferred to the waiting train. A car held 470 bales and could be loaded and sealed in just eight minutes. The longest silk train on a Canadian line was twenty-one cars. They were specially modified baggage and express cars. Passenger trains either met or passed along the routes were held at a siding, possibly for hours. Freight trains, too. I believe it was my Uncle Fred who told me about them whistling through Calgary at 60 mph. A silk train whistle must have had a good workout when you think of all the level crossings there were in those days. People who came down to the stations along the way to see the silk train go through were cautioned to stay well back lest they be sucked in by the vacuum.

A passenger train in the 1920s took 107 hours from Vancouver to Buffalo, New York. The silk trains made it in 75. The average speed, coast to coast, was 55 mph. I haven't looked at a train schedule lately, but I would be surprised if the fastest train on either line today, seventy years later, will do as well.

Silk trains ran irregularly over lines on both sides of the border as the raw silk came in from the Orient to Vancouver, Portland or San Francisco. Their demise came about for a combination of reasons in the 1930s. The Great Depression, the appearance of synthetics and the railroad unions demanding pay for passenger schedules on the silk runs were some of those reasons.

A resident of the Blindman Valley, Ambrose Montalbetti of Forshee and Bluffton, is said to have fired on the silk trains, but I have been unable to learn any details. Ambrose maintained his seniority as fireman on the CPR by working the required number of weeks each year right up into the 1940s, well after the silk trains had ceased to run. He usually took his stint during the summer, and some summers he fired on the *Peanut*, which ran right past his house.

Much of this information on silk trains I found in the book titled *I'll Take the Train* by the late Ken Liddell of Calgary. No mention of silk trains in *The Canadian Encyclopedia*.

THE SLOP BUCKET
March 22, 1994

I have read scores of books and hundreds of articles in newspapers and magazines about the lives of the pioneers, about how things were done in the olden days, and I have viewed, in museums on six continents, the artifacts with which household and farming chores were performed. Some of the early methods of doing things have survived to the present. Threshing bees and horseshoeing and wool-spinning demonstrations and instruction on the use of wood-burning stoves are good examples. You can read how to churn butter, make soap or tan your own leather. Yet there is one item of pioneer times, one which lingered into relatively recent times, one that is probably still out there in scattered corners of the 1990s, that I have never seen portrayed in a museum or described in reminiscences of pioneer times. How could one possibly demonstrate or adequately display that most essential item found in every pioneer farm kitchen, the slop bucket? The slop pail was certainly one of the least attractive aspects of country living in the days before plumbing, yet it endured in many homes through most of the twentieth century. The outhouse has often been fondly written about with varying degrees of nostalgia. Not so the slop bucket. It was an eyesore, an offence to the nostrils, an attraction for flies and the bane of the tidy housewife. Yet it was one of the most essential conveniences in the kitchen. Into it went the dishwater, wash water, water the carrots or turnips had been boiled in, left over tea, anything liquid, and sometimes, before dawn on a cold winter night, that meant anything. Wash water on wash days, bath water on Saturday nights, water from the wash basin, all exited from the house via the slop pail.

Water was used more sparingly in those days, since it had to be carried in by the pail from a pump in the yard, or uphill from a nearby spring, for if there was a spring in the homestead, that is where the house and other buildings would be located. And since all water carried in had to be carried out, unless it was converted to steam by the teakettle, we were certainly not so free with it as is the modern household. I would hate to have to carry out via the slop bucket all the water a modern family uses in a day.

The Schutz house in the 1920s was a fairly typical homestead shack, built partly of lumber, partly of logs. Yet my father installed a sink in the kitchen, with a drainpipe that ran away to a low area amongst some willows. However, this pipe always managed to freeze up in winter and since it was rather small it tended to plug up even at warmer times of the year. We just couldn't get along without that slop pail. It was usually a twelve-quart galvanized water pail which my mother would empty if need be, although it was well understood in the family that this was not her job. She knew that, and when we came in at noon we would find that pail full to the brim, so that it would have to be picked up and carried with extreme care, and you no sooner had it back empty than it would be recharged with the dishwater from the breakfast dishes that had been standing in the dishpan.

THE SLOP BUCKET II
March 29, 1994

Still on the subject of the slop bucket, that lowly, unloved and almost forgotten receptacle that at one time was so essential in every household.

If there were pigs on the farm, as there generally were in the earlier decades of this century, there would most likely be two slop buckets. One received all non-edible liquids, including soapy water, deemed not suitable for pigs, especially if the soap was homemade, as it often was. Pioneer women made soap in a stoneware crock with tallow and lye, and this soap could not usually be described as mild. Into the other pail went relatively clean water, skim milk; any food that had spoiled, moulded or become tainted, or had otherwise lost its gastronomic appeal or its edibility for humans. Since there were no freezers or refrigerators, and often not even an ice box, food spoiled much more quickly than it would today. The whey that was left after making cottage cheese was good for pigs. So was the water the butter was washed in.

The terms slop pail and slop buckets were sometimes interchangeable, but more often were not. Bucket usually meant a five-gallon bucket in which motor oil had been purchased. These well-made metal containers could be found on most farms by the 1930s, whether or not that farm had a tractor or a truck, and there always seemed to be plenty around when I was a kid. Prior to that we had a World War I latrine bucket bought from war surplus, but these were too big for any but strong men, or two lesser individuals.

I have a vivid memory of the slop bucket that goes back to my teenage years. When I was in high school, I always missed the first six or seven weeks of school. I stayed home in September to do the stooking, then I went on a threshing crew to get money to buy books and clothes and the occasional five-cent ice cream cone or chocolate bar. Sometimes I even spent thirty-five cents on a movie.

I was threshing away from home one fall when we came to a farm where the chief source of income was hogs. Most farms kept a few pigs; this farm had lots, and they were not all confined, but had the run of the farm and some of the neighbouring farms as well. I am sure the man didn't know, within twenty or so, how many hogs he had. The hogs in the fattening pen got all the slop water from the house, soapy or not. It was carried out in the two five-gallon oil buckets and I would see them rolling one around the pen, tasting the last morsel while the other was being emptied of slop or chop. I came in late to dinner one noontime and two young girls, aged about ten and twelve, were washing dishes. I watched them as I ate and when they had done everything in sight, they dumped the dishwater from the dishpan into one of the empty buckets and hung the dishcloth over the rim of the other one—the exact one I had so recently seen being rolled across the pigpen.

I appreciated the grub at the next farm when we moved two days later.

THE AXE
February 5, 1969

I'm keen on axes, especially old ones, which I collect. I would rather collect an old axe than wield one, any day. To state it bluntly, I no longer feel about axes as I did when I was a boy. Then, I was keen to take out an axe and make it dull, but my enthusiasm often dulled before the axe did. The best thing about a dull axe was sitting on a stump while you made it sharp again with a hone or a whetstone taken from your hip pocket. It was so relaxing. If I ever pen an ode to the axe, I must remember that word, relax. I used an axe so much when I was young that I became ambidextrous with it, which saved me a certain amount of walking around the tree or willow bush I was working on. And while I was busy dulling the axe I was putting a sharp edge on my appetite for dinner.

The axe, in its crudest form, was one of the first tools ever fashioned by man, and I have picked up, in my years of artifact hunting, quite a number and variety of stone axes, every one of which, if it could talk, could tell a tale. I have also found a couple of specimens from the axe's transition period on this continent: Hudson's Bay trade axes, hand-forged in England 125 years ago and used for barter with the Indians. One of these in particular I wish could talk; it has twenty-three notches cut or filed into its metal, back of the cutting edge near the hafting hole.

I don't know how selective the purchaser of a new axe is privileged to be today. Not many years ago he had quite a choice. First he had to decide between a double bit and a single bit. After that, but not to go into detail, there were Swedish axes and Hudson's Bay heads and Montreal heads and Michigan pattern heads, to name a few. The heavier ones weighed three and a half pounds; a standard handle was thirty-six inches long. Then there was a boy's axe with a two-and-a-quarter-pound head and a twenty-eight-inch handle—just right for a ten-year-old. Smaller still were hunters' axes and carpenters' axes with thirteen-inch handles.

Hatchets, by and large, had shorter handles in relation to head weight than axes. Broad axes and brush axes, of which I have also acquired some interesting specimens, have only been bought at such places as auction sales and second-hand stores for years. The axe hit its peak of usefulness—at least in the West—during the second half of the nineteenth century and the first half of the present century, depending quite a lot on where you swung an axe, for it was a tool of the frontier, and a more important one in this country than the rifle.

Now that axes are being used less and less they are changing slightly in appearance, being plainer and lighter on the average, and with shorter handles, often only thirty-two inches. While just about any tool or implement you can name has undergone enormous change and improvement in the twentieth century, the axe is an exception, and the one you might buy today at a hardware store would likely be similar in quality and appearance to the one Liz Borden used.

Liz, as you may or may not know, was a young lady who went on trial in the eastern United States back in the 1890s for the murder of her father and stepmother. Some wag, long since forgotten, wrote a bit of verse about her which remains famous to this day. It goes like this:

Lizzie Borden took an axe,
And gave her mother forty whacks.
When she saw what she had done,
She gave her father forty-one.

Lizzie was, however, acquitted.

THE AXE II
February 12, 1969

The pioneers, homesteaders and farmers who lived in the wooded sections of Alberta in the days of horse power seldom allowed themselves to get very far away from an axe, for that tool was a most essential item in their way of life, and they used it almost daily.

The axe lingers on as a useful piece of equipment on most farms, but one axe lasts for a long, long time now. If you should ever see a really worn-out one any more, it is likely a relic of those other years, when it was used for so many purposes that some of them are now forgotten. They were the years when calloused hands and aching muscles were as natural to a man as the good night's rest he enjoyed after an honest day of physical labour.

Think, for a moment, what the axe has meant in the history of the bush country, where thousands of acres of brush- and tree-covered land were cleared with human muscle power combined with a mountain of determination and the skill to wield a sharp axe. Think of the axe-work involved in converting untold thousands of great pine and spruce trees into building logs, saw logs, granary skids or bridge timbers. Quite often, the logs that went into a house were first hewed, usually on four sides—a monumental chore when considered today.

Then there were the woodpiles; enormous quantities of green poplar, or fire-killed trees of any kind, had to be converted from standing timber to a pile of stove-sized pieces not too far from the kitchen door. If you have ever split one of those great piles of blocks into kitchen wood, you will know that any kind of wood, but particularly wood with a high moisture content, such as green poplar, would split 100 percent easier when the temperature was below zero. Wood-splitting did not require a sharp axe, even in mild weather.

Many of the early fences in the bush country were constructed, not from barbed wire, but of spruce or poplar rails nailed or wired to tamarack fence posts. Half a mile or a mile of rail fence meant days or weeks of axe-work. So did the corrals, pole sheds and miscellaneous log structures on any farm.

The axe was used in lesser tasks too. Wagon tongues and reaches, sleigh bolsters and runners, as well as eveners and single trees, for all horse-drawn vehicles and implements were continually being broken. New ones could be, and quite often were, cut and hewed and shaped and smoothed and fitted with an axe. Fork and shovel handles, even axe handles, were frequently fashioned the same way. An old axe, much used and thick-edged, was kept for grubbing trees and picking roots, because you never used the good axe for jobs where you would be cutting or chopping into soil. Sand, gravel and stones were ruinous to a sharp axe.

A boy usually had his own axe and didn't touch Dad's, which was a good idea until he had acquired some skill as an axe man.

In winter the axe was put to work cutting a hole each day in the ice of the pond or creek so that the cattle might drink, or to chop the ice out of the trough in the yard. Hog troughs, too, had to be chopped out quite frequently in cold weather.

Under various circumstances the axe might serve as a post mall, sledge hammer, spade, wedge, crowbar, or even as a lethal weapon to behead a chicken for Sunday dinner, or to dispatch a marauding bear, as one pioneer lady did near the turn of the century, just a few miles from where I am writing.

THE NOSE GUARD
May 25, 1966

When Pas-ka-poo Historical Park is opened next year, I hope that featured in the farm and agricultural display section will be a pair of nose guards.

This indispensable item of horses' wearing apparel, so familiar to anyone who ever drove a four-horse outfit on plough or seed drill or binder, two, three or four decades ago, has today quite disappeared from hardware stores, gone the way of gall cure and hame straps and binder whips. Perhaps they can still be purchased if one knows where to look, but I'm sure I couldn't tell where that would be.

The last ones I bought—and they were not intended for horses—came from Engler's Hardware in Winfield several years ago. They were old stock then and Mr. Engler had to dig for them but he knew where they were.

Since some of you may not be exactly sure just what it is I am talking about, I shall try to describe a nose guard to you.

It is bowl-shaped structure of wire mesh with a brim of stiff wire hemmed over with oilcloth to cover the sharp wire ends that might otherwise have irritated the horse's muzzle. It measured about nine inches in diameter by about seven inches deep when new. A wire loop attached at each side provided a means of holding the nose guard in place.

There were two main methods of doing this. You could fasten a short length of haywire to each loop and run these through the side straps of the bridle so that the nose guard became, in effect, part of the bridle, quickly removable if desired. More frequently a length of light rope or cord, or even binder twine, was run from loop to loop of the nose guard, over the horse's head behind his ears. This way the nose guard was even more independent of the bridle and could be hung over the hame or on the back of the wagon when not needed.

The primary purpose of the nose guard was to keep a particularly pernicious insect pest, called the nose fly, from biting the horse in the tender area of the nostril. Without protection from nose flies, horses working in the field might become almost unmanageable. In the pasture a horse could bury his nose in grass or shrubbery, or in another horse's mane to ward off flies. In the barn, flies were no threat. But in harness, in the field, nose guards of some kind were essential for several weeks out of every summer.

74

The nose guard's other main purpose was to prevent between meal snacks. A plough horse that was continually reaching down to crop a clump of dandelions was not only a nuisance to the driver but disrupted the rest of a four-horse team. And a horse on a bundle wagon in harvest time could also elicit strong words from the man with the pitchfork, for, if left unmuzzled, a horse considered it his right and privilege to grab a bundle from every stook that he passed, shaking and flinging it this way and that, threshing grain uselessly onto the ground in the process of freeing the portion he had clamped his teeth to. The nose guard was the answer to this and to scores of similar problems and situations. Pre-mechanized farming would have been much handicapped without this simple contrivance.

The only other use for the nose guard that I can think of at the moment was as a sieve, used by the housewife to sift the hulls from ground oats that they might be safely fed to a flock of baby chicks or an orphan piglet.

THE IRON COOKING VESSEL
December 15, 1965

One day in late fall, Harry and I were wandering about on the ridges that rim the north end of Medicine Lake, poking among the cellar holes and building sites of the Indian settlement that flourished there three to five decades ago.

We tried to visualize the scene as it must have appeared on a fine autumn day in the mid-1920s, with all those cabins above the lakeshore at various levels and in haphazard arrangement. Some of them, we noted, had been built on promontories with a magnificent view down the length of the lake. Others hadn't had much of a view in any direction.

Old wagon trails branch away from this spot in every direction, following the ridges and avoiding the swamps. It must have been a bustling place in its heyday: with the smells of wood smoke and fish cooking and meat drying; the sights and sounds of axes cutting firewood; wagons rattling, children at play, dogs barking and all the other activities of a settlement consisting of many families.

And today—only dim, half-hidden clues to show that any of this ever existed. Forest fires have destroyed the evidence and now the site is growing up to deciduous trees and brush, and the ground surface that was once tramped smooth and hard by moccasined feet lies hidden beneath layers of leaf mold and peat beneath a veil of undergrowth.

We were noting all this and remarking about it when Harry stepped on something irregular and hard, buried in the debris of rotting vegetation. So he stopped to kick away the leaves and leaf mold to see what lay beneath.

"I've found an old iron pot," he called to me, and so he had, or most of one, for when he dug it out he had two pieces which fitted together, with two smaller pieces missing. The vessel was of heavy cast, flat-bottomed with straight but flaring sides. About twelve inches across and three deep, it had rested on three legs about one and a half inches in length. The two pieces Harry had unearthed held the ears for the carrying handle which had been replaced somewhere along its era of usefulness by a length of heavy wire, doubled and redoubled, and when you picked it up by this handle and swung it slightly so that the two pieces jangled together it sounded like a heavy, deep-toned cowbell.

We cleaned it off as best we could and examined it from every angle, passing it from one to another and speculating all the while as to the stories it might tell us if it could. How many miles had it been carried, dangling from a saddle or a wagon or a Red River cart? For this was the traditional way to carry a cooking pot, except when one travelled by canoe. That its travels had been extensive there couldn't be much doubt, for the metal ears were worn quite thin at the top, and this might well have taken more than one lifetime.

How many campfires had it hung over, along how many trails? Beside what streams and lakes had it swung, and what manner of people had dipped into its steaming contents?

What ingredients had gone into meals that had been cooked therein? Buffalo meat beyond doubt: bossmeat and soupbone and tongue. Also meat of deer and moose and elk, and possibly horse and dog, too. Tail of beaver and haunch of bear; rabbit, of course, and muskrat and squirrel; boiled duck eggs, fresh and not so fresh; whitefish and jackfish and sucker; saskatoons, mushrooms and waterlily roots; and prepared foods all the way from pemmican to pancake mix. Who could begin to guess the stews and omelets and baked dishes that had been done to perfection in this old pot.

From its appearance, design and casting, I guessed its age at 120 years. It could easily be more.

Its discovery brought to us a sense of the past of that place that no amount of tramping over the spot could ever have done.

THE STOCKHOLM CREAM SEPARATOR
November 30, 1993

It has been many a long day since I last saw a cream separator in operation; more than forty years since I last turned the crank on one myself. The cream separator was once a common appliance in farm kitchens and back porches throughout the land. Almost every family in my neighbourhood had one, and since I knew few people who had back porches, it would be found in the kitchen year-round. If it had been moved out for the summer it would be brought in again on the first frosty morning in October.

Not everybody milked cows, of course. Those who didn't, like some of the bachelors, bought their butter from a neighbour, or bought the same butter, known as dairy butter, over the counter at the store, where local farm wives with butter to spare had traded it for groceries the week before. The quality of the butter in this case was often something of a gamble, for quality was not always uniform. The coming of the creamery, or transportation to a creamery, changed all that, and stores by the 1930s were selling only creamery butter. Uniformity was in. Milking herds became larger and the companies selling cream separators sent travelling salesmen out into the boondocks to market their product. Our separator was a Stockholm. It was a small one, putting through three hundred pounds of milk per hour. Its crank had to be turned sixty revolutions per minute, somewhat faster than most. If you turned it slower than that, the cream came out thinner and tested lower in butterfat at the creamery. We liked to keep our cream at 33 percent butterfat. It could go as high as 40, but that was almost too thick to pour and therefore more was lost in transferring it from one vessel to another.

Other cream separators had names like De Laval, one of the commoner ones. Domo, like Stockholm, was made in Sweden. One called Westphalia was made in Germany. There was a Vega, which everybody pronounced Veega. I suspect that it was also made in Sweden. Some of the big machine companies also marketed cream separators. I know McCormack-Deering put one out. Cream separators were sold at least as far back as 1908 when they seemed to be a hot item in the United States.

The cream cheque was a semi-reliable source of cash income. It put groceries on the table and shoes on the kids, even in the toughest of times, and often bought the cream separator as well, at three dollars a week for seventeen weeks. That would be for a small model.

For the 450 pounds-per-hour size, or for the big 600-size, the cost would be more.

On the Schutz farm, we always saved some cream for the table. We used it in tea and coffee, on our porridge and on wild strawberries and saskatoons and wild blueberries in season. Once in a while, when the time was right and we had the ice, we made ice cream. That was the smoothest, most delicious ice cream I have ever tasted.

BUTTER IN A WOODEN BOWL
July 5, 1978

I could scarcely believe my eyes. There on the counter of the modern farm kitchen was a large, old-fashioned, wooden butter bowl, worth many dollars on the pioneer antique market. The bowl itself would have caught my attention but the bowl's contents made me exclaim out loud. Piled in the centre was a large mound—several pounds of freshly-churned, freshly-washed butter, a bright golden yellow in colour, as is normal this time of year. (In winter, when the cows are on dry feed, the butter will be much paler.) Standing upright in the mound of butter was a wooden butter ladle, probably as old as the bowl. Missing were the wooden pound mould and the butter paddle, used when farm butter was printed into pounds of the same size and shape as today's pound of butter in the grocery store.

Not for forty years had I seen butter washed in a wooden bowl, and I reflected that these bowls and the wooden working tools are only seen today in museums, yet in this kitchen I learned that they have been in regular use all down through the years. It all set me thinking about the old ways of producing and processing butter, and of how few people in this land today have any first-hand knowledge of those pioneer methods. In my own farm home, no butter has been churned for about twenty-seven years.

It all begins, of course, with the cow, from which the whole milk is obtained. Then the cream has to be separated, a process that I took for granted from a time before I was old enough to reach the handle on the separator. During the next thirty years, I probably turned that handle over some millions of times at the rate of sixty or seventy revolutions per minute. Once you had speed up, the milk was let through the tap from the large bowl into a smaller bowl where the level was controlled by a float and from there through a series of discs or baffles in another bowl whirling at high speed, and the cream came out one spout in a trickle while the skim milk poured from the other. It was as simple as that, and I had turned that separator many a night and many a morning before I ever learned about specific gravity and centrifugal force, or whatever it was that put thick cream in one pail and blue milk in another.

Cream to take to the creamery for sale was kept sweet, but that kept to churn to supply the family with butter was allowed to sour. You didn't want it too sour—just enough to make it churn more easily.

It was when the cream had been churned, the butter gathered, and the buttermilk poured off that the large wooden bowl came into use. It was here that the butter was washed with successive waters and worked with the ladle to get all the buttermilk out. As long as the water showed a milky tinge when the butter was worked, it meant that not all the buttermilk had been removed. Once the buttermilk was washed away, the butter had to be reworked to get all the water out; then it had to be salted, and worked and worked again to be sure that the salt was thoroughly and evenly mixed. Salt added to the flavour and aided in storage. And take it from me, farm-churned butter always had more good flavour than creamery butter.

Butter packed into crocks, covered with a cloth, a plate, granite crock cover or wooden cover over that, and placed in the cellar, spring house or other cool place, would keep for weeks or months in those non-electric days.

CHURNING BUTTER OR CHURNING CREAM?
July 12, 1978

There was a lot of work to making butter in the days when the farm-produced product was found on most of the country's dining tables.

The cream separator itself was a chore to keep clean. It had to be washed every morning and evening, and any farm kid who had to do it hated the very sight of that machine. And of course there were always plenty of cream and milk containers to wash and rinse and scald. The strainer was possibly the worst of all, as it retained any foreign matter that got into the milk.

Looking after the cream and keeping it sweet until it got to the creamery also took some doing. If you could keep the cream cans in cold water, that was about the best method available in those by-gone summers.

Churning was another job that few farm kids loved. It was not so bad if you had a barrel churn. Few of us did. I'm not going to take the space here to tell how a barrel churn worked, but it was the easiest way to handle a large quantity of cream, tumbling it over and over into butter. The most common method of churning a couple of gallons of cream was the dash and splash system, using a cross-shaped dash on the end of a smooth stick that slid up and down through a hole in the churn's cover. The churn might be of crockery, made for the purpose, or an ordinary five-gallon cream can fitted with a wooden lid. Glass "Daisy" churns with gears and paddles were quite satisfactory for smaller quantities, but for still smaller churnings you put some cream into a five-pound syrup can or two-quart sealer and shook it by hand. This method required that you loosen the lid every few minutes to let the gas out. Allow the gas to build up enough pressure to blow the cover off the syrup can and you could have a clean-up job to do. If you just wanted enough butter for supper you could always put a little cream in a bowl and churn it with an egg beater.

You always knew when the magic moment was at hand. If you could see the cream, it was when smooth cream took on a granular appearance. Otherwise you could tell by the sound of the splashing cream, or by the feel of the churn handle, or by the way it shook in the syrup pail.

Cream consists of 30 percent to 40 percent butterfat, so when the butter was separated, what was left was buttermilk, which had to be poured off when the butter had gathered. Then came the washing, with all its elbow work. If you had churned cream that was cold, the butter would be firm, but it would have taken longer to churn. Warm cream made soft butter. In winter, butter colouring would often be added to deepen the colour.

The buttermilk we drank. It was not quite the same as buttermilk you buy, which is a product of sweet cream, but I like the farm-churned buttermilk much better. It is also good for making pancakes. For years my mother would not let her kids drink buttermilk anywhere near bedtime; then we learned that if you salted it before drinking, you wouldn't have to get up during the night. Besides, it tasted better with a little salt.

I don't often get farm-churned buttermilk anymore, but a short while ago I was given a two-quart jar of that very product. Believe me, I enjoyed it to the last drop.

THE STONEBOAT
March 30, 1993

The stoneboat was a fixture on this farm and most other farms in the area at least until the 1960s. I really don't know when I quit using a stoneboat, or when I last saw one. No doubt some are still in use. They were so handy.

The stoneboat was ideal for hauling rocks off the field, because two men could roll a three-hundred-pound rock onto it and get it to the rock pile without doing themselves any harm. You just piled the smaller stones around it until you had all the load two horses could pull, and away you went. Some impressive rock piles were established in field corners using the team-and-stoneboat method.

Despite its name, the stoneboat was a versatile vehicle, much-used for purposes other than removing rocks from the field. Manure was likely the second-most-common cargo on stoneboats in my area. In the days of farming with horses, there was always plenty of that valuable commodity to be hauled out and spread on the fields, and the stoneboat kept to a minimum the need to elevate the heavy stuff, conserving manpower that more loads might be moved in a day.

Roots probably came next. There were always roots to pick from newly-cleared and broken and cultivated land here in the bush country, and again the stoneboat had a great advantage over the wagon, in that the work was kept low. In this case, it not only conserved energy but kept those soil-laden roots from being lifted up into the spring breezes at face level, for it seemed that no matter which side of the vehicle you loaded from, the wind was always blowing toward you. Even with the stoneboat, picking roots was one of the dirtiest jobs on the farm. Picking rocks was one of the hardest.

If the transplanted cabbages and cauliflower, or new strawberry plants, had to be watered, you filled two cream cans with water from the pump and hauled them to the garden on the stoneboat. The seed potatoes might go out at the same time and the same with bags of newly-dug potatoes and other vegetables in the fall, when they were hauled in the other direction. You might use those same cream cans plus a forty-five-gallon drum to haul water to put out a ground fire. You always placed the heaviest part of the load at the back of the stoneboat so that there would be some lift on the front end of the runners when the team leaned into the harness so they would not dig in in soft places.

A stoneboat was quite easy to build. Two eight-inch logs, six to eight feet long, were squared and smoothed with an axe and bevelled at one end to make the runners. Unplaned 2 x 6s were spiked onto these for a deck. The stoneboat was pulled by a chain attached to the two runners by a steel pin through the hole just back of the bevel. Since there was no tongue as on a sleigh, stoneboats were somewhat impractical in winter as they tended to run ahead on a grade, onto the horses' heels. This summer-on-dirt principle meant that runners had to be replaced periodically as they wore down from eight inches to two.

When we got a new John Deere "D" tractor in the 1940s one of the first things we did was build a bigger stoneboat. Now we could really haul rocks.

THE WOOD BUZZERS
March 25, 1970

I stole the idea for this week's column from another central Alberta columnist, Carl Morkeberg, of the *Innisfail Province*. In Column No. 112 of the "Markerville Story," a series I have been following right from the start, Mr. Morkeberg tells about some of the wood-buzzing outfits that toured his and adjacent districts, sawing up the farmers' firewood in winters long gone by.

While my memories do not go back as far as Mr. Morkeberg's, I do know something about wood buzzing, and it is not many years since I last participated in this activity, which is not dead, even today. Most of the outfits that I remember had, as a power unit, an old car motor of anything from four to twelve cylinders that

Buzz pile, Charlie Schutz on top.

Wood buzzers. L to R: Earl Wagar, Wilfred Connett, Orville Theede, Fred Schutz, Donna Connett, Martin Blondin, Roy Barberee, Charlie Schutz.

had outlived the car body it had come in, and had been adapted with considerable ingenuity, via pulleys and belt, to turn a circular saw. I also remember very well a rugged, single-cylinder, six-horsepower gasoline engine with huge flywheels that also served as the starting crank. It was an Imperial Stover, made in 1913, and it was still winding the saw at about 1800 rpm when Roy Barberree came to buzz wood here in the winter of 1945. In the latter days of wood buzzing, farm tractors provided more convenient power.

Whatever the power source, the job itself, so far as the crew was concerned, stayed just about the same for half a century or more, and was made up of hard work interspersed with good food, and, of course, the fun and banter that ensue whenever a group of men come together for a work bee.

I always considered wood buzzing to be one of the more dangerous jobs on the farm, particularly for the two men closest to the saw—the man who fed the saw and the man who threw the blocks. For either of them, injury or death was never more than scant inches away when the saw was in motion, and anybody who has worked on a wood-buzzing crew can remember close calls and sometimes cut boots or leather mitts ripped open because someone was careless in kicking the sawdust away, or because a jagged limb caught a ragged sleeve as the pole was pushed another block closer to the whining blade. Sometimes it was closer than a near miss, and Mr. Morkeberg, in his column, cites a number of buzz saw accidents.

It was the responsibility of the farmer whose pile was being sawed to make sure that limbing had been carefully done. If he had not done the job well, someone would be sure to ask him if he'd left his axe at home when he got up this buzzpile.

The words woodpile and buzzpile were not quite interchangeable. The buzzpile consisted of logs, poles or tree-lengths piled parallel, with the butt ends even, to a height of five or six feet, sometimes higher. The length of the stick was just whatever could be loaded on the sleigh, hauled out of the bush, and handled by the buzzing crew.

Converted into blocks it was no longer a buzzpile but a woodpile, although the latter term was often applied before sawing.

A crew of less than six considered themselves shorthanded. The hardest job on the outfit, if done properly, was that of the second man from the saw. He always carried the heavy end of the stick and delivered it to a position for the sawyer to make the first cut. The job I always preferred was throwing blocks, not because it was the easiest, but if you had a good man on the saw there was a rhythm set up that made light of heavy work. You swung your body as you flung the blocks, and the woodpile grew.

Time seemed to go fast throwing blocks; still it was always a welcome sight to see someone come from the house and wave that dinner was ready, and a relief to hear the high-pitched scream of the saw drop octave by octave until it was still, and the only ringing was in your ears.

THE ROD
May 31, 1983

I learned about the rod at a very early age, and I don't mean the one you spare to spoil the child; that is another story. Nor do I mean a fishing rod nor a hot rod. The rod I learned about before I went to school was a unit of measurement, and along with the inch and the foot and the mile, it was one of the most frequently-referred-to measurements on this farm at the time. Today it seems that only a few people other than some of the farmers and some old-timers even know that a rod is a unit of length. Fewer still could tell you how long.

The reason I knew about how long a rod was when I was small is that a great deal of fence-building took place on this farm then, and for many years to follow. The standard space between fence posts was one rod, and to measure that space a slim, dry spruce

84

pole was cut. In fact, an older name for a rod was a pole, a term my grandfather often used. The pole would be carefully limbed and made smooth with axe and pocket knife. It would be measured with a steel carpenter's square to exactly sixteen and one half feet (slightly more than five metres) and it would be light enough to be carried easily in one hand. There were probably at least three of these rod measures at various places on the farm at any given time.

As I grew older and went to school and took to reading for a pastime, I learned other meanings of this simple little word. I learned from reading "Dick Tracy" that it also meant a pistol in gang-land jargon. I knew people in the 1930s who had "ridden the rods" or undercarriage of a railroad car. They resorted to this if there were no empties going their way. Men who rode the rods were considered more seasoned hobos or railroad bums than those who rode in the freight cars.

I also knew about fishing rods. My first one was made from saskatoon, by me.

Many prosperous farms with big houses and barns had those buildings equipped with lightning rods. These were supposed to conduct lightning strikes harmlessly into the ground. There were travelling salesmen who went around the countryside selling lightning rod systems. We seldom saw them, as they didn't travel the homestead country much, but kept to the older settled regions.

In school I learned about the Gentleman Usher of the Black Rod, and elsewhere I discovered the existence of piston rods, and when I first took the Model D tractor apart I found it had tappet rods, but the first meaning of the word, to me, was the distance between two fence posts. It still means just five of my paces. Rod was an easy term to get to know and learn to use. A road allowance was exactly four rods wide. Six rods made ninety feet, call it one hundred if you weren't talking exact measurements. That was thirty paces, thirty-three if your legs were short.

Most homesteads were exactly 160 acres; one hundred and sixty rods made half a mile, one side of your quarter section. If you were ploughing a field that was half a mile long, or 160 rods, the full length of your quarter, then five paces, or one rod gave you an acre of ploughing. An acre was easy to visualize. The road allowance alongside your quarter was four acres, so forty rods of road allowance made one acre. Also, a spool of barbed wire was eighty rods in length, so you usually knew where your quarter-mile mark was on a half-mile fence.

Rods, acres and quarter sections do not convert easily to metric. Yet they are the basis on which most of western Canada was surveyed. Metric is here to stay. Acres and miles will be around for some time to come, but the rod has probably had its day.

CHIMNEY FIRES
March 21, 1979

There were—and still are—some actual hazards that latter-day wood burners should be aware of: chimney fires.

Chimney or stovepipe fires were a common occurrence in homestead days in the bush country. If the stovepipes and/or chimney were in good condition, usually no real harm came from these fires. You would hear a roar as the fire got going, and unless it was the first time, you knew at once what that roar meant. The first thing you did was throw some salt on the fire. (It made a lot less mess than water.) Next you closed the stovepipe damper. Every wood stove had a shut-off damper in the pipe within easy reach above the stove. Then you climbed onto the roof via the roof ladder that was left there as a permanent fixture, and dumped some salt down the chimney, or, as was often the case, the stovepipe, for many a homestead dwelling had no chimney of brick or cement, only the six-inch metal stovepipe leading to the roof and emerging via a roof jack.

If, by the time you got onto the roof, flames were shooting out at the roof jack, there was little you could do except let it burn itself out, and keep a sharp watch for sparks that could ignite dry shingles or dry grass in the yard, or other buildings. You needed to watch indoors, too, for sometimes sparks escaped via faulty stovepipes.

Many chimney fires occurred during periods of high wind, when danger was greatest, sometimes just ahead of a thunderstorm. The fuel that fed a chimney fire was creosote, a tar-like substance that collected on the inside of stovepipes due to improper combustion of the primary fuel. Usually its build-up could be prevented, but many people, even in those days when thousands of homes were heated with nothing but wood, had little understanding of proper combustion, and often were careless about cleaning pipes and chimneys regularly.

The greatest danger from chimney fires where there was no chimney came with the second or third occurrences, because the metal of the stovepipe, with repeated burning, could be burned through, allowing sparks to escape into an attic or other tinder-dry place. The creosote itself could be quite corrosive of the pipes, and since it burned with an intensive heat, the fire could complete the job.

Regular cleaning of the pipes was the best answer but it is quite understandable why the job was so often put off. It was a black and messy and temper-fraying task, and very often, when you had the stove and stovepipes cleaned and back up, the job was only half done. It took just as long to clean up the house afterward.

The thousands of latter day wood burners can be thankful that the modern wood stoves appearing on the market are easier to control. They are usually more carefully made and give a more even heat, holding the fire for a greater degree of efficiency, and holding the fire for a greater length of time. Last, but perhaps not least, the modern wood stoves allow far less of their by-products—soot and ashes—to escape into the house. The homestead days are really gone. Thank goodness!

THE HOME COMFORT
February 21, 1979

My mother will not be ordering one of the new $900 wood-burning kitchen stoves. She doesn't have to; she still has her old Home Comfort range which she has used most days since she was married nearly sixty years ago. It was just twelve years old then—almost new—and it still doesn't look its age. Just the same, that stove has had its temperamental days, let me tell you, days when the smoke preferred to come out the front instead of rising up the chimney (a northeast wind will sometimes do it yet); days when the smoke would go up, but smoke was all you got—no flame, and no heat. The wood usually got the blame at such times.

In those bygone days, the cure for a soggy fire was one that cannot be recommended. There was always a can of coal oil behind the kitchen door, or just inside the porch, or somewhere handy, for filling the lamps. You poured a little of that coal oil into an empty tin can, lifted the stove lid and threw it over the wood, then put the lid on fast. One of two things resulted. Either the fire burned up brightly, hopefully for long enough to get the wood going, or else the kerosene put the fire out altogether, in which case you simply put in a lighted match. Once in a while, somewhere on the prairies, the gasoline can would be picked up by mistake, and then they would read about you the following week in the *Free Press Prairie Farmer*.

Coal oil is not a common household item any more, but it doesn't matter, because if the old Home Comfort won't heat up, my mother just goes across the kitchen to the electric range. It isn't nearly as old, and not so good to get close to when you come in from the cold, but it is usually reliable.

The Home Comfort has burned more coal than wood in recent years, and in summer it goes for days and weeks without being lit, but in winter it helps enormously with the heating and saves on the power bill. For the past two winters, we have been using less coal and more wood in the old girl. Coal was great when I used to haul it from the mine where it cost $4.50 per ton. All the wood you needed then was some nice dry kindling and a few sticks to get the fire started. Now with coal around $30 a ton and the hauling from Rimbey on top of that, I am more inclined to go into the woods and cut down the dead trees that always seem to be a renewable resource. I always did like working in the woods, and with modern chain saws to do the felling, bucking and cutting into firewood lengths, it is much easier than it used to be.

Woodpiles are much smaller today than in the past, but it is still a source of satisfaction to bring in good dry firewood from the wooded areas of the farm and feed it stick by stick into that old Home Comfort range from which emanates a kind of body-warming heat that cannot be duplicated by any basement furnace or electric range. That old wood-burning stove is aptly named.

BARBED WIRE
July 3, 1968

For one hundred years now, western men have been expressing themselves in forceful and often unprintable phrases on the ancestry, life history and means of demise of an individual who is anonymous to virtually all of them.

The pious, taciturn or even-tempered among them said, "The so-and-so who invented barbed wire should have been hung with the first twenty feet of it." I have heard enough of the embellishments and variations to know that they are unbelievably colourful, imaginative and infinite, and that they involved an assortment of curses, imprecations and profane invective that are fortunately unrecorded and mostly forgotten.

Yet most of these men knew, even as they blasphemed, that they were allowing their emotions to override their common sense; that in spite of torn clothes and punctured skins and scars that often lasted a lifetime, barbed wire was really a blessing in disguise, and that it was the answer to a number of problems arising with the opening of the West to settlement and agriculture.

Accepted first in the eastern states, the prickly fence ran into some opposition in the West from both homesteaders and ranchers. But then the ranchers found that a tight, multi-strand fence would hold even a herd of Texas longhorns, and fences went up across hundreds of miles of range. Homesteaders soon discovered that it was the cheapest way to fence 160 acres on the prairie where there were no rocks or logs or rails or any of the materials used elsewhere for fences.

Research has shown that there was not just one but several inventors of barbed wire during the 1860s and 1870s, but since the names and dates mean little today, I shall skip over them except to say that one Joseph Gliddon produced the first barbed wire to look like the modern product, and he went on to be a big wheel in the American Steel and Wire, the company which enjoyed the monopoly of the rapidly-expanding barbed wire market by the turn of the century.

Barbed wire has always been associated with war and bloodshed; first the range wars of 1870s and 1880s in the western states, then in a more direct way in the Spanish-American War, where it was the most effective means of halting a cavalry charge dead in its tracks. It has been a cruel weapon of warfare ever since, as anyone who has encountered the long, sharp spikes of the product made expressly for military purposes, will testify.

Most of us would be surprised at the variety of samples of barbed wire that could be gathered from virtually any rural township in the country. One could make an interesting display that would include two-foot lengths of several varieties of two-point wire used in homesteading days, and a length of the lightweight, intractable, twisty stuff that was all a farmer could buy in the days of World War II. There is less variety in today's four-point barbed wire, but early samples would have to include a kind of wire cut from strips of metal with the barbs formed of long, sharp points, twisted and turned and right-angled.

Perhaps you will be able to see such a display one day soon in Pas-ka-poo Historical Park.

THE BARBED WIRE PHONE
May 3, 1956

There are probably not very many houses in this part of the country that can boast two telephones. But we have two in ours. One is the orthodox variety which connects us with more than a score of other subscribers on a party line as well as with phones in Rimbey, Calgary, New York, London and the rest of the world. The other, which we have been using for more than a year, is far less pretentious in scope but comes in handy nevertheless. We call it the barbed wire phone, for it runs on the top wire of the fence lines. Had we known how easily installed it was, we might have been using it years ago.

Such systems have long been in use on the prairie but were not thought to be practical for bush-grown fence lines. While small brush doesn't seem to bother a great deal, trees of any size touching the wire do tend to ground it, especially if they are grown around the wire.

Our total length of line is about three and a half miles and serves four homes. Almost any kind of wire will serve as lead-in wire and to carry the line over road allowances and gateways. We have made good use of the light, insulated wire left along the roadsides by seismograph crews. Our phone boxes are homemade, using receivers and speakers from dismantled phones. We use various types of batteries, from three ordinary telephone cells to a hotshot or a six-volt car battery. A Ford coil is used to step up the power and for buzzing.

The best possible ground is the well, but if you ground to the pump, reception may be interfered with when the pump is operating.

We use signals as on any other party line. Here it is one long and one short, to coincide with our ring on the other telephone. The signals are buzzes created by the coil at the sender's set and heard through the receiver.

In spite of its restricted use as compared to conventional phones, this line is used almost daily and, in the short time that it has been operating, has saved a lot of people a good deal of time and considerable travelling. We in this house, being on the regular phone line, are frequently asked to relay messages in one direction or another, so that, all in all, the barbed wire phone is not only a boon to the four "subscribers" but it benefits other people as well.

A PRIVATE LINE AT LAST
November 8, 1988

Alexander Graham Bell invented the telephone in 1875. In October, 1988, 113 years later, I get my very own private line.

The telephone came to this house in 1941. Our number was 811. Our ring was two long and one short and there were probably twelve or fourteen other subscribers on that party line. Moreover, the demand was growing, with names on a waiting list. If I remember correctly, a household near enough to a main line to get service had to supply poles and labour. The company supplied wires and insulators and sometimes the phone box. The instrument was usually a secondhand, reconditioned, hand-cranked apparatus that required a pair of batteries that were shaped like a giant flashlight battery with both the positive and negative posts on the top.

Rural Alberta was served in those days by a system of locally-run organizations known as Rural Mutual Telephone Companies. Our mutual had Iola-Hoadley tacked onto the front of that mouthful. Our central office and switchboard was in Rimbey and there were several other mutuals using that same central, with lines radiating out in all directions. If you wanted to call someone on one of those other lines, you had to go through central. You held in a small black button on the left side while you twirled the crank on the right side of the wooden box, then you listened for the operator to answer with the query "Number please." You told her the number you wished to be connected to; she made the appropriate connections on her switchboard and rang them for you. If you asked for 606, she would press the buzzer to ring a long and a short. If you asked for 410, which was the number of the Bluffton store, operated by Montalbetti Bros. Ltd., all the phones along the 400 line would ring with two rings. If you asked for 402, the Imperial Oil station in Bluffton, the operator sent two short rings out on the line and Harry Nordstrom would likely answer. To get someone on your own line, you rang their code yourself, without pushing the little button.

In the Central Region telephone book, under Rimbey, all these party line numbers had an R in front of them, signifying rural. Numbers within the town of Rimbey were usually low numbers and did not have the preceding R. I have a thermometer issued as a Christmas gift by the Jepson Drug Co. Rimbey. Their number was 8. The Bank of Montreal was 2, the hospital was 4, the hotel was 30, *The Rimbey Record* was 1.

The line the Schutzes were on, line 8, kept expanding after the war, in 1946, until at one point there were twenty-six subscribers, each of whom heard all the others' rings. Can you imagine trying to get that line when it wasn't busy? Three a.m. was the best time to do your phoning. The line was then divided, but the two lines were still overcrowded, and still there were people waiting for phones. Presumably this situation prevailed all over the province in the 1950s, and the eventual solution was to do away with pole lines in Alberta and go to underground cable with no more than four subscribers to a party line. This was a great boon as storm and high winds no longer meant a break in telephone service. Backhoes, however, became a threat. This system served the province well for many years. Now it has been updated to give us all a private line—something the urban dweller has long taken for granted.

Yesterday a man from AGT brought me two new phones and installed some jacks. All I need now is a cordless phone that I can take out into the yard with me, but I have no plans as yet for an answering machine.

I LEARN TO DRIVE—THE 1929 ESSEX
September 2, 1980

My very first driving experience involved the fording of numerous very wet and gooey mudholes. It was a warm, sunny, Saturday morning, and I was on my own in the beautiful, shiny black 1929 Essex which was then ten years old, but which my father had recently bought, and which looked much as it had the day it came off the assembly line. My father, returning from a trip to Red Deer, had been caught in a cloudburst and forced to leave the car at Bluffton. I don't remember how he made it home from there. He may have walked the nine miles or he may have caught a ride with someone in town with a team of horses. Anyway, his misfortune was my good luck.

I was on my way home from Monte Vista where I had been at school all week, and I was on foot. I don't remember where my bicycle was. I had probably hiked down the railroad track from the water tank, and getting into Bluffton hot and tired, I stopped at the Bluebird Cafe for a five-cent bottle of pop. There, in conversation with Jack Livingston Sr., owner of the cafe, I learned that the Essex was parked out back and the keys were behind the till. No more walking for Little Freddie. I had never driven that Essex or any car before, but I knew how it was done. I had Jack drive it to the corner where Bluffton's Centennial rock now stands. There he left me to my own devices, and I left him to check on his horses in pasture there.

I slid over behind the wheel, put the gear shift into low, took a deep breath to calm my nervous excitement, and let the clutch out very slowly and carefully. I drove half a mile before I tried changing gears; another half mile and I slipped her into high. What a way to go! That Essex was a really beautiful car to drive as well as to look at. Soft springs made even our rough roads seem almost smooth, and I remember that the engine purred where other cars of that day chugged. It never occurred to me that it was some kind of desecration to put a car like that over roads like ours.

I knew that road like the palm of my hand, and I hit every mudhole just the way it should be done. I negotiated the steep little hill at which we had always called "The Canyon," where little Gus Schuman lived (Hardwick's now) and sailed past the Iola cemetery and down Schweiger's hill toward the swamp. I knew that there was a bad hole just on the west side of the bridge across a little creek, and I knew that Vic Dersch had been stuck in there with six head of horses and mules on a loaded wagon, never mind a car. "Just their ears sticking out," said Vic, who sometimes exaggerated. This was a peat bog, not clay like most of the rest of the road, and I was worried just a bit. But the month was June and the sun shone eighteen hours a day if the sky was clear, and there was a firm if not dry track right across that half mile of peat, including the bad place, and I rolled right through. All the mudholes the rest of the two and a half miles home were hard-bottomed and I knew I had it made. I breezed into the yard and parked in the usual place, turned off the motor and nonchalantly walked to the house as the rest of the family poured out the front door to meet me.

I had come from Bluffton in half an hour instead of the three hours it would have taken me to walk it. I have driven a motor vehicle perhaps a third of a million miles since then, but seldom, if ever, have I driven seven miles that afforded me greater satisfaction.

THE BENNETT BUGGY
August 22, 1995

Bennett buggies were a common sight on rural roads in Alberta during the Great Depression. They were at least as common as buggies where I lived on the fringe of the civilized world. However, whereas people who had cameras photographed their buggies, there were relatively few photographs of Bennett wagons or buggies.

(The words were interchangeable. If the vehicle were used for hauling loads, it would be termed wagon. The same vehicle on the road as a runabout behind a fast driving team would be a buggy.) Considered a make-do contraption with an ancestry that could not be disguised, a Bennett buggy was, nevertheless, an easy-pulling, smooth-running vehicle if air was kept in the tires. It could be a bit bouncy on rough roads.

If it became economically unfeasible or impossible because of wartime tire rationing to keep pneumatic tires on the vehicle, the old tires were cut down and fitted into the rims to make a more solid wheel, resulting in a rougher but less bouncy ride.

My father never owned a Bennett buggy but neighbours did and I have ridden many a mile in one in my younger days. No two Bennett buggies looked alike. Every individual who stripped down an old car to convert it to a horse-drawn conveyance did it his own way. The majority of such vehicles had begun life as a Ford or a Chev, but other makes were also used, from Hupmobiles to MacLaughlin Buicks. My Uncle Fred had a Bennett wagon made from a Ford undercarriage. It was definitely a wagon, because he did not drive it, but pulled it behind the tractor. It was the only wheeled vehicle, other than the tractor, that he owned over many years, although he had a large stoneboat. That Bennett wagon hauled lumber, firewood, roots, rocks, tamarack fenceposts and spruce poles, and sometimes a dog named Bingo.

Most of my memories of Uncle Fred's Bennett wagon centre around threshing time, when it became the gas wagon, transporting fuel, oil, grease, parts and tools from field to field and from farm to farm. At that time it was neither driven with horses nor hauled by the tractor. The last man out of the field or off a farm had to chain it to the back of his bundle wagon and leave it at the next set. Every bundle hauler got his turn at this chore, and it would slow him down on a long move. In the house at dinnertime it would be referred to as the gas wagon. In the field, away from polite society, it was called the crap wagon.

There were also a good many two-wheeled rigs on the road in the 1930s, made by mounting a box on the springs, single-axle and wheels of an old car. In Alberta these were called Brownlee carts; in Saskatchewan, Anderson carts. R. B. Bennett was Prime Minister of Canada, 1930 to 1935; Brownlee and Anderson were premiers of Alberta and Saskatchewan. The naming of depression-style vehicles after the three men was not exactly considered an honour.

MUDHOLES
August 19, 1980

The back country of Alberta was no motorist's paradise when I learned to drive, and the main roads were nothing to brag about either. The only gravelled road we ever got onto was the Edmonton-Calgary Trail, and it was no speedway. Stretches of washboard spoiled many of its miles, and stretches of dusty-when-dry, slippery-when-wet spoiled many more. As for the back roads, they would hardly be considered roads today. They were rough and dusty at the best of times; muddy when it rained, and rutted, wet or dry. Once in a while they might see a municipal maintainer, but it was frequently broken and provided only slight improvement at other times.

It was the mudholes that made driving in the country such a challenge in my early driving days. Mudholes were the main feature of most of our district roads until after World War II. How I remember mudholes! Big ones and little ones; deep ones and shallow ones. They came hard-bottomed and soft- bottomed, some with a stream of water flowing in one side and out the other. There were mudholes you could find your way around and those you drove straight through, often depending on the amount of clearance beneath the vehicle you were driving. So many decisions to make. Did one keep to right or left? Did you ease into the puddle in a low gear, or did you hit it in high, depending on momentum to carry you through to dry land on the other side?

Local drivers usually knew each individual mudhole and how best to negotiate it, and they developed a sixth sense about mudholes in general, so that with some careful probing with a stout stick, one could assess each mudhole to determine a plan of attack.

Rural drivers usually did not get stuck. City drivers, lacking our experience, often failed to make the farther shore. Very often they weren't even equipped to help themselves: no shovel, no tow chain, not likely even a pair of gum boots in the car. Many a pair of shiny Oxfords took a beating in and around a country mudhole.

Many was the time during the 1940s and 1950s, when our roads were still in the horse-and-wagon stage, that someone would knock on our door to ask if we could pull them out of a mudhole. We would have to go to the barn, or maybe the pasture, catch a team of horses and harness them, take a set of doubletrees off the wagon, find a couple of logging chains, drag the whole works (behind the horses) down the road to wherever the car was, wade into the mud and water to hook a chain under the vehicle, then ease the horses into the load and slap them on the tail with the lines, while the driver of the car roared his motor and spun his wheels like crazy.

We hauled out everyone from the local MLA to the local moonshiner, and the only one we ever charged was the moonshiner, one morning just at dawn after he had spent a profitable night. "How much do I owe you?" he asked, after we had got him to dry ground. "Five dollars," said brother Allan, who was driving the horses. He peeled off a bill from a big roll and paid that exorbitant fee without batting an eye.

THE LACOMBE NORTHWESTERN
May 15, 1963

Railroading is a favourite theme for Ken Liddell, whose column is published four times a week in the *Calgary Herald*. One day last winter, he told the story of the Lacombe Northwestern Railroad. He had been reading *Pas-ka-poo: An Early History of Rimbey and the Upper Blindman Valley.*

A couple of weeks later, he published a letter from a man named Denny Brown, who had some first-hand information about this road. Mr. Brown's comments should make interesting reading for subscribers to this paper, so I'm going to use them for this week's column. As Ken put it, Over to Mr. Brown:

"I was delighted with your story on the Lacombe Blindman Valley railway. My father came to Canada as the English factory representative who installed the first electric car, and he was talked into staying on as master mechanic.

"You will appreciate that, although I was a mere child at the time, just after the First War, I was pretty impressed with Canada as it looked from Lacombe that cold, cold winter, and later from Rimbey, which became the operating headquarters.

"When the railway built into Rimbey, it was freely predicted the whole town would move to the station. It didn't. I recall that one man did move his hotel, and that was the beginning and also the end of what they thought would be New Rimbey.

"The original car was a fancy piece of rolling stock, with polished woodwork, shining brass and elegant upholstery. The car's one fault was that it wouldn't stay on the tracks.

"The next one they brought in had the appearance of one of those present-day zephyr-type coaches with porthole windows and a really streamlined front.

"All I remember about that one was that it made a terrible noise, which appalled the farmers along the right-of-way, not to mention the horses and cows.

"It smelled to high heaven, too. However, both were forerunners of what we refer to today as dayliners.

"I don't know about backing up to pick up passengers but the mixed train occasionally did wait for someone who might have been a few minutes late getting to the station. This played hob with the timetable but was considered good public relations, I guess.

"There was a particularly bothersome grade just outside Bentley. More than once the train pulled out, reached the grade and the passenger coach became uncoupled. The engineer carried on until someone pointed out that one of his cars was missing and in the meantime the coach had rolled back down the grade to a gentle stop at the station. This was convenient for any who had missed the train.

"One of the engineers, I've heard, was particularly partial to alcohol which he could obtain easiest at Lacombe. Came time for the train to pull out, passengers and freight aboard, then the conductor would discover the engineer to be missing.

"There would be quite a hunt for the engineer. After they'd find him, we would pull out, and, depending upon his mood, it was either like a bullet or the slower but less-frightening process of shaking and rattling like crazy.

"Sometimes the engineer didn't know whether he was coming or going and the passengers shared his confusion but without his exhilaration.

"The engineer also had his own seat for the cab. He wouldn't let anyone else use it in his absence. In fact, when they rounded him up they would make sure he had his seat with him.

"The railway had a steady war with beaver near Bentley. The beaver would dam a stream just above the railway's [water] pump which filled the Bentley water tower. The work gang would tear out or blow up a beaver dam one day and within two days at the most it had been rebuilt. I think the railway finally gave in. It moved the pump above the dam and this so frightened the beaver that they went elsewhere."

THE RAILROAD SPLITS THE TOWN
March 30, 1977

The coming of the railroad may not have been the best thing that ever happened to Rimbey.

97

There was rejoicing in the streets the day the railroad reached the town, and there was a "huge celebration" that night after dark. The date was October 25, 1919. The arrival of the first train over those lines of steel was a long-awaited event in the town and district. It had been just ten years since the first steps were taken to have a track routed west and north from Lacombe, and undoubtedly the possibilities had been well-discussed before that. No wonder there was jubilation for miles around.

Now there would be no more long, cold trips with horses and sleighs over drifted roads in sub-zero temperatures to Lacombe in winter. No more bouncing over corduroy and getting stuck in the numerous mudholes, and fighting bullflies and mosquitoes on the thirty-five mile route in summer. Hogs, cattle, cream, eggs, lumber, grain, could all go out by train now, while the multitude of items to be used in settling and opening up the country, from groceries to farm machinery, could come in the same way.

Physically and economically, the railroad was a tremendous boon to the Rimbey area. Socially, it proved a calamity of the first order, one that set the community reeling. This was because, in fact, the railroad did not come to Rimbey. It missed by a country mile, and that was probably the most controversial mile in all of central Alberta for the next few years. It separated the promoters of the "New Town" from the adherents to the "Old Town" by more than the mile of distance. It destroyed long-standing friendships and caused bitterness that lasted for decades.

In short order, after the arrival of the steel tracks, came a station house, section houses, stockyards and two grain elevators. A townsite was surveyed, and plans were soon underway for a store and hotel, or perhaps these preceded the railroad's actual arrival.

The first train into Bluffton—the Peanut, *1922.*

98

Many, in the beginning, were supremely confident that the whole existing town would pick itself up and move a mile east, and many built new houses on the site.

However, people established in home and business back in the old town were not so enthusiastic about all this, and they went right on living and doing business where they had been for years, which did not really please the "New-Towners."

It is a bit difficult, nearly sixty years later, to determine why feelings ran as high as they did. That they did run high is indicated by the fact that the Rimbey weekly paper, then called *The Pioneer*, was severely vandalized because it had run a half-page ad for MacGillivray's Real Estate, advertising lots in the new townsite. The real estate office was also ransacked. Read more details of this on page 152 of *Pas-ka-poo*.

Undoubtedly, the feud between the "New-Towners" and the "Old-Towners" in the early 1920s did as much as the mile of separation to deflate the boom that the railroad might otherwise have generated, and it very likely put the brakes on the growth of either site for decades to come.

THE TRAIN IS IN!
June 29, 1977

They are ripping up the Peanut Line and it makes me sad and nostalgic.

From the time I can first remember, the train that everybody called the *Peanut* was something exciting in my life. If I could relive an event from my childhood, I would probably go down to the station with my dad to watch the train come in. We would be in the Bluffton store, having driven in nine miles from the homestead with King and Star on the buggy. Someone would phone Rimbey (or Hoadley) to see if the train had arrived there yet. (It went south one day and back the next.) That train, to the best of my knowledge, was never on time, or if it was, it would be by sheer accident and remarkable coincidence. If it was on its way, all the men and boys (and some women and girls, too, if the day was fine) would begin the troop from the store to the station, to stand waiting on the long platform.

If the train was within three miles you could tell by putting an ear to the track. A hum signified that it would be along in a few minutes, even though you still hadn't heard the whistle. Finally, around the bend she would come, and you would see, behind the

99

black smoke, the puffs of steam that, because of the distance, presaged the whistle. And that whistle! I just wish I could hear it once again, right out loud, close up. It made your hair stand up. (It would be nice to have all that hair again, too.)

I figured that engineer, sitting there so nonchalantly in that black and grimy throne, had the world's best job. He didn't have to do a thing—not even steer. He just sat there and watched the countryside roll by and pull a cord or something to shrill that lovely whistle at every level crossing and at every station. I once knew the signals he used, but I can't remember them now.

The black smoke eased off as he coasted into the station, then applied the brakes to bring that long line of eight or ten or twelve or even more cars to a grinding, clanging halt. Behind the locomotive came the coal car. I can't remember the order, but there would be freight cars, an express car, two or three passenger coaches, flat cars, coal cars, grain cars, cattle cars and, finally, the caboose. It was, for sure, a mixed train.

The excitement, for a small boy, did not stop when the train stopped. First off were the mailbags which were thrown on the dray or a truck and taken directly to the post office. The passengers were always interesting. People embarking in their best clothes, all neat and freshly pressed; others disembarking in their much-rumpled best. Boxes, cartons, bags and unwrapped freight would be unloading, some to be picked up by waiting hands, others to be stored in the room at the far end of the station until the owners should come for it. There were cream cans and egg crates to load and the empties to leave off, and so much activity that small boys were made to stand well back, so as not to get in the way. This was okay, for the engine, by this time, was uncoupled and the shunting had begun. There might be loaded coal cars to leave off and the empties to pick up, and the reverse for grain and cattle cars. What huffing and puffing and clanging and banging!

Man! It was exciting to be in Bluffton when the *Peanut* came in!

REMEMBERING THE *PEANUT*
July 6, 1977

When the autumn sky was overcast, and the wind was from the east, and October's chill was in the air, that was when the sound of the steam whistle would come wailing clear and sorrowful across eight miles of Blindman Valley to this homestead in the bush.

It was almost like a call of the wild, alluring as a loon's cry, spine-tingling as a howl of a wolf. In reality, it was more likely the call of the wide world to a little-travelled country kid. To this day, the recall of that steam whistle, which has never been duplicated, brings visions of brown Octobers and leafless trees, frosty mornings with heavy skies. Between whistles one could even hear the rumble and the roll of the train as it sped over the track between Bluffton and Hoadley, taking the wide curves at 25 mph, possibly doing 27 on the straightaway.

The *Peanut* was not its only epithet. It also got *Toonerville Trolley*, after a comic strip street car in the 1930s, and the *Blueberry Special*, and the *Muskeg Express* or the *Muskeg Limited*. Toot! Toot! "Peanut Butter," we used to say as kids, when we heard that whistle. But the names were used in fun, and the whole fibre of the country into which the *Peanut* came as the Lacombe Northwestern was woven into that railroad.

One of its institutions for uncounted years was a conductor named Jimmy, who was probably not nearly as old as he seemed to me at the time. He wore a black serge suit and a conductor's cap. Whenever a passenger asked him what time the train was expected to get into Winfield or Bentley or Lacombe, and he must have been asked forty times a day, year in and year out, he had a stock answer that varied slightly from time to time. "What do you care?" he would counter, as he punched a ticket, "You aren't in a hurry, or you'd be out there walking." He disappeared from the Peanut Line probably in the late 1940s, I should think it was, and I never knew if he retired peacefully to a little cottage somewhere, as retired conductors were supposed to do, or if he eventually went off the deep end from riding that train, day after tedious day.

Winfield, according to my memory, was the place it took longest to get out of when you rode the *Peanut*. Coming from Edmonton, you'd get into Winfield on a sunny winter afternoon, but darkness would have fallen by the time you pulled out. I think it was the lumber business that took so much time, although I heard other rumours as to the reason for the delay, but I never went up to the Winfield Hotel to verify them. The passenger cars were not always parked in the most scenic parts of town during those hours of waiting either.

Now they are pulling the spikes, unwinding the nuts from the bolts, lifting the rails and piling the ties. That leaves little except the grade to dispose of, and I'm afraid even that may go in places, what with the price of real estate these days.

A LONG FOUR MILES
April 2, 1985

I am hoofing it down the railroad track toward Bluffton on a cold November afternoon in 1939. I watch my step, for the railroad ties in most places are raised two or three inches above the level of the gravel in which they are placed. I have always wondered if they are deliberately placed to make walking difficult (legally, I am trespassing on CPR right of way), for they are set too close together to step on each one, and too far apart to hit every other one, even for my long legs. Some places I can walk on the shoulder of the grade, outside of both rails and ties. Sometimes I walk on the rails, but this takes balancing skill and some concentration and I quickly tire of it.

I hear the train whistle for Bluffton with the bulk of the water tower receding slowly behind me as I plod along, my face averted from the easterly wind. I think of the early days of September when I could ride atop a boxcar, enjoying the breeze and the autumn scenery, getting off before the train had quite come to a stop and walking a back route up to Montalbettis' store. I'm sure the train crew knew where I was riding, but I did not want to meet one of them by going near the station. If I had not missed the train this afternoon, I would be getting ready to jump as it slowed from its top speed of 25 mph; instead, I have another hour of this miserable walking. And I may have a further nine miles to walk home if someone isn't in Bluffton to meet me with a team and sleigh. I left my bicycle at home last weekend as the road was just too rough and muddy to ride it. This weekend I am thinking the road should be frozen, and I can ride my bike, reducing time and effort by more than half.

If someone had asked me, in 1939, to forecast how I would be travelling this route in 1985, I would probably have told them that I would be aboard a streamlined train doing 90 mph on the stretches. The near demise of the train as a passenger vehicle would not have occurred to me in 1939. I would have expected to be riding the Peanut Line with the speed and efficiency that has long since been standard in the British Isles. I would not likely have forecast the end of the age of steam around 1952, and that the water tower by the Blindman, a landmark all my life, would be demolished a few years later by Fred and Charles Hansen. I would have been astounded to know that the wooden trestle across the river would be razed, the rails and the ties taken up, the Alberta Pacific grain elevator at Bluffton torn down, and the little station and all the other buildings of CPR-red, gone and almost forgotten.

102

I would have to go to England to ride a train at 125 mph. Some of my dreams of world travel would come true, but, except in England, minus the train. And I would never travel by dirigible. I would drive to Calgary in greater comfort and less time than it sometimes took me to get the seventeen miles to Monte Vista, a trip I made roughly a hundred and fifty times during my high school years. I knew, in 1939, that the world was changing. I was pretty sure that I would have television in my house when I got rich, and that I would take pictures on colour film, and that I would own a typewriter, but I could never have foretold the great changes that would come in the realm of transportation. I would have been excited if not surprised to know the hundreds of thousands of miles that I would travel in comfort just within the boundaries of this province, and the further untold thousands of miles I would log by air, but I would have been a little sad to know that the miles by train would be so few.

ALBERTA'S VANISHING FERRIES
August 7, 1963

Without looking at a map, try and guess how many ferries there are still in operation in Alberta. You might be surprised to learn that there are approximately thirty. But their numbers are diminishing, and some day will reach a vanishing point.

This year alone, the Alberta government is said to be replacing fourteen of these ferries with bridges. At that rate, they will all soon be gone, and when that happens it will be the passing of an era. There will be something final about it.

We can bring back something of the horse and buggy era by hitching a team to an old-fashioned vehicle and driving them in a parade, but it might prove a bit difficult to put one of those old river ferries back into operation once its usefulness is done and it has been hauled up on the bank.

I looked at the official road map for 1963 to find just where the ferries are. The map shows that fourteen of them are plying back and forth across the North Saskatchewan. Three are west of Edmonton and eleven are east of Edmonton, one of them right on the Saskatchewan border.

There are six on the Red Deer River: at Rumsey, Munson, Dorothy, Finnegan, Steveville and Jenner. The one at Garrington was replaced with a bridge last summer.

The Bow River has two remaining ferries and the South Saskatchewan, three, including one at or very near the Saskatchewan border.

Farther north the Little Smoky, the McLeod and the Pembina Rivers boast one ferry each, and there are two on the Athabasca.

At the moment, I have no idea which ones are being replaced this summer, but the above list will certainly need revising next summer.

So I would propose right here and now that someone get a movement going aimed at persuading the provincial government to preserve at least four ferries strategically located at river crossings in different areas of the province. These could be left or placed at spots where they would create no bottleneck for traffic, and their prime purpose would be to remind Albertans and visitors to the province alike that the people who pioneered this land counted it a big step forward when they could drive down the steep, rutted trails to the river and find a spanking new ferry at the old fording place.

In this day and age, they would enable all those fortunate travellers who were not caught up in the hurry and flurry of modern living to cross to the other side of the river in a more leisurely, more fundamental way, and this might arouse in them a feeling of thankfulness that they did not have to ford that stream—with a team and buckboard.

TWENTY QUESTIONS
October 14, 1970

Here are twenty questions that may remind you of your progress along this journey on which we are all travellers. Your score should be highest if you are male, over thirty and rurally-oriented. My terms of reference are not wholly applicable to ladies, city folks, or the now generation.

Did you, as a beginner in school, learn to read from the *Canadian Reader, Book I* ("The Gingerbread Man," "The Little Red Hen")?

Did you listen to "Amos 'n' Andy," "Myrt and Marge," "Eb and Zeb," on a radio with a horn speaker, or on earphones, or on a crystal set?

Did you ever ride the freight trains in the days of the Depression, along with all the other hoboes?

Did you work on the road with four horses and a Fresno as a means of paying your municipal taxes?

Have you ridden downtown on a streetcar?

As a boy, were you given castor oil for what ailed you?

Did you swim in the ol' swimming hole with the boys, with never a care or a worry or a thought that it might one day be too polluted for swimming or fishing, or might not exist at all?

Were an axe and a grub hoe your chief tools for clearing the brush and trees from your homestead or farmland?

Was the first airplane you ever saw a single-motored bi-plane piloted by a man in a leather helmet—with goggles, of course?

Were any of your boyhood heroes Charles Lindbergh, Martin Johnson, Sam Steele of the Mounted, or Joe Louis?

Can you remember buying a big bag of candy—or a cup of coffee—for a nickel?

Have you ever chewed spruce gum?

Did you ride horseback to school?

Did you ever buy an ice-box corsage for your girl?

Were you sure and certain that no human being would ever set foot on the moon?

Did you once consider rich anyone who had money in the bank?

Are your toes today stubby, deformed, misshapen because as a boy you used to go barefoot from spring till fall?

Did you practice by the hour with a lariat on fenceposts, stumps and the barnyard calves in preparation for being a cowboy when you grew up?

If you wore a ten-gallon hat did it have a high crown that would hold a lot nearer to ten gallons than any hat on the market today?

Were you a teenager before that term was coined?

If you have answered "yes" to even half of these questions, it's time you slowed down a bit. I don't say you are over the hill, but you sure should have a good view from up there; so relax and enjoy it.

PREDICTIONS FOR 1979
January 1, 1969

These are my predictions for 1969.

There will be changes: some for the better, some for the worse; some of them trivial, some of them startling. Year 1969 will go by just a little bit faster for all of us than did 1968. And that's it. If you would like to know more about 1969 I'll be happy to tell you—twelve months from now.

If I must go out on a limb, why not go 'way out? It's every bit as easy, much more exciting, and a good deal safer, really. So what I am going to do this week, is look ahead not one year, but ten, to 1979. Now you see why there are fewer possibilities of having my limb sawed off. Ten years from now, who is going to dredge up, either from memory or from an old copy of this paper, what I have written here today?

So what will things be like in 1979? Always assuming, of course, that there will be a 1979. To begin with, some items familiar to everyone today will either have disappeared or will be on the way out by 1979. Power and telephone lines will no longer clutter the landscape, since all wiring will be underground. Gasoline pumps, as we know them, will be on the obsolescence list. Attendants at up-to-date service stations will pull a hose down from above to fill up your 1979 model gas buggy. To pay for that gas, and nearly everything else you buy, including the car, you will present a card and sign your name. Most of the bookkeeping will be done by computers. Cash of the realm will be used less and less. Numismatists take note.

Many of the magazines and periodicals that you read today will be no more. Already their numbers are dwindling. Economic pressures are responsible. Since we will rely more on television for information about the world around us, that medium, hopefully, will show some improvements by 1979, with educational television channels available to everyone. "Bonanza," even the re-runs, will be only a memory.

While some items, objects and institutions will have vanished from the scene, some others will not yet have appeared. People will still be organizing expeditions to search for the Lost Lemon Mine, the Sasquatch of the Coast Range, the Abominable Snowman of the Himalayas and the Monster or Monsters of Loch Ness.

Premier Bennett of British Columbia will still not have pushed that province's boundaries north to Arctic shores. I cannot foresee whether Pierre Elliot Trudeau will still be in office in ten years' time, but I do foresee that if he should be, he will look about twenty years older. Ted Kennedy will be serving his first term in the White House.

Monorail trains, or other high speed rail transportation, will be operating within and sometimes between cities in regions of high density population. Hovercraft travel, over land and water, but mostly over water, will be commonplace.

In 1979 you should be able to drive to Fairbanks, Alaska, on pavement. A secondary north-south highway in central Alberta will link Evansburg, Drayton Valley, Rocky Mountain House, Sundre and Cochrane. It will be only partially paved by 1979. The David Thompson Highway west of Rocky will be mostly paved but the scenery will be somewhat different, with a dam on the North Saskatchewan River backing up water past Windy Point to the Kootenay Plains.

The FUA Youth Camp at Goldeye Lake will have long outgrown summer camp status and will be a year-round institution of learning. Pas-ka-poo Historical Park in Rimbey will be one of the tourist attractions of central Alberta.

The space race will have slowed a bit, but we will know a great deal more about the moon in 1979 than we do today.

And by 1979 this limb could be looking mighty slender.

REAL COUNTRY MUSIC
July 28, 1987

Country music in 1987, say the music critics, is getting back to its roots. Not by a country mile, say I.

Country music had its real roots back in the cowboy era of the 1870s and 1880s, in Texas and Oklahoma and Kansas. Those earliest cowboy songs originated along the old cattle trails heading north from Rio Grande country to the railroad at Abilene, and they may have existed for years before being written down. They endured with little change and no widespread popularity for forty or fifty years before catching the ear of the general public. For example, I have been perusing a list of 250 titles of Edison cylinder records, produced mostly between 1895 and 1917. The two titles that come nearest to country music are "Redwing," and "The Trail of the Lonesome Pine." No sign of "The Old Chisholm Trail," or "Little Joe the Wrangler," or "When the Work's All Done This Fall."

I have lived through the evolution of cowboy music to country music. That does not mean to say that I am over a hundred years old. The history of country music as a pop form is only half as old as its chronological history. The era of cowboy music did not get underway until the 1920s, and did not hit its stride until the 1930s, with Gene Autry, Roy Rogers, and Alberta's own Wilf Carter. I make no bones about it: Wilf Carter is my favourite singer, well ahead of the other two and the scores that were to follow. I also enjoyed the Sons of the Pioneers in those days, and Eddie Arnold singing "The Cattle Call."

I was born long enough ago that every boy my age wanted to be a cowboy when he grew up. Andy, our hired man, wore a ten-gallon hat and came from Milk River; he rolled his own from a pouch filled with Ottoman tobacco, on top of which was tucked a package of Chanticleer cigarette papers with a crowing rooster on the red cover. Andy had the look of a cowboy, but best of all, he knew dozens of cowboy songs, and when he sang he had a rapt audience in

107

my younger brother and myself. "The Strawberry Roan" was one of his favourites, and "My Little Gray-haired Mother in the West," and fifty more. I wish I had written down the words. By this time, the kids who had wanted to be cowboys now just wanted to be cowboy singers. I remember that for years we would endeavour to have our morning chores done by seven o'clock so that we could get in to listen to Wilf Carter for fifteen minutes over CFAC Calgary. Even the girls were getting into the act. I remember that when radio station CFRN Edmonton first started up, they featured on their afternoon request program a live cowgirl singer and guitar plucker named Margaret (Moo-cow) McCarthy. I didn't like her as well as Wilf Carter, but I guess she was okay. She must have gotten married or something, because although she hit the heyday of cowboy music, she quietly dropped out of sight or sound without ever becoming a household word.

The original cowboy songs were sung to keep the cattle herds quiet at night on the long trail rides. They were slow-measured, and told of hardships on the trail or mishaps on the job. Sometimes they were the fantasies of a lonely cowboy in an all-male environment. Then they were sung for entertainment in the bunkhouse, and long after the great trail drives were a thing of the past, they began to be heard on that new medium of communication, radio. By the 1940s, cowboy music had evolved into Western music and had dropped the yodeling that had been so much a part of it at first. Western music, in turn, became Country and Western, and in the 1970s, just Country, by which time it bore little resemblance to its roots.

I wonder how cow-punk singer, k.d. lang, who is busy south of the border making a big name for her unique style, would treat a song like "The Old Chisholm Trail."

THE FINE ART OF STOOKING
September 20, 1956

A picture appeared in the *Calgary Herald* recently of a field of stooked grain near Sundre, Alberta. The picture was captioned, "Echoes of the Past." Well, if that photographer had come on farther north instead of going back to Calgary with his picture, he would have found a good many acres of echoes, and they would be very much in the present.

Combines come a long way from eliminating the binder in the Blindman Valley and other areas of west-central Alberta. Not only

108

Charlie Schutz on the binder, 1948.

Grain stooks on Schutz's farm.

that, but there are many binders that are drawn by horses, and not necessarily back in the sticks either. It isn't long since horse-drawn binders could be seen operating beside Highway 2 between Calgary and Edmonton.

Binders mean stooks to set up and stooking is hard work. One of the biggest advantages of the combine is that it does away with much of this back-breaking toil. Yet I am told that in parts of western Alberta, where combines took over from the binders a decade or two ago, the trend is now back to the old way: binders, stooks, and threshing machines. As anyone who owns a combine here will tell you, our climate, most falls, is far from ideal for combining. For this and other reasons, the binder, the fields of stooked grain, and the threshing machine may be with us for a good many years to come.

Yet, in other parts of the province, there will be farm boys helping with the harvest who would not know how to build a stook. There may even be some in this area. Fortunately, they may never have to learn.

Stooking doesn't mean just going out into the field and standing up the bundles, or sheaves, as Granddad used to call them. The kind of stook you build varies with the kind of grain and the condition of the crop, with the weather and with the time of year. Your experience and ability also have some bearing, though both are easily gained.

On this farm the general rule is eight bundles to a stook. Wheat is stooked in round stooks, sometimes capped with a ninth bundle. Oat stooks are built long. My method, in either case, is to pick the bundles up in pairs and deposit them in pairs.

Barley I stook with a fork, and it took me a good half-day many years ago to learn how to build a barley stook with any success. The first bundle must be set down firmly in the stubble, and the second set just as firmly beside it, so that it grazes the first, catching some of the heads and binding the two together. If you don't know this trick, there is apt to be a considerable strain on your patience and temper before you get a field set up.

If you simply lean number two against number one they will likely both fall over. If they don't, you can still have trouble with numbers three and four. And after they have all fallen down a couple of times, they get all twisted and lopsided and loose in the twine; so you throw away the fork and go to work by hand. This seems much better for about three stooks. Then the beards start creeping through your shirt just above your belt. Two more stooks and you take off your shirt and go looking for the fork. By noon you will have no doubt acquired the knack—and a nice sunburn. You will also be convinced that barley should be harvested with a combine.

THRESHING BEFORE COMBINES
October 16, 1963.

In 1950 almost any farmer in the county would have prophesied the demise of the threshing machine by 1963. Yet this fall, which seems to have been made to order for the combines, there are hundreds of strawpiles in the Blindman Valley to prove that the combines haven't taken over altogether. There might even be more threshing machines in the area in 1963 than there were in 1950. They still hum in all directions.

But the hum is not the same. It does not begin so early in the morning, or run so long into the evening twilight. The men who gather the bundles from the field and heave them into the hungry maw of the dusty, noisy, vibrating machine are, as a general rule, the men whose fields are being cleared and whose granaries are being filled; and they have chores to do night and morning and could not possibly put in an eleven-or twelve-hour day in the field as the crews once did.

And the hum of the "outfit" is increased by the noise of the tractors which have replaced the horses on the bundle racks, although a few teams of horses remain in use on some rigs. You can't lead a tractor by the bridle, or start and stop it with a "Giddyup" and a "Whoa." You have to climb onto the thing to move up to the

The Cochrane Place. Fred farmed this land for several decades.

111

next stook, or else have a driver for it, and manpower is one of the problems of those who stick by the threshing machine.

The high, steel-tired, wooden-wheeled wagons of yesteryear have nearly all been replaced by low, rubber-tired, lighter-running wagons, mounted with larger racks to carry bigger loads.

The farm wife has it easier, too, with only dinner and lunches to prepare for the hungry men, instead of the long day's cooking she once had, from 5 o'clock breakfast to 8 p.m. supper.

By and large, the threshing crews of today are a less boisterous lot than those of a generation ago. Then, they were mostly young and always ready for a bit of fun despite the rigours of a long day on an arduous job and a rate of pay that, back in the 1930s, worked out to be as little as fourteen cents an hour—plus all the good food you could eat.

Fun was where you found it. Almost every crew had at least one clown and one wit, while half or even more were pranksters. Throwing a bundle across the feeder onto the other fellow's rack just as he had it swept clean to go to another field or another farm, was a favourite trick of some. Reprisals could always be expected, however, and the prankster might find a pole shoved through his back wheels when he pulled away from the feeder. Anyone who ever drove a team on a threshing outfit has found a bundle near the bottom of his load tied securely to the back of his rack.

All loose bundles in the field, and all the ragged ones scattered by cattle or pigs which had broken into the field, were put on the back of a load for the spike pitcher. A bundle that was white with thistle down would be given a vigorous shake in the air by the man on the upwind side of the feeder, so that all the fuzzy seeds floated across to tickle the nose of the man on the downwind side. "I don't know how they grew cotton this far north" was the classic remark when a patch of seeded thistles was encountered.

Sometimes the crew slept in a bunkhouse which was trundled from one farm to the next, tied behind the rack of the last man to leave that farm. Many bunkhouses were drafty. Some leaked, in which case a lower bunk was best. Lighting the fire on a frosty morning was not a chore everyone clamoured for, but usually there was one cheerful chap who didn't seem to mind taking his turn and that of the rest as well. He was usually an expert who could stuff in paper, kindling and a few blocks of wood so swiftly and efficiently that he could be back in his bunk in thirty seconds flat with the fire starting to roar.

You fed and harnessed your horses by lantern light, then trooped in to wash for breakfast, where the boss greeted you with the words, "Ain't this a helluva country, where they wake you up in the middle of the night to feed you?"

FEEDING THE THRESHERS
October 23, 1963

Last week, in writing about the threshing crews of twenty years or more ago, I got to reminiscing to such an extent about those other days that I believe I could keep this column going half the winter with the things I remembered.

I think I mentioned the first-rate food. Next to the pay, the grub was possibly the main attraction of the job, especially for the younger members of the crew. They worked hard, loved to eat, and developed enormous appetites. Eating with a threshing crew was an adventure in itself. Most of all I remember the pie. Customs varied from one outfit to the next and from one neighbourhood to another. On one outfit I worked, you got all the pie you wanted to eat; on another, two pieces were considered the limit. I remember once we hit a place where the pie was cut into five pieces instead of four, and served to us on individual plates, with no opportunity for a second helping. Back in the field how we grumbled! And how glad we were—or we said we were—to get away from there onto a place where pie was not rationed.

It amazes me now to think of those good women who did the cooking, managing to have enough pies made up to supply two or three pieces for every member of the crew, because this redundancy served no purpose at all, except to keep the crew in good humour, and I'm quite sure that they would have maintained equally good spirits with one piece less.

There was one chap who prided himself on never finishing up his dinner with less than three pieces of pie. One day, out of the dinner-time banter, there arose a twenty-five cent wager on the extent of his capacity. He bet the rest of the gang that he could eat a whole pie, and as he had already eaten two pieces (half a pie) this was no small undertaking. He won himself a quarter but the cost to his appetite was high. I was talking to him about the incident one day some twenty years later, and he swore that in that interval he hadn't eaten so much as one piece of pie.

Then there was the day on the same outfit when we all went pie-less. All except Bingo. Bingo was a big, overgrown pup that liked to be fed grease from the grease gun. He was everybody's friend and a sort of mascot of the outfit. On the day in question, as I recollect, he came into the house undetected, and before anyone realized what he was up to, he had sniffed out the pies where they had been laid atop a large airtight heater, and had eaten the centres out of about three of them while standing in the others with his huge front feet. Any grumbling by the crew that afternoon was of the good-natured sort. The lady of the house, who had put so much effort into all those pies, was the most aggrieved. Bingo never did live the episode down. He was known as the pie-hound for the rest of his days.

"The best is none too good for the threshers" was a saying of a bundle-hauler I once worked with, and he wasn't often disappointed. Roast beef and fried chicken were favourite fare, but you might get anything from turkey to hamburgers, or leg of lamb. There were always so many vegetable dishes, and salads, and pickles, that you couldn't get more than a sample of each onto your plate. Coffee, strong enough to float buckshot, was the universal drink. If anyone preferred tea, none were brave enough to admit the fact.

And then there was the pie. I'll bet you can't name many kinds of pie that I haven't eaten at somebody's house at threshing time, sometimes three kinds to a meal. I tell you it was great to be young, work hard, get good and hungry, and come in to a thresher-man's dinner.

FEEDING THE THRESHERS II
October 30, 1963

Last week I dealt with the great quantities of good food stowed away by a hungry crew of threshers. But I also remember a couple of times when it wasn't so good. Once we dined in an elderly bachelor's shack, and while we got enough to eat, some of us were too finicky to enjoy it. The other occasion I'll describe in more detail, simply to show that there can be another side to almost any story. I shall word the episode so that identification of the farm from this account alone would not be possible. Nor is it likely that anyone to whom it could matter will ever read this.

I was working on an outfit in a district where all the women were excellent cooks, and we had been living high off the hog for about three weeks. Toward the end of the run, the boss announced that he had taken a three-day job in another area, and he hoped the crew would go along. We went, with certain misgivings.

It was worse than we had anticipated. Both the cooking and the sanitation left much to be desired. In the first place, there wasn't room enough at the small table for all of us to eat at once, and there were not dishes enough, anyway, so those who came in last to dinner had to wait for a place to be vacated by an early-comer, and probably had to wait a little longer still for his dishes to be washed— and I use that term rather carelessly. The dishwashers had a habit of hanging the dishcloth, when it was not in use, over the rim of a five-gallon bucket that was used to carry slops to the pigs, and which showed unmistakable signs of having been left in the pigpen not too long past, possibly overnight.

The flies waited for nobody.

There was no pie.

Some of the old hands ate the poorly-cooked meat and vegetables with as much politeness—if not the same jollity—they had shown anywhere else on that run, but some of the younger ones, I am sorry to relate, put their finicky appetites before their manners. We had been too well-fed and were not as concerned as we might have been about offending people who were probably doing their best to provide for us.

Be that as it may, several of us made out for the three days by eating only bread and jam when we went in to dinner.

I considered myself fortunate that I wasn't sleeping in a bunkhouse at this time, but in a private home, where I had plenty of opportunity to fill my pockets with apples, cookies, candy, or anything else that could be nibbled throughout the day. The breakfast cook could have slept 'til noon for all of me.

The boss, after the first day at the place, didn't come to the house at all. He ate breakfast and supper at home and skipped dinner completely, but he always ate one of the apples sent out with the mid-afternoon lunch.

The weeks I spent threshing each fall in my younger days would add up to months of hard work and good eating, yet the four days mentioned above are the only ones I can remember when I didn't look forward to coming in to dinner.

THRESHING CUSTOMS
November 6, 1963

Probably everyone who has ever worked on a threshing rig has found that there were certain rules and customs which you were bound to go by. Some of these are followed, in whole or in part, by threshing crews right down to today. Unless you were a greenhorn, there wasn't much point in trying to flout them. Greenhorns,

115

however, were privileged characters in some respects, being, for the rest of the crew, a prime source of fun, which ranged from mild amusement to wild hilarity. But that is another story.

One of the basic rules was: always proceed to the farthest corner of a field to begin loading bundles. The first man into a field might pick up his load around the granary to clear a place for the set and for the straw pile; otherwise, you went to the far end. Often I could have saved myself a mile of travel simply by loading at the end of the field where the gate was, but I never did it. Nobody did. It just wasn't done that way. You hunted out the farthest row of stooks away from the machine to begin loading, and that was that.

Another rule decreed that if you started down a row of stooks, that was your row to the end. Suppose, when you got your load on, there were six or eight stooks left in the row. If you couldn't take them, you went back for them next load. No one would go fifty feet out of his way to pick them up for you, although you might have a buddy on the next row whom you could persuade to pick them up as he went by, as a personal favour. Otherwise, they were your stooks.

Another thing: if there was a field pitcher, you went to the area where he was working or you would most likely be left to load up by yourself. The field pitcher walked only so far as he deemed necessary, and if you misjudged where you and he would be when the team ahead of you had been loaded and you found yourself at the opposite side of the field from where he was, it was just your tough luck. If the fault was not yours, though, he would walk across to you. This was a good rule. The field pitcher walked far enough for eleven hours.

When you got in to the machine with your load, and if there was a spike pitcher on the outfit, he jumped off the rack just emptied and walked around the engine—or sometimes stepped over the drive-belt—to climb onto your load via the back of your rack. If you hadn't left a gap in the load at that point, whereby he could get up, he would just lean on his fork handle down below until you had removed some bundles and made one. If your rack was a difficult one to get up, and some were, you would be told about it and expected to remedy the situation.

Above all, you always took your turn. If the man who followed you went in your place it usually meant that you were away or broken down for a long enough period to have your time docked, although it would all depend on the nature of your defection.

116

Your wagon was greased every Sunday, whether you threshed on Sunday or not. No one was required to work on Sundays and, in fact, some outfits never threshed on Sundays. Others ran every day the weather was good, on the premise that you could catch up on your Sundays when it rained.

I understand the thresher-man is still supposed to obtain a permit to thresh on Sunday. I don't know of anyone who ever went to the trouble of getting one, though.

THE SPIKEY'S JOB
November 1, 1978

"Spike pitcher" is defined in the *Dictionary of Canadianisms* as "the member of a threshing crew who forks the sheaves from the load into the separator of the machine." That is not too good a definition in the light of my experience. Actually, he and the bundle-hauler fed the machine together, throwing bundle for bundle, so he forked only half the sheaves, or bundles, as we call them in the West. And the separator was the machine. The terms "grain separator" and "threshing machine" were synonymous.

The spike pitcher had the toughest job on the outfit. He had to climb up on the back of every rackload of bundles that came into the machine, a strenuous exercise to begin the day. By nightfall some of the loads looked twenty feet tall. Then when one load was unloaded, he cleaned up around the feeder while the next load was driving up. So there was no opportunity to rest. Only if there was a long haul and a team was late getting in would there be an excuse to take it easy.

Normally the bundle-haulers rested from their labours both on the trip in from the field and while they waited for the load ahead to finish unloading. The field pitcher could usually find a few minutes to lean on his fork while he waited for the next team to come over. As a spike pitcher, I worked a full eleven hours at the machine, but I had no chores to attend to before or after; no horses to feed and water and curry and harness; no wagon to grease; no harness to mend.

I was lucky that first fall. We had a seventeen-day run with almost no stops for rain. We threshed straight through, Sundays and all. That first Sunday, I would have loved to sleep in and get a twenty-four hour rest, and give the blisters on my hands a chance to heal, but no such luck. By the following Sunday, my blisters had turned to calluses which I wore for decades to come. They adorned both hands at the base of the second, third and fourth fingers, and on the

117

inside of both thumbs. If I had to grab a fork and go spike pitching tomorrow, the blisters would return.

The outfit was running by 7 a.m. It shut down shortly after 7 p.m. Not very often could you stretch your noon hour to sixty-five minutes. Breakdowns were a blessing, provided they didn't last long enough for your pay to be docked. The outfit was new, so breakdowns were infrequent and usually minor. I remember one when a short drive-chain broke with a tremendous clatter, sending pieces flying sky-high. Vic Dersch had just pulled into the machine on the drive-belt side. At the racket, his team of mules took off. Instead of pulling them to a stop, Vic slapped them on the tail with the lines, drove them at full gallop in a great half-mile circle and right back to the spot they had left, where they stood panting. We were all on hands and knees around the machine, searching through chaff and straw and stubble.

"What can't you find?" asked Vic. "Three links of the chain are missing" was the reply. "Don't worry," drawled Vic, "they'll be down after a while."

NEW YEAR'S EVE ON THE HOMESTEAD
January 1, 1980

Since I have been harking back to some early Christmases on the homestead in recent columns, I may as well tune my powers of recall to remember how it was at New Year's in those bygone times.

New Year's Day was always kept as a holiday. We just did chores—no regular farm work—and we always had a special meal, very similar to Christmas. We might have had friends in or maybe it would be just the family. It was probably the last day of the school holiday and I'd have to get busy on the homework I'd been assigned ten days before.

Actually, it was New Year's Eve I remember better than New Year's Day. We always stayed up late to watch the New Year in. That meant one o'clock for the Pacific New Year. The first New Year's Eve I remember was December 31, 1929. Then, as now, we were ending a decade, and as happens every ten years, there was controversy as to whether it actually was the end of that decade. Certainly it was the end of the 1920s because the next day would be January 1, 1930. But my dad, who seemed to me to be a genius at mathematics, declared that we had another year to go in the decade, because starting from Year One, we had only completed 1929 years, and you can't divide that by ten and come out even. I haven't

118

heard much about that old controversy this time around, but wait until the end of the century!

The argument over the end of the decade is not the only reason I remember that New Year's Eve. I remember it because it was the first time our family had ever listened to the proceedings on the radio. It was the Big Band Era, and radio was becoming sophisticated enough that local network hookups were one of the wonders of the time, and it was exciting to hear, live, what was going on in the big hotels in Edmonton, Calgary and Banff. I don't believe there were any national networks in North America in 1929, but they came in the thirties, and New Year's Eve programming would span the continent via your local station, beginning with Atlantic time on the East Coast and proceeding hour by exciting hour and city by city through to Vancouver. Before the networks, you simply twirled and twiddled the dial to get the distant stations.

Our little De Forest Crosley regularly picked up Atlantic City, New Orleans, Chicago, various Mexican stations and the old standbys, KSL Salt Lake City, and KOA Denver. We also got many West Coast stations, so New Year's Eve was always exciting right at home. I'm sure the media made more of it than they do today. Our radio was best suited to earphones, although it had a horn speaker. It ran on one six-volt wet battery, two dry-cell B batteries and a small C battery—and just two tubes. To get good reception, and distant stations and, not least, to conserve batteries, we and every radio owner in those days had a one-hundred-foot aerial strung between two poles at least thirty feet above the ground. The radio also had to be connected to a ground rod or it wouldn't work. Also required by law to operate that set was a yearly two-dollar licence. My father always had that licence and a clear conscience, but many a set was operated without it—and reception on those sets was probably as good as ours.

I'm sure radio has never since been as exciting as it was in those early days. As recreation and entertainment, radio had its heyday during the Great Depression, and New Year's Eve was a special time on the airwaves.

THE OLD STOPPING HOUSE
October 11, 1961

I have prowled around in old houses all my life, but never have I seen one look so sad, nor one that looked so much as if it would like to speak, and proclaim to all who would stop and listen that it had once known livelier and happier times.

119

The front door was off its hinges, the windows were boarded up; bare and unkempt on the inside, grey and weather-scarred without; yet, when it was new, undoubtedly one of the largest and most pretentious houses for miles around, with fancy scrolled woodwork trimming the gable ends, and similar hand-sawn scroll-work around the stairwell on the second floor.

It was the old Donovan house, one of the historic landmarks on the upper Blindman, overlooking the lazy bends and horseshoe loops of the river's west branch, a one-time stopping place for travellers between Buck Lake to the northwest and Lacombe to the southeast. It was also, at one time, the location of the Nugent store and post office.

Though built in the early days of settlement on the Blindman, it is not a log house. Except for a few forest-fire-blackened pine poles right in the peak of the building, it is constructed of sawn lumber throughout. The old trails that converged on the old place from all points of the compass, though unused for many decades, can still be traced in uncultivated areas of the surrounding countryside.

Just below, on the river bottom, is the site of what may once have been a buffalo pound. Alvin Goetz, who lived in the house as a small boy, showed me where he used to play around a pile of old buffalo bones here. A few ancient and mossy fragments are all that can be seen of these bones today, yet one can easily visualize the spot as an ideal site for a pound, with natural barricades of river and bank to help form the enclosure where the beasts would be slaughtered.

Now, a short distance away, a modern stream of motorized traffic speeds along Highway 12, and the passengers on the streaking vehicles give never a thought to the fact that they are moving through ancient haunts of Cree and buffalo, and crossing many a winding wagon trail cut by the settlers and pioneers. In their perpetual hurry they rarely have time to see the things that are on the surface: the green fields, the farm buildings, the mail boxes, highway signs, and the steel bridges across the rivers.

They never glimpse the shadowy, buckskin-clad figures astride their wan and weary ponies, who, paying not the slightest heed to the roar of traffic, follow the buffalo trails by the river's edge, crossing at the ancient fording places and proceeding in a ghostly file over the hill and out of sight into the dusk and the poplar shadows.

It is only the favoured few who hear the wind-muffled creak and rattles of the settler's wagon on a stormy night, the sucking of horses' hooves in the mud, the clank of tires on the stones in the river's bed as it, too, crosses at the fording place.

Rarer still is the person who hears—or fancies he hears—faint snatches of an old song drifting downriver out of the darkness, or the scrape of a distant fiddle playing an almost forgotten tune.

But such a one will know he has been especially privileged, and will speak to no living person of the things he has seen—or heard—or fancied—but for ever after he will know a deeper respect for the people who followed the buffalo, and for the pioneers who came when the buffalo were gone, and who never thought of themselves as pioneers, but as ordinary people, doing what must be done, carving a homestead out of the wilderness. And that, of course, was what they wanted to do. And because they did it, we owe them much, and honour them by calling them pioneers, which they were.

ABANDONED HOMESTEAD
May 27, 1964

There is always something melancholy about an abandoned homestead site—something which can induce a nostalgic awareness in any viewer, whether he has ever lived on a homestead or not; that much besides the buildings and fences and gardens and

A house abandoned in 1919.

clotheslines have fallen into disuse; that something other than the flowers and livestock and people have gone from the place.

Hope, plans, ambition, proprietorship—these have also departed, and this, in fact, is immediately sensed, even by a passer-by with his thoughts on other matters.

Let me describe for you a typical homestead site, carved from the bush in the early 1930s, forsaken forever a few years later when times got better.

Phoebes live now in the old log house, their mud nest plastered atop the highest log, to one side of the door and above a bulging, water-stained section of the heavy, dirty-blue building paper that seems to have been the universal lining for a homestead shack.

Between the doorway and a small, four-pane window that let in just over two square feet of light, is a small shelf, fashioned roughly but not rustically from two pieces of rough, not planed lumber. It is still covered with a tattered piece of white oilcloth.

The floor underneath the chimney jack in the peak of the one room building is stained black with the soot washed down by long past rains. Some burrowing animal has dredged up a pile of dry, brown subsoil from beneath the floor and piled it into a corner beneath a row of four-inch nails in the sixth log up where the man of the house probably once hung his coat when he came in from outdoors.

Children had lived here. A worn-out canvas shoe, some pages from a colouring book (not artistically crayoned), a doll's arm—part cotton, part plaster—testify to this.

And out in what had been the farmyard were more homestead structures of log or pole construction, with here and there a piece of rough lumber used for some of the finer work. Less carefully made than the house and possibly subjected to rougher treatment, most of these outbuildings are now in a state of collapse. The small log barn at the back of the yard is easily identified by an unnatural, grass-grown mound that had been the manure pile. When the last forkful was added to that heap, it must have been almost as high as the barn.

There is a small building that may have housed chickens, and a log corral, the northwest corner of which had been roofed with poles and straw to make a shelter for pigs.

Just beyond the barn, the rotting ends of poplar poles nailed to half-dead trees and an occasional tamarack post show where the hay and green-feed had once been stacked.

Beside the old wagon trail leading from the road allowance, past the house into the barnyard, stand two sturdy tamarack posts about fifty feet apart and with cross arms still attached. Here one can imagine the washing that had come from the hand-turned washing machine hanging in the sun and breeze to dry, but bearing little resemblance to the wash on any line today.

The garden had been right alongside the clothesline, but, unlike the sod-bound barnyard, it is now overgrown with brush and trees.

The well, over a rise and at some distance from the buildings, is now only a crater on the bank above a small creek, but beside it lie the rotted remnants of the stock trough, hewn with an axe from a large balm (balsam poplar) log.

The creek was not always this dry, for old beaver dams are all along it, and from one of these a load or two of dirt had been taken, possibly with a team and stoneboat or maybe a wagon. Rich dirt it would be, dredged by beaver from the creek bottom long ago.

And where had this dirt been taken? To build hotbeds or cold frames; to fill window boxes for pansies, or old lard pails to start slips of geraniums and other house-plants. In short, to make the old homestead—or, rather, the new homestead—a brighter, happier, place to live.

PLACES

CENTRAL ALBERTA PLACE NAMES
June 12, 1957

Here are some origins of place names in and around the Blindman, Medicine and Battle River valleys.

Most of the information is taken from a booklet put out by the Geographic Board of Canada, and called simply, *Alberta Place Names*. Further data was obtained from the "Jubilee Edition" of *The Rimbey Record* and from various other sources. Any comments may be considered anonymous. Since there is not room to mention all this week, some will be left for next week's column.

Everyone knows, of course, that Rimbey was named for brothers Sam, Ben, and Jim, and perhaps nephew Oscar. At first it was called Kansas Ridge, but when a post office was established in 1903, a name had to be found that was acceptable to the Department of the Interior, and "Rimbey" was chosen from a short list submitted.

Bentley was named in 1903, too, after the sawyer in a local sawmill. The story says that when a name for the post office was being chosen, the postmaster's name, MacPherson, was suggested. When the men at the sawmill heard this they decided to put up the name of their sawyer, George Bentley, and since there were more mill hands than homesteaders, Bentley got the nod over MacPherson.

Bluffton was named in 1922. Reasons for this choice are obscure, although the school was called Bluff Center, which was apparently a descriptive name.

Hoadley was known as "Haverigg" until 1924, after the railroad came. George Hoadley was minister of agriculture in the Alberta government of the day. I'm sure he would have been forgotten before now, if the name "Haverigg" had been retained. Who or what "Haverigg" was, I do not know, but it has a Scandinavian sound.

Leedale, before 1917, was called "Wittenburg," for the home in Denmark of Paul Broderson, an early settler. Many names across

124

Canada which had a German sound, were changed during World War I. This may have seemed like patriotism at the time but it looks a little silly now. It does lend interest to our history, however.

Of Forshee, the book gives no definite origin, but says only, "There is a place of this name in Virginia."

Homeglen is another descriptive name and was suggested by James Burns, the first settler in the district.

Iola is another obscure one. This time the book makes two statements: "There are several post offices of this name in the United States"; and, "Prior to 1907, the district was called Ednaville." Who Edna was, I do not know. I am thankful that it was changed. I have nothing against Edna as a name, but I think most people would agree that "Ednaville" is something quite different.

Lavesta was named in 1911 after Vesta McGhee, daughter of the postmaster.

Lockhart was named for John Lockhart, early settler and first postmaster, in 1906.

Springdale is a descriptive name given to the post office in 1906.

Nugent, which is hardly a place at all any more, was the maiden name of the wife of M. Donovan, postmaster and storekeeper.

And Willesden Green was named in 1913 after a suburb of London, England, and former home of George Wagar, the first postmaster.

More names next week.

MORE PLACE NAME ORIGINS
June 19, 1957

Here are some more place name origins.

The Blindman River was so named by the Crees when a party of hunters belonging to that tribe went snowblind along the river long ago. Sir James Hector, geologist and explorer with the Palliser Expedition, called it the Blind River (*Pas-ka-poo* in Cree), in 1858.

Medicine River and Medicine Lake, together with the Medicine Lodge Hills, all have a common name source. The Cree held ceremonial dances in the hills and had at least two names for the river. One was *Muskiki* and the other a tongue-twister which meant "Sundance River." Medicine Lake is one of the sources of the river.

The Battle River carried that name as early as 1802 when it appeared on an Arrowsmith map. Cree and Blackfoot territory somewhat overlapped along this river and their frequent meetings were not always peaceful.

125

Turning northward, Breton was named for D. C. Breton, an early settler and MLA. It was the Keystone Post Office before 1927.

Winfield was named when the railroad arrived, after the Hon. Vernor Winfield Smith, minister of railways in the Greenfield government.

Pendryl was named in 1916, after an English family.

Buck Lake was Minnehik until October 1954. That is, it was and it wasn't. It was Minnehik officially, but the more popular name of Buck Lake, which was the official name of all that water just behind the town, just sort of took over, and made the change inevitable. *Minnehik* is Cree for tamarack. Buck Lake is an old name, for the Hudson's Bay Post built in 1800 at the mouth of Buck Lake Creek was called Buck Lake House.

I have no data at all on Alder Flats, perhaps because the book I am using is dated 1928. No doubt it is a descriptive name. At any rate, today the town is rapidly over-running the alder bushes.

Out to the east, the name of Ponoka is the Blackfoot term for elk.

Lacombe, as we all learned in our school days, was named to commemorate the life and work of Father Albert Lacombe, who, for more than half a century, was a force for good among Alberta's Indians. They loved and respected him as they did no other white man. Father Lacombe died at Midnapore, Alberta, in 1916.

Gull Lake is a translation from the Cree word *Kiaskus*. It was Gull Lake on Arrowsmith map of 1859.

Sylvan Lake has had many names. David Thompson, in 1814, called it "Methy Lake." On Palliser's 1859 map it is "Swan Lake." In Cree, it was *Wa-pi-sioo*; in Stoney, *Ko-gamna*. In the early days of settlement, it was called "Snake Lake," and later, "Perch Lake." Since about 1907 it has been Sylvan.

Here is an odd one I couldn't resist including: Ricinus—Latin name of the castor oil plant.

Here are the statistics. Of the 26 place names mentioned this week and last, 6 are named for early settlers, 4 are descriptive, and 2 commemorate government officials. At least 2 are obscure. Six places have undergone name changes. Five are named for the first postmaster or his birthplace, or for some member of his family. The three rivers have names going back one hundred years or more. They, plus two of the lakes, and the Town of Ponoka, have names that are Indian in origin. One, Lacombe, is named for a person famous in Alberta history.

That just leaves Ricinus.

126

BLINDMAN RIVER SCHOOL DISTRICT #4244
May 5, 1971

A little of the history of this community repeated itself this spring of 1971, though on a somewhat reduced scale. Up to a dozen men gathered at the site of an old log schoolhouse on several different days to donate hundreds of man-hours toward renovation of the building that was erected in 1934, and opened for classes the following year.

During Easter week, the floor of the original building, which was becoming rotten and unsound around the edges, was taken out, right down to the dirt, in preparation for the laying of a cement floor. The row of windows on the east side, through which many a young face had gazed longingly on sunny afternoons a generation ago, was removed and the section of wall beneath it was cut away in readiness for the construction of a twelve-foot addition along the length of the east side. This would provide for a kitchen, a stage, and a dressing room. Just after mid-April, cement, gravel, lumber, nails and shingles were purchased and hauled, and a crew of men, under the unofficial foremanship of Bert Bakx, poured the foundation, erected and shingled the new addition, and shingled the east half of the roof of the main building. The west side had been shingled by much the same crew two years ago. Residents of the district who helped in the project included Bert Bakx, Robert Brown, Gunnar Lovelie, Vic Nachtegaele, Jim Watson, Reynold Mazu, Fred Schutz,

Blindman River School, seen here in the 1950s, was built from logs cut from adjacent timber stands, hand-hewn by volunteers. The corners were dovetailed.

Allan Barker, Lawrence Pedersen, Rob Pearson, Harry Strain, August Belter, Rudolph Belter, Paul Belter, and, on a recent Saturday, Rita Belter, for the distaff side.

Of the men listed above, only one, August Belter, was a part of the original crew, which, thirty-seven years ago, volunteered its skills with hammer and saw and broadaxe and plane, to construct the much-needed schoolhouse. Work was begun in 1934, when logs were hauled, hewn square by hand, and erected on a foundation of stones on a newly acquired plot of ground on SW 16-44-4-W5 — August Belter's homestead.

It was the 2nd of July 1935, before the building was finished and furnished, a teacherage built—also of logs and with a slab roof—and a teacher hired and classes begun, with thirty-five children, grades one to eight, in attendance.

The Blindman River School District had been formed in 1925 and classes held for three terms, or parts of terms, in a rented house, known as the Wilton House, on the farm where Alvin Steeves now lives. The first teacher was a young lady named May Christie, and she was followed by Lucille Duffy and Clark Richardson. Later, in the early 1930s, school was held in a newly-built house owned by John Birch and now occupied by Harry Mahood. Teachers at that location were Eileen Woods and Evelyn Brady.

By this time an influx of settlers was changing the very appearance of the Blindman River School District. Whereas in the years following the formation of the district the number of school-age children had varied from one to ten or twelve, suddenly there were enough to require a full-sized school building. But there was no such building, and the country was right at the bottom of the Great Depression, and the combined financial resources of all the ratepayers in the district would probably have not been enough to build and equip a tepee. However, there was a will and a way. That log schoolhouse, followed by a teacherage, then a barn for the horses, and, finally, two diminutive structures on the opposite sides of the schoolyard, went up with very little cash outlay, either for materials or labour. Even the desks for those thirty-five kids were made on the spot, of locally sawn lumber, some of it hand-planed. The sense of pride with which those people viewed their achievement must have been enormous.

The first teacher in that much-admired building was a young fellow named Douglas Sargent, who also had the honour of being the first occupant of the little log teacherage.

128

Its last occupant before the amalgamation of the rural school districts into one centralized system was Kathleen Macdonald, who, with two very pampered cats, lived and taught at Blindman River for several years. In between there was Alec Jacobs, Lois Newman, Pearl Kroening, Mrs. Long, Ida Hamilton, Mr. Green and Mr. Ferguson.

Although a black-and-white-painted board on the front of the building gives the name of the district and the number, 4244, the building continues to function, as it always did, as a community centre. After twenty-two years as a school, it became, when the buses came for the kids in 1957, the Blindman River Hall. When power came to the district, the building was wired and hooked up, so that the 1971 crew were able to make use of power tools and equipment in a way not dreamed of by the folks of 1934.

Down through the years, the centre has been the scene of many and varied gatherings and its hewn walls are familiar to people from Hoadley and Bluffton and Rimbey and Meadowvale and points nearer and farther in all directions.

In recent months, it has been a busy place, with numerous bingos, bridal showers, community picnics, Christmas concerts, card parties, talent shows, agricultural meetings and work and clean-up bees. It is also used for golden- and silver-wedding celebrations, 4-H meetings, quilting bees, and educational short courses. In the past, it was used as church, theatre and dance hall. Who knows how it may serve in the future.

It is anticipated that with completion of the improvements and alterations now being carried out, the building will be given a new lease on life, and it can look forward to increased use and greater service to the community.

THE HISTORY OF BLUFFTON
December 13, 1994

The history of settlement in the Bluffton area probably began with the land survey around 1903. A Metis family named Pocha seems to have been the first to homestead, a short distance to the south and east of the present hamlet. Pochas had done some farming in the 1890s. By 1907 there were enough families in the vicinity to form a school district. It was called Riverside #1735. A school house was erected in 1908 across the river north of the present school.

World War I (1914-18) slowed settlement, as it did in many areas, but after the war, with the coming of the railroad to Rimbey in

1919, and in anticipation of its coming on north, homesteading spread up the Blindman and its tributaries. It was partly on the strength of rail extension rumours that my father took a homestead in the Iola district nine miles west of Bluff Center in 1921.

The late John Christian (Jack) Hinrichsen also came to the Bluffton area in 1921. He was very soon one of the district's chief boosters, promoting the Blindman country at every opportunity. It was he who, with the railroad on the way, did the organizational planning and laid the groundwork in 1922, for a store. It could never be said of Jack that he was all talk and no action. He called a meeting of interested citizens at the school house and one of the first things done at the meeting was to form a committee of eight men, each of whom was assigned a compass direction. The committee's allotted task: to thoroughly canvass each segment for funds with which to erect a store building. They needed $1,200. They collected $400.

I have the names of seven of those canvassers. Who took the north segment I cannot say. McCullough had the northeast, Evans had east; in the southeast it was Jerome Donnelly, Jesse Lloyd was south and George Donnelly, southwest. J. C. Hinrichsen took west, and Jim Donovan, the northwest.

Apparently undaunted by the shortfall in funds, the committee went about acquiring the site and arranging to have it surveyed. The southwest corner of NW 31 had just been separated from the rest of the quarter by the railroad survey, and it seemed the most

Bluffton main street, 1950s.

130

suitable parcel available. Evans owned the quarter section, or said he did, but it turned out that the CPR held the title, necessitating more than one trip to Calgary by members of the committee. Red tape and consequent delays behind them, arrangements were made with Imperial Lumber Co. of Rimbey for building materials on credit, and construction of a store got underway in 1923.

Now the committee found themselves faced with another problem. None of them, nor anyone else they approached, wanted anything to do with running the store. Then it was learned that Felix Montalbetti had owned an interest in a store at Blairmore. Would he be agreeable to managing the store at Bluffton, as the railroad was now calling Bluff Center? He would. Felix and sons rented the building from the committee for twenty dollars a month. The committee had done its work and eventually Montalbetti Bros. Ltd. took over lock, stock and barrel. Their slogan, "The Most Up-to-date Store in the Blindman Valley," would go unchallenged for decades.

The Bluffton Creamery burned down in 1959.

THE BLUFFTON ELEVATOR
May 14, 1996

A group of young men and older teenagers were hanging around outside the Bluffton grain elevator one afternoon. (We didn't hang out in those days. We hung around. A hang-out was a rustlers' hideaway.) One of the group challenged one of the others to see if he could throw a stone over the elevator, expressing serious doubts that his friend could get a missile over that lofty roof-top. Soon we were all trying, and we all failed but one. I remember that it was one of the Donnelly boys who selected a pebble of just the right size from the gravel beside the railroad track, and without bragging, and without deriding those who had failed, he sailed that stone up and over.

It looked so easy. Here were a bunch of guys who could wing a baseball in from right field to home plate, all trying to get a small rock the more than eighty feet into the air plus a considerable horizontal distance, and all failing. Most of us were familiar with that elevator, inside and out. We weighed ourselves on the scale. We knew the inside of the engine room. Some of us had been in the pit and some had taken the lift to the upper levels for a view out over the country from a tiny, dusty window in the cupola. None of us envisioned a time in our lives when that tall prairie skyscraper would become redundant and, along with thousands like it, would be torn down, moved or razed.

The country elevator has been the dominant feature of prairie landscapes for more than a century, during all the history of agriculture in the West. The first one was built in Manitoba in 1881. By the 1930s, there were six thousand of them thrusting themselves into the prairie skies across three provinces. They had followed the railroads everywhere except into the mountains. Today most of those six thousand have either vanished or are doomed to disappear.

The elevator at Bluffton was built in 1922, and was the first building on the townsite. It is said that it was ready for business when the railroad arrived. It was just approaching middle age when it was torn down in the 1960s, and the rail line past it abandoned.

A grain elevator was built at Hoadley in 1934 by the Alberta Wheat Pool. It was eventually moved to another location. Elsewhere in the province, a few old country elevators have stayed put after retirement, taken over by local community organizations as museum items, non-functional reminders of Alberta's agricultural roots. One such is at Meeting Creek. There is another in the Peace River country.

I once took two young children to an abandoned grain elevator after dark. That was the thrill of the day for them, if not of the whole week. I had been in earlier, in daylight, and knew that there was no danger, but I did admonish them to be very quiet, so as not to disturb the pigeons, or the mice, or any stray skunks that might be out prowling.

And now it is Rimbey's turn to lose its elevators. I wonder how long it will take us to get used to level ground where three prairie skyscrapers stood so proudly for so long.

HOADLEY, THE BOOM TOWN
January 31, 1995

I have had to adjust my long-held notion that the railroad came to Bluffton in 1923. It came in 1922, and reached Haverigg (not yet Hoadley) late that same year.

Haverigg had been settled during the first decade of the century, when it must have been a rather remote part of the world. The year 1912 saw an influx of settlers, including John Hogarth, who that year became the first postmaster and storekeeper. Haverigg may possibly have been the name of Hogarth's home town in England. Such was the best information available in 1962, the year of publication of *Pas-ka-poo: An Early History of Rimbey and the Upper Blindman Valley.* I am a bit wary of stating definite dates right now, but it seems the post office was Haverigg until 1924, although the station was very likely Hoadley from the arrival of the railroad in 1922. A 1924 map shows both names, Haverigg to the south of the base line, Hoadley to the north. To add to the confusion of names, the school had been called Pineville since 1913, and held that name for many years to come. The school closed in 1958, having had thirty-one teachers in forty-four years. One of them was named Edith Bunker.

Hoadley experienced a small-scale boom with the arrival of the railroad, and the 1920s would be its heyday. Entrepreneurs came from all directions.

Within a year or two, Hoadley had not only a school, post office and store, but a creamery, a blacksmith shop, a hardware store, a barber shop, a pool room, a station, a cafe, livestock buying and shipping facility and a pay telephone in the general store. The Alberta Wheat Pool elevator was built in 1934, by which time many of the other businesses had closed. A hall was built in 1943, and additions at later dates. A provincial highway came from the south in 1949. Now there were two Hoadleys: the Railroad Hoadley and the Highway Hoadley, the former in decline, the latter providing necessities. Groceries, gas, auto and tractor repairs, the post office and the hall were all clustered around the corner just off the highway, which went on to Winfield in 1950. The railroad, by the way, reached Winfield in 1927. I hope I am safe in stating that date.

Hoadley certainly has an interesting past, not only the village, but the rural areas as well. Tales are told of a flourishing lumber industry. Homesteading, road building, and moonshining were other activities generating interesting stories, many or most of them lost and all but forgotten after fifty to ninety years. A whole generation gone, and their memories with them.

What of the community's future? One person who thinks Hoadley has tourist potential, based partly on its past, is Chris Harvey, a relative newcomer, but one with a keen interest in his surroundings, present and past. Some of his ideas: an historic marker of some sort to advise visitors of Hoadley's past, which might include a map of 1920s Hoadley and Haverigg; a sign along the highway such as Bluffton has; a brief, single sheet pamphlet outlining past history, for free distribution; markers at the old building sites in the old town; tours in summer for interested groups of any size; postcards with old and new scenes; a developed picnic area; a place where small groups could meet; and the formation of a club to foster the lost art of story telling.

Talk to Chris when next you meet him. He has even more ideas to put Hoadley back on the map.

CAMPGROUND BY THE WATER TANK
March 23, 1960

In the days when most of my travelling was done on a CCM "Rambler," I put in quite a bit of mileage on the old dirt road that linked Bluffton and Rimbey, and occasionally, on a summer evening, as I pedalled over the hill by the "canyon" and looked down into the green valley ahead, I would see a wisp of smoke rising out of the poplars by the river, straight ahead where the road would be had it kept to its allowance; and I'd guess at once that Indians were camping in the grassy bend across the tracks. Supposition would become a certainty when I'd catch a glimpse of a smoky white tent and odd-hued horses, picketed on long ropes beyond the wagons.

These people always made me think of Gypsies I had read about so often in story books, only these Alberta Gypsies rode in a vehicle that bore very little resemblance to the spic and span caravans of the Gypsies in the story books. Usually it was a light, farm-type wagon, liberally coated with caked mud from the clay roads and black-brown muskeg soil from farther west. The low-sided wagon box was sometimes equipped with spring seats and sometimes with just wide boards for seats.

Occasionally, as I rode slowly past, I caught a tempting whiff of what may have been venison stew—or it may have been rabbit.

There were shy papooses who ran for the tent as I looked their way; shy young girls in bright coloured dresses; old women, all wrinkles and shawls and moccasins; and old men who still wore their hair in braids down to their waist. Only the young men and boys dressed in the garb of the twentieth century, mostly in denim jackets and wide-brimmed hats, and leather boots instead of moccasins.

For these people, who were still nomads at heart, this grassy acre beside the water tower was a favourite camping spot as they travelled between Hobbema and Medicine Lake, or to Rimbey to the sports day events, or just to do some shopping.

It is some time now since the antiquated steam locomotive stopped beneath the tower to take on water, and it is even longer ago that I last saw the Indians camped among the poplars. Now the little diesel growls indifferently by, with never a stop, ignoring the tall old building that was so essential to its predecessor. Yet it is with a feeling of regret that I see the old water tower being torn down. It belonged to an era that knew a slower, more relaxed pace of living, yet at the same time was not lacking in colour and excitement and hope for the future.

Though I'll probably be told that a case of nostalgia is one of the symptoms of growing old, still, I knew that old water tower in a casual sort of way, all my life, and I wish it could have stood there 'til the river ran dry.

Postscript 1997

This is the bend in the river beside Highway 20, four miles north of Rimbey, which became a popular campground and picnic site through the 1960s to the 1990s. The site has now been closed and the picnic kitchen removed.

THE HOLY WATER STONE 1882
July 26, 1961

Mention an unusual rock to me and I'm all ears.

I have forgotten who first told me about a rock with writing on it, that lay near a spring up along the east branch of the Blindman, but ever since I first heard of it, some years ago, I knew I would never be satisfied until I had seen it for myself.

People I questioned about the rock all agree that the two most prominent words inscribed on it were HOLY WATER. Some said there was a date, and one or two named the date as being 1882.

135

Several people offered to take me to the spot, among them the Lundstroms, the Linds and the Fenwicks. The latter were most favourably located, and so it was that one fine day last June I set out to see this rock with Mr. Fenwick Sr. as my guide.

We drove north past several abandoned farmsteads, left the gravel for a road that could only be called rudimentary, crossed a swamp that would be impassable in an ordinary summer, and came out on a good gravelled road that led back toward Winfield. We didn't want to go to Winfield, so we followed the road to its very end in the opposite direction and parked at an oil well site.

Our destination was about a mile away on the other side of the river. We walked an expanse of swamp that in any other summer would have been knee deep in water and mosquitoes, crossed the river on an old grassy beaver dam, and headed into the woods.

"I have never come in from this direction before," said Mr. Fenwick, "so first we'll find the old trail that follows along the hillside; then it shouldn't be hard to find the rock."

So we climbed the slope, and before very long came upon an old wagon trail, which Mr. Fenwick told me was originally a much-used Indian trail leading from Pigeon Lake to all points south, and used in later years by the early homesteaders, some of whom came here as early as 1910.

Mr. Fenwick looked up and down the partly overgrown trail. "I haven't been here for more than ten years," he said. "But the rock should be right here close. We'll walk north for a way and see what we can see." We had gone about thirty feet when he said, matter-of-factly, "There it is."

And there it was: a piece of grey-brown sandstone, forty-two inches long by twenty-two inches high, flat on one surface, somewhat rounded on the other, and weighing, we later estimated, around two hundred pounds.

It was propped against a poplar tree and had been there so long that the tree had partially grown around it. On the flat side there were some marks, almost indiscernible on the weathered, lichen-covered stone. But knowing what to look for, it was possible to make out the words HOLY WATER carved in letters two and a half inches high, on the uppermost part of the rock.

"The spring is just a few yards down the hill," said my guide, "and I'm going to get a drink." So we both went, and lay full-length on the moss, and after chasing away a frog, drank of the cold, clear water.

We carried some water in a plastic bag to wash off the rock, and when it was dry I carefully went over the words with the head of a nail that I found in my pocket, so that the inscription could be photographed.

Mr. Fenwick was first shown this rock by one of his neighbours, Roy Counic, about 1925, and the writing may have been old then, if those words were actually carved nearly eighty years ago.

Who did carve them and why? Did Father Lacombe pass this way on some of his trips to Rocky Mountain House? Who can say?

THE SITE OF INLAND FORT
June 27, 1962

Block's Creek is drawn on many Alberta maps, but the only map I have seen that names it is the map that comes with your angling permit. Block's Creek, in case you are not a fisherman, is a tributary of the Medicine River, southwest of Leedale.

Here is a region of wide, flat, fertile pastures and meadows; of hills too high and too steep to be arable, which I would have thought were mountains when I was a youngster; and between the flats and the peaks, an area of intermediate terrain, where rolling fields of somewhat sandy but fertile soil are sown to grain.

I drove out onto this area the other day, and called at the home of the man for whom the creek was named. Seventy-six years of age but spry as a man of fifty, Mr. Block is well-qualified as an old-timer in the district. He settled on this creek more than forty years ago, and before that he carried the mail between Lacombe and Leedale. He told me he also operated the first motion picture shows in Rimbey and Bentley somewhere around 1920. Mr. Block is far from being retired, and spends a good deal of time looking after the numerous and varied livestock on the farm. Most of the field work, however, is taken care of by his stepson, Bob Campbell.

It was Bob's collection of artifacts that led me here to begin with, and when, after several years of not getting around to it, I finally saw them, I was astounded. I had no idea there was a site in Alberta that could yield artifacts in such great abundance. Bob has something like five hundred arrow and spear points, counting both perfect and imperfect or broken ones. He has uncovered scrapers and skinning knives, and possibly a score of hammer-heads and stone axes. Other assorted items include a stone tomahawk, one arrow point of iron of the type used by the Hudson's Bay Company as trade goods, one iron HBC trade axe, and two rocks with long, smooth, narrow grooves worn into them, which Bob says an aged Indian woman who once saw them told him they were used for making a fire. Bob also has an assortment of other unusual rocks, including a huge petrified stump.

The explanation Bob has for the profusion of artifacts on this land comes from Indians he has known and talked to, including the late John Strawberry, who died last year at the age of 111 years. According to them, the Cree and Blackfoot once fought a major battle here, during which the Blackfoot were driven far to the south.

Another thing that interests me very much is the site, a few rods south of the Block house, of Inland Fort, the history of which I know nothing. The old chimney place, dug into the side of a bank at the edge of the flat onto which the main building projected, is still plainly visible. One of the early settlers in the area found the bricks in such good condition that he hauled most of them away to build his own chimney.

I believe, judging by the great wealth of artifacts, and also by the ancient appearance of some of the Yuma-type points, that the Indians may have camped there thousands of years before the fort was built.

At any rate, the whole northern part of the farm is strewn with unlimited evidence of the stone age in Alberta. You may see chipped stones wherever you look, in field or pasture or farmyard. Heat-broken rock fragments from cooking fires and steam baths are equally common. Flakes of stone can be seen all over the fields, and I venture to say that a person could go out any time of the year when the ground is not covered with snow and pick up a worked artifact or two—a dozen under good conditions.

"Come back when I've got the summerfallow done," said Bob, as we were leaving. From one artifact hunter to another, that invitation isn't to be overlooked.

THE "OVENS" OF BOGGY HALL
September 23, 1959

Historical landmarks are preserved because they are a tangible link with the past. They tend to bring historical events out of the country's beginnings and fuse them with the present. They make our history seem closer and more real to us and help us to appreciate and understand it in a way no textbook can. They foreshorten time for us, and when we are in their vicinity, if we are in anything approaching a contemplative mood, centuries are reduced to decades and yesteryears are merely yesterdays.

I have felt these things in various spots: at old stopping places along the Caribou Trail, in the ruins of old Spanish missions, at the site of the old fort at Rocky Mountain House, and even right here in the Blindman Valley after reading Anthony Henday's description of how it looked in 1755, or John McDougall's glowing picture of it ninety years ago.

But at Boggy Hall site, there was little evidence of this feeling of history when we visited there on September 6.

In the first place, it was a chilly, unsettled sort of day, and rain cut short our explorations before they had even begun. Then there was the matter of getting back to the upper levels from the broad, flat bench along the river where the site is located. The road down— or up—can only be described as a stretch of rather second-class mountain-type road that is best navigated in dry weather, but Larry, our driver, didn't seem in the least worried about regaining the top in any kind of weather, so we poked around for an hour or two after it had stopped raining.

It was disappointing to find no concrete evidence of the post itself, but we found much of interest in the way of knowledge of the region and the site and information concerning it. I only hope the rest of the party considered the afternoon as well-spent as I did.

Near the north end of the meadow where Boggy Hall is supposed to be, there is a place where quite a number of flat stones are scattered about. These have apparently been carried from the river as the soil of the meadow and of the freshly-graded road that goes past the north end of the meadow to a well site on the river's edge, seem to be fairly free of stones of any kind.

Several times that day I had heard mention of the "ovens" that used to be on the site. When I enquired about the nature of these structures, I was referred to a man who had lived there forty-one years ago, Mr. Ganske, who lives near Violet Grove. He and his brother ran horses and cattle there in 1918. This is how he describes the ovens.

They were dome-shaped, about six feet across and four feet high, and were constructed of flat sandstones which sloped down to the outside to act as shingles and keep the interior dry. He is inclined to believe they were burial mounds and were called ovens only because they resembled the outdoor cooking ovens used in eastern Canada.

Mr. Ganske remembers eight of these structures in an area about a hundred feet across. They were left severely alone by the Ganske brothers in 1918, possibly because they felt that the Indians who were in the region at the time would not have looked kindly on any tampering or destruction. In later years, someone carried off most of the stones so that the field could be ploughed.

I am also inclined to believe that they were graves or grave covers, rather than ovens. In any event, they would very likely be much more recent than Boggy Hall, and I have hopes that the site of the post itself, if it is in the immediate vicinity, may still be located.

CHARLIE JOHNSON'S BARN
October 20, 1992

A wonderful old barn is falling to ruin back on the fringes of settlement in the northwest corner of Ponoka County. The land location is NE 30-44-4-W5. Knowing this much, a stranger would still have to hunt for this derelict. It is well-hidden by a forest of tall poplars grown up around it, and there are no roads leading to it. The land is owned by David Steeves.

I have several reasons for describing the old building as wonderful. Firstly, it was built in the World War I era and at that time was probably the best-constructed barn for many miles in any direction. Secondly, it was built without lumber of any kind as we know lumber today. That is to say, it was built with an axe and a bucksaw, and it was most likely built by one man.

That man, who homesteaded the land in 1914, and who built the barn, was Charlie Johnson, a onetime railroad man who had worked for the CPR. He spoke with a Scandinavian accent, probably Norwegian, and he lived alone on that remote homestead until 1927, when he moved to a quarter about four miles east. In 1914, when he homesteaded NE 30, it was thought that the proposed Lacombe Northwestern Railroad would swing that far west, and Charlie Johnson, being in the employ of the railroad, may have been banking on this, for some of the other people who homesteaded nearby at the same time were also railroad men who came in with him. It must have been a great disappointment when the railroad was routed through Hoadley, eight miles to the east.

Harry Strain told me about this barn some time ago, and he was so intrigued by it that I wanted to see it, too, and although I had looked a couple of times, it was not until the end of the summer that I finally stood beside it, and I, too, was fascinated. My imagination was fired and my admiration for the pioneer who built it was evoked.

140

Let me try to describe it. Size: approximately 28 x 20 feet, inside measurement—room enough for ten horses, with two double stalls and a single stall on either end, and a wide alley between. The wide door was on the north side. There was a small window in each end and the south side had no opening at all. The logs used in the construction seemed to be all lodgepole pine, very straight with little taper, even in the thirty-foot ones on the south side. The main frame of the building was eighteen logs high, the topmost log twelve feet above the ground. At the eight-foot level, two log beams went the length of the building, each about seven feet from the sidewalls. Crosswise on these were laid smaller hewn joists about two and a half feet apart. All were mortised into the walls. On these cross pieces the loft floor was laid, also made of hewn poles fitted snugly so that it would have been perfectly safe to walk on. The rafters were also poles, probably of black spruce, spaced about two feet apart and spiked to the top log. On these were nailed long poles, flattened with the axe to about two inches thick and spaced about their own width. Next came the shingles—more correctly, homemade shakes—split from clear pine blocks. These were nailed on, not with shingle nails, but with two-and-a-half inch nails. This, plus the fact that they were on a square pitched roof, enabled them to last for more than seventy years.

The other thing that made the building last so long was that each end of every log had been pegged to the log below it with a wooden peg. A one-and-one-eighth-inch auger had been used to drill a hole completely through the last log erected and four inches into the one below it. The pegs were expertly shaped with an axe and driven to the bottom of the hole. The corner notching on the logs was also the work of an expert axeman. An inverted V-notch, it also helped to shed water and preserve the building.

The craftsmanship that went into this building is quite remarkable; the man-hours must have been staggering. Today, some three quarters of a century later, there is so much that we could never know.

DRAYTON VALLEY OIL BOOM
August 18, 1955

I spent two hours in the busiest little place in Alberta the other day: the modern boom town of Drayton Valley, where oil is king. Now, two hours isn't a very long time in which to gain an impression of a place, but in Drayton Valley impressions are gained in a hurry.

141

In fact, the whole town is in a hurry. I don't think I have ever seen more hustle and bustle anywhere. It reminded me of an anthill that had just been stepped in, and this is in spite of the fact that it was Wednesday afternoon when most other Alberta towns take on a rather sleepy appearance.

Arising out of the hurry and scurry was something else that impressed me. Dust. Infiltrating, permeating, all-pervading dust, that on a rainy day would become sticky, gooey mud. Not that there isn't plenty of gravel about. There is. (I guess it can be called gravel, although everything under two and three quarter inches seems to have been screened out). But construction is everywhere and so there are heaps of dirt and clay that turn to mud when it rains. Everywhere, too, are stacks of building materials and equipment, and men are busy moving it from where it is to where it has to go. Absent, for the most part, are sidewalks and lawns, flowers, and trees, and quiet places. Walking is rugged, even by daylight.

Living accommodation is at a premium here. The lad who went up with me was seeking lodging, and we walked or drove down nearly every street in town before he found a place to sleep. He was, however, offered a number of jobs in the course of his search for a bed.

The town as it was before the boom is easily picked out amid the newness. To the north and east are the blocks of cabins, the trailer courts and a few new houses. Conveniently situated is a fine, modern shopping centre, together with a new hotel, where all accommodation is booked for days ahead (except in the huge beverage room). This area in the future will be the downtown business district. To the west is a surprisingly large industrial area, with many modern and permanent buildings, and more going up. Here again, of course, oil is the keynote.

Rimbey, too, experienced something of an oil boom recently, but I believe Rimbey can be thankful that its boom wasn't as big or as sudden as the one that hit Drayton Valley. The streets of that town are rougher and dustier than Rimbey's could ever have been. As for the highways serving the town, they are probably the roughest gravel surface roads in the province, and possibly the hardest used. They make the road from Rimbey to Bentley look like the Pennsylvania Turnpike.

Now I don't want to discredit Drayton Valley at all. It can't help being a boom town. And the boom is more orderly than it might have been had it come in an earlier day. It is a far cry from the chaos and utter disorganization that marked the boom towns of the continent's gold-rush days. You can see evidence of the planning that is being done, and as time goes by, conditions will improve and the boom become stabilized. The next two years may see as much change in Drayton Valley as have the last two.

HINTON, ENTRANCE AND BRULE
November 6, 1979

We are standing on a bench above the Athabasca River, looking down on the roofs of the village of Entrance—or perhaps it is the hamlet of Entrance; the latest population figure I have for the centre is ninety-four. From our vantage point, we can see that Entrance is a rather strung-out little place, having grown along the railroad. It dates back to about 1911 when the Grand Trunk Pacific was pushed westward through the Yellowhead Pass.

Entrance was so named because of its position as the first railway station east of Jasper Park boundary, long before Highway 16 had been built. Some of its buildings must be almost as old as the railroad. Others, like the huge, fifty-foot square log house immediately behind us, are as modern as the seventies.

To get to Entrance, you leave Highway 16 on the road to Grande Cache. Entrance is just off to the left a short way down this road, before you cross the railroad and before you cross the Athabasca River. As I look down over the bare poplars onto its roofs and yards, I wonder about its past and what will be its future. There is one person who sees a future for Entrance. I don't know the man's name, but he is the proprietor of the little general store and post office which we can see directly below us, and he believes that its future lies in tourism, a restoration of sorts for the sleepy little place with such a fine view of the mountains. Not a 1911 restoration perhaps, but possibly a 1950s kind. Maybe the man at the store has a vision of what Entrance has to offer the future and what the future holds for Entrance.

From Entrance we cross the bridge and turn westward once more, again off the Grande Cache Highway, to the town of Brule, where the cottages all in a row remind me of the old miners' houses in Nordegg. In Brule there is a difference, however, for here most of the houses are still being lived in. They have been kept up and improvements made; the lawns are mowed, and the street is quite attractive. In Nordegg, similar cottages are completely uninhabitable by reason of not having been occupied for a quarter of a century.

143

Brule is the French word for burn, and the name, originally complete with accents over the vowels, comes from a forest-fire burn on a nearby mountainside. Brule is about as old as Entrance and similar in size, and is also attractively situated in a mountain setting near the north end of Brule Lake which looks on the map like a long, wide stretch of the Athabasca River. The other end of Brule Lake is near the gates of Jasper National Park. Here Jasper House was once situated. I don't know if anyone has visions of the future of Brule.

We retrace our route now, back to Hinton, a thriving pulp-mill town of five thousand population. Hinton was named for a general manager of the Grand Trunk Pacific when it pushed westward from Edmonton to the Pacific Coast. Unlike its two near neighbours to the west, Hinton has thrived and prospered in spite of some reverses over its seventy-year history. Its first boom came with the railroad in 1910. By 1928 a local coal mine had raised its population to two thousand. An explosion closed the mine and population dropped to one hundred and eighty. The boom created by the pulp mill in 1955 is still going strong, and all seems to be well with Hinton's world.

I remark on this, my first visit in some years, that Hinton's bad pulp-mill smell is nothing like it used to be.

IT'S DARK IN HERE!
July 30, 1991

When my brother and I were little guys, we made a cave. We dug it out of the side of a pine ridge north of the house, using a prospector's pick and the spades and shovels that were a part of the farm. I suspect that during that period, if my father could not find his spade in the usual place, he would know where to look. He had, as a matter of fact, helped us select the location for our cave, with ulterior motives in mind. He planned to build a storage space for ice in that bank, and to that end he encouraged us to make that cave ever larger. By the end of the summer we had made it large enough to crawl into and turn around, but the bigger we made it, the slower our progress. When my father figured we had lost interest in it, he proposed the ice house, and with visions of home-made ice cream all summer long, we readily agreed to sacrifice the cave. An open-ended pit was dug (by hand, of course), a roof built over it and a load of sawdust hauled from a local mill. When the ice in the creek was thick enough, blocks were cut and hauled, and we did, indeed, have home-made ice cream in the summer time.

That was my first caving experience. Since then I have been in caves in far-flung parts of the world: in South Dakota and Hawaii, in Mexico and the Galapagos, but until this summer, I had not managed to get to Alberta's famous Cadomin Cave. When I did, I was not disappointed. It is undoubtedly the ruggedest caving I have done.

There were three women and eight men in our party, and we were led by Ben Gadd, of Jasper, an experienced caver amongst all his other achievements. Just to get to the cave mouth requires a climb of about three hundred metres on a rather rugged trail that starts beside the McLeod River, follows it up a steep creek, then turns and seems to go straight up the mountain. The trouble was, we had to pack winter clothing, a hard hat, drink, plus cameras, binoculars and flashlights. The temperature within the cave is only a few degrees above freezing, and you have to crawl and slide through cave mud in places, so you have to wear old or washable clothing. There was supposed to be a prize for whoever got the dirtiest, but nobody claimed it. We left our packs a few metres inside the entrance, which is on the north side of the mountain. The cave leads downhill and to the southeast, and has numerous passages and galleries, so that you really need to go in with someone who knows caves and knows this one. I would not want to lose my flashlight in there.

We went in via the Main Gallery and down a side passage to the Mess Hall, so called because that is where some parties stop for lunch. It is half a kilometre into the mountain, and was the turnaround point for us. We returned via the East Gallery, sometimes stooping, or crawling, or slithering beneath some very low ceilings. At other times we walked upright in vast chambers where our lights barely reached the ceiling.

Cadomin Cave is a water-eroded limestone river bed, created when all the nearby valleys as we know them today were either non-existent or filled with ice. Water still drips from the ceilings in places, but all stalagmites and stalactites within reach of human hands have long since been hauled away as Alberta onyx. Only the parts of the cave that are difficult of access are in their original state.

Back in the sunshine, we shed our muddy outerwear, our sweaters and gloves, and rested for a few minutes before beginning our descent to our van far below, beside the river.

145

DINOSAUR COUNTRY
September 15, 1981

As the summer waned and subtle hints of autumn intruded into the Alberta scene with ripening grain fields and back-to-school sales, I had an opportunity to visit one of Alberta's unique—and most spectacular—provincial parks. At the end of August, I went with my friend Maxine to Brooks to deliver two of our favourite kids, Ryan and Michelle, back to their parents and school. On the way, we stopped at Dinosaur Provincial Park, a destination we've had in mind for many years, but never quite managed to reach. We had viewed the Red Deer River from most of its twenty-four crossings between the mountains and the Saskatchewan border, and we found it overall an astonishingly beautiful and different and scenic river, but the Red Deer River Badlands have always held a fascination for us, and the section that comprises 22,000 acres of Dinosaur Provincial Park we found especially exciting.

First of all there are the great skeletons, not set up as in most museums, with every bone in its proper place, but displayed exactly as they were found, partially excavated, just as they were preserved from the beginning in the mud-become-stone of those ancient inland sea margins. Some are exactly where they were found; others have been moved a few feet to facilitate viewing. Either way, they are the most realistic glimpse you will get of the way Alberta was seventy million years ago. One skeleton you can drive right to; others require short walks; one you only reach via a trip in a park bus with a tour guide (free). All are well-protected from weather and people by glass and concrete shelters. All have interpretive display panels around them to help your imagination reconstruct the Alberta scene the dinosaurs knew.

Quite apart from the dinosaur remains, this park would be worth anybody's time to visit. The landforms are incredible, similar to those in the Drumheller region, but different, too. Most of the park's area is restricted and off limits to the average tourist, both for his own protection and for the protection of the landscape. The centre of attraction at the park headquarters is John Ware's original cabin, which was made into a museum to honour this pioneer rancher and cowboy.

As in most provincial parks, there are naturalists to provide both daytime and evening programs and activities and to answer all your questions. Take a walk along the Red Deer River which is only a five-minute stroll from the campground, and you will likely see a

146

couple of exceptionally tame deer that make their home in the park. If you happen to be a bird watcher, the river banks and river flat make an excellent area for the pursuit of this hobby.

Dinosaur Provincial Park was created in 1965 to protect this area of extreme scientific and scenic value and to make it available at the same time to the tourist who likes to get off the beaten track to see something unique. The region can get very hot in the summer, so unless you enjoy more heat than most of the province gets in the course of the summer, you should probably plan your visit for June.

Last year Dinosaur Park was dedicated as a World Heritage Site because of the richness and extent of its dinosaur remains. Even while we were there, and unknown to most of the park's visitors, a recently excavated skeleton was being loaded aboard helicopters for removal to Edmonton, where it will be prepared for display in a new museum being built in Drumheller. Albertans are very fortunate to have, within easy reach of most of us, so scientifically valuable and so spectacular a site as Dinosaur Provincial Park.

THE ROMAN WALL
September 29, 1987

I came over the rise in the prairie trail and saw the rider at about the same time he saw me. He sat tall and straight in the saddle, reminding me of Ben Cartwright. At sight of my vehicle, he stopped and turned his horse toward me as I came slowly along the rough trail. A lame collie, kicked by a bull I later learned, watched also. "Here is a cowboy," I thought, "out checking his cows, and he's wondering what my business is in this remote corner of the county. I'd better stop and enlighten him." I pulled up and got out as he rode toward me; the dog limped beside the horse.

"Can I help you?" he asked politely.

"Sure you can," I answered. "I was directed here by Vern Arnold, County Field Man for Forty Mile. I'm looking for a geological formation, a rock outcrop called the Roman Wall, and I'm also interested in seeing another formation near here called Black Butte."

"The Roman Wall is just about a mile away," said the man on horseback. "My name is Art Hagen. I check the cattle out here for the grazing association. I can direct you to the Roman Wall, but I have another idea. You go back out to the road, drive down to the cabin, go in and turn the stove on under the coffee pot, and I'll head back across country. I'll put my horse in the barn and I'll come back here with you. We can check out a couple of water holes and I'll

147

The Roman Wall.

have to look over yonder hill, but we can do all that in your truck, and I can take you to Black Butte as well."

"Sounds fine to me," I said. I had a map with me that would have taken me right to the Roman Wall, although I couldn't be sure at the time, so I headed back to his little two-room cabin beside the chutes and corrals and holding pens, and in a few minutes Art was there after a ride of more than a mile over a devious route around deep prairie coulees. We had coffee and sandwiches and headed out on the road again. Art was a gold mine of information about the country, the climate, and the people of this rather remote corner of Alberta. "It takes me three days' riding to cover this pasture," he told me, "but I'm usually in early." Art has been a cowboy all his life, and it's my bet he is a good one. He can almost tell at a glance, as his eyes scan the prairie, if a cow or a calf needs a closer look.

We left the trail in places and drove across the prairie, not something I have done a lot in my time, but we came to a stop near the rim of a coulee, and just below us, completely out of sight until you are almost on top of it, was the Roman Wall, probably so named by some early British-born rancher or cowboy who knew the famous Roman Wall back home in England. The Roman Wall here, on the Writing-on-Stone Grazing Reserve, just a mile from the United States border, is actually a vertical lava dike. This one would have formed a fissure in the bed rock well below the surface. Repeated glaciation

148

plus weather and water erosion have exposed it on the lip of this coulee. A small portion of the dike protrudes from the opposite wall of the coulee. This lava, which glistens with flecks of mica, was never molten at the surface, but first saw daylight as hard, cold, igneous rock.

Art posed on or beside the wall while I took photographs from several angles. Then we proceeded back to the road and on to the Black Butte, scaring up a herd of about thirty antelope as we approached this dark, jagged bump on the prairie, this one a somewhat different type of igneous intrusion, a tiny relative of the Sweetgrass Hills a few miles to the south in Montana.

RED ROCK PARK—JERUSALEM ROCKS
October 13, 1987

Before I left Alberta's far south in mid-September, I had two more sites to check out. Both were worth the effort. I was deliberately not visiting places I had been before, like the Cypress Hills and Writing-on-Stone, although the temptation was great when I was so close. On my first evening in Foremost, I had coffee and an enjoyable visit with Ed and Hazel Simanton. Hazel is a sister of Daisy Stuart of Rimbey (and of Helen Cooke at *The Rimbey Record*). It was Darrel Stuart who first told me about the Roman Wall, described earlier. It was a friend of the Simantons who drew me a map that would take me right there and who suggested that I see Vern Arnold, County Field Man. Vern told me about an outcrop of rock similar to the Roman Wall, called the Rooster's Comb because it arched over a hill. It is likely also a lava dike, but I just didn't have time to hunt it up. These dikes are of the same igneous rock as the Sweetgrass Hills and would therefore date back forty-five million years. Like the Sweetgrass Hills, they are rock upthrusts that pushed up through the sedimentary deposits that earlier formed the Rocky Mountains.

Another natural phenomenon that I went to see was Red Rock Coulee, recently made a provincial park. I drove about fifty kilometres east of Foremost, then turned north near Orion on the road to Seven Persons, which is southwest of Medicine Hat. Leaving the highway at the sign and proceeding up a dirt road, I soon came to the site where hundreds of huge, round, reddish sandstone concretions are eroding out of the bentonite. Some stand higher than a man. Most are smaller than that. Many are round and perfect; others are badly broken up. They are on the hillsides and in the bottoms of the swales and coulees, quite numerous over an area of

149

Red Rock Park, 22 km south of Seven Persons, Alberta.

several acres. There is probably no similar scenery elsewhere in the province.

On the following day, I drove through the sleepy port of Aden into the Sweetgrass Hills of Montana. It was the United States customs officer who asked, when I told him I planned to cross the border again at Sweetgrass, if I had ever been to visit the Jerusalem Rocks near there. "What are the Jerusalem Rocks?" I asked.

"Sandstone formations," he said. "Hoodoos, monuments, that sort of thing. They're worth a look."

When I got to Sweetgrass, I found the road west and followed it for about three miles. Suddenly, in a long, wide coulee, I came upon them: columns and pillars, hoodoos and spires, buttresses and eroded formations as big as a building, stretching away down the east side of the coulee for half a mile. The customs man was right; they were worth a look. A few more photographs and I headed for Coutts.

This was Wednesday. I had left home Saturday. I had spent four very interesting days visiting some off-the-beaten-path geological sites of southern Alberta and Montana.

Easterners (and others) often have the idea that there is nothing to see in the West until you reach the Rocky Mountains. How mistaken they are! The prairie has its own brand of fascination. I sometimes found my vistas in southern Alberta as restricted by the rugged terrain as by the forest farther north. There is a great semi-circle

150

in the south, beginning with the Cypress Hills on the east, through the Lost River country and the Sweetgrass Hills across the border, to the Milk River Ridge south of Lethbridge, to the Porcupine Hills in the west, that is chock full of interesting scenery, geology and geography, fauna and flora, not to mention an exciting history. I found it a vacation land that was very different and most enjoyable.

I HEAR THE SUFFIELD BLAST
September 2, 1964

Five hundred tons of TNT might be expected to go off with quite a bang. Yet I have an idea that when such a blast was detonated by the Defense Research Board at Suffield, Alberta, at 11 a.m. last July 17, it did not make quite such a loud bang as had been expected.

This was the largest non-nuclear explosion ever set off, and that is probably the reason why there were some six hundred scientists and government and military officials on hand for the experimental blast. They came from the three participating countries: Canada, Great Britain and the United States.

This explosion was much the same to watch as a nuclear one, with the same huge mushroom cloud rolling upward to eighteen thousand feet before drifting out over the prairie. The blast formed a crater 350 feet long and twenty-five to thirty feet deep, according to news reports.

Since the experiment was radiation free, it was the perfect opportunity to study shock effects on all kinds of equipment, both military and non-military, above and below ground. Ammunition was one of the items tested in this way, while Bell Telephone Company made tests on communications equipment. Many other things, from structures to animals, were tested as well, and the heart of the blast was photographed from an aircraft directly overhead.

Perhaps the most interesting study, at least from my point of view, was one dealing with the sound waves generated by the huge explosion; interesting to me because I was one of many observers all over the western provinces and Montana, who were asked to listen for the sound of the blast.

It was expected that it would be heard up to four hundred or even five hundred miles away from Suffield in some instances. Actually, not many observers that far away did report any hearing of the sound. It may have been that the weather on July 17 was just a little too perfect, with no high cloud to bounce sound waves back to earth at distant points.

However, at least three points in British Columbia reported hearing the big boom. One of these reports came from Kamloops and another from a point halfway between Kamloops and Prince George. Both of these were from elevations of about six thousand feet.

Strangely enough, some observers within thirty-five miles of Suffield did not hear the sound, even though it was able to leap the Rocky Mountain chain to become audible in central British Columbia.

The results of the audibility tests have now been plotted on a map and they show that the areas where audibility was most complete took the form of two crescents, both backed up against the mountains: the first from Great Falls, Montana, through Lethbridge, Calgary, Stettler and Wainwright; and a smaller one farther to the northwest, running from Banff through Nordegg, west and north of Edmonton to Lac la Biche. Between these two crescents is an area that includes Edmonton, Red Deer and Olds, plus a substantial strip of the map on either side of these points, and in this region only three of the reports sent in indicated audibility. One of these was mine.

I estimated a time lapse of sixteen minutes between the blast at Suffield, thirty miles northwest of Medicine Hat, and the arrival of the sound waves here. Actually they came at 11:17 a.m. The sound was just audible, like the rumble of distant thunder, and had I not been listening outdoors, in an open field away from traffic or other noises, I would probably have never heard this small reverberation that originated as a $4 million bang two hundred miles away.

THE NEUTRAL HILLS
May 5, 1981

The Blackfoot believed that the Neutral Hills were made in the middle of the night. The area was once a warring ground between Blackfoot and Cree. Rich in buffalo, both sides claimed it as their exclusive hunting ground. Then the Great Manitou, fed up with all the fighting, raised those impressive elevations and declared them neutral territory. The warring tribes met next morning and concluded a peace pact.

Beside Highway 41, just north of Gooseberry Lake Provincial Park, as you come up to the hills from the south, there stands a marker of stone and bronze, briefly outlining the history of the Neutral Hills. The marker was erected, not by the Historical Sites and Monuments Board, but by a group of local people. For a tourist like myself, always interested in the history of any area I am poking around in, such historical markers are a valuable addition to the attractions of the region. We should have more of them in our own corner of Alberta.

I have had my eye on the Neutral Hills for many years now, for the whole area is rich in Indian lore and artifacts. Back in the 1960s, I had an invitation, through the Alberta Archaeological Society, to participate in a project to map boulder-outline figures that were fairly common in the region, but were rapidly being destroyed by cattle and traffic and human activity. I would have loved to have gone for a few days, but in those years it was just too difficult to get away on a date set by someone else. The archaeologists, amateur and professional, who did take part mapped over one hundred teepee rings and boulder-outline figures, including twelve medicine wheels, ten cairns, one pentagon, one buffalo, and three turtles eating snakes. These fifteen-foot turtles with thirty-foot snakes in their mouths were the first ever found in Alberta.

Maps can tell you much about a region. Palliser's map of 1859 shows the Neutral Hills as the boundary between Cree and Blackfoot, but fifty years earlier, Blackfoot territory had extended considerably farther north to the Battle River.

An Alberta government map showing land disposition, published in 1924, shows large grazing leases in the hills and vicinity, and post offices named Neutral Hill, Lloyd's Hill, Neutral Valley, Lakesend and Cousins, indications that the area was once more populated than it is now. This is borne out by the many abandoned farmsteads seen throughout the rolling countryside today. The Neutral Hills area, being somewhat difficult to access in the early days, was settled somewhat later than farmland along the railroads. An annual precipitation of about fourteen inches, plus very uneven terrain largely unsuited to the plough, indicated cattle country, and rangeland it remains today with numerous Texas gates along its scenic, winding roads.

And you never saw such friendly people. Everyone waved to us; they waved from farm trucks and tractors, or from their yards as we passed. They knew we couldn't be tourists on these roads and in mid-April; we must surely be local people, and to a degree they were right. One of us on that tour had known those hills for sixty-five years, and when you are with an old-timer of that long standing you feel less of a tourist yourself.

Research has revealed that the highest elevation of the Neutral Hills is 2,900 feet above sea level. Consort, south of Gooseberry Lake about twelve kilometres, is 2,371.

THE BUFFALO JUMP
August 12, 1964

The stench that rose on the updraft from a buffalo jump on a summer's evening a century or more ago must have been something better imagined than experienced.

I visited a much-used buffalo jump earlier this summer, and I can report that a century is not quite long enough to obliterate all traces of smell from such a site.

I am sure you all know what a buffalo jump is. It is a strategically-located spot where Indians in days of yore stampeded large groups of buffalo over a cliff or precipice to their death below. Those not killed by the fall would be dispatched with stone clubs or bows and arrows.

The jump is similar to the buffalo pound as a means of killing a large number of animals for their meat and hides. The pound was an enclosure of logs, brush, rocks and natural barriers into which the beasts were driven, surrounded by members of the tribe, and slaughtered. It was used in country where no sites were available for a jump, and was probably a less wasteful method than the jump.

The buffalo jump could only be used where the animals could be driven over a drop of thirty feet or more. That is, the drop had to be severe enough to kill or cripple them, but since there were no limitations on the number of animals that could be driven over a high drop, the opportunity for waste was much greater.

Furthermore, once the hunters had cut off part of a herd and had it moving in the direction of the jump, they took great pains to see that none turned back to rejoin the main herd, for if one did so, the Indians believed, it would warn all the rest never to go near that jump again.

One of the best known of Alberta buffalo jumps is "The Old Woman's Buffalo Jump" near Cayley, where the Glenbow Foundation conducted digs that shed much light on Alberta's pre-history. Jumps are dotted all over the prairie provinces, wherever a suitable site could be found in an area grazed by the great herds.

For many hundreds of years, Indians chased buffalo over the precipice at the site I visited on two different weekends last month. The number of animals to leave their remains on the slope below the jump must have reached into the hundreds of thousands. Below the rock face that formed the drop, the slope fanned out steeply for several hundred feet to the coulee bottom, and this area, possibly an acre, was saturated to a depth of two or three or more feet

154

with buffalo bones, many of them still in a remarkably good state of preservation. Below this depth, there are layers of ash incorporating goodness knows how many more thousands of buffalo skeletons.

A rank growth of wild parsnip, or wild rhubarb, as some prefer to call it, covers what must once have been a highly offensive scene, but only some of the stench seemed to be from rotting vegetation; it seemed to be the wrong time of year for that particular odour. Indeed, I was later assured by an archaeologist that decaying bones could very well be the cause. While the bad smell was quite noticeable at first, one soon became accustomed to it, even forgetting it entirely after a few minutes.

Next week I'll go into more detail about this particular site and tell why I visited it twice, and why I haven't revealed its location.

THE JUMP DESCRIBED
August 19, 1964

The location of the buffalo jump which I mentioned last week cannot be disclosed, for reasons I'll deal with later, but it surely must be one of the most significant and interesting pre-historic sites in the province. It excited my imagination as no other historic site has ever done, partly because of its magnitude, and partly because evidence of its use is so readily apparent, but mostly because it is so easy to visualize the spot as it might have looked on a slaughtering day hundreds of years ago.

Above the drop, the lay of the land was perfect for the purpose, sloping gently from all directions to a shallow draw which led directly over the cliff. Below, the bones and debris compacted with dirt and covered with growth, spread out like an alluvial fan at the base of a mountain. The valley floor for hundreds of yards in either direction was strewn with the remains of further thousands of buffalo. Almost any bone that ever helped hold a buffalo together can be picked up here right on the surface. We did not see any complete skulls, only broken pieces, and I wondered if the skulls here were not always broken to get at the tongue, which was a delicacy, and the brain, which was used in tanning hides. Teeth, remarkably well preserved, were scattered everywhere.

So here are the reasons I can't mention the location of this jump. First, it is on privately owned land and the owner is well aware that once the public finds a spot of this kind it leads to all kinds of trouble. There are too many people who refuse to respect either property rights or the value of a historic site. And that brings up a second point. A number of people have already visited this spot, and some of them have done their best to despoil a rare and historically valuable work of art.

You see, on the broad smooth face of the rock below the overhang, where they are protected from the weather, there are pictographs: symbolic pictures outlined in red ochre by Indians long ago; but the drawings have been desecrated by modern vandals who have sharp instruments and lipstick to scratch and smear their names across the face of the rock as high as they can reach. Fortunately, the artists of old could reach higher, and there, above the uppermost scratchings, a number of distinct pictographs remain.

They feature such recognizable objects as trees with objects hanging from the limbs, human stick figures, circles with feet. They have been dated by archaeologists at about 1700 AD, some years before the Plains Indians had horses.

I consider myself fortunate in getting to see a jump of this kind, and certainly did not expect to visit it twice; but on the first visit, I lost my rock hammer just as we were leaving, and didn't have time to make a thorough search for it. But knowing pretty well where to look, and since it was a valuable tool that had been given to me as a gift some years ago, I determined to go back later and look again.

And that is how I came to be back at this fascinating place just two weeks later, in the company of three companions to help me search. And how we searched for that pick! But two weeks of wet, warm weather had produced such an increase in growth that we were just about to give up, when the last man away gave me a yell, and there, at his feet, lay my hammer—a bit rusty—but otherwise none the worse for wear. Apparently, it had fallen from my bag as I was jumping down a slope.

Finally, my sincere thanks to all the fine people who made it possible for me to observe at first hand this tremendously exciting link with a rather gory aspect of Alberta's past. If I don't name them one by one, I'm sure they'll understand.

TURNER VALLEY—GAS TO BURN
October 23, 1968

As a boy, I was witness to one of the most flagrant, but at the same time most spectacular, examples of wastage of a natural resource since the slaughter of the buffalo.

It was the thrill of a lifetime to come in to Turner Valley after dark on a summer's night in the 1930s, to come over the hill and see

156

the valley below illuminated by hundreds of huge gas flares that roared and belched orange flame like a phalanx of subterranean dragons, lighting the sky and the hours of darkness over thousands of acres with an eery, pinkish, unsteady glow.

I had no thoughts in those days about the wastage or misuse of a natural resource, nor about whose it was to squander. I was free to marvel at the light and colour and spectacle. Never before had I been so far away from home; everything was different and within an hour or so I was even used to the smell. Excitement and adventure were all around. We went down to the site they called Hell's Half Acre, where some of the flares were directed downward into a coulee bottom for some reason I never learned. One of the flares had been turned off and the ground below was spread with a thin but rather rough layer of glass, a result, I suppose, of the silica in the sand being fused by the heat.

Next morning we visited the deepest man-made hole in the world, the wildcat drilling far below the production zone, between seven and eight thousand feet at the time, if I remember rightly. Progress was slow because most of the time was spent raising the bit, lowering the mud bucket, raising the bucket and lowering the bit again. Each raising and lowering operation took about fifteen minutes and filled—or emptied—a huge spool of cable, for that was the method in use in those days. Once the bit (or the bucket) had been raised clear of the hole a tremendous blast of natural gas roared out of the well-head, hurling mud and pebbles high into the air above the wooden derrick which fairly shook for the several seconds before two men manoeuvred a heavy metal cover into place.

The first time this eruption occurred in my presence, I was right on the derrick floor, about twenty feet from the well head. I was not prepared for the deafening roar, and headed for the open prairie, sure that the whole thing was about to blow sky-high.

Remembering back and writing this account from those memories, I have wished a dozen times that I had been old enough, or, rather, smart enough, to have set down a written account at the time.

On that first visit to Alberta's oil capital of the day, I was with my father and my Uncle Fred. Uncle Fred hauled tractor fuel from the Turner Valley field for farmers in the Bentley, Lockhart, and Rimbey area. His load was made up of forty-five-gallon drums, which he delivered to the farmers' yards, picking up their empties for his next trip. In spring and harvest seasons, he was a busy man.

I think the stuff he hauled was high quality crude, filtered but not refined. Many people burned it not only in their tractors, but in their cars as well. You could tell everybody who used "Turner Valley" by the very distinctive smell they left in their wake.

When the wind was directly from the south, you could even smell Turner Valley this far north (Township 44) directly from the field. Quite frequently, too, we could see the red glow in the southern sky that was the reflection of that great field of flares.

The year of discovery in Turner Valley was 1914. Not until 1938 was any effective move made to curb the waste which continued on a major scale right up to 1952.

WAINWRIGHT, PAST AND PRESENT
March 8, 1983

As we came out of the restaurant after a hearty dinner of Chinese food, I looked up at the large neon sign that hung over the sidewalk above the entrance. Something was wrong. I took a second look. I had read it correctly the first time. The sign read "Wainwrigt Steakhouse." The letter "h" had not fallen off; the sign had been made and erected that way. I looked up a short distance to the Wainwright Hotel. Its sign was correctly spelled. I walked back a few paces to look at the other side of the misspelled sign. "Wainwrigt Steakhouse," it said. I'm sure there was a story there, but we were a long way from home and I didn't have time to pursue it.

Everything else about Wainwright that sunny, February afternoon seemed to be in apple-pie order. It was Saturday; the shops were busy; the whole town looked prosperous. There were no dilapidated store fronts, at least not on Main Street; no closed businesses as we noted in some other centres that weekend. Perhaps one of the reasons that Main Street looked so busy was that it is the town's shopping area, or most of it. The Co-op is off one block to the east, and there is another large department store a block to the west, but there is no large, new shopping mall off on the edge of town to draw shoppers from the downtown area. Wainwright's population, I think, must be close to five thousand. I can't find an up-to-date figure.

Main Street runs north and south, and at the centre of the most important intersection is a clock tower with four faces, honouring the war dead. The town's symbol is the buffalo. A large statue of one of these great animals stands near the end of the business

158

section and a somewhat smaller buffalo in bas-relief adorns the front of the post office. Back in the 1920s, a large stuffed buffalo dominated the entrance to the CNR station. One day when the train came in, a crew of men got off, loaded the buffalo on the train, and it was never seen again, at least not in Wainwright. Who owned the beast at the time I didn't learn. Perhaps it was the railroad. At any rate, some old-timers in Wainwright are said to be still upset about the incident.

The association of Wainwright with the buffalo began about 1908 when a bison reserve of about 234 square miles just south of the town was fenced and stocked with some of the buffalo from the Montana purchase. The animals flourished, and by 1925 the reserve was becoming overcrowded. Thousands were shipped north, over the next few years, to Wood Buffalo National Park. The Wainwright reserve was closed in 1939 when it became a military camp and training ground. The bison were moved, sold or slaughtered.

In the buffalo years, the neighbouring towns, like Hardisty, were given a dressed buffalo to barbecue on their sports day each summer. Wainwright has seen no live bison herds for over forty years, but they haven't forgotten their past and their buffalo. Photographs dating back to 1912 are displayed in Armstrong's Department Store. I learned that Wainwright had a disastrous fire on July 27, 1929. About half the business area was burned, including the famous Wainwright Hotel, a replica of which is a feature of Heritage Park in Calgary.

Wainwright is about thirty-three miles from the Saskatchewan border on Highway 14. It was settled around or after the turn of the century, and was a noted tourist centre in the days when the buffalo were there. It was also a division point for the CNR. Today the surrounding farming area and the adjacent military base help keep the town prosperous.

FLORA

THE DEATH ANGEL
July 20, 1960

Death angel. Not the title of the newest teenage song hit but the name given to one of the most innocent-looking mushrooms—or toadstools if you like—to be found in the woodlands of central Alberta.

Heavy rains and hot sunshine ushered in the mushroom season late last month and that combination of weather can produce a profusion of fungus growth right through to October.

Of the one hundred and fifty or so species of mushrooms and similar fungi that grow in this area, most are edible, and most of the rest are only inedible because they are tough or bitter or otherwise unpalatable. A few are poisonous to some degree, but two species can be placed in a special category. Should you partake of either of them for lunch, you won't be needing any supper.

One of these deadly variations is called Fly agaric because in early days a very lethal fly poison was made by stewing its juices. *Amanita muscaria* is its Latin name. Fortunately, this is one of the showiest and most attractive of all our mushrooms, and therefore easily recognized. It is large; in the button stage it is usually tennis-ball- or even baseball-size. Mature specimens measure six or eight inches across.

Its colour scheme is distinctive, usually bright orange-yellow with white detachable spots that are remnants of the membrane that enclosed the plant in the early stages of its growth. When very fresh it is often orange-red, but old, decaying specimens may be drab tan with little traces of the white spots left.

This species is fairly common in shady, deciduous woodlands after rains.

Amanita muscaria has a cousin, *Amanita phalloides*, the notorious death angel. Less common than Fly agaric, it is perhaps even more

160

dangerous since it is not so easily recognized. It is taller than its relative, with a slimmer stem and smaller cap. The cap is white or any of several shades of off-white, from olive-grey to greenish brown. The gills are white.

Both the above species have, at the base of the stem, what is commonly called the "death cup," out of which the stem emerges. Some other kinds, not necessarily poisonous, have this feature, too, but it is a help in identifying the deadly ones.

Death by mushroom poisoning is not quick and easy, but usually involves several hours or even days of horrible agony. A list of symptoms is long and gruesome and not for a column such as this.

I haven't wanted to scare anyone out of eating mushrooms. The common field mushroom, properly prepared, is food for the gods, and many other kinds are even tastier. But don't take chances. If you can't tell one kind of mushroom from another, eat onions with your steak. Nutritively speaking, mushrooms are about on a par with turnips anyway.

THE FLOWERS OF JUNE
June 21, 1978

Along the roadsides and fence rows, on the edges of fields or in the deep woods, or out on the prairie hillsides, the wild roses of Alberta come to blossom in June. First to bloom is *Rosa acicularis,*

Roses and an old iron plough.

161

often called prickly rose because it has thorns. This is the one that was adopted in 1930 as Alberta's floral emblem. A little later in the month, in most of the same areas, comes *Rosa woodsii*, or Wood's rose, after botanist Joseph Woods, also called common wild rose. It is the most widespread of Alberta roses and is found both in the woods, where it hybridizes with *acicularis*, and out on the prairie alongside of the prairie rose. It has smaller flowers and fewer thorns than prickly rose. The prairie rose is *Rosa arkansana*, a low plant with rather small flowers of light pink to white. Wherever they grow, the roses go a long way toward brightening the Alberta landscape in June.

Roses are not the only flowers to colour the Alberta landscape outdoors in June. The western wood lily, commonly called tiger lily, blooms later in the month and into July. The lily and the rose I have always associated with the end of the school term, as they could always be found in bloom at that time.

The orchids of Alberta begin to come into their own each June. The calypso orchid, pink and delicate, blooms under the pines (sometimes under spruce) quite early in the month. The yellow lady-slipper is not often seen in my area until June is ending. Pale coral-root is another orchid of early June. Round-leafed orchids and the bog orchids come later.

Blueberries and cranberries and *kinnikinik* (Cree for bearberry) come into bloom this month, all with delicate, urn-shaped flowers in shades of pink—worth getting down on your knees for a closer look. Labrador tea, with its clusters of bloom, brightens many a sphagnum bog. (If you look closely at the bog you will find some beautiful plants among the moss family). Look on the hillsides for twining honeysuckle, its terminal leaf-cups filled with bloom.

Mertensia, our early bluebell, may have begun to bloom last month, but its lush blue beauty peaks in June and lingers toward the end of the month. Along a rotting log in evergreen country, you will find the pretty, sweet-scented twinflower, so-called because it produces two blossoms to a stem—tiny, pink, bell-shaped flowers hanging down. No need to bend down to smell the sweet perfume; it wafts on the lightest breeze. Twinflower's Latin name is *Linnaea borealis*, named for Linnaeus, father of modern botany.

If you travelled about much in central Alberta in June, you could hardly help noticing how many pastures and hay fields were yellow with dandelions this year. To some this may look like a weedy field, but those dandelion plants are rich in iron and other minerals.

162

However, to get the most good from them they would be pastured before they go to seed. Even many lawns were peppered with the beautiful golden blossoms, and I suspect that more and more people are taking my stance—that dandelions are not only beautiful and harmless, they are universal, omnipresent and ineradicable. To wage endless, futile, unproductive war on them just does not make sense. A great amount of time spent fighting dandelions could well be put to less frustrating, more creative activity.

HEMP IN THE GARDEN
April 21, 1987

My mother chose a new garden spot one spring just about fifty years ago. It was on recently broken land just east of the buildings, and the soil was new and rich. Trouble was, the chosen site had no shelter from the west, so my mother decided to plant some. She usually got seeds from McFaydens' Seed House, for prices varying from three to eight cents per well-filled package for most common garden vegetables. The year of the new garden plot, her order included a package of hemp seed, recommended for planting on the windward side of prairie gardens, to protect the young, tender rows of garden plants from wind damage.

Around the end of April or the first of May, before field work got seriously underway, four horses would be hooked onto the eight-foot disc, and then onto the five sections of diamond harrows, and the garden site, which would likely have been plowed the fall before, or might have been summerfallowed, would be double-disced and harrowed, then disced and harrowed again. While that job was being done, two stakes, a length of binder twine, a pair of thirty-inch measuring sticks to keep the rows even, a hoe and a rake and a pail of seeds would be assembled and carried out to the garden. In due course, row on row of beets, lettuce, radishes, carrots, spinach, parsnips, turnips, peas and a score of other vegetables would be seeded into the moist, loose soil, leaving a few rows for corn and beans and a large area for potatoes, to be sown later when danger of frost had lessened.

The first row to be seeded, the outside row on the west end of the garden, was planted to hemp. The seed was not sown too thick or the plants would not grow tall and perform their purpose in life. About eight inches of spacing was probably about right. The soil was good, rich with years of leaf mould. The rains came when needed on this farm in the 1930s, in contrast to the southern prairies, and

163

those seeds germinated. The turnips sent up their two little heart-shaped leaves per seed; the carrots, a pair of thin grass-like ones, the onions, tinier ones still. I can't remember the first leaves of the hemp.

With the land so new it was relatively free of weeds, but that garden grew like the proverbial weeds, especially the hemp. Nothing grew like that hemp. In no time at all the outside row had produced a line of stalwart soldiers to defend against the northwest wind. They were performing guard duty by the time the radishes had gained their second leaves. And they kept right on growing, and growing, five or six feet tall, well-branched with large multiple leaves composed of many serrated leaflets. The plants interlaced and their strong stems kept them upright and they kept the winds at bay. That was their sole function. In the fall, still green, they were pulled and piled with the corn stalks and potato tops, later hauled onto the adjoining field to be plowed or disced under, back into the soil.

One spring there was no hemp listed in McFaydens' or any seed catalogue. A small notice informed customers that it was no longer legal to sell hemp seed, as it could be used to produce a harmful drug. Its nickname was Mary Jane, more correctly called marijuana.

My mother was quite annoyed. She hadn't planned to smoke it.

THE COUNTRY GENTLEMEN
March 30, 1966

Our friends, the country gentlemen, have been with us on this farm for more than forty years—in our garden, in our cellar and on our table, and we would not trade them for all the netted gems in Alberta.

Our good fortune at having this fine variety of potato on our menu, month in and month out, is even more apparent right now, because our supply has run out and we have had to resort to buying potatoes, something we have rarely had to do in all the years we have been on this homestead.

We did, however, keep back enough country gentlemen for seed, hand-picked to keep the traditional conformation.

The saga of the country gentlemen began, for us, with the burning of a neighbour's house about 1924. The neighbour was Old Bill Sherman, as everybody called him, a white-whiskered bachelor with eccentricities galore. Mean and suspicious and developing homicidal tendencies in the years to come, Sherman, at this time, seemed harmless, if a little on the queer side. When his ramshackle home

164

burned early one fall morning, some vegetables in the cellar remained uncooked, and the old man told Mrs. McLeod, who lived close by, that if any of these vegetables were usable, to salvage whatever she wished.

Amongst the cellar's contents were the country gentlemen, and Mrs. McLeod, who was and still is a good friend of my mother's, gave my mother enough of these reddish-skinned, deep-eyed spuds to sow a few hills in the spring. Since that small start we have never been without our friends, the country gentlemen. I know of only one other garden in this or any other area where they are grown, and that garden is tended by Bill Saunders of the Willesden Green district. And his country gentlemen are descended from the eyes obtained from our cellar many years ago.

Enthusiastic as I am about them, I am not claiming that the country gentlemen are the perfect spud. While they are good producers, they grow so near the surface that they have a tendency to sunburn if they are not carefully hilled. And they are quite unsuitable as a commercial potato because of their deep-set eyes, but they are excellent keepers and seldom sprout in the bin except following a milder than normal winter.

Finally, the country gentlemen are superior on the table, either fresh out of the garden in August or out of the cellar the following July. Given a reasonable amount of care, last year's potatoes will be found dry and mealy, long after the new potatoes are ready to use, and long after some of the other varieties grown in central Alberta have turned dark and heavy or have spoiled altogether.

There may well be other varieties which incorporate all the good qualities of the country gentlemen and none of the bad. I wouldn't know. I am not at all knowledgeable about the merits and shortcomings of different varieties of potato. You see, I have never had to experiment. And so far as I can see, I will likely be eating country gentlemen for some years to come.

THE TAMARACK TREE
January 17, 1973

If Alberta ever decides to adopt a provincial tree, my vote would go to the tamarack. It is a tree of exquisite beauty, and at the same time it is the most rugged and enduring of all our native trees; and its role in the development of this province is often overlooked.

Thousands upon untold thousands of miles of barbed wire have been strung across the province on untreated fence posts taken from

165

a thousand tamarack swamps. Being the nearest thing to hardwood to be found here, it is still in demand as fence-post material, and a good, dry tamarack post still commands a good price on the market. Instances can be cited where fences built with tamarack posts have stood for half a century, given some repair, of course. Right on this farm there are tamarack fence posts still carrying barbed wire that were driven by my father and uncle as they worked together to fence their adjacent homesteads back in 1921. Strangely enough, all the larger posts in those original fences have been replaced long ago. It is only some of the slim ones with no more than three-inch tops that have stood the test of time.

Tamarack, fire-killed and dry, made excellent firewood in homestead days, but it had to be used with caution, for it was too hot a fuel for some kitchen stoves and many a warped stove lid resulted from shoving in too many sticks of dry, split tamarack at one time.

The tamarack is a larch, *Larix laricina*. It is found across Canada from the Atlantic to the Yukon; it is common throughout the swamps and wetlands of the wooded portion of this province, and is undoubtedly the king of trees here in terms of longevity. Somewhere within our borders, there is an ancient, hoary monarch, thirty inches through and eighty or ninety feet tall, towering dead-topped and mossy-trunked above all others in its swamp, that may be Alberta's oldest living thing. It would have been a big tree already when the first white man came to Alberta more than two hundred years ago. Wherever this old-timer stands, it will be in some remote, inaccessible place, because it is hard to find a mature stand of tamarack anymore anywhere close to a settlement or near a seismograph line. Legally or illegally, they have all been cut down.

A tamarack tree is an object of beauty at any time of the year. In the fall of 1972, when autumn colours among the non-coniferous species were far less brilliant than usual, the tamaracks stood out strongly in their bright oranges, yellows and buffs. To walk into a tamarack forest in late September or early October, even on an overcast day, is like walking into brilliant if shadowless sunshine. And the tamarack's colours last for days longer than do the colours on neighboring poplars, willows and birch.

To stand on a tamarack swamp in winter and view the trees as a forest is to find that they are still very colourful, and the colour now comes in bands, or layers, with the pale green moss that is common to such trees as spruce and tamarack lending its hue to the lower six feet of the forest. Next comes a purplish layer, imparted by the new growth on the branches where they are at their most numerous. This muted shade makes up most of the forest's height but shades to a dull grey-brown-green at the highest level where the branches are lacy and delicate looking.

In early summer, the tamarack is clothed in the most wistful shade of light, ferny green, until every tree looks bewitchingly feminine for so rugged a species. This colour darkens with summer's advance but always stays two shades lighter than the poplars beyond and the willows below and three shades brighter than the evergreens.

I admire the tamaracks.

THE LOFTY LODGEPOLE
September 22, 1976

The lodgepole pine and I have been very closely associated for all the years of my life. In fact, right here in my own back yard, in my childhood play area, all around the house and right across the farm, the pines and I have grown up together.

Not that the farm, even in homestead days, was dominated by pines; they were only part of the picture. When my father homesteaded here in 1921, the ridges south of the creek were already coming yellow-green with young lodgepoles following forest and bush fires which had left much of the country scarred and desolate and bared in spots to the subsoil. Poplar, balsam poplar, spruce and willow were rejuvenating other areas. But the pines were the prettiest of all and the quickest to hide the acres of ground covered with "downstuff," as the fallen, fire-killed timber was called.

Hordes of rabbits in the 1920s and 1930s thinned the stands considerably, but a good many thousands survived and some of those ridges are covered with tall pines to this day.

Lodgepole pine.

167

As boys, my brother and I wandered amongst them, climbed the larger trees, collected cones, admired their "pineapples" (male blossoms) and shook off the yellow pollen in spring.

Early in the 1920s, my father placed an old Ford headlight rim over a pine sapling near the house. That rim was one of the large kind found on early cars, perhaps twelve or fourteen inches inside measurement. In 1940 we had to cut it off with a hacksaw because it was choking the tree, cutting into the bark all around. Another tree, planted near the foot of the lawn in the 1920s, attained a spread of fifty feet before a June snowstorm of a few years back broke off many of its long branches and left it only a shadow of its former magnificence.

The lodgepole pine is the only species of pine to be found in this part of the province. It acquired the name because young, slender, straight trunks, peeled and dry, were much used for teepee poles by all the Indian tribes of the western prairies. Its Latin name, *Pinus contorta,* or contorted pine, is a huge misnomer. No straighter, more symmetrical, or better looking tree can be found in the West. It got that name back about 1830, when the Scottish botanist, David Douglas, sent a dwarfed specimen back to London. He probably got it out on the west coast somewhere, for the lodgepole pine grows right down to sea level, but does not really thrive there. An Alberta stump rancher would never recognize the lodgepole pines which grow in Pacific Rim Park on the west coast of Vancouver Island. They have a decidedly different look out there.

Our lodgepoles often get called jackpine, which they resemble. Jackpine grows in the northeastern portion of the province, lodgepoles in the southwest. In the places where the two overlap, northwest of Edmonton and north of Grande Prairie, they may hybridize. Jackpines have much shorter needles and much smoother cones.

You will sometimes read that the lodgepole pine is also called firepine because it requires a forest fire to open the cones and release the seeds. This simply is not true. Two-year-old and older cones open on the tree. But it is true that following a forest fire in lodgepole country, this species is often the first and most prolific natural reforestation tree to appear. Therefore, it must be true that millions of seeds do survive a fire.

Whatever the reason for their appearance, I am one who will always have a real affection for the lodgepole pine.

THE ARTIST'S FUNGI
July 11, 1962

July is the only time of year when you can pick fungi for etching.

There are at least three species of etching fungi to be found in the woods in our section of Alberta. All grow on dead wood. One grows only on spruce, one on balm, and one prefers birch. These types of fungi are also known as bracket fungi and shelf fungi. They differ in size and appearance, but all have similar characteristics. They grow horizontally from the sides of dead stumps and logs, and their upper surface often resembles a large clamshell. Unlike most fungus forms, they are perennial, and show their age as a tree does, by well-defined rings marking each year's growth. An old fungus may often reach a width of two feet—if the stump lasts.

The upper surface is woody; the lower surface is smooth and soft and damp and velvety, like a thin layer of frosting. On the spruce-dwelling variety, the under surface is white; on the others, it is a light chocolate-brown. This is the surface that is used for etching purposes. Touch it with a stick and the delicate velvety frosting is crushed, exposing a dark background. This is the secret of the saprophyte's etching possibilities.

To become available for etching, the fungus must first be broken from the stump or dead tree to which it is attached. This may prove difficult, since the under surface must not be touched. A mark once made on the delicate growth cannot be erased, although it will grow over if the fungus has not been removed from the stump.

When you have it removed, you must etch your picture before it dries, be it a portrait, a scene, or whatever comes to mind. Even if you are like me, and can't draw a straight line, you can still make a fairly decent picture with a bit of practice, or else you can print or write something for posterity. When this etching has dried, which may take twenty-four hours in a warm, dry place, depending on size, it will last indefinitely. A portrait drawn on a fungus has been known to last for half a century without undue deterioration. I myself think they are more suited to nature sketches than to portraits.

The species that grows on spruce wood is perhaps the most attractive when finished because of the white underside, but the others are almost as good. The largest species is the one found on decaying balm logs or stumps. The ones on dead birch trees seldom grow to more than a few inches across, but they grow downward along the tree trunk outward from it, and this gives them a bell shape rather than a shelf form. They grow all up and down the trunk of the dead birch, whereas the other two species like to stay close to the ground.

I didn't pick up any of this fungi last summer. The season was so hot and dry that they made little growth, and the under surface was not moist enough for successful etching, but this year they are in splendid condition to serve as an attractive canvas for the outdoor artist.

TRY SOME SPRUCE GUM
March 1, 1961

Youngsters of today began chewing gum just as soon as they were old enough to understand that they mustn't swallow it, but for all their experience, there still is a great deal that they don't know about the habit. For not one in a hundred of them knows anything about chewing spruce gum.

When I was a young gaffer, spruce gum was much more commonly chewed here in the bush country than were any of Mr. Wrigley's products, for even in those days, a package of Spearmint cost a nickel, and nickels were not handed out helter-skelter to buy things as unnecessary as gum. Of spruce gum, however, there was never any real shortage. If there was none in any of your pockets, or in the handleless cup in the kitchen cupboard, you could soon go out and find some.

Now, spruce gum is nothing but spruce sap that oozed from the tree and hardened on exposure to air. It generally appears as dullish brown globules on the trunk of the tree, and often forms in clusters. Any number of things may have punctured the bark to let the sap escape: the bite of an axe, hailstones, porcupines, sapsuckers, or even climbing bears. Frost and wind fractures lengthwise of the trunk frequently produce the best clusters of gum.

To make good chewing, spruce gum must be ripened enough so that it won't stick to the teeth. On the other hand, if it is over-ripe it makes for hard chewing and tired jaws. Only experience can tell you when a piece is just right. It must be a rich amber colour on the inside and a drab brown on the outer surface; it may be quite soft, easily and quickly chewed up, and very sticky.

If it is rough and rather dirty-looking on the outside, and dark when broken, you will have to let it soak for a long time before you can chew it; then it will be hard to gather into a wad, and when you do, it will be so stiff you won't be able to chew it very long. All spruce gum becomes harder to chew the longer it is chewed.

Indians made use of spruce gum by melting it and mixing it with rendered animal fat to make a sealing compound for birch bark canoes. It must have been quite a trick to get the mixture just right, for it had to contain enough gum to prevent the tallow from melting in the sun, and enough tallow to keep the gum from becoming brittle in the cold water. However, when I come to think of it, I have never heard of the Indians chewing spruce gum.

Now, I haven't said anything about the taste of spruce gum. If you have never tried it, you might be strongly inclined not to, but it is really quite good, with a pleasant spruce flavour, and not at all bitter, as might be supposed. And if you have chewed it from childhood, you will always find it good.

SYRUP FROM A BIRCH TREE
April 30, 1969

The pangs of genuine, gnawing hunger that come from lack of food are quite unknown to me, but there was a time when I was so hungry for a thick layer of orange marmalade spread over a big slice of bread that I would have bid pretty high for the opportunity to sample that delicacy. It was wartime, and all sweet things were rationed; and marmalade, if I remember correctly, was especially hard to come by, which is probably why the thought of it tormented me for so long. But there were no coupons left from the week's allotment to waste on anything so nonessential, and so, like many another, I waited it out until the use of ration books was discontinued.

In the meantime, I had an idea, which I got, indirectly, from the Indians. A picture in a magazine about Canada's North (The Hudson's Bay Company quarterly, *The Beaver*) showed Indians in the Northwest Territories collecting birch sap for sweetening. Well, sweets were in short supply, birch trees were plentiful in the windbreaks close by, it was spring, and the sap was risin'!

I went to the tool shop for the brace and bit to bore holes in the trees. I found some copper tubing which I sawed into short lengths for spiles, those items being nonexistent and unobtainable hereabouts, central Alberta not being the Land of the Maple, exactly. The Indians used birch bark for spiles. They also made containers for collecting the sap from the bark of the tree, although by the 1940s they were showing a preference for empty gasoline cans picked up along the Canol Pipeline. They boiled the sap in big iron kettles right among the birch trees.

171

I did it differently. I got some kettles and ten-pound lard pails from the kitchen, hung them under the dripping spiles, and I was in business. I lugged the sap from the windbreak back to the kitchen where I strained it to remove the assorted flies and bugs that were attracted by its sweetness. I built up a good fire in the old wood-burning Home Comfort kitchen range and put the sap on to boil in my mother's biggest kettle.

It took six gallons of sap to make one cup of amber-coloured, fairly thick and surprisingly sweet syrup. Although it was not particularly flavourful, it was pleasing to the taste, and I have an idea that with the addition of some maple flavouring it could have been converted to a good facsimile of the syrup that comes from a maple tree.

I was quite unable to make any sugar from birch sap, possibly because I experimented with too small a quantity, and it scorched before reaching the sugaring stage.

I never tapped those birches again. It was just not worth all that effort for the small amount of sweetening obtained. If, however, this was a person's only source of sugar, I can see that it might then be considered well worth the time and trouble required. A sweet tooth can be pretty demanding.

IT'S NOT PEMMICAN
August 22, 1962

With all the land clearing that has been done in the bush country west of Highway 12 this past winter, I am surprised that there have not been more reports of buried "pemmican" being turned up by the breaking plough.

There could be a couple of good reasons why any such reports haven't reached the press. For one thing, much of this new land being brought under cultivation is not ploughed, but disced. The heavy, brownish-hued, irregularly spheroid objects of baseball- to basketball-size are not so apparent on land that is disced as they are on a field that has been ploughed to a depth of eight or ten inches.

The second reason is that most weekly newspaper editors are now aware that these objects are not petrified pemmican buried by Indians of long ago, but Canadian tuckahoe, an underground fungus growth that is rarely encountered until turned up by the breaking plough.

Fifteen years ago, I acquired a large authoritative book on Canadian fungi, which contained illustrations and a complete description of this interesting plant growth. I had never believed it to be

172

pemmican anyway, and with the book to back me up, I didn't hesitate to argue the point with anyone who mentioned buried pemmican.

I could have saved my breath. Those people had no wish to find anyone debunking the romantic notion that the stuff in their fields was genuine buffalo meat and blueberries. They just didn't believe that they and I were talking about the same thing. So, for added ammunition, I took a piece of the famous Cheddarville "pemmican" from the farm of Rex Bancroft, south of Rocky Mountain House, whose "historic find" had been publicized from coast to coast, and I sent it to the soil testing laboratory of the University of Alberta. They, of course, told me what I already knew, but the letter, from the chief analyst, A. Zitnik, concluded:

"I am in doubt whether this information will be enough to up-root the conviction of those who believe that it is a piece of buried pemmican."

Today I find that most people who turn up pieces of tuckahoe know what it is, and I think that Kerry Wood, of Red Deer, is largely responsible for this. For years now, his enlightening articles on the subject have been appearing in daily and weekly newspapers and periodicals across Canada.

The myth of the petrified pemmican has all but vanished, which is a pity, in a way because, myth or no myth, it was a real link with our colourful and exciting but now rapidly-receding past.

THE BLUEBERRY PICKERS
August 15, 1962

There may not be any blueberries to pick this year, at least not anywhere close to where I live, but I well remember the years when there were blueberries on every bush—every blueberry bush, that is.

There have been many such years in the past, but the year that stands out in my memory as the blueberry year of a lifetime was 1943. This was three years after the fire that came from the west and burned right to the edge of settlement all across this township, halting on the rise of land that marks the divide between the Medicine and Blindman Rivers.

So all we had to do was hitch a team to a wagon and drive west along the trails made by the settlers and homesteaders who took up land on the Medicine side of this township in the hungry thirties. An hour's drive would bring us to the wide expanse of burned-over country where the ground was, in places, quite literally blue with berries.

Usually, members of several families went along, and we took a picnic lunch. All we took for dessert was sugar and cream.

I remember being out there one day with Wilfred and Margaret Connett and daughter Donna, Mrs. T. R. Evans, Essie Peabody and sons, Lorne and Dick, and I have forgotten how many others. We must have taken two wagons that day. Sometimes, when there wasn't room for everyone in the wagon, some of us would ride horseback.

We soon learned that the best picking was somewhere between the ridges covered with fire-scarred poplar, dead willows and birch tree skeletons, and the stretches of swamp or muskeg with their black and grey snags of spruce and tamarack. Added up, the acres of blueberries must have run into the hundreds.

If there were children in the party who were too young to pick into a pail, they were plumped down in the middle of a small patch and left to their own devices. You never saw such blue and purple kids as those would be in half an hour's time.

Each picker, if he was leaving the wagon any distance, took with him three utensils: a berry picker, either "boughten" or homemade; a small pail to pick into, usually a five-pound lard pail or a ten-pound syrup pail; and a large milk pail to be kept nearby to empty the small pail into. More than once I remember having to hunt for that large pail. It was easy to lose track of your position when your eyes were always on the ground.

When we left for home in the evening, after eating what was left of the food, the wagon would be loaded down with berries: wash-tubs and wash-boilers full; cardboard boxes full; and the milk pails, that had been stacked one inside the other on the way out, took up so much space, now that they were full, that there was no place to put one's feet. Sometimes even the picnic dishes and the metal pickers would be full, too, and everybody had a purple tongue.

I don't think I'm exaggerating when I say that besides the berries picked in this one locality that season, which must have been hundreds of gallons, thousands of gallons went to waste on the bushes.

And do you know, we never so much as saw a big black bear, or a snarling cougar, or a great long snake, or any of the fearsome things that other people picking in this region had reported to us. We did see one frightened deer.

And when we closed our eyes that night, all we could see were blue, blue blueberries.

CRANBERRIES, CRANBERRIES!
September 17, 1975

I can't find enough blueberries to make a brace of pies, and if anyone else knows where there are some, they are not finding enough to feel they can tell me. So I think it is safe to say that it is not a good year for blueberries. I went looking for some sign of the delicious blue fruit one day, in places where I had found them other years, and I might have come home with enough for a pie or two, except that they were still on the green side, and a good many of them lay scattered on the ground, for it was evident that a late August hail storm had wreaked considerable destruction in the area.

Late frosts last June, when the plants were blossoming, could be one reason for a poor blueberry crop. A dry summer probably didn't help either. You don't need gum boots to walk across the swamps and swales this year, for there is little water among the hummocks.

There are not many cranberries in the back country either, although had I picked what I saw instead of hunting for blueberries, I'm sure I could have gathered enough to make jelly for Christmas turkey. There is absolutely nothing to compare with wild cranberries, sauce or jelly, but it seems that more and more often, in recent years, we end up spooning cranberry sauce from a jar with the Kraft label come Christmas time. Most of the cranberry ridges I used to know are long since logged and grown up to alder bushes, or cleared and ploughed for pasture. Cranberries, the kind we used to pick by the bucketful, prefer the acid soil under pine trees.

I remember the day, many years ago, when my brother Allan and I discovered a fabulous cranberry patch on some vacant land; to be more specific, it was on the old Pickett homestead west of Iola, where Dan and Gladys Neufeld presently live. The ground was literally red under the pines, wherever you looked. The first day we could get away, we packed our lunch, a couple of berry pickers, buckets and flour sacks, loaded it all on our bikes and were in the cranberry patch before the dew had dried. Well before noon we learned that others had also discovered our cranberry patch; they were picnicking and picking all around us. But we tended to business, and by evening we had picked our bags almost full, and we were wondering how on earth we were going to get all those berries home. About this time, a young fellow from Ponoka came along and offered us five cents a pound for all we cared to sell. Our problem was solved. We sold him a hundred pounds, pocketed $2.50

apiece, which was a good day's wages in those times, and we still had thirty-five pounds to take home; no problem for our bikes.

"My goodness!" exclaimed my mother when she saw our bag of berries. "Just look at all the berries these boys have picked! My, you must have found a good patch."

"We sure did," we said. But it wasn't worth going back to.

MY ALPINE FIR TREE
August 24, 1982

I live on the eastern limits of *Abies lasiocarpa*, a species of fir that has been called by at least four English names since I first saw it here, more than forty years ago.

My lawn is dominated by one of these smooth-barked trees, dense and symmetrical, more than twenty feet across at the ground and close to forty feet in height. I planted that tree as a fourteen-inch seedling in 1948. I called it balsam, or balsam fir, to be more correct. Then, in 1951, I obtained a better book, *Native Trees of Canada*. This was (and still is) a beautiful, well-illustrated, 290-page book, published by the King's Printer, which sold for $1.50. From it I learned that my tree, or trees—for I had transplanted several—were properly called alpine fir. The balsam fir (*Abies balsamea*) is a tree of eastern Canada, coming west as far as northeastern Alberta. The slightly different alpine fir grows in British Columbia, western Alberta, and the Yukon.

Alpine fir presently grow as far east as Winfield and Rimbey, and probably were once found around Gull Lake. Mine came from a logged-off woods about three miles west of where I live. Many had been cut for lumber, although lumbermen did not like the species, for the lumber is soft and not very strong. Whether any species remain in this area, I cannot say.

A wave of nostalgia comes over me as I think back to the day I brought those alpine fir seedlings home. My father and I harnessed up the driving team, I think it was King and Bob, on a Sunday morning in spring, hooked them to the buggy, loaded up spades, axes, a Swede saw and some wet sacking to wrap the trees in, and headed west. We stopped at Hreshenski's and picked up Norman, then a young boy, and followed old trails into the woods to where the trees grew. We dug up about six, ranging up to two feet in height, then wandered around in the woods for awhile before we came home and planted them in selected places in the yard. By the time this was done, that spring Sunday was about used up, and it was chore time. It doesn't sound like much of an expedition, but I remember this one well.

The tree that I have described, I planted at the foot of a stout, spruce pole that braced the twenty-five foot telephone pole which stood directly in front of the house. When that pole was taken down, the tree, then grown several feet, was left, more or less in the middle of the lawn, and there it has flourished to become one of the main features of the yardscape.

About three years ago, it developed a witches'-broom on one of the branches. Witches'-broom is abnormal growth in which hundreds of branchlets or twigs grow from a single spot on a branch or trunk. It is fairly common on spruce trees. The one on my alpine fir is now a mass of growth about three feet across, which weighs down the branch until the tree looks lopsided. I can't decide whether to cut it out and have a normal tree again or to leave it as a curiosity.

For many years now, this tree has been my Christmas Tree, as I have decorated it in December with strings of coloured lights, but it is a long time now since I have gotten lights anywhere near the top.

I brought a book home from Montana this summer, called *Native Plants and Early Peoples*, published by the Montana Historical Society. This book gives the English name of *Abies lasiocarpa* as subalpine fir and gives alpine fir as "another name." I think I may name my tree "Maria" and be done with all these name changes.

NOTABLE TREES ON THE FARM
January 22, 1985

I suppose it is little wonder that I love trees. I have lived in close proximity to them all my life, and they are a part of my earliest childhood memories. When I was small I would beg my dad for a ride to the "big trees" when he went back to work in the field after dinner. There he would let me out of the wagon or down off the harnessed work horse he was riding and I would walk home. The big trees were a group of huge, round-topped, rough-barked balsam poplar which we called "balm," usually pronounced "bam." They grew in a moist draw within sight of the house so that my mother could watch for me coming back.

Not far away, were the twin spruce, a pair of very old, very scraggly black spruce, well away from others of their species. They were a landmark on this farm for decades, even after the first one—and years later the other of the pair—died of old age and blew down. Across the creek was Magpie Bluff, occupying a wet area at the end of a field. The black and white birds nested there yearly in the great, gnarled willows, or sometimes in one of the big spruce which were, and still are, the largest white spruce on the quarter. North of Magpie Bluff, right on the north fence, was Cherry Bluff, the highest point on the homestead, where chokecherries grew tall and thick in the rich outdiggings of a coyote den, located within the almost impenetrable tangle.

As boys, my brother and I climbed the big trees of this farm and the surrounding countryside, sometimes to rob a crow's nest, or just to sit in a huge nest of a red-tailed hawk sixty feet above the ground, and sometimes just for a look around. In haying time, we regularly lunched in the shade of a huge, heavily- branched spruce that grew close to the creek and which we reached via a footbridge made of three long, heavy slabs. Beneath that bouncy bridge, in the cold waters of the creek, we kept our jars of lemonade. When lunch was over, while the horses were still eating and resting, we would lie with our heads in the shade of the dense top of that tree, and there we learned that the summer sky, for as far up as we could see, was full of flying objects: willow fluff and dandelion seeds, and a great variety of insects, from butterflies and grasshoppers and wasps and bees and flying ants to gnats and ladybirds and no-see-ums. There we learned that spiders also can fly, for in that small area of sky back-lighted by the sun, we saw numerous long strands of spider web drifting in the breeze, often with a spider attached to one end, being borne to new territory.

I knew many places beneath big spruce where rain never fell, and many a time, while after the cows or just out for a walk, have I taken shelter from a storm, crouched with my back against a large trunk. I was often saddened, in my boyhood days, to see one of these favourite trees, or a stand of trees, felled to make way for agriculture, but that was the only way to make homesteading pay. I later felled my share, with cross-cut saw and double-bitted axe, taking them for many purposes: dead, fire-killed trees of any species for firewood; dead tamaracks for fence rails, the heavier ones for corrals; large pine and spruce, even poplar and balm, for saw logs. There are still a couple of log buildings on this farm, one of them erected in 1926, but the farm never boasted a log house.

ALBERTA TREES OF RENOWN
January 29, 1985

I really intended to write this column last week. What prompted me to write about trees was a thirty-two page booklet titled *Alberta Trees of Renown— An Honour Roll of Alberta Trees*. Being a great fan of trees, and aware of all the things trees do for people, I found it of more than usual interest. The booklet was the idea of a man named C. H. Geale of the Alberta Forestry Association, and I remember seeing requests for nominations in the papers of 1983. Suggestions for further trees of note, presumably to be included in another edition of *Alberta Trees of Renown* are still being called for.

There are many categories. The oldest known tree in Alberta is a 720 year-old Engleman spruce, growing in Jasper Park. It was a big tree when this country was discovered. The oldest Douglas fir, at 674 years, is in Banff Park. The largest Douglas fir known is 30 metres tall (nearly 100 feet). It is to be found in the Porcupine Hills. Even larger trees than this one have long ago been cut for lumber in this province. A white spruce was felled near Hinton in 1980. It was the tallest known tree in the province at 48.8 metres (147 feet).

A tamarack with a record circumference of 145.5 cm (57 inches) was nominated from the Edmonton area. It was 152 years old. I have a cross-section of a tamarack tree that measures only 106 cm (41.75 inches) in circumference but it has 294 annual growth rings. This tree was already dead when it was felled by my friend Harry about twenty years ago, and it had likely been dead since the 1940s which means that it would have been a young sapling reaching skyward at the time the Hudson's Bay Company was incorporated in 1670.

Alberta Trees of Renown lists many trees for other than record age or height or girth: the crooked trees near Jasper, for instance, for which there are various explanations. I have seen these lodgepole pine, and their appearance is very similar to that of small poplar I have seen deformed by snow drifts on this farm.

Several Manitoba maples are recorded in this book, more for their historical significance than for their age or size. These include the Dunvegan Maple, planted by James McDougall over one hundred years ago, and one planted in Edmonton by Richard Hardisty in 1875. Then there is the Stockdale maple at Provost, planted about 1918 in front of a large, two-storey house, ordered from Eaton's catalogue for $833.

Another tree shown is familiar to many. It is the "tree-in-the-road," briefly dividing Highway 1A west of Banff. A tree of most unusual interest is a lodgepole pine standing near Pinto Lake. This tree was blazed and inscribed in 1924 with the name of a family that had over-wintered there and met with severe misfortune. The name was Pierce. Another inscription gives the names of the Alberta Provincial Police who rescued them in the spring.

The famous "medicine tree" of High River is also shown and described, as is a lobstick tree near Jasper, and a pine tree that once stood near Lower Kananaskis Lake with the figure of a woman realistically carved into it.

A HUGE WASTE
March 29, 1983

The windrows of brush and trees were high and straight and well-spaced. They were parallel with the road and with each other. It was a better-than-average job of piling. I scrambled over the smooth and slippery poplar logs to gain the top of one of the rows, and stood more than my own height above the ground, gazing out over eighty acres in two directions. It would make an excellent field for agriculture, well-drained with no potholes, and no water courses to cut it up. It would grow fine stands of forage crops or make excellent pasture.

Out in the middle of the field, a clump of spruce, perhaps half an acre, had been left standing. Virtually every other tree on the quarter section was gone. Part of the quarter had been cleared of lighter brush cover some ten or twelve years earlier. This new clearing had been mixed wood forest, mostly aspen and balsam poplar, but interspersed with stands and scattered large trees of white spruce.

First, the waste. Thousands of tons—or tonnes if you prefer—of biomass are being destroyed. Many of those trees, both poplar and spruce, were of sufficient size to make lumber, thousands of board feet of lumber, enough to build many houses. The smaller trees could have made heating fuel, enough to heat hundreds of homes for one year. Everything else—brush and branches—could be processed and used for a wide variety of purposes: mulch, organic fertilizer, fuel, insulation, even feed for livestock; or it could simply be chewed up and left on the land to add fibre to the soil.

This brings us to the economics of converting a forested tract to agriculture. It costs an enormous amount of money today to brush, pile, burn, re-pile and burn, break up the land, work it smooth, and finally bring it to the required stage for the seeding and harvesting of field and forage crops. By harvesting instead of burning the wood products on that land, it should be possible to reduce by several years the length of time it will take to get returns on the investment via the agricultural route.

In the third place, I am disturbed at the totality of the conversion. To clear a large acreage of all trees and forest cover not only drastically alters the prospect of the acres concerned, but it has a bearing on whole regions, even on the province and the country in terms of climate, water pollution, downstream flooding, agricultural markets, loss of wildlife and natural areas, tourism, and other aspects of living that we cannot now foresee.

I have been saying for many years, sometimes in this column, that it should be mandatory that for every 160 acres opened for agriculture, a reasonable amount, say thirty acres, be left in a natural state. There could be some flexibility in such a regulation, but its effect would be to prevent the total conversion of forest, bush and parkland to bald prairie, and to lessen the effect of a resultant change of climate with its unpredictable results.

It seems foolish that we should be spending so many millions of dollars clearing land and torching the wood by-product when already we are spending huge sums for winter fuel and for young trees to plant as shelter belts. Yet all our economy is geared for us to waste one resource to gamble with another.

FAUNA

THE PICKLED BUMBLEBEES
August 24, 1960

Here I was, surrounded by wilderness and a good twenty-five miles from the nearest pub, and right before my eyes was one of the most flagrant displays of intemperance I had seen for quite a spell. It was not merely a case of mild inebriation, either. The little rascals were drunk and seemed to be enjoying it.

Perforations in birch tree bark made by a yellow-bellied sapsucker.

The little rascals I am referring to were bumblebees, and their "pubs" were large thistle blooms, somewhat past their best.

It seems that recent rains had soaked into the purple heads, and the combination of water, nectar and hot sunshine had fermented up a pretty stout brew.

Drunk they may have been, but they were not disorderly. They mumbled and grumbled in a good-natured sort of way as they crawled from one sticky flower head to the next. I took small risk when I picked one up and placed him in a more favourable position for photographing.

It was not just an isolated occurrence that I noted, either.

182

Wherever these large native thistles, commonly called bull thistles, grew on the open hillsides along the river, or beside a short creek that I followed for a short distance, there would be a few of these imbibing bees, all blithely oblivious to their surroundings.

This wasn't the first time I had seen tipsy bumblebees, but it was the first time I had seen them in such numbers.

Sometimes, in the spring, they can be found, along with a wide assortment of other creatures, drinking at the "wells" drilled by a sapsucker in the bark of a birch tree. If the weather is warm, birch sap ferments and Mr. Sapsucker has a host of freeloaders at his tree.

Probably the most ridiculous thing I ever saw at a sapsucker tree is a tipsy chickadee. He was affected by the brew in much the same way as a person might be. He certainly couldn't fly straight and he barely kept out of my reach when I tried to catch him. Most of his flying was up and down, and when he said "chick-a-dee-dee-dee" it came out "shicker-ree-ree-ree."

I have seen squirrels lapping up the stuff, too, but since squirrels are frisky to begin with, I can't actually say I've ever seen one under the influence.

P.S.
I wonder if bumblebees get hangovers. I'm not sure I would like to meet one the morning after.

WILD HONEY
June 23, 1955

The weather is warm and the bees are buzzing. They are on the dandelions and the chokecherries, the Iceland poppies and the caraganas. Tame bees from the bee yard and wild bees from all over. We won't sample much of the honey made at this time of year, for it is used by the bees themselves in raising their ever-increasing brood. Dandelion honey is not too good anyway. It is dark and strong and scratches your throat. The good honey is made later in the summer—mostly from clovers of various kinds. This is the light, fine-tasting honey familiar to everyone. It is ordinary fare throughout the land.

But did you ever taste wild honey? Real wild honey made from wild flowers by large bumblebees? Well, I have, and it just isn't possible for me to describe the delicious taste sensation that ensued. For richness of flavour and aroma, there is nothing to compare with honey made by bumblebees.

Bumblebees may make a nest almost anywhere, but usually it is in, on, or near the ground. It resembles a mouse's nest in outward appearance, but inside the ball of fine, dry grass is the irregular comb, made up of brood cells and honey cells intermingled. They also make good use of old straw or hay stacks, or a recess in the wall or under the eaves of a building; and once I found one in a rather unusual manner.

I have a habit, when I see a tree with a woodpecker-built hole in it, of giving a sharp rap or two with a stick, just to see what the opening will produce. In the spring you may stir up a woodpecker, chickadee, swallow or wren. At any time, you may disturb a flying squirrel, or a chipmunk, or a horde of angry bees. I drew the latter one summer's evening when I whacked a half-rotten, ten-foot high, poplar stump that had a hole near its top. I had to remove myself in a hurry to a safe distance as they poured buzzing from their round doorway.

I knew by the numbers that this was a larger than usual colony, and I did a hit-and-run act on that stump every now and then for the rest of the summer and fall, just to keep tabs on them. Then I forgot them completely until early the following spring when I passed the stump again. This time, since it was quite unsound, I shoved it over and broke it open at the nest hole, just to see where all those bees had come from when they were annoyed. I found that they had been at least the third occupants of that tree abode, for, below their nest, was one of twigs, perhaps a wren's, and on the bottom was a bit of sawdust, which is all a woodpecker ever needs.

It was the usual type of bee nest and the brown comb inside was still intact. All the outer cells on this fist-sized hunk of wax were empty. They had contained brood and honey; but on the inside of the comb was a group of six cells of sealed honey, just as the bees had left it. I squeezed it out onto my hand; about a teaspoonful altogether. It was liquid, transparent, and amber in colour; and the flavour was out of this world.

Nectar of wild rose and honeysuckle, of fireweed and goldenrod, spiced with wild parsnip, and aged in the comb. Honey fit for the gods. I wished for a gallon of it. If I could raise that kind of honey in commercial quantities my fortune would be made. Oh well—I guess I'll go and spread a slice of bread with good old clover honey.

GIANT WATER BEETLES
November 2, 1960

The killer whales of the insect world.

That might be the best and most concise description of a couple of creatures presented to me one day last month by Mrs. Rees Evans, who found them in the soft water tank by the corner of the garage.

They were giant water beetles, insects which breathe air but live in the water. Their food consists mainly of other, smaller insects, which they capture and hold with two sharp claws, one on either front leg.

When you consider that the two beetles saved for me by Mrs. Evans measured more than three inches in overall length from extended claws to the tip of the short, sharp, needle-like appendage at the opposite end, you realize that these are among the largest and most ferocious members of the insect world; and for their size, they may well compare with the most vicious of whales.

Actual body measurements were about two and a quarter inches long by one inch wide. They can remain under water for long periods of time by taking their air with them, held in bubbles against their body.

And how did they get into the water tank? Well, they have one great advantage over the whales. They come equipped with wings. Whales, fortunately, have to stay in the water.

I don't know much about the life history of giant water beetles, but it may be that from time to time individuals of the species take to the air with the idea of finding and colonizing new bodies of water. I should think, however, that it would be possible to find a more suitable spot than a galvanized rain tank.

I took one of the insects over to show Harry, carrying it in a glass jar half filled with water. Harry thoughtfully placed a fly in the jar, and, after a few moments, it grabbed the fly and appeared to suck the fluid from it with its mouth parts, but did not actually devour the whole insect. Then Harry dropped in a small morsel of pressed meat and the big fellow also seized that and began to chew on it. There must have been a food shortage in that rain barrel.

The other one of the pair was dead when I got home—starvation possibly—so I dehydrated it, which process shrunk it just a little, and put it on display in a small plastic box.

The water beetles that I mentioned in a previous column, which emerge from subterranean streams in the water from Harry's spring, are seldom more than half an inch in length, and could be either a different species or very young members of the giant species. Anyway, Marge (Strain) hasn't quite gotten used to finding them in her water when she goes to fill the tea kettle.

I can only guess at what she would do if confronted with one of the king-size variety in the water pail some morning.

THE FLUTTERBYS
September 28, 1993

Some are blue and some are orange; some are startling white and some are camouflage brown. Some are bright and showy; others are dull and inconspicuous. They fly silently on scaly wings. They are butterflies.

As a small boy, I knew the names of most of the butterflies that I saw, and in those days, butterflies were far more numerous than today. Like the waterfowl and the songbirds and the grizzly bears, they are in trouble everywhere as their habitat disappears. I knew the names of butterflies because both my parents knew them, somewhat imperfectly as I would find out later, for in those days there was no checklist for butterflies of Alberta. They learned butterfly identification from the pages of the *National Geographic,* and, in the summer of 1919, they collected and mounted all the species they could find on the prairie in the Trochu area. One grouping, complete with wildflowers and grasses and leaves, was mounted under glass and framed as a wall hanging. The other, and similar display, was mounted as a serving tray. I still have those butterflies. The flowers with which they were posed have faded completely, but the wings of those ethereal creatures are as bright as they were that summer long ago. They have never been hidden from light, but have hung on the walls of the Schutz home for seventy-four years.

Late in the fall of 1919, when the butterflies had all migrated south or found shelter locally in which to hibernate over a prairie winter, my mother and father were married. They had little time for netting butterflies after that, but their pre-nuptial hobby fostered in their firstborn a lifelong interest in these fascinating and beautiful insects. I learned to tell an admiral from a mourning cloak, a tortoise shell from a painted lady. Most butterflies have fancy names. There are satyrs and wood nymphs, sulphurs and little blues, swallowtails and checkerspots. One of the best and most widely known, but one which I did not know as a boy, is the monarch. Monarchs do come into Alberta, but I have never seen one here. I think the

Medicine and Blindman and Battle Rivers may be the northward limit of their range on the continent, because it is the northern limit of the milkweed plant on which monarch caterpillars feed. The only place I have seen milkweed in central Alberta is in the Open Creek area.

Like most insects, butterflies have a three-part body with very narrow restrictions between each part: head, thorax and abdomen. Look at the word insect. It comes from the Latin *insectus* and means in sections. Butterflies, like most other insects, have six legs, two pairs of wings, one pair of antennae. The antennae have knobbed ends. Moths have hair-like or feather-like antennae.

There are four stages in the butterfly's life: egg, larvae, pupa and adult. The larva is a caterpillar; the pupa is a chrysalis. Complete metamorphosis.

Some butterflies emerge from their winter retreats to fly about on very mild days or in late winter, but we won't be seeing many now that the flowers are gone, until late April.

THE FOREST TENT CATERPILLAR
May 31, 1961

If you should be walking in the woods some day this summer, and a forest tent caterpillar happens to drop inside your collar, you won't find him exactly cuddly. In fact, he will be so covered with stiff brown bristles that he would feel like a miniature, wriggling, bottle brush. At the same time, if he isn't handled with care, he will prove as squishy as any worm.

Where you find one of these two-inch long creatures with the blue stripes down his side, and black back marked with white, there will likely be more. There may be a few more, or a thousand, or there may be millions.

Government entomologists are forecasting a plague of forest tent caterpillars in central and northern areas of the province this summer, provided they get the right kind of hatching weather this spring.

If there is a big hatch, and the poplar trees are crawling with the insects, it won't be the first time. The first recorded scourge in Alberta was in 1887, when they were noted all across Canada. In 1925 tent caterpillar moths piled up to a depth of two feet under some Edmonton street lights.

They were last thick here in 1952, when there were reported to be six thousand insects to every poplar tree on twenty-two thousand acres west of Rimbey.

Last summer they were working east of Edmonton and in the Peace River area, but I saw one cluster on this farm, feeding on a willow branch, the leaves of which they stripped before they disappeared.

When they are bad they take the leaves from whole regions of poplar and willow growth, eating and moving on, covering hundreds of square miles in a summer; and once they start moving they aren't easily stopped. They crawl over buildings, up and over fence posts and telephone and power poles, just because their brain is too small to think of going around. When they come to poplar or willow or fruit trees, or to any of a wide variety of ornamental shrubs, they stop to eat.

Trees are seldom killed by them, or even permanently harmed. Hence they are not too important, from an economic standpoint. They are certainly a nuisance, however, especially when they invade resort and beach areas. It's no fun to walk or work or play near the trees where they are feeding. They may even make paved highways slippery when they are travelling in search of food.

Because of the insect's stiff bristles, few birds will so much as look at a tent caterpillar. One bird though, the cuckoo, regards them as a favourite food. This bird's stomach has a special kind of lining, to which the bristles of the caterpillar become attached. Stomachs examined have appeared to be fur-lined, and when this lining can hold no more bristles, it breaks up and is shed, leaving a brand new lining.

Unfortunately, the only cuckoo found in this province, the black-billed cuckoo, is rather rare in central and northern Alberta, but if we have caterpillars this summer, we may catch a glimpse of this slender, brown-backed, white-fronted bird, which is twelve inches long, including six inches of tail.

THE SMALL BLACK TOURISTS
July 18, 1995

Two small, black tourists from down close to the Mexican border showed up in Rimbey the first week in July. They came separately, secretively, and were not exactly welcomed by the people who received them in their homes. They were not totally black, either. Each had a red hourglass configuration on its abdomen, and their legs were barred with brown. As you have now guessed, they were black widow spiders, and they hitch-hiked here in boxes of grapes.

Forty-four years ago this summer, I hunted one afternoon for a black widow spider in a garage in Pico Rivera, a suburb of Los Angeles. "You can always find one in a dark corner here," my uncle reassured me. He was wrong, and I was most disappointed.

Since they are closely related to the smaller common house spider, black widows like dark, slightly damp, indoor locations. The female has a body about twelve millimeters or half an inch in length. The male is half her size. Both Rimbey specimens are females. As in many other spider species, cannibalism is practiced by the female. After mating takes place, she eats the little pipsqueak.

The black widow spider is found all across the United States and is known in southern Canada as well. In Alberta, Medicine Hat and Taber are known black widow areas. Because of their name and lifestyle and their extremely poisonous venom, black widows are among the most notorious spiders on the continent, yet they are not at all aggressive and wish very much to be left alone. They will, however, bite in self defence if hurt or threatened. The venom is powerful stuff, and has a paralyzing effect, especially on the digestive tract. It is the cause of considerable pain to the human victim. It is not fatal or even lastingly harmful to healthy adults. Those at greater risk are babies and adults whose resistance is low, or whose immune systems are defective.

Black widows in Alberta produce shelves are not to be taken lightly, and the consumer, I believe, should be aware. On the other hand, there is no need to panic, and no reason to shun grapes in the grocery store. Black widows, or any other spider, in no way harm the grapes, which should be washed thoroughly in any case. As an extra precaution, submerge them for a few minutes. Grape growers actually consider spiders an asset, as they prey on insects that do cause harm to the crop.

B. C. grapes are now on the market, and the likelihood of finding a black widow in a cluster from that province is remote indeed.

There are two reasons for the appearance of black widows in Alberta this summer. First, this is a very good year for them in the southwestern states. Like other wildlife species, their populations are cyclic, and there are more in 1995 than for several years past. Second, there is a strong swing away from spraying vineyards and market gardens with chemical pesticides. This is due to public pressure and is viewed by most of us as a desirable shift in agricultural practice.

Neither retailers nor distributors, when contacted, expressed any surprise at black widows turning up alive and well in Alberta grocery stores.

Black widows certainly practice a weird system of raising their families. The female will lay several hundred eggs in two or three waterproof, silken cocoons. When the eggs hatch, the young feed on each other, until a few survivors emerge as adults. It is hard to say if this is survival of the fittest, or the luck of the draw.

I LIKE SPIDERS
September 26, 1995

I was out walking in the woods one day this summer with three-year-old Stephanie and other members of her family. Part of Stephanie's early education has been—and is—to make her aware of nature and sensitive to the environment, to respect and enjoy it, as her elders do. "Oh, look at the big spider," said one of the big persons. Being a spider buff, I hurried over to look at the creature on the path. Stephanie got there at about the same time, and before I had laid eyes on it, and before anyone could protest, or even speak—STOMP! End of spider. It seems that reverence for lower life forms may be an acquired personality trait, and a natural fear of little-understood creatures may have to be deprogrammed. Will we have to de-emphasize or eliminate from children's literature such seemingly innocent nursery rhymes as Little Miss Muffet?

I have long been partial to spiders. I find them much easier to like than many insects. Spiders, as I am sure you have been told many times, are not insects. They belong to a different class of invertebrates called arachnids, and there are more than forty thousand species, worldwide. That is not counting other arachnids such as scorpions, mites, ticks, chiggers and such unsavoury characters. Daddy longlegs are also arachnids, but I have always thought of them as being more like friendly spiders.

Spiders, unlike ticks and chiggers, are mainly beneficial to man. They are all carnivores, and eat insects and sometimes each other. Big spiders even eat small birds that become entangled in their webs. Spiders like their meat fresh and go to some trouble to keep it that way. Some species paralyze their victim until next mealtime.

Not all spiders make use of webs to catch their prey. Trap door spiders are one example. Chapters of books are often devoted to this creature. In central Alberta we have jumping spiders, and I have watched them hunting insects, leaping several inches at a single bound. They are a compact little critter with specially adapted legs.

Spiders that depend on webs to make their living, display a magnificent variety of form and structure in their weaving. Webs often identify the spinner. The best known and the prettiest is the classic web of the orb weavers, in which the circles are sticky, to enmesh the victim, while the spokes are dry and serve as runways for the web's owner. A common orb weaver in central Alberta is large for this latitude and yellow in colour, with red markings. These are probably our most useful spiders in the garden and orchard, and should not be wantonly harmed or molested.

Another common spider here weaves a funnel web in the grass. This funnel is wide and shallow and tightly woven and the spout leads to a retreat at ground level. Since they catch mostly hopping and crawling insects, they do not compete with the orb weavers.

All spiders have eight legs and most have eight eyes. I have seen tiny red spiders on my back forty, so small I needed a ten-power magnifier to see what they really looked like. I have seen huge, saucer-sized beasts catch moths around the lights in an out-door restaurant in the tropics. And I have seen more than a few of the thousands of species in between.

I may have stomped spiders when I was three; I don't remember, but in adult life I have regarded them as fascinating fellow travellers on this earth.

THE SWARM
August 4, 1992

I knew the sound as soon as I became aware of it coming through the screen door. I jumped up and went through that door and saw above me, over the lawn, a great swarm of bees, many thousands of them. There is no sound in the world of man or nature that is exactly the equivalent of a swarm of bees on the wing. It is a loud, homogeneous hum that defies accurate description. Think of the buzz of a single bee as it gathers nectar from a flower. Multiply that by about twenty-five thousand and you will have some idea of the auditory effect. It is not a dull sound. Those bees are in a state of excitement. They are on a great adventure. Either they have just left their old home forever, not knowing where their new home will be, or they are following an advance party to a new home and are anxious to get settled in. If you know bees, or even if you are not familiar with them, you can sense the excitement. People who are ignorant of the ways of bees may be terror-stricken if they see a swarm approaching, and little wonder. A great ball of insects, several metres deep, that casts a shadow on the ground, is not something that the average person cares to encounter at close range. Fortunately, bees in a swarm are not prone to sting. Although they are excited, at the moment they have no hive to protect. They will still protect their individual life, however, or that of their queen, so it is only prudent to keep a reasonable distance; and don't go swatting at any that come near you.

I was quite sure as soon as I saw the swarm that they were about to take possession of new lodgings, that the hunt for new digs was over. I have a building that has housed a colony of honeybees between the inner and outer walls for many years. I have come to expect them here, although most years I am not lucky enough to see them come in. They never survive the winter there, so the first thing a new swarm has to do is give the place a good cleaning. I went and stood a few metres back of the building, where I could see the opening, and waited for the swarm to come. The mass of bees moved slowly, the bottom of the swarm about five metres above the ground, the topmost bees perhaps ten metres up. As they came over the roof of the building they held their position, the formation became looser, less compact, and they began to funnel down toward the hole in the wall. I could not spot the queen in that great throng, even though she is twice the size of the rest, but I presume she would go in early. Since the hole is small, with only one or two bees being able to enter at a time, it was going to take them a long while to all get in and so they began to collect about that entrance, and within minutes they were massed about the hole on every side, one on top of another, several deep. I watched for twenty minutes until only a remnant of the swarm was left in the air.

It was mid-morning when they came. By late afternoon, only a few hundred were left outside the hole. Next day all had found their way in and a new hive was in business.

THE HATEFUL HOUSEFLY
September 4, 1968

He is a most unlovable creature. He is hairy and dirty and he likes to crawl with his sticky feet into the smelliest, germiest, gook he can find. He wallows in filth and revels in it, then, if he can, he comes into the house and eats the food prepared for you and me. He can't eat solid food, so he spits on it first to soften it up. He has other repulsive habits, too, and even his scientific handle, *Musca domestica*, has an unlovely sound. Because he is one of the most prolific creatures on earth, he will always be with us. He is the common housefly.

The housefly has, however, seen better times. Fifty years ago, he almost ruled the West, but the decline of the horse as a source of farm power and the advent of DDT, together spelled serious trouble for the housefly. So when I see a modern housewife panic at the sight of a single fly in her kitchen, I cannot help wondering what her reaction would be if she were to find herself plunked down in a pioneer kitchen of thirty, forty, fifty or more years ago. No DDT, remember, and horses everywhere, for, even in the 1930s, people in the bush country were saying, "Tractors may be all right on the prairie, but they'll never be any good here. They would be stuck all the time."

So the horses pulled the tillage implements and the haying and harvest machinery. They furnished transportation and they pulled trees to clear the land. They built the roads and mowed the lawns and did a hundred other jobs throughout the land. Now all this work took a great many horses and all those horses produced some pretty huge manure piles, and if there is one thing above all others in this world that makes a perfect habitat for housefly larvae, it is a huge pile of horse manure.

These piles, one to a homestead, usually accumulated during the busy spring and summer months. Eventually, as the farmer or his hired man cleaned out the barn every morning with a wheelbarrow, the pile grew so big that something would have to be done about it, so, late in the fall, generally around freeze-up, it would be hauled out and spread on the nearest field, where it made the best of fertilizer. This meant that during the warm months of the year, the pile just sat there and grew and produced flies in clouds. When a young fly emerged, he was only seconds away from the kitchen door, which, quite naturally, was the first place he made for.

Now most, though not all, kitchens in the 1930s and earlier were equipped with screen doors, but these were banged by kids and scratched by dogs until they were seldom fly tight, and any flies not smart enough to find the cracks and holes only had to wait a few minutes until someone opened the door for them.

The housewives of the day made some pretty heroic efforts to combat the housefly in his teeming millions, and to relate the means and methods they used in this unending and unequal struggle requires another column.

THE HOUSEFLY BEFORE DDT
September 11, 1968

When the pioneers get to reminiscing about days gone by, they tend to dwell on the good times, and to gloss over or treat casually the woes and tribulations that beset them. But since historical accuracy is necessary to any proper assessment of the present, I have decided that I should document, as well as I am able, one of the most lopsided struggles in the annals of pioneering—the contest that featured the housewife on the losing end right up to the 1940s. That was the decade that marked the end of an era and the beginning of another. The day of the workhorse as the backbone of agricultural economy in the West was over; and DDT, a wartime development, was introduced on the pesticide market. With far fewer flies and a more efficient means of control, the tide of battle turned.

No one born this side of the 1930s can visualize the black, buzzing swarms of houseflies that once plagued so many farm and even urban homes. Many just accepted them. Others made a valiant effort to stem the tide. Few met with anything approaching complete success.

Many and varied and ingenious were the methods used. Fly coils and fly pads and fly spray could be purchased in the local general store. A fly pad was a round, blotter-like piece of heavy paper which was impregnated with some kind of poison, which was also toxic to humans. You placed it on a plate and added just enough water to saturate it. Flies were attracted, partook of the potion, and turned up their toes.

Fly coils can still be purchased today. They consisted of a roll of very sticky paper about two inches wide. These were uncoiled and hung from the ceiling. They hung down about two and a half feet and were left until there was not room on them for another fly, when they were burned and replaced. They were something of a nuisance, I remember, especially in low-ceilinged rooms, because if you accidentally bumped your head on one, you came away with sticky dead flies in your hair.

The best known brand of fly spray, I think, was "Flit." I am not sure but I suspect that "Flit" was a mixture of peretheum, the most common insecticide before DDT, and a light oil similar to kerosene. Attached to each can was an L-shaped spray which you activated by placing one end in the can of "Flit" and blowing into the other, creating a mist very similar to that which comes from today's spray cans. Later you could buy a hand sprayer which was never quite leak proof and always dribbled down your arm.

194

Peretheum could be used in powder form, too. You placed an ounce or two in a tin and oilcloth poofer, which, if I remember, was a little larger than a box of snoose with a two-inch spout on the side. It was spring-loaded and you pointed it at the flies in the window and pumped it with your thumb.

For those who did not have the money—and many didn't—to buy powder and spray and fly coils, there were other methods that were more or less effective, some of them in use well back in the nineteenth century. More about these next week.

HOUSEFLIES IN PIONEER TIMES
September 18, 1968

Everyone dreads the first hard frosts of autumn. They herald the end of a summer that was all too brief, and they sadden us with their portent of the winter to come. No more summer flowers or summer greenery; no more robins on the lawn or birdsong in the windbreak; no more insects buzzing in the balmy summer air. No more the freedom of dressing lightly; no more weekends at the beach.

I have been wondering, though, if our pioneer grandmothers might not have viewed the frosts of October in a different light. I think they may even have welcomed them, for they knew that a few sharp frosts were the one and only means of ending the plague of houseflies that invaded their kitchens and every other room in the house, for that matter, during the late summer and fall each year. With the coming of those first killing frosts, the pioneer housewife could breathe a sigh of relief and look forward to eight or nine months' respite from the pests, while she devoted her energies to more rewarding endeavours. For the war with the flies was one she could never hope to win, although she felt compelled to try.

One of her weapons was poison, which she brewed herself from mushrooms gathered in the woods. The species she used were of the *Amanita* family, most likely *Amanita muscaria*, called Fly agaric, a beautiful fungus fairly common across the country. Or she might have used *Amanita phaloides*, or death angel, which is even deadlier. I am not too sure, but I believe that all she did was brew the mushrooms, strain off the liquid and sweeten it with sugar, then place it where the flies could find it but well out of the reach of children. Because of the element of risk, especially when there were small children in the household, many homemakers were reluctant to use this method.

195

Another method of fly control practiced in pioneer times went somewhat as follows: darken all the windows, making sure there are no flies behind the shades, then, with shakers made from scores of strips of brown paper fastened to the end of an old broom handle or other stick, chase the flies to the open door and out. Repeat the procedure until the flies in the house have been reduced by noticeable proportions.

Fly traps were used too. I don't know much about these. The only one I ever saw was one my brother made when he was a boy, and which I still have. This was a screened-in cylinder about nine inches wide by fourteen inches high which stood upright on short legs. The bottom was an inverted funnel. Sugar or jam or meat scraps were placed beneath the trap as bait. When the flies rose from the repast, the funnel led them into the trap. It caught quantities of flies but had no noticeable effect on the overall situation.

Then there was the smudge. This was usually a fire built in an old pail and covered with green grass to produce copious quantities of smoke. This was carried from room to room, forcing the flies to seek the purer air outdoors. What it did for the decor of the rooms, I can only guess.

These are some of the measures taken to combat the housefly before the advent of DDT. If you know of any other methods used by the pioneers, I should be interested in hearing about them.

DDT FELLS THE BEDBUGS
July 8, 1970

It has been said that there were two kinds of people living on the frontier in homestead days: those who had bedbugs and those who said they didn't. This division of the populace came to an end immediately after World War II, when practically everyone could say, and truthfully, that they did not have bedbugs. DDT had arrived on the scene and it came in the guise of one of the best and most miraculous friends a housewife ever had. How she loved it, and how she used it, never dreaming that it would someday prove to be so disastrous to world ecology that nobody would have a kind word to say about it.

It was not only frontier areas that spawned bedbugs. They could easily be found in some long-settled regions as well, and in urban areas, too. A log house was much to their liking. I don't know how they fared in a sod shanty.

Today I can't imagine how far one might have to travel to find some of these obnoxious little insects in their favourite habitat. Thanks to DDT, it might be quite a good hike.

DDT was a direct result of the war effort, developed under a crash program to produce a chemical that would effectively control lice on humans, one of the unsolved problems of World War I, and one of the obstacles to the control of typhus. DDT was also used to combat mosquitoes, thereby reducing the danger of malaria. When perfected, it seemed to have everything required of it, and was hailed as one of the chemical wonders of the century and a boon to man's future in peacetime as well as in war. And it took nearly a quarter of a century to recognize the monster that had been created.

It is one of the sadder facts of our technical era that too often our most brilliant scientific minds are single-tracked and shortsighted. They set out to create a product for a specific purpose, and when the requirements of that purpose are fulfilled they look no further. They came up with DDT to kill insects, with "1080" to kill coyotes, with mercurial compounds to kill fungus on plants, and with phosphate-loaded detergents to get things clean, to name but four of the most infamous poisons and pollutants of the 1960s. But research scientists, governments and manufacturers have too often refused or neglected, in the past, to look ahead for potentially undesirable side effects, and they have added insult to injury by scoffing at and deriding as alarmists those laymen who have undertaken to point out some of the real and possible dangers of such compounds as DDT, which has now become a potential poison in the bodies of nearly every living creature on land, air or sea.

DDT does its deadly work by accumulating in body fats, and when the fats are used, the chemical, now broken down into one called "DDE," affects the nervous, digestive and reproductive systems, and may upset genetic make-up as well. DDT may already have doomed several species of wildlife, and many more are threatened with extinction from the earth. It even threatens the existence of man himself on this planet.

But it was great for killing bedbugs.

BEDBUGS? IN ALBERTA? IN THE SEVENTIES?
October 27, 1971

Bedbugs? In Alberta? In the seventies? After a quarter of a century of DDT?

A professional pest exterminator, guesting on a TV panel show recently, stated that many of his calls (in the city of Edmonton)

197

were from people who wanted him to get rid of the bedbugs in their houses. It would not have surprised me to learn that these age-old parasites of man could still be found in some remote outposts of civilization, (though at the moment I can't think of any likely location in Alberta) but to learn they exist in a modern city like Edmonton....

Bedbugs were one of the very real hardships of the pioneers that we hear very little about. Universal as these highly objectionable little pests once were, and in spite of the fact that they were easy to acquire but difficult to control, it was considered some kind of disgrace to have bedbugs in your house. It seems they were somehow associated with poor housekeeping and careless sanitation practices. The stigma still exists, for the man on the quiz show said he still had to park in back alleys a lot.

They were a hush-hush that could not be easily hidden, and a discerning school teacher in her one-room rural school might have told you that the small but tell-tale red spots of inflammation that were bedbug bites might appear almost any morning on the skin of almost any pupil, regardless of their standard and mode of living.

The people most afflicted were probably those who lived in log houses, where there were myriad cracks and crevices into which the nocturnal insects could retreat in the daytime. A government pamphlet on insect control, published in 1950, after the advent of DDT, states that bedbugs can live for a year without food, and can withstand the winter temperatures of an unoccupied house. If there are no people about they can live on the blood of rodents and birds, so that an unoccupied house, particularly in past decades, might have harboured them indefinitely. But they could not live with DDT.

In occupied houses, they could usually be found in the creases in the mattresses. Here, and in any other places they could be reached, they were treated by the pioneer housewife with a feather soaked in coal oil. A farm auction sale presented the day of truth if the beds and mattresses were sold. The stains left by bedbugs could always be detected on these items, and sometimes the bugs were there, too, ready to move to a new home. They were also spread on clothing, in borrowed books, and by other devious means, even by mail.

One more scrap of information about bedbugs should not be omitted here. If squashed they gave off a pungent stink that would put to shame any ordinary stink bug in the raspberry patch.

There is some talk of allowing controlled and limited use of DDT for specific purposes. If it is found that this can be done without further harm to the ecology, one of the allowable uses should certainly be for the control and elimination of bedbugs.

PIONEER MOSQUITO PROTECTION
June 3, 1970

It has sometimes been hard, down over the years, for a mosquito to make an honest living. Of the many defences used against him, a smudge of thick smoke was probably the best, but a smudge was not always practical, and besides, the constant smoke irritated the eyes and soaked into clothes and skin until one soon smelled like walking buckskin.

Explorers, travellers and outdoorsmen in the early West often wore a kerchief over the head and gloves on the hands. Exposed skin was smeared with a messy and unsightly concoction of bear grease and ashes, a trick learned from the Indians. Whether the mosquitoes were repelled by the smell of the ashes, or attracted, caught and held by the bear grease, I am unable to say.

Farther north, in the land of the musk-ox, the Native people, both Indian and Eskimo, used to wear what early explorers called a "musketoe wig." This was a band worn around the head, from which hung a fringe of long musk-ox hair, the same as you might find hanging from the underside of any musk-ox. They also used a "musketoe fan," a handful of these long hairs attached to the end of a short stick. It must have been difficult, during musketoe season, to tell just who was the Medicine Man!

The homesteaders, when they could afford it, used citronella, once the only repellent on the market, but it was not too effective by today's standards, and had to be reapplied about every ten minutes. Unfortunately, citronella was also repellent to some people, who declared they would rather have the mosquitoes, but I can remember using citronella up to about 1943, and I didn't mind the smell. In fact, I am sure I can detect the citronella scent in some modern repellents.

In the days of citronella, every country general store sold mosquito netting by the yard. The housewife tacked it over windows and hung it across doorways to keep out the insects, and used it to cover the baby's crib, and sometimes to hang around the beds to insure a good night's sleep.

One of the very best defences against the mosquito was immunity. After a few days or weeks of exposure to their bites, you found them much less annoying. They would still get your blood, but the swelling and itching would be minimal.

If all else failed, one could always resort to the spoken word—not too effective, yet not without some psychological benefits. The mosquito has undoubtedly evoked more lusty curses, more weird imprecations, and more heartfelt profanity than any other species of fauna in the history of the Canadian West.

Some people are more susceptible to the bite of the mosquito than others. On the other hand, mosquitoes are a lot fonder of some folk than they are of others. If you should happen to be both susceptible and appetizing, you had better not leave the protection of your campfire smoke without your musketoe wig and some citronella.

COYOTE WATCHING
March 27, 1963

This week's column might be titled "An Hour in the Life of Old Mr. Coyote."

When I first saw him on this warm, sunny, St. Patrick's afternoon, Mr. Coyote was dozing atop a strawstack a quarter-mile away. At least, he was trying to doze. The magpies were pestering him. They would light close by and taunt him in voices that fairly invited mayhem, but Mr. Coyote had long ago resigned himself to the fact that he was not equipped with wings, and that magpies were just another of life's vexations. Once he got to his feet and they flew off a bit. He turned around and lay down again—and back they came.

At this point I gave a shrill whistle. The coyote raised his head and looked around, then seemed to decide that it was just the starlings that were calling back and forth from two tall trees nearby. Anyway, he laid his chin on his paws again and took no notice when I whistled a second time. But the magpies did. They all took to the woods. Now he could doze in peace.

At this juncture, I moved down the field about thirty rods for a better look at the lazy old rascal. Here I could see him very clearly with binoculars. I would not care to have to sleep the way that coyote did, with one eye open and the other half-shut. His head was seldom down for more than thirty seconds. Then, for a somewhat longer period, he would scan the scenery in every direction. Sometimes he yawned. Once or twice he raised himself to a sitting position.

Just when I was getting tired of watching this dull perform-ance, he decided to come down from his castle. Walking in the most leisurely manner, he took a diagonal course across the field almost directly toward me, so I squatted down when he looked the other way, and continued to watch him closely.

He was very light in colour, almost a dirty white, and while he had a black nose, there was no black on his tail.

Some distance from the strawstack and much closer now, he heard a mouse under the snow and began to stalk it. He chased it out of its snow tunnel and onto bare stubble, and there he played with it as a kitten would, taking dainty swipes at it with its paw, head lowered, great tail wagging like a spruce bow in the wind. Finally, he grabbed it in his teeth, shook it furiously a couple of times, then carried it to the bank of snow and proceeded to devour it. He smacked his lips and came on his way, still not in the slightest hurry.

Here I virtually proved that some coyotes, at least, are colour blind. I was wearing my red hunting jacket, of a red that would have been noticeable to human eyes a mile away. Yet the coyote walked through a gate where I was in full view fifty feet away, walked right past me at a distance of fourteen paces and continued on his way without ever seeing me or being aware of my existence!

He was a beautiful animal—fat as any coyote I have ever en-countered. The breeze ruffled the long cream-coloured guard hairs on his coat, disclosing the fine, dark grey fur beneath. His legs were tawny. Ten inches on the end of his tail was golden brown with shades of red, and the backs of his ears were distinctly orange. It was a coat to be proud of.

He was making for my tracks near the spot from which I had first seen him, so I watched closely to see what effect they might have on him. I was not disappointed. Suddenly, he stopped, sniffed twice with his nose close to my footprints, raised his head and took a fast look round, then turned abruptly and trotted briskly into the willows along the creek, not exactly alarmed but now very much on the alert. He had not set a paw across my tracks.

A few minutes later, still at a trot, he disappeared through the windbreak onto the next quarter half a mile away.

I had watched his every movement for about an hour. He had only seen my tracks.

WOLVES AND THE POISON 1080
March 22, 1961

Earlier this winter, according to the feature by Dick Decker in the *Calgary Herald*, a pack of wolves were reported west of Red Deer. Almost overnight, age-old fears and superstitions concerning wolves took hold of the imaginations of whole groups of people. Farmers were concerned for their livestock. The Fish and Game people had visions of badly-depleted game herds. Calgary hunters planned wolf hunting expeditions. Everyone talked about wolves.

And the worst happened. The government was pressured into strewing poison pellets, stated in this story, to contain "1080," by plane, along the Nordegg and Brazeau Rivers. Then, after the damage was done, an investigation into the wolf situation was begun, and it was found that "west of Red Deer" meant a long way west, in mountainous country accessible only on snowshoe.

So the Calgary hunters gave up on the idea of a coveted wolf skin trophy, the Fish and Game Association turned its attention back to fishing, the farmers let their cows out of the barn, and the whole thing sort of blew over—except that a quantity of deadly poison had been spread where it might take the lives of goodness knows how many mink, foxes, lynx, jays, hawks, owls, ravens, eagles, nuthatches, and too many more species to list; and all for what? To kill a wolf or two, or a pack, or perhaps no wolves at all.

This indiscriminate and widespread poisoning of wildlife is just one of the reasons I would like to see the placing or distributing of 1080 baits banned forever.

Not far from here, in the area west of Hoadley, four valuable farm dogs have died, presumably from 1080 poisoning, not because they were feeding on a 1080 bait where they would have no business to be, but because a large bird, probably an eagle, died in a farm field approximately one and a half miles from a 1080 bait. At least one of the dogs was known to have chewed on this dead bird. It has not been proved, of course, that either the dogs or the eagle died of 1080 poisoning, but the circumstantial evidence is great. Hawks and eagles are especially vulnerable to poisoning by 1080. Dogs (wild dogs) are what the poison was created for.

All four of these dogs, I am told, were exceptionally able cattle dogs.

There is a very real question as to whether some of these baits are even killing coyotes. One bait, situated in the far western part

202

of the county, well away from any farming activities, appears to have been dined on solely by birds and small mammals in recent weeks, while close by, in stands of young pine where rabbits abound, coyote tracks also abound. Here is a case of coyotes seemingly determined to benefit man in spite of his perception of them; for snowshoe rabbits, even in winters as mild as this, can do tremendous damage to stands of young pine, sometimes destroying them by the acre. And the coyotes understandably prefer fresh rabbit meat to the dried-out portion of horse carcass set out three months before.

Meanwhile, Canada jays, chickadees, woodpeckers and flying squirrels continue to peck and nibble away at the poisoned bait, and with their dying, spreading the poison farther and wider.

Then there is the question of actual economic gain or loss due to the actual destruction of coyotes. That there is plenty of room for argument on this question, more and more people are coming to realize. When all the wildlife that is destroyed is taken into account, there can be but one answer: the direct economic loss to the farmer, and the loss to all nature lovers in aesthetic values can never be written in dollars and cents.

THE WOLVERINE
March 15, 1994

Not many people living in Alberta today have ever seen, or will ever see, a wolverine in the wild. Civilization, in any degree, does not suit this largest member of the weasel family which was once known throughout the wooded areas of Canada and Alaska, south along the Rocky Mountains into the northwestern States, and north, far into the treeless tundra. There was one in the vicinity of Bathurst Inlet when I was there last summer, but I was not fortunate enough to see it. Wolverines are circumpolar, being found from Scandinavia to eastern Siberia.

I have seen two wolverines in the wild in my lifetime. One was on my own land around 1940. The next sighting was near the headwaters of the Highwood River in what is now Kananaskis Country, about 1970. I had a good view both times. In the 1980s, I saw wolverine tracks about eighteen kilometres northwest of my farm. Seeing tracks doesn't mean that the maker is anywhere near. A wolverine on the hunt will range over a thousand square kilometres. Jasper naturalist, Ben Gadd, once tracked a wolverine for four days, but gave up on the chase when the trail got too cold.

203

Wolverines have been declining in numbers ever since man invaded their territory, yet man is their only enemy. No other carnivore of any size cares to take on a wolverine. Pound per pound, they are said to be the most ferocious animals in North America, and have been known to kill deer, caribou, mountain sheep and even moose. Yet they weigh from twenty-five to fifty-five pounds. A big one can reach four feet (1.2 metres), including a bushy tail. They are heavyset for a weasel, but not as roly-poly as a bear cub. For all their fierce reputation, I read about a pair raised from kittens that made wonderful pets. That was in the Caribou.

The wonder is that the wolverine has survived at all, so hated has the species been by trappers and by anyone living or travelling in the wilderness. The individual wolverine was traditionally seen as a thinking, scheming, malevolent being with powers of reason that were often more than a match for the wits of a simple trapper. The animal often followed the trapline at night, removing the catch or removing the bait, with or without springing the trap. Then in daylight, while the trapper was investigating the damage and becoming more and more frustrated, the wolverine would be breaking into the cabin, ransacking and befouling everything therein. Maybe the wolverine had something to do with the term "mad trapper."

The scent glands of the wolverine produce the most obnoxious smell of any of the weasel clan, including the skunk. The scientific name *Gulo gulo* means Glutton glutton, an apt and descriptive name. The North American sub-species is *Gulo luscus*, weak-sighted glutton.

There is a place in northern Alberta named for the wolverine. It is Carcajou, the Metis name. Indians called him skunk-bear. Trappers have called him a long list of names which shall not be repeated here.

THE ALASKA BROWNIE
February 10, 1955

This is the story of the third-biggest bear of any species ever recorded from any part of the world. This remarkable old bear was a huge Alaska brown, and he was shot just about one hundred miles from Rimbey by George Bugbee, guide and outfitter of Ricinus, south of Rocky Mountain House.

In the fall of 1950, Mr. Bugbee had taken out a party of big game hunters from North Dakota, and they were at Limestone

Creek in the Clearwater Gap, on the return leg of their trip, when they encountered the giant bear.

The party had been following a narrow game trail through a thick growth of young pines when they came to a place where the trail led out of the dense cover, and down a ten- or twelve-foot sloping clay bank into a relatively clear area. The guide had gone down the slope first and had turned to see that the rest of the riders and the pack horses descended safely. At this point, pandemonium broke out.

The bear had just killed two moose and was feeding on one when he heard the approaching hunters. He stood up on his hind legs and waved an enormous head from side to side, trying to get their scent and direction. That is how the hunters first saw him from less than a hundred feet away, and they said he stood ten feet tall. The horses were terrorized at the sight and smell of him and went rearing and plunging and trying to turn back up the trail, piling their riders and deranging their packs.

Bugbee had instinctively reached for his rifle at the first sign of trouble, and managed to get it out of its saddle sheath by the time he was free of his terrorized horse. In the meantime, the bear had charged and was coming fast, covering about twenty feet to the jump. He was three jumps away when the guide shot. One shot was enough. The bullet went in his open mouth, nicking a front tooth and entering the brain. In seconds from the time they first came upon him, the bear was dead. No other member of the party had retained his gun.

They rounded up their horses, skinned the animal and resumed their journey, almost playing out a packhorse taking the hide into Rocky. It weighed four hundred pounds, including head and paws. According to measurements, the bear's total weight had been around sixteen hundred pounds. After seeing the pictures of the hide and head, I thought that figure seemed conservative.

Forestry men, old-timers, big game hunters and all who saw that hide and head were puzzled and amazed at the huge size and unusual markings of the animal. He had none of the silver hairs of a grizzly and no white on his chest. His well-worn, finger-length claws were black instead of ivory, and he was several hundred pounds heavier than any grizzly ever seen or heard of. He was over nine feet from head to tail and his skull was nineteen inches from front to back.

Mr. Bugbee tentatively identified him as an Alaska brown, and this was later officially confirmed by the Natural History Museum of Fairbanks, Alaska. The measurements are on file with the Boone and Crockett Club at the New York Natural History Museum. The hide is in the Prince Albert Museum.

The big Brownie was evidently an old fellow, and how many years it had taken him to wander down the mountain chain from his home in southwestern Alaska would be hard to guess. The Alaska brown bear is the world's largest carnivore and is seldom found far from the coastal areas and islands of his home range. Specimens of the Kodiak bear, a sub-species on Kodiak Island, are said to attain a weight of two thousand pounds, but if they do, none apparently has ever been recorded.

For this story about the biggest bear ever taken in Alberta, I am indebted to Mrs. Freeda Fleming of Rocky Mountain House. Based on her newspaper account in the *Calgary Albertan*, it was supplemented by information she gave me on later occasions. She also showed me many pictures taken in Rocky Mountain House which showed the size of the hide, the huge head and the nine-inch front paws.

He was some bear! But his luck ran out when he met Mr. Bugbee.

THE BUFFALO'S GRANDFATHER
October 6, 1981

Dinosaurs are reptiles, buffalo are mammals; yet in decades of prowling the parklands and badlands with an eye out for the remains, fossil or otherwise, of both dinosaur and buffalo, I always knew there had to be a connection, though I could never quite put my finger on it. In September, this year, it was revealed to me.

Buffalo bone fragments lay strewn all around a granite erratic that lay on the prairie below an escarpment of sandstone cliffs. Also in evidence were many quartzite chips, cores, and crude tools of stone, indicating that the granite boulder had probably served as a work bench, not only for making tools of stone, but perhaps for breaking bones to get at the marrow, and for other butchering and meat preparation chores. The date was September 20, and I was on a field trip with a group of naturalists out of Lethbridge following the fall meeting of FAN, the Federation of Alberta Naturalists. The sandstone cliff was the site of Head-Smashed-In Buffalo Jump at the extreme southern end of the Porcupine Hills west of Fort Macleod. This classic example of a prairie buffalo jump is expected to be made a world heritage site in the near future.

Earlier, in September, I had visited Dinosaur Provincial Park, where skeletons of dinosaurs from the earth's Cretaceous period are preserved in situ, just as they were first uncovered after being buried for seventy-five million years, give or take a few days. This park is already a World Heritage Site and you can't do much prowling around on your own, but it is right at the southern end of a vast stretch of badlands; and farther north, along the Red Deer River, there are still areas where one may wander more or less at will, and find bits and pieces of dinosaur material from bone and sinew and tooth, to associated fossils such as oysters, shark's teeth and petrified wood, and other fossilized vegetable matter from seeds and leaves to copralite (dino-doo).

Sometimes in these same badlands you will find non-petrified or partly petrified bones that obviously are not dinosaur remains. They may very well be buffalo bones, but unless you find a skull you may have difficulty in deciding whether you have come on buffalo remains or those of an early settler's horse or cow. At Dry Island Buffalo Jump Provincial Park there are scads of buffalo bone, but of course it cannot be removed from the park.

It was Dave Spalding who made the connection for me between the bison and the dinosaur. Curator of Vertebrate Palaeontology at the Provincial Museum, Dave was guest speaker on September 24, at the annual banquet of the Red Deer River Naturalists. He spoke to us about Alberta dinosaurs and the men who first discovered them, and about the men who later made a living excavating the skeletons and shipping them to museums all over the world. The height of this activity occurred in the 1920s.

The first scientist to discover dinosaurs in Canada was G. M. Dawson, in 1874; but even before that, a would-be scientist, priest, explorer and anthropologist named L'Heureaux, if I heard Dave Spalding right, was travelling through the badlands with a band of Indians when they came upon some exposed skeletons.

"What great animals were these?" he asked his Indian friends.

"The Buffalo's Grandfather," came the ready answer.

So now I have the connection.

SOME BUFFALO LOST THEIR HEADS
July 19, 1961

I suppose it would be stretching things just a bit if I said I went buffalo hunting last weekend. Well, anyway, I did go looking for buffalo bones last Saturday evening. Found some too.

It all started one day a week earlier when I was admiring a buffalo skull which Phil Pearman, who lives in the Monte Vista district, northeast of Rimbey, has displayed on his lawn.

"I know where there are two or three more, not too far away," said Phil. "If you want to come with me some evening, we'll drive out and have a look at them."

And that is the explanation of some otherwise incomprehensible tracks made by Phil, my brother Allan who is visiting from Vancouver, and myself, as we meandered about on some mud flats which in more normal summers are under water.

What we were really looking for of, course, were skulls, and since no buffalo have roamed near the Blindman Valley since the 1880s, any skulls or bones found in this area today cannot be less than seventy-five years old and may be much older. Of the untold millions of buffalo that died on this continent around a hundred years ago, only the barest traces remain, and such bones as do turn up have usually been preserved in wet peat soil or under water.

Phil found the first skull. The portion that protruded from the muck had already been bleached by the summer sun, and shone whitish-pink in the sunset light.

Some minutes later, Allan made another find. "Two discoveries in one," he told us. This skull was lying face-down in somewhat drier ground, and when he bent to pick it up he noticed that the cranium cavity, or that portion that was left, was serving as a nest for some shore bird, possibly a killdeer, as there were several around, and the single egg was about the right size, colour and shape. However, the egg was cold, so Allan appropriated skull, egg and all.

The third skull should have been found by me. I didn't find it but earned it. It was considerably further out in the mud than the others had been, and since I was the only member of the trio wearing knee-length rubbers, I was automatically elected to retrieve it. I got about halfway out to it and had to turn back, and I was afraid for a moment that I was going to lose my boots into the bargain. I had so much difficulty just getting turned around in that knee-deep, stinking, sucking mud that I began to have some idea of how these buffalo bones got there. I wished out loud for my snowshoes. For the first time this year, I could have made good use of them. I got mud in my boots getting back to firmer ground.

We wanted that skull, so the three of us went to work pulling rushes and flinging them onto the mud to form a causeway to it.

This took a few minutes as there was a stretch of about seventy-five feet to cover. "It's lucky nobody is around to see us," said Phil, "or someone would be sending for the boys with the straitjackets."

But it worked. With the rushes to support part of my weight, I managed to reach the skull and bring it in.

So we had one apiece, and in addition I was carrying a couple of pieces of vertebrae, one of them with a sixteen-inch blade on it that had formed part of the bone structure of the buffalo's hump.

Old buffalo skulls are seldom found complete. Usually, they consist of the forehead down to about the eye sockets, the cranium, and the bone structure of the horns, the outer shell of actual horn having disappeared long ago. But for those of us interested in the province's history, they are a prized trophy.

Our expedition may have lacked some of the thrills and excitement of a nineteenth-century buffalo hunt, but it made for a thoroughly enjoyable evening.

Back at Pearmans', Norma served us coffee and a hearty lunch, and didn't complain at all about us coming into her kitchen smelling like three muskrats.

THE COW
July 15, 1964

Did you know that cows have babysitters? They do. Not dairy cows. Dairy cows don't have much to do with the raising of their offspring. They live in a welfare state, and so do their calves. With range cows it is a little different. They enjoy more freedom. They are milked by their calves and never see a loafing barn or a milking station. You might think of the range cow as being unfettered by any routine, grazing and lazing the days away in some far pasture, her calf at her side. The picture is close to reality except for one thing. The average range calf doesn't spend a great deal of his time alongside his mama. Only at mealtime, or if something frightens him, and at other irregular intervals does he seek her comfort and company.

It is usual, when you go amongst a herd of range animals, to find most of the calves in a sort of loose cluster. They might be close to the main herd or they might be at the opposite end of the pasture. But suppose they are all together. Young calves, for all their friskiness, do a lot of lying down. As the herd moves off, many of the calves remain where they are, and remaining with them will be one or two or more cows. These guardian cows are usually older ones, and they lie there chewing cud after cud, while their sisters

209

are lapping up grass. It is quite common to see two or three cows left with twelve or fifteen calves. It is also quite usual, if one of these cows decides to get up and wander in the direction of the herd, to see four or five calves get up and go with her but, should a calf leave, the cows take no notice, unless one is the calf's mother.

Even if all the calves and cows are together, it is likely that many or most of the calves will be as a herd within a herd. Like children, they seem to enjoy each other's company. Try chasing one though and you will soon learn who is his mother. He'll head straight for her whether he has a sitter or not.

I have watched this calf-sitting aspect of bovine life many times but since I have never made a serious study of it, there are many questions you might ask that I couldn't answer.

For instance, does every cow take her stint on the calf-watching detail, or are there some who shirk their duty here? Or do a few of the older cows do it all? When one of the sitters leaves, are the calves that leave with her that cow's responsibility, or is this merely a matter of chance? How old does a calf have to be before he requires no guardian?

The practice seems most common when the calves are quite young, just days or weeks old. And I believe it is less noticeable as the size of the herd increases.

Paradoxically, a newborn calf is quite often left entirely to himself for the first day or two, and will lie quite motionless when approached by a person, keeping his head down and his ears flat, just the way a young fawn will do.

Perhaps it is time—if someone has not already done so—to make a proper study of bovine behavior. The resulting report, I am quite sure, would provide more interesting reading than some that are currently being compiled and published by various government and non-government agencies all across the country.

WHO SAID, "COWS IS JUST COWS"?
July 22, 1964

Still on the subject of cows this week, and still trying to show that cows are as different from other cows as people are from other people.

This individuality can be easily discerned, even in a group of uniform, two-year-old Hereford steers in a feed lot. For instance, there will always be one that is boss, or tries to be, and there will be one at the other end of the scale who will be pushed around by the

210

rest. And guess which one will bring a little better price come marketing time.

There is usually one that is first—first through the gate, at the feed bunkers, up the chute. And there is usually one that prefers to be last.

Some of the group will be quiet, unexcitable, easy to work with, but there may also be one or two that are wild and sometimes unmanageable. As in human society, the wild ones and the bad ones tend to corrupt the rest, and the whole group has, in some measure, to pay for the shortcomings of the few. They get the dog, or the rough treatment occasioned by the shortness of human tempers, which in turn is occasioned by the troublemakers in the herd.

Having once milked cows, I think I am qualified to say that there is a great variation in the temperament of individual milk cows. I would even say that most dairy cows are somewhat temperamental and the contented cow is so much the exception as to be almost a myth.

Nor are any two bulls alike. There are some who simply would never harm any person, but because there are others who would, none can ever be trusted. Bulls are said to be especially tolerant of children, and there is a real-life story about a small girl who wandered from the picnic site and was discovered out amongst the cattle in a nearby pasture. She was sitting on the back of a large and very untrustworthy bull as he lay contentedly chewing his cud.

She was called from a distance and left her friend to return to her frantic parents.

Cows are conscious of strangers. A herd that knows only one person may stampede in terror if a stranger suddenly appears. Likewise, cattle who have never seen children might just break down the corral fence if a youngster climbs onto the top rail on the other side. Yet, when they overcome their initial fear of a strange person, be it child or adult, they will show real curiosity toward that person. If the stranger stands motionless, they may form a circle about him, heads to centre, and some of the braver ones may move in close enough to sniff at him with a sticky, cold, wet nose, or taste him with a warm, rough tongue. One sudden move though, and the stampede is on again.

Dairy cows mostly have names. And such names! They range from the fanciful to the ridiculous, from Veronica to Clementine. We once owned one called Rattles because mud balls always formed on her tail as a result of wading the creek, and these dried and rattled when she walked. The one I hear about most this summer is Mary Anne, who lives across the road and sometimes does not want to go in the barn at milking time.

Names are very useful. They immediately identify any animal in the herd. Range cows, being less familiarly known, rarely have names. When one has to be identified, it is described by age, colour, horns, temperament, condition, offspring, size, or anything else that will serve the purpose. They are bound to have some distinguishing features.

And don't ever let anybody tell you that "Cows is cows." It just isn't that simple.

TEACHING A CALF TO DRINK
December 14, 1993

Most farms in the district where I lived did not have a large herd of milking cows. Milking was thought of as a sideline, although it sometimes provided a substantial portion of the farm's cash income. The Schutz's herd of cows milking at any one time varied from six to twelve in the 1930s and 1940s. There were always one or two dry cows and some heifers due to freshen at a later date. The cows were, of course, milked by hand, by all members of the family, from Granddad down to the kids. My brother Allan was not very big when he sneaked out of the house one morning early, before anybody else was up. About the time the rest of us were rising, he came in with a pail full of milk, and announced, proud as punch, "Look! I milked Bessie, all by myself."

"Good for you," said my father. "You can milk her every morning."

My mother only milked seasonally, mostly during seeding and haying and harvest, when she felt she was needed. She seldom milked in the winter months.

Not every member of the family taught the new calves to drink. Newborn calves were separated from their mothers before the milk was useable in the cream separator. For the first three days, the milk is thick and yellow with colostrum, which is essential to the calf's start in life. From the first day or two, that poor little guy was expected to drink milk from a pail. He knew that this was unnatural and behaved accordingly. Educating him was some fun, although I don't remember ever seeing the humour at the time.

How do you teach a calf to drink? I can take you through the whole procedure, step by step, and I can speak from experience

212

and with authority. First, you straddle the little beggar, clamping him between your knees. It's best to have him backed against a manger or a wall of some kind; otherwise he'll have you running backward. His head will be pointing skyward, in more or less the position that it would be had he been allowed to get his milk in the natural way. He is trying to reach your chin or any other part of your face. This makes it easy to grab him by the snout and insert four fingers into his mouth. Now you have him frantically sucking and you force his head down into the pail, which you have been holding in the other hand all this time. Now he thinks you are trying to drown him and he bucks and snorts and shakes his head and spills some milk. You spread your middle fingers to make a passage for the milk and he finally gets a taste. At last you have his interest, if not his cooperation. He still fears death by drowning and wants his head up, so you try again, and again, and you keep trying until the pail is empty, and you hope there is at least as much milk in him as there is on you and on the ground. And you say to this little, orphaned, bewildered and still-hungry creature, "Okay, Stupid. I hope you got enough to keep you alive until morning. That's when you get your next lesson."

Some calves learn to drink in the first three minutes. Others take three days. Most are somewhere in between.

THE COWBIRD AND THE COW
July 1, 1964

Let us say you are driving past a small herd of cattle in a green pasture by the roadside. Some of the beasts are grazing; some are lying quietly, contentedly chewing a cud. Perhaps some calves are off frisking by themselves while their mothers seem to be keeping a benevolent eye on them.

This scene will not be complete without some birds, and most of these birds will be blackbirds of some kind, plus a magpie or two. A few, especially any perched on the cows' backs, may be cowbirds; and now I have got down to my subject for this week.

Cowbirds were called buffalo birds in the early days on the prairies, for the same reason they are now called cowbirds. They followed the herds, living off the insects that were attracted by the animals or were stirred up out of the grass by their hooves.

Cowbirds are the dullest coloured of the blackbird and oriole family, which also includes the meadowlark. To say that they are the black sheep of the family is to speak very, very figuratively, for

213

they are not nearly as black as the blackbirds. At the same time, it is putting the case bluntly, for cowbirds are parasites, the only species in North America to be so classed. Some old world cuckoos are also parasitic.

Cowbirds build no nest, but lay their eggs in the nests of other, generally smaller birds. So the parent cowbirds, once the eggs have been foisted onto the care of other species, have no further responsibilities—no nesting territory to maintain, no eggs to incubate, no offspring to feed.

In the meantime, the host bird, which may be a warbler or a song sparrow—but in this area often a junco—may be overworked to feed the rapidly-growing young cowbird which, being larger than the rightful occupants of the nest and hatching sooner besides, soon has the nest to itself. And a young cowbird's appetite is enormous. The nest's rightful youngsters simply perish from lack of food, or else are pushed over the side, to die of exposure and neglect.

Even after he has been shoved, fully grown, from the nest by his foster parents, the young cowbird continues to mooch. He huddles on the ground and utters a very plaintive cry that birds out foraging for their own families just can't seem to resist, for it gets him many a juicy bug intended for the mouth of a more needy youngster.

I see I haven't nearly enough space left to tell all the things I intended about cowbirds and their interesting, if unorthodox, habits. In fact, I have enough material left for another column so you may be hearing about the cowbird again in this column.

THE COWBIRD AGAIN
July 29, 1964

Now that I've done with cows for a while (in this column, that is) I'll get back to the cowbird again.

And here is one bird who has it made. Or has it?

The cowbird goes south in the fall and returns north in the spring, just as do hundreds of other species of birds. But, unlike any of the other species on this continent, its springs are not spent in the care and trouble and toil attendant on hatching and raising a nest of young to maturity. All this is done for it by other birds, either willingly or unknowingly, while it goes its carefree way, and with no censure or abuse, no recriminations of any kind from the society in which it lives.

It might be argued that the cowbirds are missing much that is worthwhile in life: forfeiting, as they do, the joys of parenthood,

214

the challenge of bringing up a family in the way they should go, and the satisfaction—when the fledglings have flown—of having done the job well. And where, it might be asked, is the cowbird's normalcy of family living as practiced by other birds? Where, in fact, is its pride?

If these questions provide food for human reflection, it is safe to say that they bother the cowbird not one whit. The other birds accept the situation and the culprit suffers no degradation whatsoever.

The books usually mention a single cowbird egg being placed in another bird's nest, but it is quite common to find two and occasionally three of the nearly always larger eggs in a smaller bird's nest. However, Alvin Goetz reports that he found a junco's nest containing *seven* cowbird eggs, and buried under the heap were two of the junco's own small eggs. What is more, every one of the cowbird eggs was warm.

"It beats me," said Alvin when he told me about it, "how so small a bird as a junco could keep so many cowbird eggs incubating."

Now, the question arises: were all those seven eggs left in that nest by one prolific cowbird, or were they deposited by seven different cowbirds? No one seems to know for sure just how many eggs, on the average, a cowbird lays, or how many may be laid in one nest. For all anybody can tell, Mrs. Cowbird may lay a dozen eggs, or twenty. What's to stop her if she can find nests in which to drop them?

Another question arises. With all the potential for easy increase, what keeps the cowbird a far less numerous species than most of its hosts? There must be limiting factors; there always are.

Here is an opportunity for some budding young ornithologist with time on his hands and patience to spare, to fill in some of the gaps in ornithological knowledge.

Meanwhile, other birds slave away each spring, doing the cowbird's household chores, raising a gluttonous young monster to maturity, often at the expense of their entire brood for that season.

SNOW BUNTINGS
March 3, 1965

Different species of wildlife have been leaving tracks this winter in a field where stooks of hail-damaged wheat have been left, as they seem to think, for their special benefit.

Strangely enough, the creature that has made the greatest depredations in this field, in terms of bushels of grain consumed, is a small bird, but what this bird lacks in size it makes up in numbers. There are only hundreds at the present time, but a month ago, in late January, thousands of rusty black and white snow buntings flew about that field all day every day. And when the whole flock settled on a row of stooks and spread out along that row and to the rows on either side, the snow became covered with a solid mosaic of tiny tracks, each like a long-handled "Y" with an extra stroke bisecting the middle of the letter. If it didn't snow now and then, the whole area where the stooks remain would soon have become saturated with snowbird tracks.

As it is, all the bundles are lightened by reason of every exposed head being emptied of grain. Not that they were ever very heavy, but now I have to reach into the stook to find heads of grain in them.

I think this may be the reason that the major portion of the flock left. It is simply a matter of depletion of the food supply.

I was not aware, before this winter, that snowbirds ate wheat, but these birds like nothing but the best, spending most of their time in a part of the field where the crop was heaviest and the hail had left more grain.

The bird books describe snow buntings as being seed eaters, meaning, I suppose, either native or weed seeds. No mention is made of them eating a seed so large as wheat, but this may be because they so seldom have the opportunity.

The books also say that snow buntings, being hatched and raised on the tundra north of the tree line, seldom or never alight in trees. It is true that when they come south for the winter they seem to prefer the wide open spaces, no matter how bitter the day; but they do perch in trees, at least on this farm, and in fact, spend quite a bit of time so perched.

When they have satisfied their hunger, they look for a place to slake their thirst, and any place where water or wet snow can be found, there they will congregate. A bit of exposed summer fallow also attracts them; even a bit of dirt scratched onto the snow surface by spinning tractor wheels or the subsequent use of a shovel will cause them to pack the spot in their search for grit. It is for the same reason that you will see flocks of these birds on a newly-snowploughed road.

They do everything by flocks, whether it be feeding, drinking or perching. A flock of many hundreds rising from the ground en masse will make a sound like miniature thunder. They will wheel and dip and swoop and rise again, and, if the day is sunny, they will show brilliant white against a blue sky. This is in contrast to a very dark appearance when viewed against the snow as they are feeding.

When snowbirds alight in a tree, they furnish it, temporarily, with both foliage and bloom. They will festoon a naked poplar until it rivals an Okanagan cherry tree in blossom time.

Gregarious as they are, and beautifully as they bank and spiral and swoop in the winter sunlight, snowbirds are a quarrelsome lot. Observe them carefully when they are on the ground feeding, and you will notice several individual quarrels between two birds, and as one quarrel ends another will begin. This goes on continually, and I have noticed that it is even sometimes apparent when the flock is in the air.

Like a great many other wild creatures, snowbirds have some traits that are almost human.

"MR. BLUEBIRD" ELLIS
June 9, 1971

I visited the operations this spring of two of the best friends our native birds have anywhere in central Alberta. One is the "Mr. Blue-bird" to whom Red Deer author, Kerry Wood, has dedicated his book, *A Time for Fun*. In that book, Mr. Wood mentions thirty-four occupied bluebird houses on this man's property. Last year and this, there are over forty pairs of nesting bluebirds and over a hundred pairs of swallows, as well as scores of other nesting birds from purple martins, barn swallows and flickers to blackbirds, robins, finches, orioles and many more.

I was with friends Bill Buckingham and Alvin Goetz on this visit to "Mr. Bluebird" and, while Alvin has an impressive array of bird life nesting in the environs of his own home, even he was amazed at the number and variety here, and at the trust these birds place in their benefactor and visitors alike. So tame were they that one could lift the hinged front of some of the swallows' houses and peer in at bi-focal distance eye-to-eye with the incubating bird. We amused ourselves repeatedly by holding out white feathers and having the tree swallows fly in and take them out of our hands, or by tossing one onto the breeze to see the birds compete for it and snatch it on the wing. Tree swallows, even though their nest may

Board of Directors, Ellis Bird Farm. Back row, L to R: Howard Fredeen, (Hog Manager, Lacombe Experimental Station), Fred Schutz, Ken Larsen, Dell James. Front row: Orest Litwin, Winnie Ellis (sister of Charlie Ellis. Neither ever married.) Charlie Ellis (Mr. Bluebird), Walter Lindley (Union Carbide.)

have been completed days or even weeks before, cannot seem to resist another white feather to add to their home. "Mr. Bluebird" always carries a pocketful and a couple in his hat for them.

Some of his birds are so trusting that as they perch on the fence wire near their nest box, "Mr. Bluebird" can touch them with his cheek. In winter he carries on an extensive and also costly feeding program, and then it is waxwings and grosbeaks and chickadees that know him as friend, and swarm all over him when he comes out with their breakfast. Even in summer, feeding is kept up for some species; robins in particular seem crazy about a mixture of ground apples and raisins and also johnny cake.

House sparrows are trapped as fast as they come to the premises. The traps are large enclosures of wire mesh, and since they must be baited with live sparrows to attract and capture other sparrows, the birds are fed and watered daily and treated humanely, if with less affection than the other birds. Starlings are controlled by making the openings in swallow and bluebird houses too small for them to use, but if they have to be trapped they are more sternly dealt with. Wrens, too, are considered undesirables

218

on these premises because they puncture eggs or kill young in any other nest to which they can gain entrance.

We arrived at the farm about 9:30 a.m. while there was still a great deal of activity and song overhead. It is much quieter in the middle of the day, but even then it is a fascinating place for a bird watcher to be.

Like Kerry Wood, "Mr. Bluebird" ties an old hat—or sometimes a new one—onto the roof of many of the nest houses, on the theory that this helps to keep the sparrows from harassing the rightful occupants.

That same day, on our way home, we visited at the home of Mrs. Hrycyk at Sylvan Lake, and she, too, puts old straw or old felt hats on her tree swallows' nests, but her specialty is purple martins, and that is another story.

THE PILEATED WOODPECKER
December 6, 1988

I was standing with a man from the power company underneath the line on my property, when a large bird flew in, lit on the side of the nearest power pole about twenty paces away, began to drum, "bap-bappeta-bap, bap-bapeta-bap." It was almost as large as a crow, but slimmer and more colourful and with a decidedly different stance. It had a bright red crest and white stripes down the sides of the neck. Even before it landed, I had recognized this beautiful bird as a pileated woodpecker.

Its long toes seemed to grasp the relatively smooth power pole with ease. When it hammered, the long, stiff tail was propped against the pole, and the bird leaned back at a thirty-degree angle. This way it could see what it was doing and also had room to manoeuvre that strong, pointed bill.

The trouble-shooter stared for a moment. "What kind of bird is that?" he asked. I told him what it was. "My Gosh!" he said, incredulity in his voice. "I never knew woodpeckers got that big."

The woodpecker, or one just like him, was back on that same power pole a couple of days ago, and I thought again of the surprise on that man's face and in his voice at his first encounter with this absolutely marvellous wild bird.

I have known this species of woodpecker as long as I can remember. I have been lucky in that all my life I have lived near an area of mature and even over-mature and sometimes fire-swept (1930s and 1940s) mixed wood forest. Here pileated woodpeckers, no more than one pair or one family, have always been resident, and occasionally they fly as far from their home base as my yard. I learned as a boy to recognize their call and tell it from the flicker's, which it resembles. The call is louder and somewhat lower than the flicker's and is often made while the bird is in flight. Like most other woodpeckers, the pileated drums on dead wood as part of the courtship ritual, and one book tells me that they drum before going to roost. They roost in specially excavated cavities, and usually have two or more of these roosting holes.

One observer, who is to be commended for his patience, noted that the bird entered its roosting cavity half an hour before sunset and left it just before sunrise. These roosting holes, usually not far from the nesting cavity, are often taken over by buffleheads or goldeneyes, and as often by flying squirrels. Wasps and bumblebees also make use of them, as do small owls and kestrels. This woodpecker, as you can see, is a very useful denizen of the forest, providing homes for creatures unable to use cavities made by other woodpeckers. Just one pair will provide numerous suburban houses for other wildlife. They will excavate a 20 x 50-cm hole as high in the tree as that can be done, and this often makes the opening difficult to spot.

The favourite food of the pileated woodpecker is the grubs of large carpenter ants which it digs out of stumps or dead trees near ground level. It also eats other insects as well as some berries and nuts if there are any about.

The range of the pileated woodpecker is eastern, northern, western, but not central North America. Each pair requires a rather large area of mature mixed forest, probably eighty to one hundred hectares as pasture when raising a family.

The first syllable of the bird's name may be pronounced either "pile" or "pill." I usually say "pil-ee-ate-ed." The name means crested.

LISTENER'S GUIDE TO THE GREAT HORNED OWL
April 5, 1988

Great horned owls make some of the weirdest, most astonishing noises to be heard in the woods. The normal call of the bird, and the one we usually hear, lasts about four seconds and translates into English as "whoo, wh-whoo, whoo, whoo." The second word is normally of two syllables, but may sometimes have three. As with most bird sounds, there are variations amongst individual birds—considerable variation in pitch. Some are high, some are

220

Great horned owl's nest. Fred made this 20-foot ladder on the spot, by nailing several 20-inch boards on two slim spruce trees so he could satisfy his curiosity about the wildlife on the school quarter, SE 11-44-4-W5, 1948.

low, with the females generally higher. I also believe that calls vary according to geography, for the great horned owl is found from the edge of the Arctic tundra all the way to Central America, and from the Atlantic to the Pacific. It is unlikely that a bird of this species in Alaska would sound the same as one in Guatemala, since they do not migrate.

I have done a good deal of owl listening during February and March this year, as a pair seem to have established themselves in a wooded area close by. I can often hear them from within the house. They started hooting in earnest in January, but it was in February before they got into the different squawks, squeals and croaks that pass for love songs in official owl language. These strange sounds are not unusual at mating time, and since nesting in our area usually takes place in March and April, sometimes even February, the courting songs begin in the dead of winter.

Only three or four months earlier, I had heard these sounds at close range, this time combined with the begging of a juvenile. It was in October, at a campsite in eastern Washington. The loudness of the calls brought me out with a flashlight to see if I could see the birds, and I was rewarded by the ghost-like image of the adult bird as it flew against a patch of starlit sky just over my head. This bird was making two types of calls, one the normal hooting sound made at any time of the year, and described above. Interspersed with the hoots was a loud "houk," much higher-pitched and just a single note. Sometimes it translates into a two-syllable "hou-uk."

The second bird in the vicinity made a similar sound but never came close to us. The third bird was close but I could not get it in my spotlight. It was a juvenile, for the only call it was uttering was the well-known begging call used by more than one species. This call, if heard in the deep forest on a dark night, by someone who is not familiar with it, is enough to raise your nape hairs. If you try to approach it, it will most likely prove maddeningly elusive as near-silent wings carry the bird to another tree. The only way I can translate this call into English is "kwee-e-e-e-k." Juvenile great greys make an almost identical call. I was surprised to hear this call so late in the year. The bird making it could have been six or seven months old.

Owl calls in early spring are even more bizarre, louder and more strident than the ones I heard in the fall. It seems to be the female that utters the most un-owl-like noises. During courtship the owls seem so intent on each other that a human observer may approach quite closely.

Bird watchers are usually also bird listeners, and many listeners rely on recorded bird songs to help them identify a species. The problem with this aid is that many birds, including owls, have a far wider range of songs and calls than are to be found on most recordings. Many of the call recordings are made at a nest site, and what you are hearing is a bird doing its best to defend the nest. With the owls, this includes a loud clacking of the mandibles.

In my younger days, when neighbours were fewer and so were my inhibitions, I often hooted back at horned owls. They were

Great horned owl.

easily mimicked and therefore an easy bird to talk back to. In mating season this can make them quite excited. I was present at one such incident when the owl caller had to desist, as the male bird attacked the female, thinking she was fooling around.

A PAIR OF OFF-COURSE WHOOPERS
May 25, 1982

Now and then there comes a day in the life of every bird watcher when he hits the jackpot. I have had a number of such days over the years. The latest was May 5, 1982.

I was working indoors just a little before noon when I heard the high, rough bugling of sandhill cranes. I ran outdoors to see where the birds were, and found a pair of them circling almost directly overhead at the height of perhaps two to three thousand feet. With the aid of binoculars, I watched the two birds riding a thermal, going higher and higher, their rattling call coming down to me steadily as they rose. But I could hear, interspersed amongst the normal crane sounds, a different sound that did not seem to be coming from the birds I was watching. I searched the surrounding sky with the binoculars, and came upon two more large birds, much higher than the pair I was watching moments earlier. And these were not sandhills. They shone brilliant white in the late morning sun, and they had black wingtips. I recognized them instantly, although I had never seen one living before. They were whooping cranes! I could plainly see their long necks fore and their long legs aft. I was looking at more than two percent of the world's population of whooping cranes!

I forgot the sandhills then and watched the whoopers as they rode to the top of their thermal at an estimated six to seven thousand feet. Then they made a beeline to the south and I saw or heard no more of them. I could still hear a sandhill, however, and found one bird winging west at a fast clip, and soon the sky was empty and quiet once more.

I was elated. Living, as I do, well west of these birds' normal migration route, I had never expected to see one in the sky. Usually, on their long flight from southern Texas to Wood Buffalo National Park, they fly up western Saskatchewan toward northeastern Alberta.

This is the second sighting of whooping cranes in the Blindman area in three years. In June of 1979, a single bird was seen on the ground, and while the sighting could not be confirmed, I am sure that it could only have been a whooper.

I keep wondering if there isn't a possibility that a pair of these rare birds have been nesting or attempting to nest somewhere in a secluded, swampy area near the headwaters of the Blindman. There may still be such a spot of the required four-hundred-acre extent where a pair of birds could spend the summer undisturbed. I would like to think so.

WHOOPING CRANE SPENDS THE SUMMER
October 24, 1995

The whooping crane that spent the summer of 1995 west of Rimbey was something of a puzzle to the world of ornithology and to the Whooping Crane Conservation Association. Virtually every whooping crane in existence is accounted for, their whereabouts known most of the time. This has been the case for decades, both as regards the wild population which nests in Wood Buffalo National Park and the smaller breeding populations scattered across the continent.

The Rimbey bird had no band and was usually seen in company with two sandhill cranes. Ernie Kuyt of Edmonton, a leading authority on whoopers, having spent decades on their conservation program with the Canadian Wildlife Service, believes this bird to be a 1994 chick, hatched in Wood Buffalo, that got separated from its parents and spent last winter in Oklahoma with a flock of sandhill cranes. It was later reported in Colorado. While its future is uncertain, Ernie is optimistic that this fall it will get back with its own kind at the Aransas Wildlife Refuge on the Gulf Coast of Texas where the Wood Buffalo flock winters.

I heard about this stray whooper back in July. I made numerous trips, in company with other bird watchers, to look for the rare bird, but its pasture covered a rather large area, and we were never in the right place at the right time. It was Ed Brown, who lives a few miles west of Rimbey, who got word of the bird's whereabouts one morning, came in and picked me up, and took me right to the spot where the three birds were foraging—two big, tall, long-legged brown ones and the single, noticeably larger, white bird that stood nearly five feet.

Few garden-variety bird watchers have ever seen a whooping crane, but it was not a lifer for me, merely the first I had seen in fourteen years. On May 5, 1982, I had observed two, high in the clear blue sky, four or five thousand feet above my house, circling on a thermal. I am quite certain that I saw two more last month, at Last Mountain Lake, Saskatchewan. While this sighting was

224

unconfirmed by any other observers up to the time we left there, I am sure enough to be able to state that I now have a lifetime total of five whooper sightings.

The whooping crane is North America's most famous endangered species. Large sums of money have been spent over the last half-century to try and save the magnificent birds from extinction. Progress has been made, but not to the point where the future of the species is assured. There were a total of fifteen birds left in the world in 1941. The count as of summer, 1995, was 320. That may look like a good gain over fifty-four years, but the number is woefully small for a bird that has been a spectacular part of the continent's wildlife for tens of thousands of years. The intensive conservation program will have to be continued for many years to come. It is interesting to note that the number has doubled in the past six years.

The 166 birds counted in Wood Buffalo National Park this summer constitute the only wild flock breeding in a natural setting. The other 154 birds are in breeding flocks scattered across the continent, in Maryland, Florida, Wisconsin, Texas, Idaho, and Alberta, at a site south of Calgary. Chick production from these captive breeding flocks is spotty.

The summer count of 320 will be somewhat reduced before next spring. There are always some casualties in migration, and some yearly loss by attrition. But the outlook is good; barring some natural disaster, either in Wood Buffalo National Park or at Aransas, Texas, the flocks should continue to increase.

MAGPIE DEATHS BY HYPOTHERMIA
February 21, 1989

Did the blizzard cause the death of a flock of magpies?

Magpies are tough, resourceful birds that seem to thrive, despite a century of persecution. What would cause them to die by the dozen on a morning in early February, in a wooded area not far from Rimbey? Was it poison? Disease? Or was it the inclement weather? Gus Jehn, on whose property the birds perished, believes it was the weather.

It was bitterly cold this particular morning. As residents of central Alberta will well remember, it was the worst winter storm in at least a decade. When Gus walked out into his yard, he saw a magpie in the snow. Expecting it to fly as he approached, he was surprised to find that it was quite unable to do so. Then he spotted

225

another magpie beneath the trees, and this one was dead. When he looked further, he found eleven more dead magpies in the snow, and later, talking with his neighbours, found that they had also observed dead magpies.

Gus discounts the possibility of poison. There is no evidence of any being placed out in his neighbourhood, he says, even though magpies are still on many people's hit list. Unfortunately, none of the dead birds were saved, eliminating the possibility of a post-mortem in a laboratory.

Gus Jehn lives in the midst of a dense stand of mostly young spruce, a third-generation remnant of the great spruce forests that covered much of the shallow valley east of Rimbey one hundred or two hundred years ago, and exactly the sort of cover that magpies seek on cold winter nights. "They flock into these woods to roost every evening," Gus says.

While we can never be sure, the theory is that these magpies fell victim to an unusual circumstance of weather. While hunting and foraging on Sunday, January 29, they became wet with a rain that continued into the daylight hours of Monday morning. The rain was followed by a sudden and drastic temperature drop, accompanied by snow and strong winds. In their dampened state, the birds succumbed to hypothermia. No other wild birds were found to support this theory, however, and not all the magpies of the area died. There are still numbers about, as well as gray jays and smaller birds. Only magpies were found dead by Gus.

The magpie is a striking black and white bird that is quite unfamiliar to people from the East. Related to crows and jays, a magpie can be silent and furtive if it is on that kind of mission, or it can be bold and noisy at other times. Black and white also describes the bird's economic status as seen by rural eyes. His black side will rob the nests of other birds at every opportunity. It picks at wounds in large animals, preventing them from healing and eventually causing infection. These bad habits raise the ire of farmers, cowboys, duck and grouse hunters and even bird watchers who have witnessed the robbing and plunder of song birds' nests.

On the positive side, magpies are eaters of carrion, and provide a service by keeping the landscape cleaned of dead flesh. They also eat quantities of grasshoppers and other insects and catch not a few mice.

The magpie is a controversial but probably economically neutral species that came to Alberta with settlement from regions farther south. It was apparently not known here in the nineteenth century and is perhaps not quite so hardy in our climate as we had supposed.

I NEVER HEAR 'EM
May 24, 1972

I visited a man once who lived alone, far from neighbours, and surrounded by woods and wildlife. It was June when I went to his place, and bird calls and birdsong came from every quarter. Thrushes, warblers, jays and song sparrows poured down a barrage of wilderness melody. The man was working in his garden.

"You certainly have music to work by," I said to him, after our initial greeting.

"Music?" he said, puzzled at my remark.

"The birds," I explained. "Wouldn't you call that music?"

"I never hear 'em," was his reply.

Now I know that most of us go through life without being fully aware of our surroundings, but this, I thought, was unawareness in the extreme. Here was a man who lived by himself and liked it that way, which is not uncommon, and he knew enough about wildlife to be a successful hunter and trapper, and made a part of his living that way, yet the mating calls and territorial quarrels and warnings to intruders and cries of alarm that told of the life all around him held no meaning for him. Here was a man apparently concerned only with his own existence, and certainly not with the total ecology. The presence or absence of other species did not bother him except as they directly or immediately affected his livelihood. Yet there were good books on his shelves, and he could discuss the writings of H. G. Wells and Henry David Thoreau and Jack London, and did not consider himself uneducated.

It seems to me, as I think back on it, that the education meted out to this man (and most of his contemporaries), while it may have been adequate to their needs, was most inadequate to the preservation of the world's resources. The man is gone now, but he was one of many who lived as he did, a day or a month or a year at a time, only half aware of the world that enveloped them, and with never a worry that the future, due to their passiveness, might be one of great disaster.

Thinking has changed a great deal since that man went to school. More often than we used to, we look at things in terms of total environment, and it may have been products like DDT and writers

227

like Rachel Carson that brought the lesson home to us. Conservation, as a movement, has made rapid headway in the past ten years. Unfortunately, as the conservationists become stronger and better able to make themselves heard, their adversaries spring up from unexpected quarters. "Let's get what we can before the conservationists put a stop to our operations," seems to be the attitude of some industries and of some governments, too, and the deterioration of the environment is accelerated. Governments shun any drastic remedial measures, fearing to disrupt the economy, and are even subsidizing huge corporations like Proctor and Gamble with millions of dollars of the taxpayers' money in order to attract more industry, while industry continues to produce great quantities of sometimes nonessential and occasionally harmful goods, their only criterion being, "Will it sell?" So we preserve the status of the economy at the expense of the environment.

It is true that we are changing our way of thinking about these things. We are just not changing it fast enough. Too many of us never hear the birds singing.

FRISKY TRIXIE
December 6, 1956

Trixie is past thirty years of age but doesn't look—or act—more than half of that. Perhaps this is because, even for a pony, she has had an easy life. She was born on this farm in August 1926. Her mother was a white-faced, blue-grey cayuse named Baldy, who never did a day's work in her life. Baldy was a genuine mustang whose ancestors were likely brought into Alberta by the Blackfoot Indians in the days before the white man came.

Trixie is pretty much a chip off the old block, both in appearance and in temperament. Her blue is a little darker hue at most seasons of the year than was her mother's, and the white on her face is smaller in area. She is spirited but not mean. She loves freedom but submits to discipline. It takes about four people to catch her in an open pasture—after they have her well cornered. And on short trips she simply hates to walk. Never trained for a cow pony, she has nevertheless shown, at times, a natural inclination to be one. She would keep the strays bunched and the stragglers well up. Without being told, she knew instinctively what to do. But she lacked at least one of the attributes of a good cow pony. If you left her standing with the reins on the ground, you could expect to walk home. She had to be tied, and tied well.

Dorothy with Trixie, the farm saddle horse and school pony for many years.

While she made thousands of miles between home and school, she was never a children's pony. She wasn't broken, either to saddle or harness, until she was seven or eight years old, and she was too frisky for me to ride for a year or two after that. But although she maintained a frisky streak all the days of her life right up to the present, travelling to school five days a week and going after cows every summer evening quieted her down so that my brother and sister made better use of her than I was able.

In those days, the population of saddle horses in this community almost equalled the human population. The school barns were usually full, and most people depended to some extent on saddle horses for transportation. As might be expected, there was always a certain amount of genuine horse trading going on. Trixie was so pretty, so alive and young looking, and so well-built, that long after she was past her prime, I had many offers for her which the would-be owner no doubt considered generous. But I was never tempted. She had been given to me by my Uncle Fred, who was Baldy's owner, and I vowed I would never sell her. That is why, when a big truck called one day to load some of our surplus horses, Trixie was not included.

Today she is as fat and frisky as ever. She never eats hay or straw or grain, but munches green grass in the summer time, and paws through the snow in winter months for grass that is not so green. In spring she is far healthier and in better shape than if she had been kept in the barn all winter.

It was two years now since I have ridden her, and at that time she was a bit jerky of motion but otherwise her old self. Some day when I have the time and the help available to catch her, I'm going to throw the saddle on her and ride her up to the old log school house, just to give her one last look. Then I'll turn her back out to pasture for a few more years.

FAREWELL! GYPSY, JESSIE AND BOB
November 22, 1966

We said goodbye, a short while back, to three old friends: Gypsy, Jessie and Bob. They were the last of their kind on this farm. For purely sentimental reasons, we hated to see them go, representing, as they did, a tangible link with the homestead days. From a practical angle, we have no regrets. Each passing winter seemed just a little rougher on them, and it is always after a hard winter that old horses succumb to their age.

Gypsy, at twenty-seven, was the youngster of the trio. She had led an easy life, being born after most of the really hard work on the farm had been done, and just a few years before the advent of the tractor on her home acres. Gypsy was black, well-proportioned, and with a gentle nature, but she had poor feet; her hooves split easily and she was frequently lame.

Gypsy was usually paired with Jessie, who was two years older; heavier but not taller; less steady, less reliable and trustworthy; and neither black nor bay in colour, but a roan, off-shade brown. Like Gypsy, she had been born here on the farm.

Bob we acquired by purchase. We bought him from neighbour Fred Schweiger in 1944. "I won't lie to you about this horse's age," said Fred at the time. "He's twelve years old; born in the spring of 1932 but he should be good for a few years yet." He was good for quite a few.

There was no tractor on the farm then and Bob worked alongside the other horses—Gypsy and Jessie, Ted and Dan, Ginger and King—hitched, in season, to plough and disc, harrow and float, seeder and binder. With King, his driving mate, he pulled mower and rake and hay wagon, and hauled many a load of bundles to the threshing machine in the fall. And with King, he made a weekly trip to Bluffton with up to six cans (thirty gallons) of cream in the back of the democrat. We tried him on the garden cultivator a time or two, but he had trouble keeping his big Clyde feet between the rows and the job reverted to King.

King and Bob were the chore team. They hauled cords of firewood, tons and tons of hay, untold loads of manure and thousands of bushels of grain. Both were bays, but while King was well built, Bob had oversize joints, protruding hips, big feet, a long head with a heavy black forelock that should have obscured his vision but never seemed to. He looked a bit on the wild side.

Bob's tail, like his forelock, grew long and thick—when it got a chance. It was severely combed at periodic intervals, for horse hair was one of the sources of a farm boy's spending money in the days of horse power. Tail hair fetched a good price—forty cents per pound, if I remember right. Mane hair was about ten.

My nephew and nieces in Calgary and Victoria will, on future visits to the farm, miss the horses. For them, a farm without horses is something less than a whole farm. It is just possible that this is one of the subconscious reasons why we did not make more effort to dispose of them sooner. But none of them were ponies that kids could ride, and what other function do horses perform these days than be ridden?

Anyway, they are gone, gone from the pasture and the barn and the old strawstack. No more will their heads come up as we come into the field where they are grazing. No more will we see them coming down to the creek for a drink, or standing neck over neck in the shade on a hot summer's day, switching flies with tails uncombed for years. They are gone, but not forgotten.

And no, Niece Loa, I did not kiss Bob goodbye for you.

HORSES ON THE HOMESTEAD
November 29, 1967

The farewell to three old horses which made up this column last week set me thinking about the part played by horses in the development of these acres from a raw bush homestead to something resembling a farm.

Horses are a part of my earliest memories, and names like Chip and Bessie, King and Star, Lucy and Bill and Baldy were probably among the first hundred words in my vocabulary.

Horses, hitched to a buggy, brought my father to his first view of this quarter section back in 1921. The following year, they were used to transport household goods and farm machinery from the dry prairie to this lush, green, newly-settled land.

231

Then began a task unknown to either horse or man back on the prairie: the clearing of the land, by muscle and brawn, of the brush and trees that grew thereupon, that it might be turned by the plough. Trees under four inches or so were cut off at ground level with an axe. Larger ones had to be pulled out by the roots, else the sixteen-inch, wooden-beam breaking plough, pulled by four or sometimes five horses, would not be able to cope with the large, tough roots. To facilitate tree-pulling, roots were exposed with a grub hoe and severed with an axe. Grubbing trees was sheer drudgery, as I remember it, but pulling them over with a four-horse outfit and thirty or forty feet of logging chain was something else; it was an exciting operation. As I write I think I can smell the strong, clean smell, fresh and good, of newly exposed earth—and feel the moist coolness of it on my bare feet as I followed behind the plough.

There was much for horses to do on a new homestead besides clearing and breaking the land. They hauled fence posts and spruce rails for fencing and cross-fencing, for the quarter had to be separated into fields and pastures and gardens and barnyards. There were buildings to erect, corrals to build and haystacks to fence and creeks to bridge; and horses hauled the logs and lumber and wire and materials and tools.

Horses served as cow ponies and school ponies and as just plain saddle horses, for a saddle horse was often the most satisfactory way—often the only way—of getting from where you were to where

Dorothy, Allan, and Fred, near the farmhouse, with some of their horses, 1938.

you wished to go.

With the aid of a team of horses, the roots and the rocks were picked from the fields. Granaries were moved from one location to another. Our horses ploughed fireguards when bush fires threatened, and they hauled thousands of gallons of water in a wooden barrel on a stoneboat to put out ground fires that burned all winter in the peat if not quenched.

Today's horse, compared to the farm horse of yesteryear, leads the life of Riley, and may live to a ripe old age of thirty-five or even forty. By contrast, the work horse was old at eighteen, or even sixteen. Few lived past twenty-one and those still alive at twenty-four were on their way to being famous. School ponies and cow ponies frequently lived longer.

Some of these beasts of burden in the days preceding mechanization were rewarded with good care: plenty of hay and oats, some salt to lick, a clean stable and sometimes green pasture overnight. Many fared less well.

THE SMELL OF HORSES
December 8, 1971

The smell of horses is so much a part of daily living on your bush homestead in the mid-1930s that you are never really aware of it unless it comes in massive doses, and even then you easily become accustomed to it. You find nothing objectionable about a faint aroma of mixed horse sweat and manure. Compared to the way a pig smells, or even a sheep or a cow, a horsey smell is a wholesome sort of smell, but it is, after all, an animal smell, and mildly unpleasant in some instances.

If you drive horses, and feed them and groom them, and clean out their barn, there is no escape from the smell, and as long as you remain outdoors, who cares? But bring the smell into the house, where it is an alien smell, and you may get a few wrinkled noses. You come in for breakfast, say, after doing the chores, and you bring in the horse blankets to warm up and dry out because you will be using them this day, and you spread them over the backs of chairs beside the heater, and throw in another block of wood, and the smell will rise off those blankets, though you hadn't noticed it out-of-doors. But horse blankets quite naturally smell of horses, for it is usually a sweating horse onto which they are thrown. If a horse is not sweating, or has not been warmed by travelling, he has little need of a blanket.

233

Horsey smell comes in on your own clothes, too. You brush and curry the horses in their stall and the acrid dust swirls all around you and gets in your nostrils. You throw the harness on and do up the hame-straps, and snap the hold-back straps to the martingale, and buckle the belly-band, and pull the horse's tail out from under the britching (breeching if you prefer that spelling). In winter you do all this with your mitts on, then you straighten up and wipe your nose with the back of your mitt, and you are aware of horse smell for a moment.

When you are driving in winter, you are much lower to the ground than in summer when wheels instead of runners are beneath you. So, in summer you are elevated above most smells from the horses; in winter you are closer and more directly in line. Horsehair, for example, is something you learn to live with when your team is shedding, which seems to be most of the time. Push them a little too fast on the trail, and especially if the day is warm, your horses will lather: a creamy-white foam appears wherever harness comes in contact with the animal, a product of sweat plus friction. Flecks of it, lightened by evaporation, fly back into your face as you whisk along. Then, horses sneeze a lot. If you are driving with any speed, or into the wind at whatever pace, the moist spray of those sneezes also hits you in the face. Flying lather and sneeze on the breeze are such common, ordinary things that you don't even think about them, but they contribute to the total aroma that emanates from you and from your clothing but which is only noticeable to folks who have not recently been in contact with horses and such.

If, when you came in for the night, you could shower and put on clean clothes, you might rid yourself of horse smell for a short time—at least until morning—but the idea is so impractical and redundant it never even enters your head. Everyone is in the same boat, and it would never occur to anyone to complain. It wouldn't do any good, anyway. You'll be a few years older before you can forget about smelling like a horse all the time.

THE UNLOVED PORCUPINE
January 8, 1969

His lack of social grace or value bothers the porcupine not at all. It suits him to a "T" that in our eyes he is neither handsome nor pretty, neither cute nor cuddly, or that he smells even worse than he looks. He finds it greatly to his advantage that his meat is powerfully strong, and that his pelt is of no value to anyone but himself.

Few are the people who are able to find a soft spot in their hearts for this unfortunate creature. His surly disposition, easily triggered defence system and anti-social behavior have led him into the role of martyr in the animal kingdom. And that seems to be the way he likes it. He has other negative attributes. He is a menace to livestock and to such pets as dogs. He disfigures, deforms and even kills valuable trees of forest and orchard. He tramples grain in the field and chews holes in granaries. He will masticate fork handles, horse collars, or a pair of gloves for their salt content, and has, on occasion, reduced a pair of high top boots, left outside the tent, to sandals by morning. He is stubborn and stupid and can't be discouraged from unneighbourly actions or behaviour. His main ambition in life is to be ignored, to be left alone, so his friends are few or none at all. Who would want to be a porcupine?

The most extraordinary instance of porcupine harming livestock that I have heard about occurred in the Cremona district about four years ago. A farmer in that area was in the habit of turning a small herd of about seven milk cows out to pasture each evening after milking. One morning the whole herd came home in a painful plight. Their heads, legs, and underparts, including their udders, were a mass of porcupine quills. It took until noon to pull them out except for a few in the legs that could not be removed. The reported yield was two milk pails full of quills. Even when you consider that one porcupine may wear as many as thirty thousand spines on his back and tail, it seems likely that more than one animal may have been involved. And why did all the cows get into the act? They must have attacked the porcupine or porcupines for some reason, to have collected so many quills.

Never a year goes by without porcupines doing some damage on this farm. Sometimes it is considerable. Over the past two years, they have completely ruined our raspberry patch, breaking down and trampling the brittle new growth to nibble on the tender tips.

A porcupine has more lives than a cat. He is extremely difficult to kill, but after you have had to pull hundreds of quills from the face of a dog, a heifer or a colt, sometimes even from your own shins, and sometimes from the tires of your automobile, you may well be in the mood to make an attempt on the life of the next quill hog you see.

Yet I never kill one just because he is a porcupine, for even so abject a creature has some right to existence, and he doesn't need my hand against him to give him a huge persecution complex. Besides, he does have a few things going for him.

IN DEFENCE OF THE PORCUPINE
January 15, 1969

Last week I pointed out all the faults and blemishes we as humans see in the poor old sad-sack porcupine. I think that this week I should try to make some amends and cite the two redeeming features that I can think of concerning this myopic, grotesque rodent, and then list a few interesting fragments and details of porcupine life and behaviour that not everybody knows.

To begin with, the porcupine makes his greatest contribution to the good and welfare of the outdoor scene by helping to sustain a few coyotes and lynx, and perhaps several other predators as well, including eagles and larger owls, during the lean years following a rabbit crash, thus serving the old balance of nature theory. Secondly, he provides one of the raw materials for some wonderfully decorative artwork on birch bark and buckskin.

Porcupines range up to twenty-five pounds or more in weight, and they also range over much of the continent, from sea level to timberline. I have been surprised to find them on the bald prairie south of Lethbridge and in other treeless areas of Alberta. Since in summer they eat mainly new plant growth they could subsist on this prairie, but in winter, when the inner bark of pine, willow, alder, birch and other trees forms their staple diet, I should think they would have to head for the woods.

To think of the porcupine is to think of the quills that he wears. The myth that he could throw his quills probably had its basis in the fact that they are not very firmly attached to his hide, and when he swings his heavy muscular club of a tail some quills might easily shed, even without actual contact.

If you do get stuck with a quill, it will leave an insignificant wound and will almost never cause infection if pulled right away. It won't do you any good to cut off the end of the quill to let the air out though, as it is filled with pith and won't collapse. Nor will vinegar soften it. The best way to remove it is with a quick yank.

Light and buoyant, all those quills make porky a fairly good swimmer. They are usually white, tipped with black, and overlaid with long, black, brown or yellow guard hairs. They are two and a half to three inches long, lie flat when the animal is not alarmed but become erect when danger threatens. Lost quills are quickly renewed.

The usually single porcupine baby comes fully armed. The quills are soft for about fifteen minutes after birth, but quickly harden in air.

A porcupine in a tree moves so slowly and carefully as to be sloth-like, perhaps because he lacks the prehensile tail that is enjoyed as an extra safety feature by some South American cousins. On the ground, a motivated porcupine can gallop as fast as a man. I can also testify there is nothing sluggish about the way he will turn to attack someone or something running after him if he is caught in an open area and can't find a tree or any shelter.

There is a reliable and accepted method of picking up and handling a live, wild porcupine—you use his tail for a handle. I have never had need or occasion to try this, but apparently there is nothing to it if done right. The animal cooperates by always turning his tail toward you. You just grasp it from behind, stroking backward as you do so. Zoologists and wildlife biologists do this all the time.

Those people who know and take an interest in the porcupine, as opposed to those who merely dislike and castigate him, are convinced that we have in our woods an animal that is every bit as interesting as the duck-billed platypus from Down Under, or as diverting as the anteater of South America. They feel that his presence in the forest is worth a few trees. As for myself, I would rather lose a few bushels of grain to him than to see him eradicated altogether. I'm glad I wasn't born a porcupine, but if I had been, I would want to be treated with a little more consideration than most of us presently accord the poor little fellow.

PORCUPINE TALK
February 19, 1969

Imagine yourself walking alone, after dark, through the coniferous woods. It is late September and a waning moon has risen in the northeast, but deep in the pines its only effect is to cast an eerie, feeble light on the very tips of the trees and to make the shadows below seem a little blacker, the darkness a little more somber. There is that indefinite something in the air that tells you summer is finally past and a long winter lies ahead. You hear it in the topmost branches of the tall pines where a light breeze is making sad, whispery sounds, heightening the mood of melancholy that already pervades the darkness and encompasses you within that darkness. You quicken your pace, not because it has ever occurred to you that there is anything sinister about either the place or the season; it's just that you feel more comfortable where there are lights and people. Though it is not yet Halloween and you are miles from a graveyard or even a house that might prove haunted, you are, without even being aware of it, in a receptive frame of mind for intimidation by goblins, specters, or manifestations from the unknown.

Right at this point, from some indeterminate region in the darkness overhead, a sound comes to your ears that brings you forty thousand goose bumps and sends a procession of chills marching up your spine. It filters down through the branches like a series of ghostly wails, not overly loud, sometimes rising to a high note then descending to little more than a growl, and you think of the Indian medicine man of yore, and of how he talked to the spirits, and of the spirits answering him back.

So totally unfamiliar are the sounds that you might find them scary at ground level at high noon if you couldn't see their source. Coming down this way from the impenetrable gloom up aloft, they are positively spooky.

You want to run, but instead, you stand there, scalp prickling, not quite frozen to the spot, trying to identify that sound, for, once the first shock has worn off, you know that it originates, not from the supernatural, but from living flesh. And, of course, you are right.

The creature responsible is one of the most familiar denizens of the woods, the common porcupine; and you probably didn't even know he owned a set of vocal chords. Even people who have seen countless porcupines in their travels have not often encountered one in vocal mood; in fact, there was once a widespread belief that the animal was mute, for, even when attacked or severely injured, it utters no sound.

For most of the year, the porcupine is a silent and solitary bundle of reticence, but in the fall of the year, with the approach of the mating season, he may become almost loquacious by spells, with a repertoire of grunts and growls and whines, in addition to the tree-top serenade. All or any of these, falling on human ears for the first time, may be difficult to identify.

The first time I heard a porcupine talking, there were three of them, ambling around right under my feet as I stood motionless in the moonlight, so I had no trouble whatever in identifying the source of the sounds. It was a revelatory experience, and no doubt would have been more so if I could have understood porcupine.

THE UNINVITED PORCUPINE
February 14, 1989

A porcupine has become a star boarder at my place and I don't exactly welcome the intrusion. It isn't that I object to his race *(Erethizon dorsatum myops)* or his colour (mostly black with creamy-ended quills) or his social status (below the median), but I must admit to some intolerance of his eating and sleeping habits. I am much less kindly disposed toward this individual than I was toward the almost cute little thing I had a conversation with last fall.

I became aware of my unbidden guest on Groundhog Day, February 2, when I found fresh tracks going into the old chicken house during the aftermath of the blizzard. I store firewood in that building these days, and since I did no sawing all that frigid week, I went in there to take some of my reserve. It was not warm, but it was dry and out of the incessant wind, and there was old straw in a corner for a bed, and no predators anywhere in the vicinity. In short, the Porcupine-Hilton, with a four-star dining area right in the same compound, with numerous pine trees on the menu.

Pine tree denuded by porcupine. Porky stayed up there for months in the cold and wind. Bark and needles on the ground showed the fruits of his labours.

The first pine he chose to chomp on was a rather slim fifteen-metre specimen that was probably already doomed, since it had been girdled part way down by a porcupine two winters ago, but later I found him working on healthier trees that had been planted near the house by my parents more than fifty years ago. You might think that an animal that will eat pine bark and pine needles would not be a finicky eater. The truth seems to be that porcupines are very fussy about their food. What other explanation could there be for him eating twigs and needles only in the first tree he attacked, but when he moved to another, better-looking tree where he has been for the past four or five days, he ate

239

nothing but the bark from that trunk? That tree, now girdled in several places, will have no more growth rings.

When twigs and needles are his dish, the porcupine may climb to the very top of a tree, sometimes less than his own length from the very tip. Over the days, even weeks, he will work his way down, sometimes going to the very end of a branch so slender that he hangs down and sways like a pendulum in the breeze. This may leave the tree, in time, looking bare as a skeleton, but with small tufts at the ends of branches where he was unable to reach. If he chooses to eat bark, he is more likely to start at the bottom, and, if he likes the sample, take patches here and there higher up until the tree trunk looks like a jig-saw puzzle with half the pieces missing. Any bare patch that goes more than halfway around the tree will likely result in the tree eventually dying of starvation. If it is completely girdled anywhere on the bottom half, no sap will rise in the spring, and the tree will die within a short time. Birch, willow, alder and spruce bark are also grist for the porcupine's digestive system in winter. Once spring comes, porcupines leave the trees for more succulent fare.

Sometimes, especially if the winter is fine, a porcupine will remain on one tree for days at a time without descending. The porcupine in my yard is not like that. He likes his comforts, and comes down each evening to take shelter in that building where he is a perfect nuisance. So far, I have taken no drastic action. I keep hoping the weather will warm up to resemble spring and the prickly problem will go away. It may be wishful thinking.

PORCUPINE PROBLEM RESOLVED
March 14, 1989

The saga of the porcupine in my pine trees is ended—I hope.

My porcupine was a very lucky porky—lucky in that he chose my yard and my outbuildings and my trees as his home and food supply. Elsewhere he could have met an untimely end, and on this farm in an earlier time he might not have been so lucky, for people with dogs and colts and cattle, and ornamental or fruit trees, and grain in storage, do not have much tolerance for porcupines. It can take half a day and a great deal of trouble to relieve a heifer or the family dog of a face full—and often a mouthful—of quills, while years of work to get an Alberta orchard into production can be severely set back in one or two unmonitored weeks by a prickly, gnawing rodent.

240

My porcupine destroyed three lodgepole pine trees close to the house, trees that my parents planted there more than half a century ago. I was sorry to lose those trees, yet I was extremely reluctant to extract the ultimate penalty from this porcupine, for he was only doing what porcupines have always done, and I do find porcupines to be unique and interesting dwellers of the woods. I have had to dispatch porcupines in the past when they persisted in chewing holes in a granary, either letting the grain out onto the ground, or making their bed in a bin, leaving quills and droppings all through it and rendering it unfit for cattle feed or for sale. I would have done almost anything to avoid so unpleasant a task, for porcupines are not easily killed, even with bullets.

This time I tried a different tactic. I brought home a live-trap one day, used as a skunk trap by Alberta Fish and Wildlife. I baited it with green alfalfa hay, but it took the animal several days to get used to it, and in the meantime my trees were taking a beating. Then one morning my brother Allan, visiting from Vancouver, came in and announced, "The porcupine is in the trap." We wasted no time in getting the trap into the back of the truck and heading for an area where there are no cows, no dogs, no planted trees. There, with several cameras primed, we lifted the door of the trap and released ol' Porky into unfamiliar territory, many miles from the area he had known. He emerged into the bright light of a sunny winter's day, obviously disoriented. He looked left, then right, then all around for several seconds before he struck off with the rolling gait for which his kind is known, leaving his peculiar patterned-trough trail in the snow as he headed for the trees.

One might think that porcupines have few enemies. The truth is that they have several, including coyotes, wolves, lynx, cougar and grizzly bears. In the days when fishers were plentiful, these animals hunted the porcupines even in the trees where they fed.

The porcupine is the only member of its family found in North America. It may be found wherever there are trees and quite often out on the open prairie where trees are scarce. Should you be skiing through pine woods and notice the snow beneath a tree littered with fine bits of bark, a few green twigs with some needles attached, and numerous pellets that are very similar to moose droppings, look up—there may be a porcupine above you.

THE CRIES OF THE UNGULATES
March 5, 1969

Some animal sounds are so infrequently heard by the average person as to be puzzling, even disturbing to a one-time or first-time listener. I was walking along a narrow trail through the bush one extremely dark and overcast night when I was startled, to put it mildly, by a sound that was some kind of combination of violent snort and piercing whistle, something like a wild stallion might make at being taken by surprise, and about that loud.

I stopped short, for the blast was close and somewhat ahead of me. It came again, and was answered by another, off to my right, and this one, too, sounded less than a hundred yards away. All I could think of were horses, but I knew that there were no horses in the vicinity. Besides, there were no other sounds, and horses' feet make noise, even on soft ground. The whistle snorts came several more times, but each time from a little further away, still no other sound came to my ears. Only when they had receded some distance then ceased altogether, did I continue on my way, completely baffled as to what creatures I had heard.

Much later I learned their identity: white-tailed deer which at the time were rare in the area, seldom seen or heard by anyone. I have heard that sound a number of times since and I still thrill to it but never the way I did that first time when it was beyond my education and experience.

Prior to the episode with the white-tails, I had heard mule deer make vocal sounds, but this was no help at all as I stood mystified in the darkness that night, because the only cry I ever heard a mule deer make was a weak little "ma-a-a" that could easily be mistaken for the bleat of a sheep. The alarm signal of a white-tail, particularly when heard for the first time at close quarters on a very black night, is something quite different.

I have never heard a moose, so all I can say about their call is that I get the impression that it is the most preposterous and unmusical animal sound this side of Africa, alluring only to some other moose. I have heard experienced big-game hunters demonstrate a moose call that was likely pretty close to the real thing, and I always intended to try it for myself, but never felt sure that there were not armed men closer than the moose were.

A sound that I have heard is the wild, eerie, far-carrying bugle of the bull elk, and I can say that this ranks with the cry of the loon and the howl of the wolf as one of the soul-stirring sounds of the

Canadian outdoors. It can take you back a thousand years and more to a time when man did not seek to control nature but was merely a part of it. The first time I heard an elk bugle, I was picking blueberries on a dull, September afternoon, and, as with the white-tails, I was not sure at the time what I had heard but I had the feeling that it was one of the great sounds of the wild.

There is another sound made by a game animal which I have heard about but never heard with my own ears. This is the resounding report sent echoing and reverberating across the mountain valleys when two bighorn sheep with trophy heads back off from one another, then charge full speed, meeting head-on, horn to horn, hard enough to lift both animals off their feet, and do this over and over and over, sometimes for hours on end. I would rather watch this performance once, and photograph it if I could, than possess the biggest sheep head in the Rock

THE CRIES OF THE PREY
March 19, 1969

The most hair-raising calls and cries to come out of the wilderness are generally attributed to the larger predators, but the prey, especially when caught, may also blare forth with some bizarre yelps and screams and assorted cries of anguish.

If you have ever slept out in the woods with not even a tent between you and the sky, you will know that you have to be dog-tired to get much sleep on the first such night. Your ears will be assailed the long night through with so many squeaks and grunts and squeals, such a variety of hoots, chirps, twitters, peeps and yips, not to mention clicking, snapping, thumping and gnawing sounds that you wonder if it is safe to even close your eyes.

It isn't a steady chorus as it might be in the tropics. There will be frequent lulls that let you get to the verge of sleep, or you may even catch forty winks. Then you are brought wide awake by a sharp cry of terror and pain as some small night wanderer becomes a meal for one of the forest's nocturnal predators, and all you can do is lie there, wide awake, wondering just what took place to evoke that cry, and puzzling about who the participants in the drama could have been.

I think the most heart-rending sound in the whole outdoors is that of the snowshoe rabbit (more correctly, the snowshoe hare) caught by whatever means. He doesn't even have to be hurt or

243

harmed to set the countryside ringing with a shrill, penetrating cry of such volume and intensity and such a note of excruciating pain that it would wring pity from a tamarack stump; and he can keep it up interminably. Years ago we used to set up snares and traps around some fruit trees, which, although we had them wrapped in tar paper, were apparently exceptionally tasty to the rabbits that were overrunning the bushlands. Every so often, a rabbit would get into either a trap or a snare and set up his clamour in the middle of the night. I would waken and lie there listening for a few minutes until I could no longer stand it, and I would have to climb out of a warm bed, dress for sub-zero temperatures, and go out and quiet that rabbit.

More cheerful and less interesting are the noises made by our largest rodent, the beaver. This is another animal whose vocal abilities are not well known, but which are somewhat more predictable than those of the rabbit or porcupine. That is, you may listen at the top of the lodge in early summer and expect to hear the mews and murmurings of the kits within. Or you may visit the beaver pond on an autumn evening when all are out working, and you will hear them apparently talking back and forth in nasal sounds that can be defined neither as grunts nor whines, but which are akin to both.

The most dramatic call I have ever heard a beaver make was loud and full-throated and neither a whine nor a grunt. It was nothing less than a bellow and it came from one of a pair of adults far from any beaver dam, probably in search of new territory. I heard it from a quarter-mile away and was sure it was a cow bawling, but investigation proved to me just how loud a beaver can holler. A better known beaver-produced sound is the whack of the flat, scaly tail on the water, used as an alarm signal, and sometimes, too, there is the crash of a poplar tree in the middle of the night.

MY BEAVER TELL THEIR STORY
November 18, 1970

I really didn't expect to find a message when I picked up the short length of peeled poplar log I found floating in a small patch of open water near the broken dam. The tooth marks on the white wood looked like columns of hieroglyphics, irregular, yet orderly. Are beaver learning to write, I wondered? After all, they are among the cleverest of animals. Suppose these tooth marks were a record of events kept by the beaver who occupy the stick and mud house that looms like an island from the middle of their pond. I looked at the carvings more closely.

By using my own knowledge of the beaver and their way of life, and by employing a liberal helping of literary license, and by exercising my imagination as well, I managed, in time to come up with results of a sort. Here, rather freely translated, are some excerpts:

September 1, 1970—For several months now, we have been busy rimming the crest of the dams with a waterproof mixture made up of mud dredged from the pond bottom, and long, coarse grass from the pond's edge. This job will keep us busy for some time to come, as we want to raise the water level several inches in preparation for the winter we can tell is coming. Already we have backed the water under the old bridge and onto the land across the road. When we go up that way we are always thankful that we can swim beneath that decrepit old structure instead of having to travel over it.

September 20—With the water rising gradually, we have had to do some work on the lodge, enlarging it and raising the level of the interior rooms. Another day or two hauling long willow branches onto the sides and roof, and outside work will be finished.

October 1—A big truck came down the road the other day and dumped a huge steel culvert near the creek. At long last they must be going to replace that rotten old bridge, though how they are going to work in three feet of water, we don't know.

Beaver dam.

October 20—There has been a lot of parading up and down along the ponds and out onto the dams by any number of people during the past few days. Many of them are strangers and some were wearing uniforms. We are a bit uneasy at all this sudden interest in our territory and our construction activities. Is it of a friendly nature or is there something fishy afoot?

October 23—What a day! What a night! Now we know some of the answers. Yesterday the two uniformed men returned, accompanied by the one who lives close by and whom we see often. They tied some small sticks together with a cord and shoved them deep into the mud of the dam. Those sticks turned out to be dynamite and they packed a powerful punch. They blew great holes in the three upper dams and let about two acre-feet of water go rampaging down the creek, water that had taken us weeks and months to store. And the noise they made! It was frightening and badly scared the kits in the lodge. Don't those people know there is a winter coming? It will take days to raise the pond even a few inches, and already the nights are cold and ice forms almost to the middle of the pond.

MY BEAVER TELL THEIR STORY II
November 25, 1970

Here are some more excerpts from my none-too-literal interpretations of the peculiar tooth marks found on a peeled, poplar log near the ruptured beaver dam:

October 23—We worked around the clock last night, and before daylight this morning we had stopped all water going over the dams. We concentrated on the second dam because it will take days to plug the hole in the main dam, and only days are left to us to raise the water as much as we can before thick ice curtails our activities and seals us into this pond for the winter. We only hope there will be no more dynamiting. It seems to us that people think only of people. No one else seems to rate.

October 26—Just as we feared, cold nights have frozen thick ice on the pond's surface and now an early fall blizzard has buried everything under a foot of snow—just the kind of weather we could least afford. Large sticks and brush needed for repair work are now inaccessible beyond the shoreline or are frozen in the ice. As an emergency measure, we have had to use all the loose brush on the roof of the lodge, and we have even taken some of the upper portion of our pile of winter provisions, which was now above water and of no use to us anyway. It is a problem, these cold nights, to keep enough open water between the house and the dam to do even this much. The lodge looks like a big pile of mud once more and it will not hold the layer of snow and air spaces that help to keep out the cold when severe weather comes; and if the winter should be a long one, we could be short of food by spring as well.

November 1—The ice is now solid enough for people and animals to walk about above us, although they are careful to avoid the thin places where we have been trying to keep the water open. We are still able to haul a little brush to the dam, but it is now only a token activity and can do little good. And it can be very uncomfortable. Did you ever try walking with wet feet or sitting with a wet tail on ice that is well below freezing? There is a tendency to stick.

November 8—We have raised the water about a foot since the dams were blown, but this was not enough to fully cover the east entrance to the lodge, and we have had to make some alterations there. We have made repairs to the limit of our ability in the short time we had, and there is little likelihood that we will see a mild spell that will allow us to do more. We must wait for the spring and hope for the best, but we are wondering what will happen then, for the big steel culvert still lies uselessly where it was dumped several weeks ago.

We are more convinced than ever that humans could learn a lot from us about planning ahead.

THE NIGHT HUNTERS
December 6, 1972

This week's column is taken largely from a news story in the *Edmonton Journal* under the by-line of Richard Finnigan, dated November 24, 1972. His story deals with the unscrupulous practice of night-lighting and the use of aircraft in apprehending night poachers.

With the plane flying at an altitude of two thousand feet, wildlife officers have been able to spot night hunters up to seven miles away. With direct radio communication to patrol cars below, they can patrol an area of three thousand square miles three times a night and they are able to follow a spotted car even when it drives without lights. At the time this story was written, game officers had been able to lay a charge every time they took to the air.

247

"Of course we have to be able to satisfy the courts that the parties involved are hunting," says chief wildlife officer Ernie Psikla. "Many of these people will argue they were out looking for cows, but if they're caught with loaded guns and hunting knives ... we don't have to catch these people with game in their possession to establish their intent."

One biologist cited in this report believed that 80 percent of the deer taken in this province were taken illegally, and of these, 90 percent were taken by jack-lighting. There is no doubt that poaching has a very detrimental effect on deer populations. Areas where poaching—particularly night hunting—is impossible because of the terrain will support up to five times as many deer as can be found in areas accessible to cars and people.

The story goes on to point out, as I have done in this column more than once, that quite apart from its effect on the deer population and apart from the contempt displayed for the law and the infringement on rules of sportsmanship and on the rights of others, this is a very dangerous practice. Fire a rifle at night and there is no way to be sure what lies beyond your range of vision. There could be livestock or buildings, high-priced machinery, oil or pipeline installations, power lines or even people in the line of fire. Mr. Psikla thinks that if the practice cannot be stopped, a human death will eventually result somewhere in this province.

Jack-lighting is so prevalent in the Kinuso area, says the story, that one farmer placed a sign in his fields: "NIGHT HUNTERS— Please Watch for Horses and Cattle." In the meantime, the honest hunter and sportsman is penalized in reduced hunter success, a shorter hunting season, and a strengthening of the ban-hunting movement, just because some people with twisted minds and no consideration for anyone but their greedy little selves find it sport to flout the law and shoot a spellbound deer. One man was caught with six deer. Was he planning on putting them all in his freezer?

The legal hunting season here is over, but the period for night hunting, when it isn't safe to walk or drive or be within a mile of deer-feeding areas at night, will not be over until snow gets too deep to drive into the fields.

WILDLIFE AT A WILDERNESS LAKE
May 31, 1976

Happiness, for a naturalist, is a wilderness lake in spring. Here are some reasons why.

I have to begin with the loons. They protest loudly at sight of me, and I react perversely, as humans do to loons, and enjoy their protests. To be thoroughly scolded by a loon in his native tongue is one of the great wilderness experiences.

After the loons, beaver are the most evident of the lake's inhabitants. Two lodges, in different parts of the lake, rise dome-like from the deeper shallows beyond the reeds. Felled poplars, their branches all gone for salad, lie all along the shore where these trees grow. Slightly weathered stumps show recent work by these industrious animals; old rotting stumps indicate they have been here for many generations. Finally, there is the series of dams at the outlet by which they control the level of the lake, and which, incidentally, made it possible for us to get our canoe here.

Beaver, like the loons, seem to resent intrusion. Let a strange object appear on their lake, as our canoe, or on the shore, as our tent, and we are very likely to see a huge old beaver swimming back and forth, back and forth, periodically hitting the water a resounding whack with his tail.

Muskrats don't seem to be bothered by an alien presence as do loons and beavers. They go quietly about their business and only if we come too close will they dive with a plop.

The marsh wrens become quite excited when the canoe comes close to their nest in the cattails, but we are not much wiser about where their home is, because they build several false nests in their cattail jungle, most of them inaccessible from a canoe.

Morning is the best time for bird sounds. Snipe whinny in the air overhead, sandpipers peep from the beaver dam, yellowlegs send up a clamour and yell from a dead snag near a swampy bog until we are glad to leave the place to gain some peace and quiet. Once they have simmered down we can hear the song birds again, sending forth their territorial warnings from tall trees, thick willows and low perches all around the shore. Woodpeckers hammer from drowned dead trees; flycatchers and swallows skim out over the water for insects; warblers and kinglets sing from the spruces; a grouse drums, grebes call, a squirrel chatters. I mustn't forget those attractive birds so symbolic of places where cattails grow, the red-winged blackbirds. Most red-wing nests are built over water.

Strawberry Lake, November 17, 1975.
L to R: Alvin Goetz, Bill Nesbitt, Dennis Andersen.

A period of relative quiet falls on the lake in the afternoon, but it is not quiet after sundown when sounds, having no visible source, take on an aura of mystery. Some we can identify, some we can't. There is splashing and gnawing of muskrat and beaver, mice rummaging along the shore. Ducks, grebes, and coots all make noises in the darkness, while the white-throated sparrow sings his Canada song all through the short night.

A quarter of a mile down the shore from our tent, water sounds, splashing and tinkling, tell us a moose is feeding. Every little while we hear the sounds of wings overhead, owners unseen and unknown. From the woods come larger sounds: thuds, grunts, brush-breaking, and we wonder if all our food is out of reach of bears. Then we conclude that it is a passing elk, as we hear it no more, and our attention is diverted to the yodeling chorus of coyotes across the lake.

It's one of those nights when you hate to climb into the sleeping bag, but the dew is damp, the fire is low and the night chill is settling. Tomorrow is another day.

THE GLIDING SQUIRREL
September 14, 1982

The nest was occupied, but not by swallows.

Each year a pair of tree swallows raises a brood in a nest box that I provide for them at some distance from the house. It is a modern type of bird house, and in order to look into it to see what's doing, all I have to do is raise the roof, which is hinged on the back. I had last looked in several weeks ago, in July, when four nearly-grown swallows opened wide their faces expecting to be fed. Now it is almost autumn and I happened to be walking by that nest. "A good time to clean that box out," I thought. "I won't be seeing the tree swallows again until late April next year."

The nest was nailed to a poplar tree facing an open field on a ridge not far from the creek. It is about five feet from the open ground, a height that suits the swallows and makes it easy for me to monitor or to clean. I opened the top and looked in. There was a swallow's nest, lined, as most of them are, with white chicken feathers and looking as if it had just been built. "You'd never know that a brood of swallows had been fledging in here," I thought, and put my hand in to pull the whole thing out. When I did that, I got a surprise; something soft and furry ran right through my hand, out of the box and up the tree, stopping only a foot or two above my head. I don't know which of us was more surprised, old Freddie or that flying squirrel. I very likely wakened the animal, as flying squirrels sleep by day. As the pretty fellow watched me from part way around the tree with one unblinking black eye, I carefully closed the top of the nest box and quietly backed away, for flying squirrels are very timid creatures, and one disturbance such as this might be enough to cause this animal to abandon a home that must be near perfect for a flying squirrel.

It is not the first time that a flying squirrel has taken over a nest box intended for swallows on these premises. Rather, it is a fairly common occurrence. I always have flying squirrels about. Sometimes I know where they live and sometimes I don't, for I am reluctant to go searching lest I frighten them away. When my attic was less well insulated than it is today, I would often hear them scampering over the roof on moonlit nights. I still hear them at my bedroom window, and sometimes I see one in silhouette against the night sky as it clings to the screen.

There are more flying squirrels about than most of us realize, because they are nocturnal animals, unlike the red squirrel which

251

stays in its nest at night. In the years when I had cattle, I would sometimes find a flying squirrel drowned in the water trough.

Flying squirrels do not actually fly. They glide. Instead of wings they have a membrane extending from the body and stretching from the ankle of the front foot to the ankle of the hind foot. This is simply a double thickness of skin covered with fine soft hair. To glide, the animal climbs to a high place, usually up a tree, leaps into space and extends its legs straight out. It can swerve left or right, dodging trees and branches, and its flight path turns upward as it lands, so that it can break and light softly against the lower trunk of a tree. Flying squirrels can glide two hundred feet or more into or across a clearing, using their flat, furry tails as rudders. I have found their tracks in the snow that far from the launching tree on many occasions when they have come down short of the target tree.

PLAYING IN THE MOONLIGHT
September 21, 1982

The moon will be full on October 3. There will be no better time in the next six months to observe flying squirrels. There are several reasons for this. Firstly, flying squirrels love to play in the moonlight, and are most active on nights when the moon is bright and the woods are still. Secondly, some family groups should still be together. During the winter the animals become solitary and do a lot less cavorting. The next best time to observe them might be around the next full moon next March 28, about the time the mating season is getting underway. Thirdly, the leaves may well be off the deciduous trees by the first week of October, making viewing a great deal easier.

The best place to find flying squirrels is in a mixed-wood forest where the trees are tall and not too thick, and where there are numerous woodpecker cavities in old or dead trees. These are favourite homes for flying squirrels, although they sometimes make their nest or dray, in an old magpie nest, or against the trunk of a thickly-branched spruce tree in the manner of the red squirrel.

To locate flying squirrels at night, go into some suitable habitat and sit still for a few minutes. If the little animals are about and frolicking, they will be making soft, rather musical sounds, in sharp contrast to the very unmusical repertoire of the red squirrel in daylight hours. Some naturalists tell us that flying squirrels are one of the few species that sing in group harmony, as do wolves on occasion. Although I once heard the wolves doing this, on a moonlit night, I have not had the experience of listening to the squirrel chorus at night.

Once you have located them, your best chance of seeing them at play is from the edge of a small clearing where the moonlight can penetrate. Some naturalists believe that the age-old connection of witches with Halloween came from early New Englanders who had really seen flying squirrels gliding across a clearing in the autumn moonlight.

Flying squirrels range over temperate North America wherever suitable habitat is found. Our race is the Hudson Bay flying squirrel, *Glaucomys sabrinus*. In the mountains to the west is the Rocky Mountain flying squirrel, *Glaucomys sabrinus alpinus*, while in the very southwest corner of Alberta we find *Glaucomys sabrinus fuliginosus*, or dusky flying squirrel *(The Mammals of Alberta*, Dr. Dewey Soper, 1964). The dusky is the largest race; in eastern North America there is a smaller, tawnier race.

Flying squirrel fur is soft and fine but, fortunately for the squirrel, it has no commercial value, to the annoyance of the trapper when he finds one of the silky- haired animals in a trap where it has been attracted by the bait.

Flying squirrels do not hibernate. While the red squirrel will sleep through a severe cold snap, the flying squirrel is active at any temperature. For one thing, he doesn't store much food, and has to go hunting for wild rose hips, dried berries and other plant seeds; meat if he can find it. Often at night, flying squirrels will come to a bird feeder for suet and other goodies.

THE RICHARDSON'S GROUND SQUIRREL
April 23, 1991

The question has arisen: do gophers, more correctly known as ground squirrels, bear their young in the burrows before they first emerge in the spring? Or do they have them later? "Later," I said, when the question was put to me. But I was not one hundred percent sure, so I said I would go home and check it out. I went to two eminent authorities: Dr. J. Dewy Soper, who wrote the first reliable book on *The Mammals of Alberta*, which was issued by the Queen's Printer, and Ben Gadd's nine hundred-page book, *Handbook of the Canadian Rockies*, a bargain at twenty-five dollars. The two books give similar answers, but disagreed on some minor points. In addition I posed the question to two outdoors friends with 125 years' experience between them. Same answer, "Later." A month to six weeks later, in fact.

This is how it goes for the Richardson's ground squirrel, the common gopher of the prairies and parklands. The males emerge from hibernation first, usually during the second half of March, in a normal winter. The day has to be mild, and if the weather turns severe again they will go back in and stay until the next warm spell. The females emerge a week or ten days after the males, and not until then does mating begin. Add another four weeks until the young are born and the time of year will be somewhere around the first of May. The little ones are born in a nest in the recesses of the burrow, and there they stay for weeks—at least seven or eight—to show up as cute but inquisitive and vulnerable half-pint versions of their parents. There may be five to eleven of them, but before they get big, these numbers will be drastically reduced by red-tailed hawks, coyotes, badgers and automobiles. If these were not problem enough, there are still .22 bullets, traps, snares and the farm dog to take a toll. Enough survive to go into hibernation in September and repeat the cycle the following spring. Since a ground squirrel's year is only about six months long in the central part of the province, they only have time for one family per year.

Times have changed for the Richardson's ground squirrel in that he now has a few friends amongst the human population, but he is still far from popular in the agricultural community, where he is still persecuted with gun, trap and dog. I have seen well-populated gopher knolls where whole acres have been denuded of grain or grass. If a pair of badgers move in, they may decimate the ground squirrel population, but the large deep holes they leave in the process are almost as great a nuisance as having the gophers.

On the plus side, they are a favourite food for red-tailed hawks, and who does not like to see these graceful and beautiful birds soaring over the meadow? They are also a favourite meal for a coyote in summer, and if coyotes are destroyed, the ground squirrel becomes a greater nuisance.

MY FIRST WHITE-TAIL SIGHTING—1953
November 15, 1983

I saw my first white-tailed deer on a sunny mid-summer day about thirty years ago. Harry and I had hiked about two and a half miles west onto the Hudson's Bay section, prospecting for blueberries. The berries were green as grass yet, but they grew in profusion on a good part of this land that had been burned over by severe forest fires in the summer of 1949. It takes a forest fire to make good blueberry country.

We were tramping through brush, and wading through grass and peavine in rolling terrain when Harry stopped, his eyes on the ground. "Deer tracks," he said, speaking quietly, "and they're fresh." I looked where he pointed. There were trails through the peavine all right. "About three of them," he said, still speaking low, and after a few seconds' pause he added, "I think they're white-tails." He looked around, sizing up the lay of the land. "They are probably on the sunny side of the next ridge," he went on, "lying down where they can get the breeze." The breeze was light and westerly.

How does he know all this, I wondered, but I did not question. Harry was, even then, a hunter of considerable experience who knew the ways of the animals. He started up the little ridge immediately in front of us, moving slowly but deliberately, bent double, almost appearing to walk on all fours. With his fingers, he removed any dry twigs or dead leaves from the spot where each toe would be placed as he advanced. I followed closely behind, carefully tiptoeing in his exact tracks, also bent low to the ground. As we neared the crest of the low ridge, I moved up beside him, doing as he did. When he lowered himself into a grassy patch and began to inch forward on his elbows, I followed suit. We were moving about as noiselessly as two humans could do.

Finally, we were able to peer through the grass to the opposite side of the little swale. There, on the ridge, in the sun and the breeze, lying down in a three-metre triangle, perhaps a hundred metres away, were three white-tailed deer, right where Harry said they would be. I should have been astounded. The truth is I expected them to be there. I would have been disappointed had they not been.

We watched them, through binoculars, for some ten or fifteen minutes, until it became boring. All that those three sleek, tawny animals were doing was chewing their cud and flicking an occasional fly off their ears. Harry looked at me. I knew what we were going to do. It wasn't the first time. As one, we leapt to our feet, waved our hats in the air and hollered "Yahoo!"

We got action. From a lying-down, at-ease position, and without appearing to stand first, those three left their beds, white flags flashing, and came down on all fours seventeen to twenty feet away, as we learned moments later when we measured their leaps. Only a slow-motion replay could have revealed exactly how they accomplished this. And they had left that spot travelling in three different directions, another survival tactic.

We felt no remorse at having scared our wild friends like that, instead of backing ourselves quietly down the ridge the way we had come. We were just keeping them on their toes, we told ourselves, with hunting season just three months away.

I learned some lessons in stalking that day that I have made use of ever since, but I never did figure out how Harry knew there would be three white-tails on that ridge.

HENRY'S BONE FIELD
October 31, 1962

I have never seen a field before like Henry Macareavy's "bone field." Twenty-eight acres in extent, it lay newly-turned by the breaking plough—and as nice a job of breaking as I have seen in many a day. Each furrow led the eye straight to the far side of the quarter, and each furrow was a dark, flat ribbon of soil that exactly matched the one beside it. That soil was mostly dark brown peat, but some was black and loamy and there were patches where the familiar grey wooded soil had been turned up.

And why does Henry call it his "bone field"? Apart from the small patches and fringes of grey wooded clay there was hardly a place on the whole field where you could stand and not see old bones within a few steps. There were thousands of them—all sizes and every shape. The ones in the peat were the best preserved, for peat contains tannic acid, used in tanning leather, and a natural preservatory of animal remains. When the bones were first turned up, they were much the colour of the peat, but when I saw them, they were bleached in the sun, and easily seen.

There were leg bones, rib bones, vertebrae and shoulder blades. There were jaw bones, foot bones, skulls, antlers, teeth. They occurred in ones, in pairs, in groups, in clusters. No wonder Henry calls it the "bone field."

But the number and variety was not the only remarkable thing about these bones. In one cluster that must, at one time, have been a pile, there were both buffalo and moose bones, including a buffalo skull and one moose antler; and intermingled in the same group were some smaller, finer bones that did not belong to either a moose or a buffalo. Unfortunately, there was no skull visible to go along with these small bones.

Buffalo skulls were there in all sizes, from the broad-fronted skulls of old bulls to the small, short-horned one that must have belonged to a nursing calf. Neither skulls nor antlers were what might be

256

called well-preserved, although many of the bones were in excellent condition.

The moose antlers that were turned up were something to wonder at. These were not the wide, platter-like trophy sets. These made you wonder what on earth the moose who wore them could have looked like. Not that they were small. They came in all sizes, but the largest one was probably the oddest.

Thick and heavy at the base, its spread was commendable, but the palm, or spade as it is sometimes called, was more saucer-sized than platter-sized, while the tines were long and spreading.

How did all these animals die? Were they trapped in muskeg when the land was far wetter than it has ever been in recent years? Were they slaughtered there by the Indians? Did they all die in one year, or over a span of many years? That moose with the big, thick antler: what year was he born? 1870? 1835? 1799? And how about the buffalo calf, or the bull, for that matter?

It may be indicative of something that there were no artifacts, or any campfire stones in the field or among the bones, so far as I could see.

CARIBOU ANTLER PLOUGHED UP
June 12, 1968

What would a young caribou be doing in the swamps and peat bogs along Muskeg Creek, about ten miles south of Pigeon Lake and many miles south of what must have been his normal range, even in the days before the white man's coming?

Perhaps it was a hard winter that year in the northern woods, and the animals, in their quest for food, had been driven south by Arctic storms, south of the North Saskatchewan River, into territory unfamiliar to their kind. Here, right beside the creek that would be called Muskeg, the young caribou had drawn its last breath. Whether it had succumbed to exhaustion and malnutrition, to wolves or grizzlies, or to a hunter's arrow, we have no way of knowing. So, preserved by the acids in the peat that covered them, the animal's bones lay for a hundred summers, or perhaps two hundred, or even longer than that. Their disinterring came one spring day this year when Benny Falt was working up his meadows with a deep tillage cultivator. Benny is one of the hunting fraternity. He knows about big game and what they wear on their heads, and he scarcely could believe his eyes when he saw that the cultivator had dragged to the surface a caribou antler, not a large one, but well preserved. It came from the farthest, lowest corner of the field, just a few yards from the creek, and when I attempted to dig in the spot, hoping to uncover more bones, or another antler, I encountered frost about eight inches below the surface. That was on the Victoria Day weekend, and the dry peat on top was serving as insulation to keep the frost from coming out.

It was Julius Lind, a neighbour of Mr. Falt's, who told me about the discovery, and he also told me that, years ago, before the land had been cleared, he had seen two live caribou in the area, easily recognizing them by their antlers and their whitish neck patches. These could possibly have been mountain caribou that were exploring beyond the fringes of their normal habitat.

The present range of the woodland caribou comes no nearer to central Alberta than the Lesser Slave Lake area, possibly as far south as Athabasca. According to the Alberta government publication, *The Mammals of Alberta,* no caribou of any kind ranged south of the North Saskatchewan River in central Alberta, or south of Banff Park in the mountains; so both Julius Lind's sighting and Benny Falt's antler would extend that range by some miles. Either or both occurrences, of course, could have been casual strays, beyond their normal territory.

Mr. Falt is curious to know how long that antler and a few other bones, including a portion of skull, have lain buried in his field.

I wish I could tell him.

ELK ANTLERS OF OLD
April 28, 1989

I was a kid in grade three at the time. There was no school at Blindman River, the school district in which I was resident, so my parents were paid seventy-five cents a day by the Department of Education to drive my brother and me to Iola, four and a half miles away. It was just too far for two little kids to walk, so my father or my mother or my granddad took us with team and buggy each morning and came for us each evening with the same team, King and Star, as the horsepower. Our teacher was a young and pretty nineteen-year-old named Joan Williams. Most people in the Rimbey area know her today as Joan Freeman.

The road north from the house along this quarter section crosses two creeks and a stretch of low ground which, in the 1920s, was made quite swampy by a spring in the very northwest corner of the quarter. Some road work had been done on this piece prior to 1921, the year my father homesteaded this land. A quarter of a mile of corduroy had been laid and ditches dug to channel the spring down to the creek, but the ditches were mostly filled in and the corduroy had worked up through its cover of dirt; and the logs were in such disarray that it was impassable for vehicles, so a trail was made in the soft ground alongside the corduroy. That trail was used twice a day, five days a week, on our way to and from school. It became very soft in wet weather, and in many places the buggy wheels would be in up to the axles, the horses scrambling for firmer ground.

At one spot in this trail, one of the wheels would hit something solid with a jar that would rattle the teeth of those in the buggy. Supposing it to be a rock, the driver of the buggy would try to avoid it by guiding the vehicle a foot or two either to right or to left, but still the wheel would hit that solid object. A rock had no business to be in peat soil in any case, and puzzled by the unseen conformity of this annoying obstacle buried a foot or more beneath the surface, the whole family went down there one Sunday morning with spades and shovels, determined to either dig it out, or at least have a look at it. It didn't take long to uncover it, and to everyone's amazement, it turned out to be a petrified elk antler, weighing a good deal more than when some bull elk had shed it there long, long ago. It was a large, six-point antler with a heavy stem and a rather massive butt. It would be a long time before I would see another that big. We brought it home, cleaned it up and used it as a hat rack for the next sixty years.

There were no elk in this part of Alberta at that time, and so far as I have been able to learn, there had not been for forty years before that time. An extremely hard winter in 1887 had taken the last of them. A few survived that winter east of Edmonton and became the nucleus of the herd in Elk Island National Park, which was established in 1906. It would still be many years before elk, more correctly known as wapiti, were to re-establish themselves in this area, coming in from Banff National Park. The first elk known to hunters of this area was shot west of here along the North Saskatchewan River in 1929, long before there was a season on them, and about the same year as the Schutz family dug an antler out of the muskeg.

In later years, other long-shed elk antlers were unearthed from the peat soils on this farm in the course of breaking the land for cultivation. Preserved first by the tannic acid in the peat, and later petrified from minerals brought up by adjacent springs, these antlers may go back centuries, perhaps at least to the time of Anthony

259

Henday, who wintered in this part of the province in 1754-55. He noted "herds of hundreds, passing and re-passing in front of the tent." I suspect that it would have taken at least two hundred years for a foot of peat soil to build up over that first antler we found by striking it repeatedly with a buggy wheel.

MUSHROOMS, ELK AND RHINOS
June 11, 1991

Some things just do not add up. My friend Frank and I were talking about the big magic mushroom bust east of Hoadley. Frank has land in that area, and so the news story was fairly close to home. I haven't talked to anybody who admits to knowing this chap, and few have even seen him. The rumour is that he also raised German shepherd dogs, possibly more as a security measure than as a business. In any case, the dogs were known to be deer chasers, so perhaps that will come to an end at the same time as the cultivation of the psilocybin mushrooms. This is a $1.5 million operation, according to the paper, and the police waited more than twenty months to pounce, just as the guy could expect some returns on his investment, which likely was considerable. Some people will take major risks for money.

Frank thought of it first: a remarkable similarity to another Alberta enterprise that involves big money and preys on the gullibility of uninformed people with more money than good sense. I am speaking about the elk farms in the province that harvest summer antlers which sell for high prices as an aphrodisiac. The game-ranching industry doesn't like that word. When they have to admit the reason for the antler market, they prefer something like "reputed medicinal properties." And herein lies one major difference between raising elk and raising hallucinogenic mushrooms. The mushrooms contain a drug, which brings them under a drug act, and makes them highly illegal. Powdered elk antler contains no drug and not much of anything else and therefore is as legal on the market as oil or wheat or most other kinds of mushroom. The magic-mushroom grower lives under stress and secrecy and in the end stands to be registered at a bed and breakfast place in Fort Saskatchewan, at the taxpayer's expense. The elk rancher gets grants from the government and legislation to make it legal (not moral), and if his animals become infected with disease and have to be destroyed, he becomes an instant millionaire via the compensation from the taxpayer. The taxpayer just can't win.

All this makes me think of a story about the rhinoceros and his horn. It is this animal's horn that has put him on the endangered list. Thousands have been killed just for that horn, which is a double whammy for the rhino as it is exceptionally valuable on two counts: first as a dagger handle in a land where the rhino has been extinct for centuries, and as an aphrodisiac in a lot of other places. Now the rhino's horn is composed of compressed hair, and hair is mainly a substance called keratin. Keratin is what your fingernails are made of. So why pay big dollars for powdered rhinoceros horn? Save a rhino! Learn to chew your fingernails. Or you could chew each other's.

The mushroom grower runs afoul of the law, the game-ranching industry is booming, and the poor old rhinoceros faces extinction— all because people are never satisfied. What a strange world this is!

THE JOLLY JACKRABBITS
April 24, 1984

Once, in the days when I hauled hay with horses, I had a most interesting insight into jackrabbit life and behaviour. I was coming home with the last load on a winter evening. The sun was down and not quite a full moon was well up in the eastern sky, so the light was a combination of twilight and moonlight. The trail led off the meadow into a small, natural clearing before going through a wooded area. On the edge of this clearing, as I approached, I saw a couple of jackrabbits jumping about in the snow. It was early winter, not mating time, and out of curiosity I said,"Whoa" to the horses and stopped to watch the antics for a minute.

The hyperactive animals paid me no attention, although they were only twenty paces away. Getting near to wild animals was often much easier when I drove horses. As the twilight deepened and the moonlight took over, more rabbits appeared, whether from off the hay field or out of the bush I never knew. In a few minutes, there were eight of them, bounding about, chasing each other in circles and figures of eight, and frequently leaping over one another. It was perfectly obvious to me that they were playing, having fun, enjoying a sociable get-together in the moonlight, in an arena no larger than my front lawn. I only went on when my horses got restless and I began to feel the winter chill seeping through my parka.

This was the first time I had seen that many jacks in one spot, and it was the most I had seen together until last month on the

Little Bow River, when I saw much larger groups. The rabbits I am writing about, and the ones I saw on the Little Bow, are members of the species *Lepus townsendii*, otherwise known as the white-tailed jackrabbit. The scientific name used to be *Lepus campestrus*. An adult male is 60 cm long (about 2 feet) and will weigh 3.5 kg (2.2 pounds per kg). Females are slightly smaller. I have clocked more than one jackrabbit in the headlights at 35 mph and that without pushing him as I did not want to risk his life. If a jackrabbit is going flat out, he takes long, low leaps, yet hardly seems to touch the ground. Kerry Wood once measured a jackrabbit jump of twenty feet, three inches (convert if you wish). Longer jumps have been measured but most are much shorter than that. If a jack is running from something but not particularly frightened, every so often he makes a high jump for a look around. The greater the danger behind him, the fewer the high jumps.

Jackrabbit tracks, like those of other hares and rabbits, are fairly distinctive in that the marks of the hind feet are ahead of those made by the front feet, and the set of four seem to point back the way the animal came. While the jack is much larger than his cousin—the snowshoe hare, *Lepus americanus*—the snowshoe hare has bigger hind feet, and tracks are easy to differentiate.

The third Alberta rabbit is the cottontail, *Sylvilagus nuttalli*. His name is different because he is a true rabbit, not a hare like the other two. The cottontail is the smallest of the three and the most southerly. While the snowshoe or varying hare is the animal of the north woods, and the jackrabbit range now extends north of Edmonton, the cottontail likes the short grass prairie to the south. It ranges north up the Red Deer River valley to Delburne, possibly to Red Deer. I have never seen one in the central part of the province, but I shall not be too surprised if someday soon I do.

SAW-WHET OR TREE FROG?
April 12, 1994

I have a naturalist friend with whom I often exchange information about the comings and goings, the activities and antics, of wildlife on our back forties and in our respective areas in general. We were talking on the phone one evening in early spring. "The tree frogs are out," he said to me. "I heard one peeping after dark tonight." I was puzzled by the statement. Not only are there no tree frogs in Alberta, early March was rushing the season by several weeks for any frog. I was wondering what he had heard.

"What do you mean, tree frogs?" I asked him. "There are not supposed to be tree frogs in western Canada."

"This has to be a tree frog," he answered. "It sounds just like the ones on the tape, and there is no water out there in the woods where I heard it."

"What does this frog sound like?" I asked. "Can you do an imitation?"

"It is a single note, rather high-pitched, repeated over and over," he said. Before he was finished telling me, I began to simulate the call into the phone. "That's it," he exclaimed, with just a trace of excitement. "So you know it, too."

"Sure, I know it, but it isn't a tree frog." I was restraining an impulse to laugh, trying to figure out how to break the news gently. My mother had taught me that it was not polite to laugh at another's honest mistake.

"If it isn't a tree frog, what is it?" asked my friend, scepticism in his voice.

"It's a saw-whet owl," I told him. "I have heard them calling at this time of the season for years."

"It doesn't sound like an owl. It sounds like a frog, a tree frog." I knew that he wasn't convinced, but I had planted the seeds of doubt, and I knew I had planted them on fertile ground. He wouldn't rest until he had settled the thing one way or the other. For the following nights and weeks, through March into April, he traced that sound until he eventually saw the creature that made it, a saw-whet owl.

All this took place many years ago. I had learned much from this well-read and keenly observant naturalist, and I was happy that this time I had been able to return the favour.

The saw-whet owl is a very small owl, which may be why it peeps instead of hoots. Like most owls, it is an early nester, and begins its monotonous mating song as early as late February. Its nesting site in the wild is often a cavity excavated in a large tree in a previous year by a pileated woodpecker. It will use any suitable cavity and may be induced to nest in man-made nest boxes.

I fear that in 1994 a great many saw-whet owls, along with the woodpeckers that provided them with nest sites, will find that their habitat has disappeared by reason of extensive logging throughout Alberta's woodlands. Forest birds deprived of habitat must eventually perish. They cannot simply concentrate their numbers elsewhere.

MOOSE IN THE FENCE
November 12, 1996

Barbed wire twangs. There is a soft thud, then silence. A young moose has entangled himself beyond his own ability to escape, held fast in an unnatural position by the strands of a new, tight, four-wire fence. His mother, a few paces ahead of him, had cleared the fence with a graceful leap. Junior is small, less experienced. His left hind foot goes between the second and third wires, bringing him up short in a very ungraceful descent on the other side. He ends up on his back, completely helpless, his hoof pointing skyward, held by two taut wires on either side of the lower leg. He will not survive for long in this predicament.

But this youngster is lucky. He is right beside a well-used county road and in plain view of any traveller on that road. Still, it is several minutes before traffic appears, in the form of a pick-up truck. "What on earth ...?" asks the driver, as he slows and stops beside the distraught animal. The moose is not struggling. It is not his nature to do so.

The man sees at once that it is still very much alive. Another truck approaches, slows and stops. "What can we do?" asks that driver.

"I have pliers," replies the driver of the first truck. "Phone Jack and tell him I am going to cut two of his wires." A cell phone appears. Jack is there in minutes, with a tractor on which is mounted a front-end loader. Presumably he also has brought some short lengths of wire and wire stretcher to repair the fence.

In the meantime, the two men first on the scene approach the young animal cautiously. They know that this is a risky operation. A trapped and very frightened wild animal deserves the utmost respect. One wire is snipped, then the second, but the young moose remains still, awaiting what fate he knows not. His foot is still between wires and must be freed. He cannot be left to disentangle himself, which he could probably do now, for he might lie there, disoriented, soon to die.

A length of rope is brought from one of the trucks and looped over the foot. A wire is raised and the leg pulled free. The men quickly put distance between themselves and the animal, which rolls to an upright position, then gets unsteadily to its feet, like a newborn. The hoof will not bear weight, but buckles under. It could well be "asleep," having been cut off from circulation for a time. As the men watch, the moose takes a few steps, hobbling along the fenceline for a few paces. As the seconds go by, the leg and foot seem to regain some of their usefulness, and a minute later the animal trots into the poplar forest, still limping painfully, but fully mobile. He will soon rejoin his mother. It is to be hoped that he has learned something, so that he will not again find himself in such a plight. Next time there might be no rescue.

When I was a boy and for some time after, moose had not learned to jump fences. And most fences those days were only two wires. Into or through, but not over, was their way, tearing the wire from a dozen posts if they were going the right way, often breaking it if they were not. This was actually safer than jumping, since they would be unlikely to ensnare themselves.

The story above is a heartwarming one, the most recent (October 1996) of several such tales I have heard over the years. I don't like to think about the animals that are found too late, and written off as fence kills.

THE ELUSIVE SIDE HILL GOUGER
February 13, 1963

I had a phone call one morning not long ago. A feminine voice which I could not identify asked me to describe a side hill gouger, mentioned in a previous column. I hedged, wishing to know who was on the other end of the line before I divulged the requested information, but the lady didn't stay to listen.

However, she seemed genuinely puzzled, which, when I stop to think about it, is not at all surprising, as side hill gougers are never seen by people who don't take the trouble to look for them, and if they don't know them, how can they look for them?

Never very common, this very strange creature shuns man as does no other critter except the Abominable Snowman of the high Himalayas. The gouger has been forced back into areas so remote that he has never even seen a 1080 bait.

A side hill gouger is hard to describe, for even if you are lucky enough to encounter one, you never get a really good look at him. He is not at all photogenic, and only in rare instances does he appear in the sunlight, preferring misty, overcast days for his perambulations. A thick fog suits him even better. In fine weather, he is sometimes glimpsed at dusk on the shady side of a mountain, or on moonlit nights.

Many an old-time woodsman or prospector has claimed to be familiar with the habits and appearance of the side hill gouger, but their descriptions vary widely. In general, the following should serve to identify the species. In size the gouger is much bigger than a small dog but much smaller than a large dog. His tail is neither long nor short, and his colour is a dull neutral, about the shade of an old stump.

In fact, his one distinguishing feature is that which gives him his name. His two left legs are shorter than his right legs, so that he has to travel along a slope, and furthermore, is confined to travelling in one direction only—counter-clockwise.

In early days, side hill gougers were sometimes found well out into level country, having followed the ruts made by the Red River carts across the plains. With their right feet in the rut they trotted off the miles at a great rate.

In Montana the side hill gouger is known as a side hill dodger, while in the high peaks around Mount Assiniboine lives a species known as the Rocky Mountain gouger, which has legs of four different lengths. That is, the left front leg is shorter than the left hind leg, and the same goes for the longer right legs. The Rocky Mountain gouger, then, not only has to travel on side hills, but also has to always travel uphill. If he tries to go downhill he invariably ends up going head-over-heels, so when he gets to the top of a mountain he stays there until he gets hungry, then has to back carefully down, a tedious business. For this reason, Rocky Mountain gougers are only found in the very high country. They never back more than halfway down a mountain.

All side hill gougers are descended from the Glyptogon, a prehistoric, reptile-like monster that wasn't much different from other dinosaurs, except that it lived on the hillsides. This trait saved the Glyptogon from extinction when the Rocky Mountains were formed. All the dinosaurs around Drumheller got buried in the mud and ooze as the plain sank into the great inland sea, but the Glyptogon, on higher ground, survived, and it is rumoured that a few still exist on top of Castle Mountain, where they are sometimes seen against the skyline by travellers along the Banff-Jasper Highway.

LAND AND SKY

THE DANCING DEADMEN
November 9, 1966

The Dancing Deadmen have been active on several occasions during September and October, and more than once when I have been an observer the choreography has been fantastic and varied, running the gamut from a slow waltz to a polka, from ballet to the watusi.

The Dancing Deadmen is the name given by the Eskimos long ago to the aurora borealis. They believed the restless lights in the sky overhead were the spirits of departed Eskimos cavorting and making merry.

This belief was just about as plausible and much more colourful than the one that the supposedly educated white man was setting forth a surprisingly short number of years ago. The auroral capers, he theorized, were due to the reflection of the sun's light off the polar ice cap, or from Greenland's icy mountains.

In recent years, scientists have discovered that the aurora is the product of disturbances on the surface of the sun coinciding with disturbances in the earth's magnetic field and reacting on gases in our upper atmosphere. Height of aurora is easily measured by triangulation, and sixty or seventy miles is about usual. Colour varies with height, the reds being very high.

Scientists have a great deal yet to learn about this spectacular phenomenon, and they are going about it in many ways, using many complicated methods and instruments. The aurora are being photographed by night and checked with radar in the daytime. Rockets are sent into them from the base at Churchill, and they are being produced in miniature in the laboratory.

It is important to learn everything possible about the northern lights because when the Deadmen commence their dance they can play havoc with radio communications around the hemisphere.

The northern lights take many forms. They may appear as nothing more than a glow in the northern sky; more often they take the form of an arc, sometimes with discernible movement, sometimes without. Sometimes the observer will see isolated rays or streaks of light, usually with thrusts of light along their length. Again, the light may be seen as a spot or a patch.

Well-known is the curtain effect, with ripples undulating along the curtain. Now and then they appear as flames dancing and leaping along a line that has been likened to an advancing prairie fire.

The corona form is seen when the lights are directly overhead, with rays radiating to all points of the compass.

The Dancing Deadmen can provide spectacular entertainment when viewed in black and white, but when they perform in colour they may rank with the wonders of the universe—rippling, shimmering, white and yellow curtains fringed with green and violet, and above the curtain a mass of pulsating, rosy red light that blots out the stars.

I have seen this red aurora cover the entire sky from horizon to horizon in every direction, and once, on January 24, 1949, I saw it so intensely bright that it was visible even in the twilight before the stars had appeared. It lasted all night on that occasion, and was seen from Manitoba to British Columbia. It was 20 below here at the time, but I spent a good bit of the evening outdoors.

Lucky indeed is the person in these latitudes who sees the aurora in such magnificent display. It is a sight to wring wonder from the most scientific mind.

But the scientific explanations tend to minimize the mystery and awe that has always been associated with an auroral performance. Perhaps it is time, now that we know a little of their nature, to begin referring to the aurora borealis once again as The Dancing Deadmen.

ROCKHOUNDS AT GENESEE BRIDGE
October 20, 1987

I straighten my aching back and look about me for a moment. I am seated on a large stone at water's edge. Before me the river flows swiftly, not swiftly as over rapids, but about as fast as a long-legged man might walk. The river is the North Saskatchewan. I am just a mile or two upstream from the Genesee Bridge, within the sound of the church bells at the St. John's Boys' School. I am quite sure it was their bells that we heard in the distance last night about 9:30.

The river flows south here and a little west, but turns southeast against a high, unstable bank that is slumping soil and trees and a seam of coal into the water below. There are tracks in the mud at water's edge, tracks of beaver and coyote, mink and skunk, moose and deer. Small flocks of Canada geese fly up and down the valley, not yet rising into the migration flight. A few mallards and teal are also still about; and I repeatedly saw three kildeer, plus a lesser yellowlegs and a solitary sandpiper hunting in the muddy margins, for the river shows signs of frequent fluctuation, probably due to regulation on the upstream dams.

Although it is well into October, a few flowers are still in bloom: asters and fleabane, the odd dandelion and the ubiquitous, scentless mayweed. Trees are mainly bare except for a willow-covered island between the main river and an old side channel, where remaining top leaves on the thick growth turn the island orange. Last night the coyotes howled from among the entering ravines on the other side of the river as we sat around a campfire telling bear and other stories. Above the river on this side is flat farm land of rich alluvial soil.

I am sitting with my rubber-booted feet in the water, my gold pan in the space between my knees. I bend again to my task, dipping the gravel-filled pan to the water, tipping, swirling, shaking—agitating the contents so that the coarse gravel, then the finer stones are washed over the edge, leaving only the sand. I repeat the process again and again, with more care as the sand diminishes. Finally, I am left with only a tiny amount of black sand, perhaps a quarter of a teaspoon. I swirl the last few drops of water over this, spreading it over the burn-darkened bottom of the metal pan, and I see what I have been looking for—six or eight tiny flakes of gold, plus a line of flour gold. It isn't much, but it's the best I've done yet this morning.

I am here on an outing with the Rimbey Rockhounds. Eight of us camped here overnight in recreational vehicles. Down river from me, Lester is shovelling gravel into a small sluice box. It will be a while before he knows how well he is doing. Beyond him, John is bent over his pan. He seems very interested in the contents. This should be a good spot for panning, as someone has been all along the shore here with more sophisticated equipment, sluicing the gravel back from the water until the overburden of the crumbling bank made the workload prohibitive. We easily find the few shovelfuls needed for our pans, but, as I straighten my back once more,

269

I conclude that panning for gold in the North Saskatchewan River will never make me rich. Even as a hobby, I think I shall pursue it only occasionally and in easy doses.

THE NOISY LAKES
November 18, 1954

November always seems to me the quietest month of the year out-of-doors. It is probably no quieter than the cold, quiet months to come, but only seems silent after the hubbub of summer and of autumn.

There are sounds to hear, of course, if you just listen. A prairie chicken, or a dozen of them, talking across a field at sunrise; some magpies and jays berating an owl in a thicket of spruce; a squirrel chittering behind you, and a chickadee saying "Dee" three times in front of you.

These and other sounds you may hear in November. You may hear them in December or February, too, but there is one sound of the outdoors that belongs to November alone, in this part of the world at least. It is a hollow, rolling, echoing, far-carrying sound that cannot be accurately described. It is the booming of the lakes at freeze-up. The noise is made by the cracks forming under the pressure in the ice of a lake, or pond, or slough, when the ice has been frozen to a depth of some inches.

A crack may shoot across the surface of a small lake with a report like a cannon shot. Snow on the ice will muffle the sound, and it may reach your ears like an underground explosion. It may be loud as thunder or soft as an owl hooting. The first time you hear it, you may not know what it is, but forever after you will remember it. Its varying qualities depend on many things: temperature and atmospheric conditions; size and position of the lake, together with your distance and direction from it; amount of snow; thickness of the ice and depth of water; and whether the shores are open or wooded.

I discovered a small, spruce-rimmed lake once, just by following the booming sounds to their source. I walked out on the ice which was about seven inches thick, and so clear that I could see the water bugs swimming beneath it and the water lily roots on the lake bottom. Suddenly, a crack shot down the ice from right under my feet, with a report like a high-powered rifle. I scooted for a mossy shore, even though I knew that ice to be as safe as a cement sidewalk.

Within fifteen miles to the west and northwest of where I live, there are about forty of these lakes and ponds, varying in size from little three- to five-acre ones, up to 160-acre Island Lake and two-mile-long Medicine Lake. If you are out there in November, you can hear them in all directions, booming and rumbling away. Sometimes I can even hear the thunder of Buck Lake, several miles to the northwest.

NOVEMBER
November 18, 1959

It is November, by tradition the dreariest month of the year. A sad and quiet month outdoors; nothing growing; no singing birds; no flowers. The sun is brief and low and distant. Frost in the ground; ice on the pond; snow in the air.

Our northern autumn is over; summer is far behind; spring a far-off time in either direction. Next month is a festive month; last month a busy one. November is a month of in-between; of transition; the month of freeze-up; of nature going to sleep.

Yet not all November's moods are sad and sombre and subdued. For November has her livelier moments, her splashes of colour and motion.

All plant growth is dormant. For the annuals of life have been infinitely— almost unbelievably—condensed into a very tiny, very dry, very durable thing called a seed. Perennials, having produced seeds or not, have compressed life into their root systems, while trees and other plants with woody stems have drastically reduced their water content. Even so, some trees, especially poplars, will be split by the frosts of deep winter.

Small rodents are snug in insulated nests. Some are already in hibernation. Porcupines have been reduced to a diet of pine and willow bark after a summer in the grain fields. Beaver, their busy season over, are imprisoned but safe beneath the pond ice.

Early winter is the time of uncertainty for the weasel and the snowshoe rabbit. The first snowstorm may find them conspicuous in a summer coat of brown, but if November goes by without snow, they'll be more conspicuous still in winter pelage of snowy white against a brown and snowless landscape.

Game animals in November are harassed and gun shy. The deer that last mid-summer looked back at you from a little distance are now alarmed at the slightest sound and bound away in great, frightened leaps.

The cheerful, friendly robin has left for a softer climate, but his place is taken by the equally cheerful, equally friendly, pine grosbeak.

271

They are the robins of November, rosy red and burnished brown on the dry, dead delphinium stalks. Their cousins, the evening grosbeaks, adorn the Manitoba maples, yellow and black and white in the frosty dawn.

Birds return to the feeding station. They come with the first fall of snow, revealing memories that reach back at least to the previous spring. Bluejays come looking for wheat and the heads of dark, ripe sunflower seed. Redpolls, jewelled heads flashing in the pale morning sun, are hungry for weed seeds. Canada jays and chickadees and two quarrelsome, downy woodpeckers come seeking the suet bags.

Out in the fields and woods, if we are lucky and observant, and keen of vision, we may sight a snowy owl on a fence post, or a raven flying low, the one from the Arctic tundra, the other from northern forests or western mountains.

Even more rarely seen are the flocks of white-winged crossbills, birds of exotic plumage, showing little fear of man, shredding spruce cones with bills unsuited to any other purpose.

And when the first fall of new snow covers the ground, a walk through the November woods will tell us that nature is not so much asleep as we supposed. Tracks and trails in the snow reveal much about what goes on out-of-doors that we would not otherwise be aware of.

WILDERNESS LAKE, JUNE AND NOVEMBER
December 4, 1979

What a difference the seasons make to the appearance, the atmosphere, the very ecosystem of a wilderness lake! Here I am walking where I so recently glided in a red canoe, and all is different; the colours, now mute; the bird sounds, now stilled; the temperature much lower. November puts a whole different perspective on this 140-acre lake in the wilderness that I have known and enjoyed for thirty years now, in winter, spring, summer and fall.

I think back to a day in June. The afternoon sun is high in the heavens. The lightest of breezes makes patches of dark ripple on the lake's farther side, toward the beaver dam. Our canoe leaves a wake that survives our passing for a longer than usual period of time, so still is the air and the water. A long-billed marsh wren scolds us as we pass by the impenetrable cattail clump, where the enclosed nests, made from last season's cattail seed, and which we can see near the margin of the stand, are all false ones. The one where her

272

eggs are hidden will not likely be where we can reach it from a canoe. At the next clump, a red-winged blackbird berates us as intruders. Marsh marigolds are still raggedly blooming where ice lay late, while the pond lily buds, purple and perfect, can be seen below the water surface.

A muskrat leaves his own smooth wake as he goes about muskrat business. Near the north shore, grebes gabble and a loon hollers to tell us, "Canoeists go home." We glide quietly and easily, almost lazily around the circumference of the lake, photographing the loon's eggs, peering into redwing nests and generally making a nuisance of ourselves. We rest our paddles and listen to bursts of song from a ruby-crowned kinglet in the black spruce swamp.

Now, a surprisingly short time later, it is mid-November. The afternoon sun hangs in among the spruce tops, pushing their elongated shadows far out across the frozen surface. I walk the perimeter this time, on an eight-inch thickness of water turned to rock, for that is exactly what ice is, and the present surface of this muskeg lake is every bit as interesting as its unfrozen surface was in June. Lightly depressed lily pads make beautiful impressions here and there, and the geometric patterns on the ice surface are worthy of a modernistic floor-covering design. Everywhere there are fractures, glistening in the sunlight as you pass over, and they are continually being made with strange accompanying hydroponic booms.

A wilderness lake, 1976. Andy MacKenzie's 20-30-acre hay meadow, under this lake, was flooded by a beaver dam built in the 1950s.

Though I can walk amongst the cattails now, there are no redwings or marsh wrens here to care; no sight or sound of a living thing, only past signs, tattered nests, frozen muskrat roofs, a lynx track in a bit of snow by an abandoned beaver lodge, a coyote's paw marks frozen into ice near the north shore. Were one to look beneath the ice, however, life would be in evidence there.

Shadows cover most of the lake surface by the time I get around. One day soon, snow will cover the ice, and this brief, fascinating period in the lake's year will give way to yet another, longer, colder, but equally thought-inspiring. Before I know it, the redwings and the marsh wrens, the loons and the grebes will be calling once again.

CHRISTMAS WEATHER
December 17, 1958

What kind of weather can we expect for the Yuletide holiday? What will Christmas be like? Cold or snowy? Sunny, with hoar frost on the trees? Or will the weatherman make us a last-minute present of a beautiful warm chinook? I'm afraid I can't tell you. Nor, I fear, can the Indians on the Kootenay Plains, or Dr. Chase's *Almanac*, or even the *Country Guide*.

But if I can't forecast the weather for Christmas, I can go back over my records and tell you what our Christmases have been like since 1944.

That year Christmas morning heralded the first really cold weather of the season, a cold snap of fifteen days' duration. In 1945 Christmas was just another winter day, weather-wise, with above zero (Fahrenheit) readings. Christmas 1946 missed being a beautiful day by just twenty-four hours. December 24 was sunny and 44 degrees above from morning 'til evening—a genuine chinook. But on Christmas Day the weather was heavily overcast with light fog and 20 degrees above.

Nineteen forty-seven, however, produced Alberta's mildest Christmas since 1919. The high here was 52 degrees. It was 56 at Rocky Mountain House, 53 at Calgary and 50 in Edmonton. There was very little snow.

We were back to normal again, temperature-wise, on December 25, 1948, but it was a black—or brown, or green—Christmas that year. No snow until January 1. In 1949 the day was marked by a weak chinook that sent the thermometer to 27 above, one of the few breaks in a six-week-long, cold spell that proved to be one of the severest on record in the history of the continent.

Alberta had the best Christmas weather in Canada in 1950. White from Calgary north; sunny and 30 above here. Very ordinary weather for Christmas in 1951, with a high of 19 and not much sunshine.

Christmas 1952 was green again—or brown, or black—sunny and 32; almost autumn-like. And the following year, 1953, it was also snowless on Christmas Day, 34 above and partly sunny. Winter and snow came that year on December 27.

Two snowless Christmases in succession must have been something of a record, but it was evident by Christmas Eve, 1954, that Santa and his reindeer were going to find it tough sledding in our region for a third straight year. However, the day itself, although it started out as a brown—or black, or green— Christmas, ended up a bit on the grey side, with dull skies and a light skiff of snow. Prior to December 25 that year, we were basking in a record-shattering warm spell, with highs around 60 on December 21. It was 62 in Rocky on that date.

Much different was Christmas 1955, with plenty of snow and sub-zero readings. Next year was warm again—48 above and mostly sunny. Nineteen fifty-seven gave us fine winter weather over Christmas and into the New Year, with highs around 30 and all the sunshine we could hope for during the shortest days. Christmas 1958—Who-o-oa! I'm getting ahead of myself.

But whatever the weatherman has in store for us this year, you can see that we have had some really wonderful weather in Christmases past, and none that was at all nasty.

And I am going to make one prediction after all. Indoors, with all the excitement among the small fry, all the gladness that comes of the getting together of families, all the Christmas music and lights, and all the wonderful things to eat and the crackers to pull, and the beautiful tree sheltering all those mysterious and exciting parcels, it will be a bright and cheery Christmas Day, whatever the weather outside.

And from "West of the Blindman,"
A MERRY CHRISTMAS!

WINTERS OF OLD
January 2, 1996

I have a much younger friend who likes to kid me about the olden days, when the winters were really rough; how my generation had to walk five miles to school, uphill both ways, and through five feet of snow. I just smile and tell him we'll get one of those winters again one of these times, and a whole generation won't know how to cope. I don't mind the kidding, but I don't dare to tell him how close it is to the truth.

It was actually only four and a half miles to Iola School, and I walked it many a time when I was in grade nine, and there was uphill both ways, although I have to admit that they were different hills. Sometimes I skied, and that was much faster. Then, when I rode my pony, I could make it in an hour, easily. Walking took at least twenty minutes longer.

As for the five feet of snow, that would have been one of the easy winters. I remember walking for the mail after one blizzard, and I could walk back and forth over the telephone wires, and that was not the barbed wire phone, and the wires were not down. They were fastened to the insulators and the insulators were on the poles where they were supposed to be, and the ground was far below. I can't say precisely how far, but at least twice five feet. That was after the blizzard of March 15, 1951. Amazingly, the telephone still worked. Fortunately, I didn't have to walk to school. I think it was closed for a few days, and, anyway, I hadn't gone for about ten years.

Despite the gale force wind that blew on that occasion, my recollections tell me that we had a good deal less wind in those winters than we have in the 1990s. Most old-timers I talk to corroborate that observation. I had considered that perhaps I was less aware of wind when I was young. Maybe it was little Freddie, rather than the winter that was tougher then, and perhaps the wind's bite had less effect on my exposed skin. Certainly there were more trees to provide protection from whatever the winds that blew.

One thing I can say for sure: I have never liked any wind above the level of a breeze, summer or winter. Strong wind, if I have to be out in it, makes me owly. Windy days I have always tried to spend indoors. That went double when the thermometer ranged far into the minus figures. Cold I could get used to, but cold and wind combined made me owly and growly.

I remember a winter when the thermometer did not get above zero F, for the whole month of January, and the *Edmonton Journal* printed up fancy certificates whereby you could declare yourself a survivor of that bitter month.

At the beginning of winter, a few years ago, I was in Jackson, Mississippi, and I had a discussion about Canada's weather with a native of that city. "I cannot imagine, I cannot conceive in my mind what forty below would be like," he told me, "and I don't ever want to know." I am becoming a little like that Mississippian. At forty below, I don't go for my mail.

The Journal
EDMONTON, ALBERTA

I WAS THERE

This Certifies That

DONNA AND BILL BAERGEN

lived through Edmonton's
record cold spell Jan. 7 - Feb. 1, 1969

Daily High and Low Temperatures Recorded at Edmonton Industrial Airport

	H	L									
Jan. 7	-6	-14	Jan. 12	-18	-26	Jan. 17	-10	-16	Jan. 22	-16	-35	Jan. 27	-22
Jan. 8	-11	-21	Jan. 13	-10	-24	Jan. 18	-13	-22	Jan. 23	-13	30	Jan. 28	-20
Jan. 9	-18	-25	Jan. 14	-11	-18	Jan. 19	-16	-22	Jan. 24	-6	-31	Jan. 29	-23
Jan. 10	-16	-23	Jan. 15	-13	-20	Jan. 20	-16	-31	Jan. 25	-9	-18	Jan. 30	-22
Jan. 11	-14	-24	Jan. 16	-12	-25	Jan. 21	-15	-31	Jan. 26	-15	-25	Jan. 31	-11
												Feb. 1	-10

Edmonton Journal *certificate, 1969.*

SHOVELLING SNOW
February 6, 1996

Winter on the farm, half a century ago, was hauling: transportation of farm-related loads on sleighs, with a team of horses, and later with a tractor hooked to the same set of sleighs. Hay, straw, grains (both whole and chopped), firewood and manure; these were the major cargos. Whatever the load, wherever I went, I carried two important tools—an axe and a scoop shovel. If I spent most of my time hauling in winter, those hours included a large proportion of time using one or the other of those indispensable items.

277

If I had a dollar for every ton of snow I have shovelled, I could retire from retirement and spend next winter where there was no snow to shovel. I shovelled snow off haystacks and straw stacks. I shovelled hard-packed drifts from in front of the granaries so that I could get close enough to shovel on a load of grain. I shovelled my way back onto the trail after the sleigh runners had slipped off into deep, soft snow, and I shovelled out the tractor when it slid off the packed trail. On an east west trail, the late winter sun shone against the north side of each track, softening the snow and allowing the runners to "cut off." This usually happened on the way home with a load, and it made for hard pulling. If there was no shady spot ahead, where the situation would right itself, the shovel might be the only answer.

I shovelled a track from garage to road after the snowplough had gone by, and shovelled back the ridge of snow that it had left across the lane entrance. Sometimes it was a roof that had to be relieved of its burden of snow. Sometimes it was lumber piles that had to be shovelled off. It seemed that every day there was snow to be shovelled somewhere.

If the creek flooded and the crossing became ice, then you had to shovel snow onto the trail to give the horses some footing, usually after you had gone to work on that ice with an axe to chip some roughness on which the horses' hooves could gain some purchase. Sometimes, on toward spring, warm sun would bare the trail down to the dirt, and the scoop shovel came into play once more.

When there came a period when there was no snow that required shovelling, you would slip down to the pond and shovel off the large area of ice so that you and your friends could go skating in the moonlight.

I haven't mentioned shovelling out the many paths leading from the front door and the back door, or using the scoop shovel to bank snow around the house to keep the interior warmer and save on fuel. I know that there were twenty other uses for that scoop shovel in winter that I haven't thought of after all these years, and none of these would include the purpose for which that shovel was manufactured in the first place, that is, moving grain from bin to sleigh box and from sleigh to bin, or fanning mill, or grain grinder.

I have no doubt whatsoever that *Homo sapiens* had his origins in Africa, because if he had gotten his start in this part of the world, he would grow a shovel-like appendage every October and not shed it until May.

QALI, API AND PUKAK
February 1, 1978

It is no fun getting a frozen mess of *qali* down your neck. Better to walk right out in the *api* and keep away from the edge of the *qamaniq*.

Because the English language evolved in a land where snow was not a part of everyday life, it is woefully short of concise and precise words to describe the many kinds and conditions and consequences of snow. On the other hand, the Inuit and northern Indians, whose very lives might depend on the state of the snow that was with them throughout most of the year, evolved families of words to clearly distinguish each and every type and variation of snow. Wildlife biologists and other scientists studying plants, mammals, insects or anything else to do with winter in the North and how to cope with it, need to be able to describe all the modifications of the frozen water vapour that descends on earth as snow. To fill this need, they have simply gone to one of the northern languages, that of the Kobuk Valley Eskimo in Alaska, and borrowed some very interesting words.

Qali means snow that hangs in trees. *Api* is undisturbed snow on the ground out away from the trees. *Qaminiq* is the bowl-shaped depression in the snow beneath an evergreen tree. There are a dozen or so other Inuit words used to describe snow that is no longer just as it fell from the sky. *Anymanya*, for instance, is the space formed between a drift and the obstruction that caused it. Drifting snow is called *siqoq*, while the drift that forms is *kimoaqruk*.

Snow that is hard enough to walk on for fox, wolf, caribou or man is called *upsik*. This is formed when wind picks up the light, fluffy snow that is made up of complex crystals and batters these down into fine particles that pack easily. A snow-crust formed by the sun or by thawing temperatures is *siqoqtoaq*. Practice that one for a few minutes and it may seem easier to use the cumbersome English term. Snow as it falls from the sky is *anniu*.

All these types and conditions of snow have an extremely important bearing on life in the boreal forest or taiga. Mice and lemmings, for example, avoid the *qamaniq* where cold prevails. They must stay in the *api* to survive. Caribou avoid *upsik*, preferring protected areas where snow is loose and they can paw through it for sustaining herbs and lichens. Plant and insect survival is also geared to the kind of snow cover.

Life beneath the snow is in sharp contrast to life above. At the bottom of the *api*, next to the ground, is a granular layer of partly eroded snow called *pukak*. Here the lemmings of the North and the voles or meadow mice of our climatic zone live and move about under one or two or more feet of *api*, in a world of deep twilight, high humidity and almost complete silence. Even in winter, decaying vegetation can cause build-up of carbon dioxide, a heavier-than-air gas that can settle in vole runways. Then the little animals have to push an air vent through to the surface. You may notice these mouse-size holes in the surface of the snow almost any time you are out cross-country skiing or snowshoeing. Also, the gas makes the animals hyperactive, and they may go tearing around at random over the surface, exposing themselves to the owl population.

If temperatures are low, they may die anyway, of exhaustion and hypothermia.

SNOW AND HYPOTHERMIA
February 8, 1978

Ever since I have noticed my blood getting thinner, it has been my ambition to go through two summers without seeing snow in between. I know this is only a dream, so my alternative plan is always to take as much enjoyment as I can get from that cold substance which comes in so many designs, arrangements, styles, structures, colours, compactness, textures, weights, quantities, specific gravity, densities, humidity, velocities and degrees of beauty. Snow is fascinating stuff to study, but it sometimes seems unfortunate that it has to be studied out in the cold.

Snow is not often thought of as a natural resource, but it has more uses than coal. It is a blanket, a cushion, a leveller, a sponge, an irrigation system, a disguise, a playground, a refuge, a reservoir, a freeway, and it provides the economy with thousands of jobs. Snow can also be a nuisance, a burden, an impediment, a discomfort—but I am not going to list all its negative qualities. I think there have been years when I was much more aware of those negative qualities than I was of the beauty and mystery and the many benefits. I have shovelled it until my back and most of my muscles ached, day after day. I have disliked it in my pockets and down my neck and up my sleeves. I have plodded through it for long hours until I was so tired I just wanted to lie down in it and go to sleep.

I remember one instance, in particular, although it occurred decades ago. I was twelve miles along on a seventeen-mile walk home. It was night and it was cold. Snow was deep and I was getting very tired. I came to a hill, and part way up I had the strangest urge to lie down right in my tracks and rest. I had never heard of hypothermia in those days, but I had read Jack London's books about the North, and from his drastic accounts I knew the danger; so I resisted the impulse to stop and rest on that hill, and I resisted it for five more miles, and up another hill. Even after I got home to a warm house and hot food and blessed rest, I was hours getting back to my normal feeling of well-being. Had I stopped to rest on that hill, I would likely have dropped immediately off to sleep, never to wake up, just as characters in Jack London's stories had done, and as many a person has done in actual fact.

In those days, there would have been no traffic along that road I was walking, certainly not motor traffic, and on such a night not likely any horse traffic either. The newspapers would have said, "Died of Exposure."

Jack London had written that freezing to death was the easiest of all ways to die. No fear, no suffering, no resistance—a completely peaceful and non-violent death. Not only is the body numbed and unfeeling in such circumstances, but the mind as well, since the brain is being supplied by blood cooled below normal.

There have been occasions since when I have been tired, hungry, cold and sleepy, a potential victim of hypothermia, miles from home and protection from the elements of winter, but I have always remembered Jack London.

FOGBOW OVER EDMONTON
April 5, 1994

I saw a rainbow on the last day of February this year and there was no rain. I knew that this was no ordinary rainbow, although it was in the right position to be a rainbow. It was opposite the sun, and had a 42-degree radius, as with regular rainbows, but a regular rainbow would have put it to shame. Its colours were not at all bright, but appeared rather faint, as though muted by white light. In fact, all I could see at first was an arc of white against the grayed white of the cloud cover. Yet the colours were there, because the people I was with could see them. A little later, as we came under slightly more dense cloud cover, I began to see the upper or red band of the spectrum, but still could not see the inside or blue bands.

We were coming into Edmonton from the west on Highway 16 when the phenomenon was noticed, and as the time was near noon, the arch of the bow was in the north. Farther west the sky had been clear, but near Entwistle we had come under a very light, fairly even overcast, through which the sun shone with only slightly reduced strength. Within a few minutes the light began to appear diffused, and when we noticed the bow, its refracted light also appeared diffused.

How can there be a rainbow when there is no rain? It was not exactly a rainbow we were seeing, but a fogbow. I had to get home and get into the books to confirm this. However, to add to the confusion, there was no fog, none at least anywhere near ground level. This is what I think was happening. We had left Hinton that morning in temperatures that were above freezing and several degrees above those of the cold air that blanketed the Edmonton area. As that warm air blew in from the west, it overrode the cold air and either created the fog conditions above where the two layers came together, or else it turned existing ice crystal to tiny water droplets. Either way, it had to be unfrozen moisture up there to cause the rainbow effect. Fog is composed of very small water droplets that refract the light differently than do large raindrops.

At the same time as the fogbow, another light phenomenon was observed. The cloud (or high fog) outside and to the right of the fogbow, as we drove toward the city at 11 o'clock, was a pale, even pink. This, say the books, is called iridescence, and it also requires water droplets rather than ice crystals.

Ice crystals, of course, do refract light into the colours of the spectrum, red, orange, yellow, green, blue, indigo and violet. The best-known example of this is the appearance of perihelia, or sundogs, when the sun is fairly low to the horizon. These are bright spots with the rainbow colours, seen on either side of the sun at 22.5 degrees distant from the sun and at the same height above the horizon. They are caused by refraction of light from ice crystals in cirrus type clouds. Sundogs are said to foretell cold weather, but all they tell me is that it is darn cold up there in the sky where those ice crystals are.

THE WILDEST NIGHT
March 17, 1976

"The wildest night in the history of the West." So said the Edmonton Weather Office on the morning of March 16, 1951, just twenty-five years ago this month.

And it was a wild night, I can tell you, and a wild day to follow, even though we on the upper Blindman missed the full brunt of that spectacular, ripsnorter of a blizzard.

The weather office had issued storm warnings on the fine, mild afternoon of March 15, and we on this farm were well prepared. We had plenty of feed for the livestock and wood for the stoves, and we always had an adequate supply of groceries on hand in those days, for at any time during the winter a storm might keep us from getting to Bluffton for several days.

I had gone out to the meadow over a mile away to clean up the butt of a haystack, and was on my way home with half a load on the rack. The horses were lazy, the air was mild and I was in no hurry. Abruptly, at 6 p.m., the wind changed from west to due north, and snow began to fall. The temperature dropped, though not alarmingly, but the horses sensed the change and picked up their pace a bit, and I arrived home in a rather ordinary March snowstorm. We finished the chores before dark, and by suppertime it was really storming. By midnight it was down to 8 above zero, Fahrenheit, and the winds had increased to about 40 mph. In the meantime, the storm had slammed into Calgary at 70 mph with gusts to 80. Visibility in Edmonton—fifteen feet.

Our entertainment that evening was to sit by the radio and listen to the reports from across the province, and listen to the howling blizzard outside. There is a degree of excitement in a storm of this calibre, and we sat up late.

Miraculously, the telephone line remained open so that we had all the local news. Our miles of pole line were in fairly good state of repair, having been badly damaged by a storm in July 1949, and subsequently repaired.

The morning came late, with the wind still howling, snow still falling and the temperature at 3 above. The morning news told of twelve deaths from the storm in Alberta and Saskatchewan. All roads in both provinces were blocked. Our road would not be open until the snow melted in the spring. The oil companies opened some roads, but many were left to thaw. There were still many horses in use in 1951, and, of course, they could go where motor vehicles could not.

Bluffton postmaster Ben Odenbach kept the post office from overflowing by sending out all the mail he could with everybody who came in, and though our rural delivery didn't resume for weeks, we got our mail frequently.

High drifts appeared where no drift had ever been known before, and they towered ten feet high in many places, and they were so hard-packed that men and horses and even cars could go right over them and scarcely leave a track. Rudolph Littman drove his Model T into Bluffton after the storm, and there were places where one could climb over the telephone wires along our road. The train through Rimbey and Bluffton missed one day. The bus missed several. Many people still residing in this district can tell you stories about that storm. Ask Martha Lovlie, or the Kreiger boys, or Marvin Becker. There has been no storm like it to hit this area before or since, for which we are thankful.

As I sat writing this story from my weather notes of 1951, I had the feeling I was repeating myself, but I could not find any "West of the Blindman" column about the 1951 blizzard, so went ahead with it. Then I remembered. Look in *Tributaries of the Blindman* if you want to read more about that mad March night of twenty-five years ago.

THE CHINOOK
April 19, 1956

One thing we get in Alberta in great variety is weather, and of all the weather's many facets none is more famous than the chinook. Faith in the ultimate appearance of this balmy breeze from the southwest has sustained us through many a prolonged cold snap in the past. But for most of this past winter, the chinooks let us down badly. Only brief and feeble traces of them leaked through this far north. For four solid months, there was hardly a sign of the springlike breezes that in other winters have shoved the thermometer up 50 or 60 degrees in a matter of hours, or 30 degrees within minutes.

We, in the Blindman Valley, are normally within range of the chinooks. People living east of Number 2 highway and north of Red Deer feel them much less frequently and less spectacularly. This year, however, they seemed to be already in a weakened condition by the time they got through the Crowsnest Pass.

The story of how the name "chinook" came to be applied to the wind is an interesting one. It all began with the Chinook Indians, a warfaring tribe who dominated a good-sized area of the Pacific Coast and the lower Columbia River, a couple of centuries ago. They made their living partly by capturing slaves from one tribe and trading them to another, and partly by catching salmon, and drying them for food. The smell of tons of drying salmon, together with the stench from the piles of rotting entrails, was mighty powerful in combination, and when the warm Pacific breezes blew, they wafted the smell far inland, so that tribes far from the sea held their noses and exclaimed, "Chinook!" Thus the warm southwest wind was named, and whether or not it had lost its smell by the time it had passed east of the Rockies, it retained the name for so far as it blew.

A northwest wind, however balmy, is not a true chinook. A genuine chinook is usually prefaced by a chinook arch, which is almost as famous as the wind itself. Indeed, there is hardly a more spectacular sight to be seen in all of Alberta than that clear-cut, often geometrically perfect, segment of blue-green sky, pushing back the cold, gray overcast of a February afternoon. From east of south on the horizon to your left, it stretches unbroken to the northwest on your right. Gold-rimmed its upper margin, its lower edge is the sun-brightened serrations of the snow-covered Rockies.

Little wonder that the chinook wind and the chinook arch have inspired so many poems and paintings and tall tales, or that such a wide variety of ventures from fast trains to drive-ins have been named "Chinook."

The tall tales? Well, one is about the farmer who went to town with a team and sleigh. By the time he had finished his business, he noticed a chinook arch coming up. Without delaying another instant he untied his team and headed for home. Luckily, he lived east of town for he barely made it into his barnyard. By the time he got there with his horses in a lather, only his front bobs were on snow. The back ones were in the mud.

A SNOWSHOER'S DREAM
March 24, 1965

Today is March 17 and as I sit here beginning a column that will appear a week hence, I realize I have given less thought during the day to the Patron Saint of Old Ireland than I have to the unnamed Indian who invented the snowshoe—and for all I know he may have been a contemporary of St. Patrick.

It has been a day of blue skies, Arctic air, and a chilly, northerly breeze, and on the ground anywhere from sixteen to thirty inches of compact, hard, frozen snow—the kind that will support about half a man's weight before dropping him knee-deep with every step through the firm top crust into the heavy, granulated stuff beneath.

There is no time of year when a walk in the woods has less appeal for the outdoorsman—unless he owns a pair of snowshoes. With these ingenious contrivances harnessed to one's feet, there is no better time for a hike across the fields and into the woods, than during a March cold spell, following a period of warm, snow-softening weather.

285

This is the first winter for some years that I have gotten much use from my snowshoes. Other winters during the 1960s, it has taken about the same amount of effort to walk a mile with snowshoes as it has without them. For the greater part of this winter, the snow has been deep enough that it required considerable effort to go any-where across this country, even with the webs on your feet. With-out them, it was best to stay away from untrammelled snow, if this could be done.

Today, however, was the kind of day a snowshoer dreams about. Conditions were absolutely ideal, and since I had to go to a part of the farm where no vehicle has been all winter, I made the most of the opportunity and went the long way around. In fact, I spent four or five hours roaming over several hundred acres with an ease that I had never enjoyed before, for it was actually less arduous travel-ling around the farm today than it is on foot in midsummer.

Look at some of the advantages: you are above much of the underbrush that tends to hold you back in summer, although you have to duck more tree branches. Swamps are comparatively level expanses of deep snow; no jumping from hump to hump. Sloughs, beaver ponds, water courses—none of these present any obstacle. There is no mud. Rough ground does not exist for you. You walk over logs, hummocks, anthills, soft sphagnum beds, and, in many instances, even fences.

During a winter when chinooks are few, and snow is perhaps two or more feet deep and uncrusted, snowshoeing is arduous work and is barely an improvement over ordinary foot travel. Under such conditions, the snowshoer usually stays on the trail, for once bro-ken out, a snowshoe trail is easily travelled.

But this week snowshoeing is a fun thing. You get a feeling of satis-faction—even exhilaration—at being able to walk on two feet of snow with such ease. It is probably a little like walking on clouds, and reminds me of the time when I learned to ride a bicycle. Equipped with a pair of snowshoes, you can go places now that you can't reach at any other time of the year. Or you can visit favourite haunts for the first time since November, after sixteen weeks of staying on roads and paths and routes that are either packed or cleared of snow.

And every so often you look back at your trail, like the tracks of some prehistoric monster, and you know the satisfaction of having conquered, to some degree at least, one of the elements.

I should go for a walk in space? Nothing doing. I'll take a pair of snowshoes in preference to a space suit on any St. Patrick's Day.

THE SETTLING SNOW
July 21, 1965

I am writing this column in early April 1965, but because it is about snow, and because I am assuming that everybody is sick and tired of snow right now, I am not going to send this copy in for publication until snow is only a memory.

I am going to wait until July, when the nasturtiums are in bloom and the lawn needs mowing and there is no ice on the creek. July, you know, is the month of the year least likely to produce snow.

But snow does produce some interesting phenomena and it is about one of these that I am writing now. Goodness knows when I'll get another opportunity, and if it should be simmering in the 80s on the day you read this, here's hoping it has a cooling effect.

I don't know what to call this occurrence that I am about to describe, except to term it the settling snow. It happens this way. You walk out onto a large expanse of crusted snow, say a field of several acres. Suddenly, the snow about you settles, perhaps an inch or more, and this drop spreads across a large area, possibly the whole field, with a noisy, swishing sound, like a whispering avalanche, while you stand in your tracks, startled and in wonderment.

This is not a rare thing. It happens nearly every spring and is commoner when snow is deep. I have observed it many times in the past, but never have I had so much fun with it as I did on this morning of April 8.

There was a firm crust on the snow this morning, the result of a sharp frost following a mild day yesterday which had softened the snow right down to the ground.

I left the yard on snowshoes, for snow is still deep, varying from sixteen inches on the fields to two feet in the woods. Not far from the buildings there is a small pasture field where the only traffic all winter has been me on snowshoes. I had walked out only a few yards onto it this morning when I felt the crust drop about an inch, and in a second or two an acre-sized patch had settled with a swoosh. Most of the remainder of that field settled in the same way as I walked across it.

I knew that, as the morning advanced and the crusted surface of the snow began to soften, the phenomenon would be more easily triggered and the result more startling and more far-reaching. In the next field, which was larger, I did a little better, settling several acres at a time, but it was in the third field that I got the best effect. Forty acres, dazzling white under the April sun. I walked out very gingerly for several paces, then gave a little jump. About thirty of those forty acres dropped in something like seven seconds.

For the first few rods, the phenomenon is visible as well as audible. You can see the line of drop racing away from you, and I estimated the speed of this movement at about 120 mph.

The sound is difficult to describe and the words I have used above do not seem adequate. It is not a roar but it is loud enough to carry back from a quarter of a mile. It will startle horses when they start it going by stepping off a trail, as I have witnessed in years gone by when I hauled hay with a team.

I was wishing that Allan, my ten-year-old nephew, could have been with me this morning. He would have had a great time. I'm sure I wouldn't have gotten him home until we had settled every field on the farm.

SNOWBLIND ON THE BLINDMAN
September 1, 1955

Many years ago, a small party of Cree Indians were hunting in a valley well-stocked with game of every kind—moose and elk and buffalo, snowshoe rabbits and grouse and beaver, and a host of other creatures large and small. The party was some distance from their main camp, and severe hardship was to be theirs before they all returned. There is no written account of this event, but let us try to reconstruct the story from the meagre information we have.

The time of year was probably March, the "Month of Crusted Snow," when the snow was still deep, but settling and becoming heavy under a warm sun now quite high in the sky at noon. A fall of new snow had come in the night while the hunters slept. When the morning came, the sky was clear and the early sun was dazzling on the absolute whiteness of the fresh snow. The men broke camp early for they were possibly a day's journey from the others and the travelling would be hard. Also, they would be taking in some of the meat they had killed.

As the sun climbed higher in the unclouded sky, the brilliant whiteness became more intense and the hunters' eyes began to water and become sore. Still they kept on, their eyes half-closed in a permanent squint, the burning sensation becoming more severe. Long before noon, their vision blurred and the pain became severe. Eventually, they were forced to halt, for they were blind and in great distress.

Snowblindness is a terrible thing. It renders one helpless and in torment for two days and two nights, and that is what those people endured, for the story says that they all returned to their home camp.

Since that time the Crees have called the river *Paskapiw* or *Pas-ka-poo*. This can be translated as river of the blind, or Blind River, or, as we call it, Blindman River.

Just when this event occurred is not possible to say, but it was probably more than one hundred years ago. David Thompson, in 1814, called this river Wolf River. If the artist, Paul Kane, knew its name when he crossed its swollen current on a raft in the spring of 1848, he failed to mention it in his journal, but James Hector apparently knew it by that name when he crossed it in 1858. Anthony Henday, who spent a month on the Blindman River two hundred years ago (January 1755), referred to it as "a branch of the Waskesew." Waskesew meant "elk" and was the Cree name for the Red Deer River. The Stoney Indians had their own name for it: Dead Standing Timber River. So it seems that for about half of its history, this river has been known as the Blindman.

A small, quiet river as rivers go, the Blindman has its beginning in several small streams, all known as Blindman and originating in the swamps and hills of Township forty-five, in Ranges 2, 3, and 4, west of Meridian 5. It flows south into the Red Deer at that river's northern-most point on the map. An unspectacular river, it boasts no deep gorges or roaring falls, no badlands or mountain panoramas—just a peaceful, quiet beauty that sometimes leaves one almost breathless.

Across the hills to the west flows the Medicine River, which also empties into the Red Deer, and both river and valley are similar to the Blindman in many respects.

To the northeast lies the drainage system of the Battle River, longer and more varied in its wanderings than the Blindman and perhaps more famous in history. But for sheer loveliness, season by season, for amazing fertility of climate and soil, and for its appeal to the hearts of those who dwell on its gentle slopes, the Blindman Valley will vie with any in the land.

The lower part of the valley was homesteaded and settled in the 1890s. The upper portion, from Rimbey north, saw few permanent settlers until after the turn of the century, and much of the land along the river's upper reaches was not homesteaded until the 1930s. The earliest settlers came right on the heels of the buffalo. The bones of these wild cattle were everywhere and their trails were well defined. Today almost no trace of these trails remain, but an occasional skull of one of the great beasts may still be found.

It was well for the inauguration of agriculture in the Blindman Valley and in the whole Canadian West, that the buffalo had vanished by 1890. It was unthinkable that agriculture in any form could ever have been possible if even a part of those great herds had remained on the prairie. The passing of those huge, shaggy and independent animals from their former domain cannot be mourned by us.

Green is the valley's predominant hue in spring and summer and fall, green and black in May, when the soil is being prepared for seed. Squares and strips of green appear in the summer, with each kind of grain and grass and clover reflecting a different shade, all blending one with another to form a restful patchwork of growth. Green and gold is the fall with swaths of grain lying pale and ripe in the stubble, awaiting the combines.

The black and green and gold of the land is relieved and enhanced by other things: herds of beef and dairy cattle wading luxuriant pastures; prosperous farmsteads along the highways and byways; and grain elevators always in sight up the long grade of the old Lacombe Northwestern, which bisects the valley almost as accurately and with far less mileage than does the river itself.

This is the Blindman Valley: rich mixed farming country, producing meat and milk and eggs as well as grain, where the farmer lives on his land and would not have it otherwise.

But the Blindman is other things, too, and recently discovered reserves of oil and natural gas have now added to its riches. Rimbey was heard of far and wide this spring, when a gas well went wild at more points on the map than one well ever did before.

The river itself even presents a puzzle. Why does it flow through those hills that lie to the west and north of the town of Rimbey? Why doesn't it flow instead down the natural valley beside the railroad track? Was this valley full of ice some twenty thousand years ago when the river was being formed? And has the deposit of gravel at the water tank anything to do with this diversion? Some geologic occurrence must surely have been responsible for this deviation from what would seem to be the Blindman's natural course.

When the dry years come and the run-off is less than normal, and when the level of Gull Lake begins to drop, that is the signal for the revival of a rather ambitious plan to divert part of the Blindman's waters into the lake. This scheme has now been picked up and laid down so many times with changes in the weather cycle, that it is a bit difficult to determine just where it originated and when and by whom. It has lain quiet for some years now, but it may easily rise again.

Two dams were built in the valley some forty years ago to provide electric power for nearby areas. One, at the scenic mouth of the river, actually had the turbines on the site when the earth fill was carried away by a flood and the venture abandoned. The other was on the outlet from Gull Lake. It was blown up by persons unknown for reasons that were obvious. Hundreds of acres of lakeshore meadow were threatened with inundation. If both these dams were financed by the same promoters, misfortune certainly was theirs.

Getting back to the gravel pit at the water tank, gold was found in the river there many years ago. This precipitated a small gold rush, and a number of claims were staked in the vicinity. The gravel was supposed to have assayed about three dollars per cubic yard. The excitement has long since died and the gold was left in the river.

But the wealth of the Blindman is not of the kind that is measured in ounces per yard. It is measured, instead, in bushels and tons per acre of grain and hay; in cents per pound of beef and pork and butterfat; in poultry and eggs and honey and wool; in seeds of clover and grasses, and even in willow fence posts.

This is more permanent wealth than gold and more evenly distributed. There will be no ghost towns in the Blindman Valley.

APRIL
May 6, 1986

Winter hates to give up in central Alberta. It is May 1 as I write this and there are shades of April everywhere. There are patches of old snow and traces of a recent fall visible from my desk, and it isn't melting. The sky is overcast, there is ice on the puddles and the bluebirds must be hungry, for no insects are moving. All this is really quite normal for the time of the year, as I find from looking back over forty years of weather records I have kept.

We must be conditioned by the Victorian poets we had to study in school to expect more of April than we get, never realizing that those poets never knew April in Alberta. "Oh, to be in England, now that April's there," said Browning in 1845. Shakespeare, centuries earlier, made many references to April's charms, but he was

291

being somewhat more realistic when he penned a line about "the uncertain glories of an April day." Scores of famous poets have sung the praises of the month, but it was left to T. S. Elliot in this century to finally peg April for what it really is. "April is the cruelest month," was how he put it in 1922.

The last week of April this year was not exactly a pleasant one, but we did need the moisture. Last year, on the 20th, we were handed the worst April storm in thirty years, according to reports in the papers, although I debunked those reports in my column of April 30 last year. Normally, however, April is a month of very little precipitation, either in showers or in flurries, according to my records, yet the same records show that the showers and flurries are frequent, if unproductive, and are so cold and miserable that they are seldom welcome.

About half of the Aprils over the years have had snow on the ground throughout. The other half have had little or no old snow by mid-month, and new snow quickly melted. Most Aprils have a few mild, warm, or even hot days. Only occasionally do the fields dry enough for the farmers to get out with the tractor and work the land. This seems in contrast with Aprils earlier in this century. Many an old-timer can still tell you that when he was a boy in the 1920s or earlier, they had a hundred acres of crop seeded by the end of April. I, myself, remember one or two such Aprils in the 1930s. I have a record of the trees in leaf by April 20. I can't lay my hands on it at the moment, but I think one year was 1934. I have a record of a different sort for 1954. That year we had a real winter for the last ten days of April, lots of snow and very cold. At the end of the stormy period, the sky cleared and the thermometer dropped even lower. When we got up in the morning of May 1, it read 4°F (-16° C), but at Clyde Lamb's place, one and a half miles south, the thermometer was below zero (-19°C) on the first morning in May. Clyde, seventy-nine at the time, likely was up and around about two hours before this household rose. He declared it to be the first time in his life time that he had ever seen sub-zero temperatures in May.

May that year went on to be a wet, cold, and horrible month for the farmers and the wet weather continued into June. The leaves didn't come out on the trees until June. May, like April, is often over-rated by the poets and can be a most disappointing month. If I were a poet, I'd write an ode to all of the Aprils and all of the Mays I've known, all of them different and all helping to make Alberta such an interesting province in which to live.

ROCKS—A ROCKHOUND'S VIEW
April 26, 1972

Any day now will find the rockhounds out in force, prowling around gravel pits, over freshly-worked fields, along streams and lake shores, up and down the canyons of the Red Deer River Badlands. Wherever there are stones, you will find them, heads down, eyes scanning as many square yards as possible, stopping now and then to pick up something for a closer look, nine times out of ten only to fling it down again. Old rockhounds will be very choosy, the pebble pups less so, and the toddlers want to take home every pebble. By summer's end, everyone will have more than enough specimens to keep them busy at the indoor phase of their hobby throughout the winter to come.

It is little wonder, when you stop to think of it, that there are so many rockhounds among us. Since the days that man first trod on this earth, rocks and stones have played such an important part in his way of life that interest in them might almost be said to be hereditary. The wonder is that there are so many people who are not rockhounds.

Rocks and stones have been the material for man's tools and for his weapons from the very beginning, and sometimes they have been his money as well. His charms, amulets, and personal adornment have often been of stone. Some rocks have been home to important spirits, while some have been fashioned into gods or homes for gods. Rock has provided shelter for the living and for the dead. Man has taken selected rocks and chipped and carved and polished them into objects of beauty and utility. In ages past, he has quarried and split and drilled and hauled and hoisted huge and heavy objects of stone using methods unknown today. And because most rock is so durable, we have been allowed a glimpse into the lives of long-forgotten peoples that we could have obtained in no other way.

Here in Alberta, rocks and stones have been important in people's lives from the time men first arrived here from far to the northwest. Cutting tools and projectile points of common quartzite, basalt and slate, and of less common but more attractive stone like jasper, flint, obsidian and agate, can be found in any part of the province. Even petrified wood and dinosaur bone have been used for making Stone Age artifacts here in Alberta. Rougher and less-easily-worked stones such as sandstone, granite and less-well-known varieties were used for such things as hammers, choppers, grinders, canoe anchors, horse and dog hobbles and fish net sinkers.

The Stoney Indians had still another use for stones—one which gave the tribe their present name. Originally Assiniboines from farther east, they did their cooking by means of stones heated red-hot in a fire, then placed in a leather cooking vessel filled with water. The water boiled, the food was cooked, and the people were called Stone Boilers, later shortened to Stoneys.

Think about some of these things the next time you pick up a rock. Tell the kids about them. Most children are fascinated by stones, anyway. You might make certified rockhounds out of one or two of them.

MY TRAVELS WITH OSCAR
April 21, 1976

I wrote this little story for *Fossil Trails*, a publication of the Alberta Federation of Rock Clubs, where it appeared in the March-April issue.

My pet rock, Oscar, and I have not been hitting it off too well of late. In fact, ever since I got him, I've had nothing but trouble with him. I do as the book suggests, and take him with me everywhere I go, but all he does is take the fun out of my travels, with his strange moods, his gloomy outlook and his refusal to take any enjoyment from anything. No sense of humour at all.

The pay-off came the other weekend when I took him on a trip along the David Thompson Highway. You think Archie Bunker is a bigot? You ought to have heard Oscar. We took a side trip from Nordegg up into the Blackstone River country. I stopped at one spot to get out and take some photographs.

"Where are we, anyway?" asked Oscar.

"Looking over the Blackstone River," I said.

"Let's get outa here," he yelped. I had noticed similar racist behavior on his part when we visited Yellowstone Park and again at Red Rock Canyon in Waterton Park.

Back on the David Thompson Highway, we proceeded west toward the Bighorn Dam. "Where does that road lead?" asked Oscar, pointing off to the left.

"It just goes down there a little way to the Stoney Indian Reserve," I answered.

"!@^{~~#}+! [............] " (whole line censored).

"What was that all about?" I asked, innocently.

"As if you didn't know," he snarled. "Those so-and-sos used to boil rocks. That's how they got their name." I could see his point.

He seemed to brighten up a bit as we came deeper into the mountains. "It seems like I'm coming home," he said.

We stopped at Whirlpool Point where I planned to climb over a shoulder of Mount Cline and down to Landslide Lake for some fishing. Up above tree line, we flushed a couple of rock ptarmigan. "Stupid, dumb birds," growled Oscar. I looked at him in perplexity. I was thrilled to see the beautiful rock ptarmigan miles south of their normal range.

"What have you got against ptarmigan?" I asked him.

"Do you know where they roost at night?" was his enigmatic answer. I looked around. No trees. Just rocks. Again, I couldn't blame him, but I was annoyed anyway. I love the mountains and Oscar was spoiling my day.

"Listen, you kidney-stone from a brontosaurus," I said, "you are beginning to bug me. You are not the only pebble on the beach you know." He just sneered. "If you were soapstone," I told him, "I'd carve you into a walrus. Since you're not, I'm going to keep my eye open for a gravel crusher on the way back."

Oscar sulked all the way home.

ALBERTA'S PROVINCIAL STONE
November 9, 1977

At the same moment that the great horned owl became Alberta's bird emblem last May 18, petrified wood became Alberta's official gemstone. The two items made up Bill 10, and both items had been before the legislature for a similar length of time.

Alberta is not exactly world-famous for its gemstones, which I suppose simply means that Alberta rockhounds are faced with more of a challenge in finding and using what we do have. And we do have an interesting, even exciting, variety when one gets down to searching.

We do have a fair abundance of petrified wood, much of which is of less than gem quality. It occurs in the gravels and beds of most of our streams and everywhere in the glacial till that covers much of the province. In the Red Deer River valley and elsewhere that the glacial drift has been eroded through to the sedimentary layers, huge stumps and logs are found, most of them of inferior quality as gemstone.

Petrified wood is of many kinds, depending on how it was formed. The low-quality pieces mentioned above are partly silicified, partly carbonized, and your eye alone will tell you that some of it is closely related to coal. On the other hand, even the poor pieces often contain cracks or fissures that have been filled with chalcedony, a bluish-white, very fine-grained material, usually smooth and translucent. Chalcedony is quite common in the Red Deer River Badlands and is also found in the Hand Hills to the east of Drumheller, where it is known as Hand Hills agate. It is not necessarily petrified wood, but is commonly formed in association with wood or bone.

After carbonized wood, more desirable forms of wood petrifaction include calcified wood, silicified wood, agatized wood, and opalized wood. We have mighty little of the latter in Alberta.

Most petrifaction takes place by cell replacement. Silica or some other mineral in solution in water invades the cells of the dead organism, sets and hardens, literally turning what was once a living object into stone. *Petros* is the Greek word for stone. Petrified wood is one of the easiest fossils to recognize, as the growth rings of the original tree are usually evident. It has been used for almost a century in Alberta to decorate rock gardens, fireplaces or other stonework. Small pieces sit on basement shelves. Large pieces repose by gateposts or doorsteps all over the province. Some of the finer pieces are taken in hand by lapidarists and sawed and shaped and polished (and polished!) into tabletop slices or into beautiful jewellery. Most of the common variety is grey in colour on the outside, but many of the cut pieces are black, brown, red or variegated.

Gravel pits are often a good place to look for gem-quality wood. Stream beds are the place to look for larger pieces and the fine-quality pieces are there, too. The McLeod River is said to be one of the best for petrified wood, but the Red Deer, North Saskatchewan, and Blindman, all yield the material, as does just about any stream that cuts very deep into the glacial drift that covers sedimentary rock.

THE MONTH OF LEAFING OUT
May 20, 1964

May, the month of birdsong, blue skies, warm showers, and things becoming green. Well, you can have it.

Last year I wrote a column on May in which I demonstrated from weather records I have kept for a score of years that May is likely to be something other than the perfect month: that it has, in fact, during those twenty months, given us drought, forest fires, killing frosts, blowing dust, blowing snow, floods, erosion, zero temperatures, temperatures in the 80s, mosquito hordes, and hailstorms. The majority of those twenty May months were chilly, with too much wind, and most were either too wet or too dry.

Fortunately, there are compensations. Winter's snow is gone. Grass turns green. Days are long once more. And trees and shrubs of all descriptions clothe themselves in summer foliage, and in doing so, clothe the landscape.

I averaged up the dates for this greening up process, and I find that the first leaves should show on the poplars and birches about May 13, and that the whole countryside should be a solid, summery green by May 25. As is the case with most averages, these figures are usually one side or the other of those for any given month of May.

For instance, on three of the years considered, green-up time actually occurred in April. The earliest was April 28, 1946, and by May 7 that year the deciduous foliation was fairly complete. That May was very dry and windy.

On the other side of the picture, there were three years when the trees were not properly leafed until well on in June. The most extreme of these was 1954, when not a leaf was to be seen around these parts until June 12, and the last ones out couldn't bring themselves to face the world until June 21.

May of that year was a dilly. May Day came in with the temperature just above zero and in some of the lower areas it was below zero degrees Fahrenheit. At that it was ten degrees warmer than the morning of April 30. We went on to have one of the wettest Mays on record that year, and, of course, the mosquitoes were terrible.

So you see, while we can expect May to be the leafing-out month, there have been years when it wasn't.

If I hadn't kept those records, I suppose I would be perennially on the lookout for those clear, sunny days and soft breezes and warm spring rains that constitute the kind of weather everyone seems to associate with May, but, armed with a written account of just what each of those Mays was really like and remembering some of them into the bargain, I suppose I may be excused for not picking the fifth month as my favourite.

SNOW DAMAGE IN MAY
June 17, 1986

One spring day in the mid-1920s, my father planted a row of native pine trees across the bottom of the garden near the house. That garden became lawn about half a century ago and the old shack was put on skids and hauled away with six or eight horses. Most of the trees survived, and one, having lost its neighbour on either side,

297

had plenty of room to grow. By 1972, at the age of fifty, that tree was fifteen metres tall and just as wide. Great, spreading branches stretched right across the bottom of the lawn, dropping pine needles with every wind, and drastically thinning the grass.

Then, on April 20, 1982, a snowstorm made a shambles of that tree, breaking most of the long, lower branches and many of the middle ones. When the snow had melted, a few days later, it took a day's work to clean up the debris. Just over thirteen inches of sticky snow fell that time, but it did much damage to other trees and shrubs as well.

In the intervening fourteen years, that tree had almost recovered its good looks. It was slimmer now, but nature, which abhors a vacuum, had filled in the holes and made quite a respectable repair job.

Then came May 14, 1986. This time the weight of the snow would be more than double the 1972 fall, and once again the poor tree, now in its sixties, was badly broken. Its damage was at least as bad as in 1972 and the destruction over the rest of the grounds was far, far worse. My honeysuckle took a severe beating. My beautiful May Day tree, ten metres high and twelve metres across, just leafing out and ready to bloom, was almost flattened and the trunks broken off. The Manitoba maples, prone to split and splay in far lesser storms, did all that was expected of them this time. The huge dogwood and the hansa roses were flattened and broken. The trees that survived best were the mountain ash and the alpine fir that spreads over a good portion of the upper part of the lawn.

There are scores of spruce and pine around my yard. They dominate the area to the north of the house. Many of them lost tops and limbs, as did their kind all over central and southern Alberta. But it was out in my woods, that stretch not quite unbroken over one and a half miles, south of the creek on three quarters, that the major damage occurred. No longer can I stroll through the pine and spruce forest where I have wandered since I was old enough to walk by hanging onto my father's hand. Thousands upon thousands of those eighty- to ninety-year-old trees, approaching maturity, were topped, broken, bent, bowed, delimbed and uprooted. The devastation is difficult to describe. Even the trails are all filled in with the debris.

I have searched my records and my memory, and the memories of residents older than I, and I have concluded that the May 14 storm was the worst spring storm in sixty years and quite possibly in this century. Its effects will be evident for many years to come.

It is perhaps just as well that I waited for a few weeks after the unseasonable blast to write about it. With summer finally here, and most of the havoc cleared from around the yard, life is almost back to normal. My dismay at the amount of damage has lessened somewhat, given way to resignation.

FROST IN THE GARDEN
April 30, 1991

When my father homesteaded this land in 1921, he was told by a neighbour, Jim Freeman, "You can't even grow potatoes in this country. They freeze down three or four times in the spring and don't have time to get any size before they freeze down again in the fall." Jim Freeman was right—for where he lived, on the west branch of the Blindman, now called Anderson Creek. The Freemans ate little potatoes.

The climate was not quite so frosty on this homestead, but it was no banana belt either. One of the first things my parents did when we moved here in 1922, was to clear and break a good-sized garden patch, and over the next few years, they raised some fabulous gardens in the rich new soil. Not, however, without some discouragements. Tin cans (called tomato cans in those days, regardless of the product they contained), were always saved to cover up garden plants. If the sky cleared in the evening following rain, and the air felt like frost, the boxes of cans were carried into the garden and a tin can was placed over each young and tender plant of beans, corn, potatoes or tomatoes. If tins ran out, paper cones were sometimes made from pages of the *Winnipeg Free Press Weekly*. These were generally weighted down with a clod of dirt or a stick or a stone. Sometimes a severe frost would freeze right through this protection. Once, in June, my mother used all her two-quart sealers, emptied over the winter, to cover plants in the garden, and it froze right through them.

Another June night sometime in the 1920s, the risk of frost was especially great. Skies had cleared following a storm and as darkness came on, the thermometer dropped steadily. The garden was particularly good that year, well-advanced and doing just fine. Such gardens don't just happen. They are the result of a lot of hard work, and my parents had visions of everything being wilted and black in the morning. Then my father had an idea. In the windbreak and in the uncleared land right beside the garden lay quantities of dead wood. It was wet from the rain, but it would burn nicely once it got going. Charlie started three bonfires equidistant from each other down the centre of the garden, right in amongst the rows of vegetables. Then both my father and my mother went to work carrying out that dead wood to feed them. Most of it was pine and still sound, the result of a forest fire the decade before. All night they chopped and carried wood and fed those fires. Back at the house the thermometer showed several degrees of frost. When daylight came, around four a.m., Gertie came in and went to bed. Charlie stayed with it until the sun was high enough to bring the temperature above freezing, then he let the fires burn down and came in, too.

Most gardens in the area were severely damaged that night. The only damage to the Schutz garden was from fire.

ROCKS IN THE FIELD FOREVER
December 5, 1989

Years ago I had neighbours who believed that rocks grew in their fields. Being much younger then, and figuring if I didn't know it all, I knew quite a bit, I argued with those men, trying to explain to them the geologic origin of rocks in glacial soil. Some rocks did grow, I admitted, but the process took eons of time, not just since last spring, as they were telling me. My arguments were not persuasive enough to change their way of thinking, and when they went out on their land in the spring to haul off loads of rocks from land that had been picked clean the year before, and each spring for many years before that, they knew they were right. There was no other explanation. And, they were quick to point out, my fields were not different from theirs, and had to be picked every time they were ploughed, for rocks left on the field were a nuisance, a danger, and damaging to farm machinery, especially harvesting machinery. I subscribed to a different theory as to why a field that contained rocks was never free of them. I figured that they were pushed up by the frost, which penetrates to a depth of two metres in an open field in central Alberta. This meant that every rock in that depth of soil would appear at the surface some day as long as the field was cultivated, and would have to be hauled off if that land were to be kept rock free. It was a depressing thought, almost as much as the growth idea, for picking rocks was nobody's favourite job.

I was further depressed one day in talking to the late Fred Plank, who had just been back to the scenes of his childhood. He had visited the farm near Guelph, Ontario, where he grew up, and where he had spent many a day as a boy, before the turn of the century, picking rocks from the fields. He was astonished, he told me, to find the owners of the old farm still picking the rocks each spring. Sixty years and more of rock-picking and what had been gained? Where did they come from? Was there any end to that dirty job?

Another theory claims that gradual erosion of the top soil exposes new rocks each year, and that the plough keeps loosening another layer, but in most fields erosion takes place more gradually than the appearance of new stones.

Now a series of studies has been done in cold climates, including Antarctica, Greenland and northern Canada, but chiefly in Spitzbergen, Norway, which proves that frost not only brings rocks to the surface, but over long periods of time, arranges them in rough circles. These are called sorted circles, their centres clear of stones, and it can all be explained by the laws of physics. A variation of this phenomenon may be seen on the top of Plateau Mountain, west of Nanton, Alberta.

I shall end my dissertation on rocks with the story about the farmer who put his land up for sale. He was walking his fields one day with a prospective buyer when the man made some objection to the number of stones in the fields. "Those stones," said the farmer, "are there to hold the moisture. Just turn one over and you'll see." Sure enough, the man turned over a few rocks and there was moisture underneath, and some bugs, and a few weeds growing around the edge.

The man was still sceptical. "What about that big pile over there in the corner of the field?" he asked.

Said the quick-thinking farmer, "Oh, them. I've been so dang busy this spring I just haven't had time to get them spread yet."

SOUNDS IN THE NIGHT
June 14, 1961

There is nothing like sleeping out under the stars on a warm summer's night, under the trees and the sky—and the dew.

It is something I do infrequently, but one night not long ago I unrolled my sleeping bag beneath some poplars on a grassy hilltop; and there is one thing I can tell you: to get a good night's sleep on your first night out in the woods, you will need to be unusually sleepy; otherwise, unaccustomed noises will keep the sandman miles away.

Some of the noises you will hear are distant and not all disturbing. The far-off barking of a wakeful dog; the clang of bells on night-grazing cattle; the murmur of water over a beaver dam; these are soothing noises and actually induce sleep.

Nor will you be kept awake by a chorus of frogs in some hidden slough; or the repetitious whoo-who-who of a horned owl in the deep woods across the valley; or by the light night breezes rustling the soft new leaves on the poplars overhead.

If these were the only sounds in the night, you might sleep like the proverbial log; but they are not. There are other, closer, stealthier noises, and there are loud, startling ones too—things that go bump in the night.

First off, there will likely be an insect or two crawling and creeping amongst the dead leaves and grass roots directly beneath your ear. You can hear them as plainly as though you had tuned in on a stethoscope, and you suddenly wonder if you have laid your bed too near an ant hill.

Before you come to any conclusions on this, a rustling noise among the dry grass and stalks underneath the poplars denotes activity by a mammal, and you try to determine, from the sounds made, the size and identity of the creature. Can a tiny mouse make all that commotion, or is it a weasel, or a flying squirrel? You will likely never know for sure.

Next, the sound of wings whistling by in the darkness overhead—not one pair of wings, but several. They didn't sound just like ducks, yet you can't say what they were.

Down the hillside a piece, a small bird lets out one cheep, as though something had frightened him. Was that his last cheep, you wonder, or was he having a nightmare?

A pair of bush bunnies go tearing by, thumpity-thump, thumpity-thump! With your ear to the ground, the noise is so magnified that at first you think they are deer. Then you wonder if there are any deer nearby, and if they have good night vision. If a 150-pound buck travelling at twenty feet to the jump should happen to land on your sleeping bag, it might be a little rough.

Then you hear what you think is a porcupine waddling through the underbrush, and you remember the stories you have heard about people waking up and finding one in the tent, and when you are down there on his level you hardly dare to move for fear he starts swinging that quill-studded, club-like tail.

Before you know it, dawn is breaking in the northeast, and a white-throat gives forth with his high, clear song, and a Wilson's snipe makes his peculiar flight over the swamp, and as you finally doze off you think that now you will at least be able to see anything that comes making noises around your bed.

Next night, if you have to sleep out again, you will likely be so sleepy that a pair of bull moose galloping by wouldn't wake you, but if you can get there, you will likely be found back in your bed indoors.

WITCHING FOR WATER
June 28,1961

Either you have it or you don't, and if you don't have it you may be just a little sceptical of the claims of those who say they do. The ability to locate underground streams of water by witching is what I am talking about—the age-old art of dowsing, or divining, with a forked stick held in the hands.

So far as I am aware, I don't have this gift. Exactly how sceptical I am of those who do profess to have it, I am not prepared to say. One thing sure, I don't believe in witchery, or magic, whether black or any other colour, or flamdoodle of any kind. Yet, from all that I have read on the subject, there does seem to be a good case for the dowsers, a good deal of evidence that some people can locate underground water using a forked stick or other contrivance. So, theorizing that there may be some eventual adequate explanation for the phenomenon, I think it might be best to try and keep an open mind on the matter.

I also think that if the water-witching business should ever prove its worth and become established as a profession, there will have to be a name coined that is more acceptable than witching or divining or even dowsing, all of which carry connotations of the supernatural, of something mystic and miraculous.

The customary method of witching for water is to cut a slender, forked stick from a live tree or shrub, and with the prongs of the twig gripped one in each hand, palms upward, to walk hither and thither until the point of the stick is pulled down, indicating water below.

Some witchers use a willow twig; some use poplar or birch. On the prairies, caragana has always been a favourite, being relatively easy to find, and, where it grows, witch hazel is usually first choice.

Some dowsers scorn wooden twigs altogether and use copper wire bent to the right shape, or even wire coat hangers as a divining rod. And there is a man in Manitoba who locates water with nothing but his bare feet. He kicks off his shoes and socks and walks about over the area to be searched. Electric shocks in the soles of his feet tell him where the underground streams are.

The number of water diviners in the West has dwindled from hundreds in the 1930s to a very few today. Many of the early ones came originally from England or other parts of Europe, where the art has been practiced for centuries.

Of the men who find underground water this way, only a few can tell you at what depth it will be found.

It was once believed that anyone who practiced the art of dowsing must be in league with the Devil, and, so far as I know, no one has ever come up with a more up-to-date explanation, and the dowsers themselves, whether they use a witch hazel twig or an old coat hanger, have one thing in common: they can't explain it either, and most of them don't even try.

WALKING FOR PLEASURE AND PROFIT
July 4, 1962

There is a danger that walking may come to be old-fashioned.

An anthropologist, speaking to the Calgary Archaeological Society one evening a few weeks ago, voiced the rather startling speculation that some time in the distant future, human beings may lose their legs. Farfetched as such speculation may seem, there is nothing farfetched about the reasoning that prompted it.

We could all make a long list of people we know who consider themselves still young and healthy and able, and who, if they had to walk four or five miles away from their car, would find it a real hardship to get back. And sometimes our own name would top the list. The percentage of North Americans who ever get more than a couple of miles from some means of transportation must be fairly small. Today's motto seems to be: "If you can't drive there, don't go."

The present-day attitude toward travel by shank's mare would have elected a snort of derision from some of the old-timers I have been reading about recently. Many an early homesteader, leaving his claim to go out and get a job harvesting, walked forty miles or more to the nearest railroad station and the chances are good that he would walk the same distance back again when he returned with a winter's grubstake to keep him in groceries while he got some more land cleared.

Now, I am not about to advocate that we walk rather than drive wherever we go, just that we should walk a lot more than we do. There are any number of reasons why we should do more walking, quite apart from the spectre of our legless descendants, so I am just going to point out some of the advantages of this time-honoured method of getting from one place to another.

Walking is one of the best means left to us to live as nature intended. It gives us time to think. Our mind is not on what we are doing, as it should be when we drive. Instead we can listen, observe, smell, feel—in other words, be alive. We can become aware of things like wind in leaves, running water, birds flying and singing, insects buzzing, children laughing or playing or quarrelling or crying.

We can smell the rain, the wood smoke, the hay curing and a hundred other smells that we are only half-aware of at 60 mph. We can feel dirt or moss or gravel or pine needles beneath our feet. We can touch the bark of trees, feel the texture of stone and wood, the wetness of rain, know the warmth of the sun and the coolness of the breeze on our face.

We have time to look at things: the architecture of an old building, the worm scrolls on a leaf, the faces of people we meet.

Walking is not merely enjoyable. It is good for us. It has long been recognized as an ideal way to let off steam, to relieve pent-up feelings. More walking and less driving by juveniles would cut the delinquency rate immeasurably.

With traffic and parking problems being what they are, and growing the way they are, we may be forced to do more walking in the years to come. The modern shopping centres are being designed as pedestrian malls, with cars relegated to the outside perimeter of the area. The same idea is even being tried out on downtown streets in large cities. In short, we are getting to the point where there is just not room for all the automobiles.

So, though we may feel that we haven't time to walk today, tomorrow we may have to take the time.

I think we should take more time for walking now, while we still have our legs.

HILLTOP SITTING
August 4, 1965

I have been a hilltop sitter for years in an amateur sort of way. It was just something that I enjoyed doing once in a while without ever thinking of it as a hobby to be shared with other enthusiasts, but now that it has been brought to my attention, I can certainly see the possibilities, and, by golly, they are almost unlimited here in Alberta, where we have no shortage of hills for the purpose.

Percy Barker, Fred's brother-in-law, hilltop sitting above 6000 feet, in Porcupine Hills, west of Claresholm.

Let me describe a half-hour that I spent on a hilltop in late June. On this occasion I was hilltop sitting the easy way. I was quite alone, a situation which is desirable if one is to reap the maximum benefit from one's elevated position. I am not suggesting that hilltop sitting has to be indulged in by not more than one person at a time, but, on the other hand, I have little doubt that any company on the hilltop with you is bound to be in some measure distracting. For instance, had I not been alone on the night described in the following paragraphs, it is quite possible that they might never have been written—or written in a style not suitable for this corner.

I was driving home around midnight after what had been a fine June day, one of the few we had in that month. But a change was in the making. It was the night preceding the extremely wet spell near month's end, and anyone could have forecast rain before morning.

I stopped at the top of the hill near the Fairview Cemetery, about five miles west of Bluffton, and turned off the car lights and motor. The night was starless, moonless, and almost overcast, but it was not at all dark. The horizon, from southeast through south and west to northwest, was ringed with six semi-connected electrical storms, and lightning flashed almost continuously from one direction or another.

The nearest storm was directly southwest, and from it I could hear occasional distant bursts of thunder. Far away to the south, flashes of lightning were trying to peep over the horizon and I wondered where windows were rattling from the thunder they generated. Crossfield? Calgary? It could well have been. Away to the northwest, another distant storm was emerging from the foothills, perhaps somewhere near Hinton.

After half an hour of watching, none of these storms appeared to have moved appreciably closer, although they did, ultimately, passing slowly and leaving a soaked countryside in their wake.

Lightning did not provide all the illumination on the hilltop that night. Behind me to the east, the high cloud that covered most of the eastern sky ahead of the advancing line of thunderstorms was tinted a dull rose by the flickering flares of the Rimbey Gas Plant. Around the horizon clockwise, the darkness was relieved by the lighter glows from a circle of gas and oil fields: Rimbey, Gilbey, Alhambra, Willesden Green, Alder Flats, Buck Lake, all adding to the eerie quality of the midnight sky. This eeriness was still further heightened by a white glow of daylight that came from a narrow strip of unclouded sky low on the northern horizon. Whether lingering dusk or early dawn it would have been impossible to say. This merged, in the northeast, with the reflected light from the City of Edmonton. The only part of the sky not giving off light at that moment was the portion directly overhead.

Although the night and the locale were extremely favourable to the appearance of spooks and hobgoblins, I sat there for thirty minutes without giving so much as a thought to anything supernatural. I was too engrossed in a spectacle that was quite within the bounds of natural law. A ghostly apparition right then would have been almost anticlimactic.

THE SMELLS OF SUMMER
July 1, 1970

Good, bad, or neutral, there is nothing subtle about the smells of summer. They are sometimes so much and so many that we tend to tune them out, taking notice only of the more obvious ones as they waft over us from all directions.

Most of us could, and some of us do, get by minus a good sense of smell, but I am sure mine would be sorely missed if it left me. A good nose, I find, is an aid to good living.

Here are some of the smells, odours, scents and emanations that I have savoured during the past weeks, and some I am looking forward to in the weeks to come:

A newly-ploughed furrow. No more wholesome smell can be found than that of freshly-turned earth. Best of all is the virgin sod, but even the moist soil of a stubble field that first saw the plough half a century or more ago, gives off a pleasant smell.

Dust in the field. Blinding, face-blackening, lung-filling, it still smells better than neutral, but dampened by a summer shower and laid to the ground, it is quite different from ploughed ground and nothing short of delightful.

The sweet, slightly exhilarating odour of crushed vegetation that arises from a newly-mown lawn.

The decaying leaves of last autumn. Although they began their decomposition before the melting of the snow, it is only later, after a warm summer rain that one can really smell the forest floor, a slightly pungent but usually pleasant odour.

A large chokecherry bush in full blossom wafts a fragrance that one almost backs away from. The May Day tree has a similar but more delicate fragrance.

A herd of cattle in a pasture. Ambrosia for a retired cowboy. For some city folk, a smell a little to the left of neutral.

A spruce forest.

Ozone after a thunderstorm.

Road construction, the smell of raw clay mixed with the smell of diesel smoke. Raw clay smells different from ordinary field soil. Often it has a slightly sour tang.

Sweet clover blooming along hundreds of miles of Alberta highways. About as sweet a smell as you can find anywhere.

Alsike clover blooming in a roadside hay meadow.

The many smells of newly-cut, freshly-cured hay. Fragrant is the word here, the aroma varying with the crop, the temperature, the humidity, and the stage of curing.

A beaver pond. A smell unique among outdoor emanations. A dank odour of rapidly decaying vegetation mixed with unmistakable perfume of beaver castor permeates a beaver pond. A drained or partly drained beaver pond produces this smell to a high degree.

Wild strawberries. You get this smell in different ways—by walking in a field where the berries are ripe, and crushing some of them under your feet, or, in just passing, in late July, a hay field where the berries have produced well and have dried on the vine. It is a wonderful, mouth-watering, nostalgia-producing essence that makes you want to linger by that meadow for hours.

THE TORNADO
August 9, 1972

Howard Penfold had some good news and some bad news last week. First, the bad news—and there's plenty of it: his farm buildings demolished, his whole farmyard a complete shambles, nothing left of his house but the floor, his household and personal possessions scattered on the wind.

(When I was there two days after the disaster, he still hadn't found his tape recorder). His fences were wrecked, his crops damaged and the beauty of an attractive farmstead setting turned to frightful chaos in a minute; and to top it off, an extensive poplar forest containing an estimated two million feet of lumber was left in a tangled mess of broken, splintered wood.

Now for the good news. Howard is alive and unscathed, having come through what must be termed one of the most violent windstorms ever to hit Alberta. "I'm glad you came to look at all this devastation," said Mr. Penfold. "Maybe you can convince people that wind damage on such a scale can happen here."

The tornado that whipped across the Penfold farm in the Home Glen district at approximately 7:10 p.m. on Friday, July 28, 1972, must have been one of the largest and most violent tornadoes in Alberta's history. Indeed, according to the literature I have been reading on tornadoes, it may be one of the worst ever recorded in Canada, or even North America, in terms of area laid waste. Had it descended on a large centre of population, thousands of people would surely have been killed and injured, while property damage would have been of astronomical proportions. As it was, I didn't so much as hear of a single injury in the Home Glen area, and one man took the brunt of the property damage.

"I had been in the construction business all of my life," said Mr. Penfold, "and I found it growing a little stale, so I decided to do something different. I bought three quarters of land here, and I was just beginning to make something out of it. Now look at it."

I had been looking at it, and I quickly deduced that this farm of Howard Penfold's was not exactly a retirement project. In fact, it appeared to me that he had been working some pretty long hours to carve a farm out of 480 acres of raw land, clearing and cropping a sizable acreage, fencing, building, getting a well drilled, and making plans to get a major logging operation underway this September. Then, in a twinkling, to be singled out as the principal victim of a storm of such immensity....

"I heard the storm coming," said Mr. Penfold, "and ran for the house. By the time I got in, the wind was blowing so hard I could hardly get the door closed. Then it hit. I saw that the house was not going to withstand the force of it and I got down on the floor. In seconds the walls and roof were gone and I had nothing to hang onto but the rug, into which I was rolled by the wind. I looked up once, and the air seemed packed with flying objects and wood and debris, so I ducked down again."

It was over in less than two minutes, and when Mr. Penfold crawled out of his rug it was to a bewildering sight. Two new plywood granaries had completely disintegrated, and I observed pieces of them more than three quarters of a mile away, when I visited the farm on Sunday. A larger storage building was laid wide open, probably exploded into the vacuum in the vortex of the storm, but since it was soundly constructed of sawn lumber, it was possible to drag the walls in with a tractor and reassemble them. The roof of this building was never found. A large shop building was demolished on the spot, damaging the newly-installed pump beside it. As for the house—it was gone—period. And gone with it were most of the owner's furniture, bedding, clothing and personal possessions. Chunks and fragments of pink insulation were scattered afar throughout the devastation. The heavy kitchen stove proved only slightly tornado resistant. It didn't get far from the house—only a few yards—but it punched a hole in the floor as it left, and wound up wrecked. A 1958 Ford car, sitting on blocks on another part of the farm, was bounced and rolled up a sixty-foot slope and left badly battered but upright in a grain field more than a hundred feet from its starting point.

The Penfold farm is an L-shaped holding consisting of the north half of Section 30, and SW 31 in Township 44, Range 1, West of the 5th. A large part of his acreage was covered with great, tall poplars, with hundreds of trees containing upwards of two hundred board feet of lumber each. From what I could see after the storm, these trees were all sound and white and I would not consider the reported estimates of two million feet exaggerated. Today that tall forest is a shambles of broken, splintered, twisted, uprooted trees, most of them horizontal, piled helter-skelter in a tangled, nearly impenetrable maze of logs and branches. It is so completely levelled that one can look right out across that forest for a half to three quarters of a mile and see the farms beyond.

Had a storm of this dimension hit a heavily-populated spot, that area would certainly have been declared a disaster area and residents would have received aid from many quarters. For one man, Mr. Howard Penfold, it is no less a disaster area. Think about it.

VOYAGEUR CANOE ON THE
NORTH SASKATCHEWAN RIVER
August 7, 1990

It is time to embark on the fast-flowing North Saskatchewan River. We are standing on a narrow sandbar, in a rather tight circle, made even tighter because we are all fat with bulky, orange life jackets around our ribs. Our canoe paddles are held blade down in a circle within the circle. A unique ceremony is about to take place. Our leader, Merle Pederson, of Voyageur Adventure Tours, Rocky Mountain House, who will pilot us in safety down the not-so-calm waters of the rolling river, pours a clear brown libation into a silver vessel and with it anoints each paddle, then the bow of the canoe, and lastly the throats of the embarkees. The concoction is rumoured to contain many of the ingredients used by the voyageurs who plied this waterway in freight canoes well over a century ago—needles of spruce and leaves of *kinnikinik*, Labrador tea and wild mint. It is a brew to savour. We drain the chalice and regret that so much was expended on the paddles, but if a safe voyage is ensured, we unanimously concur.

We are at the Rocky Canoe Club Access, some miles upriver from the town. Above us rises the river bank and the series of crude steps which we have just descended. Beside us in the water and facing upstream is the big canoe, which also negotiated those steps, and into which eleven people will now climb with care, seating ourselves in pairs, except for the bow paddler, and the sternsman at the opposite end. The evening is warm, the sun shines from amongst a few clouds in the west, and we are off, making a 180-degree turn as we paddle out into the current.

The river takes us as if we are a part of it. The big canoe smoothes anything that doesn't show a whitecap and we find it strangely relaxing and exhilarating at the same time. None of us has been in so large a canoe before. This is just one of the many field trips sponsored this summer by the Red Deer River Naturalists, and it has to be one of the more exciting ones. We zig-zag from one side of the river to the other, avoiding rocks and the faster rapids. We are making very good time: the speed of the current plus the push of the

311

paddle. Inside the hour, we have learned to rest our paddles in the calm stretches, letting the current take us, and paddle like mad in the fast water to give the sternsman better control. Contrary to what some might think, paddling a canoe is not tiring work, at least not downriver.... We watch for deer along the shore, for it is the best time of day to see wildlife, but all we see are multi-coloured cattle, grazing or drinking at water's edge. We disturb dozens of sandpipers, not in flocks, but still in small families or singles. We see several small flocks of common mergansers, and now and then a great blue heron takes off from a sandbar and flies before us down the river.

Our guide all the while is giving us a running commentary on the history of the region, about the Indians and the fur trade and David Thompson, who was here nearly two hundred years ago. From our vantage point, the river has likely changed only a little in the intervening centuries. We go ashore to stretch our legs at the National Historic Park, and learn more about the trading post, and the York boats that were built here to carry furs to Montreal, and the lifestyle of the voyageurs who manned them. Then we paddle up the Clearwater River a short way to see where David Thompson and his wife, Charlotte, lived when their first child was born.

We pass beneath the two bridges at Rocky Mountain House and on to the newer highway bridge four miles beyond. Here a delicious supper is waiting for us: buns with hot roast beef and all the trimmings, and muffins, home-made cookies and fruit for dessert. As the sun sets, we haul the canoe from the water, load it on the trailer and climb aboard the bus to return to Rocky Mountain House where we have left our vehicles. We have stretched our adventure into twilight and as we leave for home we voice our appreciation to our host for an exciting and enjoyable evening.

AUGUST
August 1, 1995

August fares little better than July in English literature, and perhaps Lord Byron knew the answer when he wrote about the English winter "ending in July and recommencing in August." Both months are named for Caesars, Julius and Augustus. I wonder if July was Julius' baby name—his diminutive—or his nickname. I'll bet nobody called him that to his face.

August in its early stages is pretty much a continuance of July. It is still holiday time. We should still be able to bank on some hot

312

days and crowded beaches. There is still the risk of hail, which lessens as the month wanes. The hayfields should now be full of half- to three-quarter-ton, shoulder-high cylinders made from July's grass and legume crops. Days are now shortening noticeably as harvest gets underway. Deciduous foliage begins to look drab and muted in colour, and some yellow creeps in. Every leaf shows marks of insects, which every August threaten to take over the world and all that's in it, then just as they have their objective in sight, September comes with frost and possibly snow, and days and nights with temperatures that slow the hordes in their tracks.

Shorebirds appear from the north in August, migrants on their gradual journey south. Snow buntings, too, come down off the tundra, though still in brown summer garb. Crows gather in flocks, fattening on grasshoppers and other insects and whatever else they can scrounge. South is in their tiny brains, too.

August was haying month when I was young. Haying is earlier now, July weather permitting, but in the old days we would be lucky to get a start before August 1. We didn't have harvest looming so close, however, even though crops were seeded as early or even earlier then. We just did not have the early maturing varieties or the farming practices to hasten development and maturity.

Snow has covered the ground on quite a few August days in my lifetime. Devastating for the farmer. What a headache that always was, with all but the lighter stands of grain flat on the ground. There was little joy in harvest those years. The only good thing about snow in August was that it protected the grain from frost damage when the storm cleared.

On the other hand, August can be a delightful month: warm sunshine to fill and ripen the heads of grain, frequent enough showers to keep the pastures productive, and just a bit of time to sit back and enjoy it. That was always the rub in August—too little time to relax. Only in your imagination would you find yourself sitting on the deck, in the shade, ice tinkling in the glass as you refilled your glass from the dewy-sided pitcher, then settling back to get in some summer reading, or when you tired of that, to just lean back a little more, shift your brain into neutral and watch the cumulus clouds change shape.

I did some of those sorts of things as a boy, but for the past sixty years Augusts have always seemed to present more important tasks to accomplish. No time for wool gathering, but one of these days, when I get caught up....

MIRAGES PAST AND PRESENT
February 8, 1961

A mirage, says the dictionary, is an optical illusion occurring on oceans, deserts, or plains, by which distant objects appear inverted, misplaced or distorted; caused by refractive conditions due to the difference in temperature between the upper and lower strata of air near the earth's surface.

You can know all this and more, and it still will not lessen the wonder that you feel on seeing a really fine mirage. The word is, in fact, derived from a Latin verb meaning "to wonder at." (The word "mirror" comes from the same root).

The desert, of course, is the place for mirages, and many a thirst-tortured traveller is supposed to have lost his last shred of reason at the sight of non-existent, palm-fringed pools of cool, clear water.

The bush country does not produce too many mirages, but you sometimes see them from a high elevation. Once, from a high point twenty miles up the Medicine River from the Medicine Lodge Hills, I saw a hill with its inverted likeness, balanced peak to peak in the sky above.

The Rocky Mountains are frequently seen in some form of mirage, especially early in the morning. Sometimes they are seen in this way from hilltops in our area which are not normally high enough to make them visible.

Some weird and exciting mirages occur out on the prairie. My mother was so enchanted by one in her first summer in the West that she wrote her impressions on a piece of note paper which I have before me at the moment. She lived at the time on her father's farm near Trochu, Alberta, and she had a young visitor this day, a little boy who lived in the valley and seldom saw a mirage. He, too, was enthralled.

"Ordinary haystacks," she wrote, "reached heavenward 'til they looked like giant trees. Little buildings, heretofore invisible, stretched up proudly from the hollows, like huge grain elevators. Ridges never before noticed by the casual observer grew up to resemble the walls of some ancient Roman city, and a little prairie shack took on the proportions of a castle.

"My little companion gazed in rapt wonder. 'Look,' he said, 'at the cemetery over there.' A row of grainstacks looked like statues and tombstones glittering in the sun in some abandoned graveyard.

"To the south, the little town of Three Hills had become a baby city, with skyscrapers and factories."

Possibly the most dramatic account of an Alberta mirage that I have ever read, appears in the book, *Pathfinding on Plain and Prairie*, by the early missionary, John McDougall. One day, well before the turn of the century, he and his wife were out driving with a team and buckboard, on the high land near the Red Deer River.

A thunderstorm had just passed and the sun shone brightly, and presently the whole country came under the spell of a mirage.

"Watching the wonderful panorama," he wrote, "I saw away beyond the mountains and there was a body of water, with land and hills in the far background. Then on the water there came in view a steamship. There she stood on her course, with a dark cloud of smoke falling astern.

"I said to my wife, 'What do you see?'

"'Why,' she exclaimed, 'I see a big lake, and there is a steamer coming toward us.'

"All this was real to our vision and sense, and if truly a picture of this world, that mirage was revealing to our vision, scenes seven hundred miles distant."

WATCHING FOR THE PERSEIDS
August 8, 1989

It was a warm August night in the 1930s. My father came in from outdoors and said, "Who wants to stay up late and watch for the Perseids?"

"I do, I do, I do," was the response from Freddie, Allan, and Dorothy. Even our mother had no objections—no warnings about what would happen to our health and good temper if we didn't get our sleep quota. Our answer to our father's question would undoubtedly have been in the affirmative even if we had not known that the Perseids were a meteor shower which appeared on the night of August 11-12 each year as the earth passes through the tail dust of a disintegrated comet. We likely all did know, even the youngest, for my father was an amateur astronomer who could explain the intricacies of the solar system to anyone willing to listen. His kids all knew the names of major constellations and first magnitude stars from an early age. One of my father's dreams, never realized, was to own an astronomical telescope. He was one of the most thrilled people on this planet when he watched Neil Armstrong step onto the moon's surface in July 1969. He was eighty that year and this was a marvel he had never expected to witness.

To get back to the 1930s:

We went and got a 12 x 16-foot tarpaulin that we used to cover loads of hay or grain or anything else that we did not want to get rained on, sometimes including ourselves, and we spread it on the grass, away from the lights of the house. Well before midnight we were all out there, horizontal on the canvas, watching for those shooting stars. It must have been a very good year for the Perseids, for there were a great many of them, in all parts of the sky, and the aggregate was greater than the number observed by any one person. Some were bright, some very faint; some left long, luminous trails. If you tracked them backwards, all seemed to come from that portion of the sky where the constellation Perseus shone forth, high in the northeast. Hence the name, Perseids.

Our aim was to stay out watching until after midnight. Meteor showers are at their best after the witching hour, for reasons which my father would have told us, but which I no longer remember. Maximum occurrence after midnight has been logged at fifty to sixty per hour, an average of almost one a minute.

I have watched for the Perseid showers many times in the years since that night, but seldom with such satisfactory results. Some years the sky is cloudy and there is no watching. Often there is a moon in the sky, and that greatly distracts from star gazing, shooting stars included. On some occasions I think the earth has barely managed to catch the fringe of that comet dust, for the meteors appeared so infrequently that one soon tired of watching.

This August the moon will be more than half illuminated by August 11, and will be in the sky at midnight. But if the night is clear, and you can find a spot away from artificial light, it might be worth the trouble to spend a few minutes gazing skyward, not necessarily in the direction of Perseus. This might be the year, as that other was half a century ago, when our home planet sails right through the densest part of that comet dust.

There are other annual meteor showers, but the Perseids are the most watchable in terms of frequency, glowing contrails and summer occurrence.

ALBERTA'S WORST HAILSTORM
August 12, 1968

I shall never forget the afternoon of August 7, 1949. I was caught out in the worst hailstorm in the history of Alberta, with only a big willow tree for shelter, and I had to share that with four other people and my dog, Ike. The Texas-style storm, with stones up to baseball-size, cut a swath several miles wide and two hundred miles long, hitting here about 4 p.m. and petering out in Saskatchewan hours later. The largest stones were not baseball-shaped, but measured three inches long by two and a half inches wide by one and a half inches thick. There were no small stones there, the smallest being the size of a large grape.

I was caught about a mile from home, along with seven other people. This is how it happened. Nelson Donnelly's horses, pasturing on the northeast quarter of the school section, had gotten into our pasture on the southeast quarter. They had been there for a few days without causing anyone any concern, but August 7 seemed a good day to put them back where they belonged. There was a picnic at Iola that day, which had been hot, with temperatures in the eighties. About mid-afternoon Nelson picked up Charlie Carey, who lived just north of Iola, Dudley Bloxham, a man of indeterminate age who lived just south of Iola, and three fourteen-year-old boys who were at the picnic. Their first names I have forgotten. Their last names were MacKenzie, MacLennon and Schweiger. The latter was probably Walter. I think that Dudley and the other boys came with Gilbert Donnelly, who left his car parked on the hill three quarters of a mile north of our house while they walked across the half-mile to the pasture. Nelson, Charlie and I walked from my house, and I hope my memory is not too much in variance with those of the other people involved.

I noticed a high cauliflower cloud in the west before leaving the house, so even though the sun was hot, I took my waterproof canvas dry-back along. We also carried enough halter ropes to lead out the several horses, once we had caught them, which proved to be no problem. I was leading a horse from the south side of our pasture quarter north toward the other quarter when the sun disappeared, and the thunder and lightning in the west gave me some apprehension, for this was one of the blackest, most awesome-looking clouds that I had seen for a while, and it was coming up fast. I was not with the others, who presumably had the rest of the horses caught and were heading in the same direction. I was still some way short of the fence opening when I heard the unmistakable roar of the pounding hailstorm. Within another minute or two I knew I was in for it, and began looking for shelter. I knew of a big willow not far from me, so I turned the horse loose to fend for himself, slapped him on the rump, and headed on the run for that tree, which had grown several trunks of ten- or twelve-inches thickness.

I reached the willow ahead of the storm, but found Dudley and the three boys already crouching beneath it. They made room for me and for Ike, but we were on the edge of good shelter. However, there was not time to look further; the storm was upon us with a roar that would have terrified the Old Boy himself. The first hailstone I saw was the size and shape of a hen's egg. It hit the ground beside us and bounced several feet back toward the sky from whence it came. Within seconds the large stones were bouncing like tennis balls on pavement, for the ground was still dry and hard. The lightning was flashing close around us, but the thunder could scarcely be heard above the roar of the hail. Ike was shivering, shoving as close to me as he could get. My left side was protruding past the trunk of the willow and an occasional hailstone was getting to me there. I had bruises on my ribs when I got home.

Within short minutes, the ground was deep in several inches of hail, and the storm had let up, roaring off to the east. I was lucky; my canvas coat had kept me dry. Even so, I was cold, for the temperature had plunged drastically from the 80s before the hailstorm, into the 30s, the air cooled by so much ice. The three boys were miserably cold. They wore only thin, cotton shirts which were now soaked. They ran back to the car through the ice and in near winter climate. I went to look for the others. Charlie Carey had not found shelter in time and had been knocked unconscious by a chunk of ice. He had a lump on his head, but seemed okay when I came upon him. The others had fared better. The horses were in our pastures for a few more days.

When I got home, I found that twenty-two panes of glass had been broken. My father was putting on storm windows, upstairs and down, on the house's five west windows. My mother was sweeping up broken glass and hailstones and mopping up the floors. Water from upstairs was dripping through the ceiling. There were tennis-ball-size hailstones under the beds. The Chev truck and the John Deere tractor, both new, carried the dents from the hailstones to the end of their days on this farm. The cedar shingles on the roof, seventeen years old, were badly damaged, but the roof did not leak. Large poplar trees, stripped of leaves and bark, eventually died. The landscape looked like spring. There was considerable loss to wildlife and to some domestic birds and animals. And we got our fall work all caught up that year. There was no harvesting to do.

WHAT A SUMMER!
September 1, 1981

Summer's contract does not run out until September 21 or thereabouts, but I have trouble thinking summer anytime after September 1. Summers in Alberta have a way of going when they've only just come.

Over the next month, the leaves will turn colour and be blown from the trees. One month after that, the ground will be freezing more at night than it thaws by day—freeze-up. Winter, like autumn, jumps the gun here. Fall comes three weeks prematurely, but ends about seven weeks ahead of its full calendar term. That leaves winter with a long head start. Like the Bard of the Blindman Valley complained many years ago, "We're too fur north."

I don't know what I'm complaining about; I've had a fantastic summer, even if it has seemed to go by at 190 km/h. Come to think of it, a good many hours were spent this summer moving over the face of the earth about 990 km/h. At another time I was travelling at 125 mph and not even in the air. I was on one of England's fastest trains, going from Reading to Bath, a distance of about eighty miles. That trip seemed to take only minutes, but since I didn't time it I can't be very precise. I know it took a scant two hours from our arrival at Heathrow Airport to collect our bags, clear Customs, catch a bus to Reading, transfer to the train and find ourselves in Bath at 10 a.m., having come 6,500 miles from Johannesburg since sunset the night before.

"What did you do, fly?" asked cousin Margaret when we phoned her from Bath to come pick us up. We had phoned her about 8:30 from Heathrow.

Back in Alberta, my mind still filled with the wildlife, the people, the problems of Africa, and the rose gardens and the history and the different problems of England, I hardly had time to sit down and get myself sorted out before I was off again—to Hinton and the Wild Sculptures with Bill and Adeline Nesbitt, the Red Deer River Naturalists, and the Federation of Alberta Naturalists. Then there was a visit to Brule and its interesting history, and an old-timer there named Mr. Garneau. From there it was into British Columbia, to McBride and an interesting visit to the one-time town of Eddy; down through Valemont, Blue River, Kamloops and Vernon to Lumby where we visited Reynold and Marion Mazu, my neighbours here ten years ago. Later, at Nakusp, we visited Johnny and Margaret MacLean, who moved there from their Meadowvale farm this summer.

Back home I got in some canoeing with friends Alvin and Dennis and Doreen, on Island and Medicine Lakes one weekend, on Burnstick and Swan Lakes another weekend. Then it was back to Hinton for a weekend, with more back-country exploring around Brule, with Maxine and daughter Diane and friends, and a day of mountain climbing at Miette, then home via Mountain Park and Smallboy's camp and Nordegg.

All in all this summer I spent some exciting times with old friends, made some interesting new ones, had the first prolonged visit in decades with brother Allan, saw portions of the globe from 26 degrees south latitude to 70 north, from 120 degrees west longitude up to 40 east, and had some once-in-a-lifetime experiences in the process. I felt the warm waters of the Indian Ocean and the cold of the North Atlantic, and I gazed down from thirty-nine thousand feet on two of the world's famous mountains, Africa's Kilimanjaro and Europe's Matterhorn.

Like I said, I've had a terrific summer. I'm just not ready to let it go.

HILLTOP SITTING II
September 7, 1966

It is quite some time now since I have done a column on that fascinating and rewarding pastime of hilltop sitting, which *Calgary Herald* columnist Ken Liddell did much to popularize and make socially acceptable a couple of years ago. Mr. Liddell, having bought himself a place somewhere in the foothills, can now pursue the hobby from his own front window.

I have indulged in the sport since I was a boy, and, as a boy, I used my own muscle power to climb most of the hills on which I sat, using either shank's mare or bicycle. Today I seem to be doing a good deal of my hill climbing with horsepower—or maybe tiger power.

So it was that I stopped the car recently on a hill just a mile or so south and west of the little centre called Forshee. Forshee consists of one grain elevator, a general store complete with hand-operated gasoline pump, a small railway station and some miscellaneous houses and buildings. It is situated right beside Highway 12 in the very heart of the beautiful and fertile Blindman Valley. As a matter of fact, it was once called Centre Valley, and why the fates decreed that it was to remain unchanged for half a century while the towns of Rimbey and Bentley grew, is a point to ponder. And so this was a

320

part of my ponderings as I sat and gazed from across the Blindman. And I pondered, too, how to describe in black print on white paper the intensity and variegation of colour that was spread before me in the light of the late afternoon, late summer sun. A string of shower clouds, stretching halfway around the horizon, had just passed to the east, leaving the valley soaked. The sun had appeared in plenty of time to make a brilliant rainbow, and now the remaining northern end of this, complete with inverted reflection, was directly above the elevator. The backdrop for the rainbow and for the rest of the picture was the rain cloud, dark steely-blue but not quite black, the way a storm cloud often looks when the sun comes out low in the west behind the storm.

In brilliant contrast, and brighter than the rainbow even, the sunlit, silver-white grain elevator drew the eye like a beacon light. This was set off by the red roof of the store and by a cluster of farm buildings just beyond.

A quieter, more peaceful spot than Forshee would be hard to imagine—except for one thing. The highway, with its continuous and noisy flow of traffic bisected the picture from left to right, but the traffic did add to the colour, and it is amazing how colourful are today's cars and trucks compared to two or three decades ago.

Below the highway and as parallel to it as a meandering river can be parallel to anything, ran the tree-shaded Blindman, and its valley was a sight to behold. There was nothing in sight that was not Blindman Valley, and it made one wish to be a landscape painter or an expert photographer or a philosopher or a poet—or a bit of all of these.

It was typical Alberta parkland and the clumps of trees, with their lengthening shadows, lent an added touch of drama to the scene. Fields of ripe barley, some in the swath, alternated with green alfalfa patches, rich with the colour of second growth. Other grain and other forage fields varied the shading but not the basic colours, while a few expanses of black summerfallow told almost as much of the richness of the soil as did the crops beside them.

Directly ahead, road and river met and parted at a bright green steel bridge, a green that almost contrasted with the green of nature. And all this colour, remember, was wet and glistening and intensified in the clear air and the westering sun.

I had not been on this hill before and I may not stop here again, because I stopped this time when the scene before my eyes was beyond the ordinary and that is how I would remember it.

HILLTOP SITTING III
November 5, 1969

Very little in the way of deliberate, premeditated, hilltop sitting did I get in this past summer. Like so many of the things I fully intend to do every summer, hilltop sitting takes a fair amount of time if one is to savour it properly and gain the maximum therapeutic value from this delightful form of outdoor recreation. And time, it seems to me, is in shorter supply with every summer that passes.

Schutz farm home, 1987, where Fred wrote these columns. The wheels came from the hose carriage of the Winfield Fire Brigade, 20 km north of Rimbey.

Even if I am able to tell myself that I don't need the therapy, not being plagued with jangled nerves, peptic ulcers or a worried mind, I feel I should still make time for more hilltop sitting because, like fishing, it is probably a preventative for the above and other afflictions, as well as a form of cure.

I did manage to get in one brief stint of hilltop sitting on a hill where I had never been before, but where I am determined to go again. I had been to Sylvan Lake, and, as I sometimes do on a return trip from that area, I was driving up the west side of the lake, intending to reach home via Leedale.

As I came northward near the northwest corner of the lake, I could see a high prominence looming ahead, and I thought it must

322

be the hill referred to locally as the Ski Hill, where the ski slope is situated, but on coming closer I could see that the nearest hill to me and to the lake was not the Ski Hill, nor even the tower hill, which is crowned with a tall radio mast, but a somewhat lesser knob about half a mile to the south. By turning at the right corner, I found I was able to drive right to the foot of this elevation, and it looked even higher from close up. The southern slope appeared mostly bare of trees and seemed to be pasture, ungrazed at the moment. I had no idea on whose land I would be trespassing, but there was no way to resist the impulse that I had to climb to the summit.

It was midsummer and the countryside was green with a variety of rich, lush shades, tones, tints and intensities as would bewilder a painter of landscapes, and even before I reached the sitting point of that prominence, I knew that I was going to see much more than just green fields and trees and pastures. And I did; much more. To the southeast the whole expanse of Sylvan Lake was spread out before me—about twenty square miles of water looking little more than a pond in that vast area of Alberta countryside that lay within my field of vision. At the far end of the lake, almost twelve miles from my hilltop, the town of Sylvan Lake appeared through a haze as a thin bright line rimming the foot of the lake. With binoculars it showed up as a populated centre with individual buildings. About the same distance away to east and north, I could see the southern portion of Gull Lake, with the town of Bentley, about nine miles off, appearing somewhat plainer than did Sylvan Lake. The northern part of the lake was cut off from my view by eastern ramparts of the Medicine Lodge Hills, which begin their rise not far west of Bentley. Gull Lake is over a hundred feet closer to sea level than is Sylvan at 3065.

To the west and southwest there was no visible horizon, and little view. The sun, low in the west and shining into the smoke and haze, screened all detail from the landscape in those directions.

About three miles to the north and east rose the hill called Sunset Hill, where Maskepetoon, the great Cree Peace Chief, is said to have fasted as a young brave. This whole range or cluster of hills, the Medicine Lodge group, were a well-known landmark in the early days of recorded history in this part of Alberta, and were, for generations, a favourite gathering spot for the Indians from miles around. And little wonder. I'm sure that some of the medicine made there still lingers around those hilltops. I am just waiting for another opportunity to sit and absorb some of it.

KIDS IN MY NATURAL AREA
October 23, 1990

Last spring I toured a group of youngsters and a few adults into the southern segment of the Anderson Creek Natural Area. They thought it was great, and I was asked by Lyn Stankevich if I would do it again this fall, on the northern segment. I readily agreed, and again the kids enjoyed it. Fall is almost as different from spring in the outdoors as summer is from winter.

We trooped across a small meadow, deep in grass no longer green, climbed a knoll and walked along above the creek until we came to a beaver dam. It was an old one recently repaired. I showed the group the fresh mud on the top of the lodge and the food cache of poplar branches close by and the section of the dam that had been rebuilt. A good many poplar trees had been cut by the busy rodents as they prepared for winter, and some were too high off the ground for the animals to reach. I had carried my chain saw with me and explained to the kids that I was going to cut and pile my winter firewood while I had a crew. Then I revealed my real scheme. I cut green, felled poplar into short lengths and the kids hauled or slid or rolled them down to the water behind the dam and near the lodge. We thus made use of several trees that would otherwise have been wasted.

I parked my saw beside a tree then and we all crossed over the dam to the opposite side of the creek where a few partially-dried blueberries still clung to the low bushes. It took some time to exhaust the patch, but we soon found some tart but juicy lowbush cranberries amongst the fallen leaves and pine needles, then a few highbush cranberries, even tarter and juicier. The group tasted the gritty *kinnikinik* or bearberries and the tasteless, bright, orange bunchberries, but I warned them about the white snowberries which are poisonous, especially to children. Wild berries, edible or not, were quite unknown to these kids. In my kid days we were out in the fall with syrup pails picking blueberries and cranberries for our mother to can. The gathering and preserving of wild fruit is becoming a lost craft, I fear.

We walked through pine and poplar woods, looking at lichens and liverworts and fungi and moss and lots of other living organisms on our way back to the road and the cars, and while David and I went back for my saw, a potful of boiling hot corn-on-the-cob appeared as if by magic from the trunk of a car, and there was butter and salt and pepper, too.

The more often I visit the Anderson Creek Natural Area, the more I see the value of it to present and future generations, both human and non-human. By non-human I mean the wildlife, both plant and animal that is at home on parcels of land like the Anderson Creek area which I monitor under the Volunteer Steward Program of the Alberta government. I worry a little about the permanency of these natural areas. Already an oil well (which apparently turned out to be a dry hole) has been drilled in the middle of one of the quarters, although I understand I could have prevented or at least objected to this had I known about it in time. The thing is, a designation as a natural area does not mean that the property is sacrosanct—far from it. If a government department decides to put a road or pipeline across a natural area, there is nothing to prevent it. This has happened to a natural area in the region of the Alberta-Pacific pulp mill. The answer, I think, is to give these natural sites as much exposure as possible as the preserve of native plant and animal species for which they have been set aside. If they are large enough for unobtrusive human use, as is the Anderson Creek area, so much the better.

SEPTEMBER GOLD
September 9, 1986

September, and another Alberta summer has done a fly-past and it is time to get ready for the fall-out. However, with a bit of co-operation from the weather god, there will be time left before parka and snow-boot time, for getting to know better this beautiful and ever-fascinating province. Now is the time to head for the hills to prospect for gold, for there is infinitely more gold in Alberta in September than has been sluiced out of its east slope streams in a hundred years. There is the gold of the ripened grainfields across the prairies and parklands. There is the gold of the birch and aspen, brightening and lightening the forested hillsides. And there will be a golden sunset now and then wherever you are. Before month's end, the landscape will become one glorious golden panorama with overtones of orange and red and purple, and undertones of dun and beige and muted green.

I can think of no better place to prospect for Alberta's golden riches in September than the southwest, where the prairie slides up to the mountains and the Rockies meet you more than half-way. Make Waterton National Park your target destination if you have a few days of holiday left, and you will not likely regret it, but

325

for goodness' sake, don't go straight there. Dawdle a bit; stray from the pavement, meander down side roads and really see the country. Use shank's mare and hike the mountain trails or walk the railroad ties to new vistas. Get sidetracked into the little places like Longview and Leavitt and Whiskey Gap. You can do it all in the southwest. Since one visit, unless it is a long one, is not nearly enough to more than merely discover this part of the province, here are some suggestions for making the most of your available time.

From Calgary, take a circle tour to Waterton, going via Highway 2 to Cardston, then cutting across to the park on Highway 5. On your return, take Highway 22 via Pincher Creek, Crowsnest, Chain Lakes, Turner Valley and Millarville. The September scenery along 22 will be spectacular. Make frequent stops. Visit the Big Rock at Okotoks, the country's largest erratic, which came by glacier from Jasper Park. Stop for a drink of famous Nanton water (which I find tastes much like water in High River, Medicine Hat or Lac la Biche). Visit the art galleries, museums and antique shops in all the towns along Highway 2. Take a side trip from Claresholm into the Porcupine Hills, which vie with the Cypress Hills as one of Alberta's elevated beauty spots. If Alberta's history is of interest, visit Jerry Potts' grave in Fort Macleod, located in the northeast corner of the cemetery. (I had to hunt for it). The museum in Fort Macleod is a must. At Cardston, drive by the Mormon Temple, unique in Alberta.

If you drive to Waterton on Highway 5, drop down to Police Outpost Provincial Park, close to the U.S. border, a tree-ringed prairie lake not many Albertans see. You can add a foreign flavour to your trip by taking Highways 2 and 6 from Cardston instead of 5. You drive into Montana at Carway and out again at Chief Mountain an hour later. The mountain scenery is magnificent, dominated by the Chief.

There are many ways to spend time in Waterton National Park. Some of the more interesting: drive to Red Rock Canyon and hike the nature trail, and on the way back hike up to Blakiston Falls. Take tea in the stately Prince of Wales Hotel; go for a horseback ride; take a two-hour boat trip on the lake; rent a bicycle or a trike at the Texaco station. Drive up to Cameron Lake. Relax in the sun in your lawn chair.

And I'd need another column to finish your trip.

326

UFOs I HAVE SEEN
February 20, 1996

It is now half a century since Unidentified Flying Objects came to the fore in news headlines. It was 1947 when the media of the day decided that there was something that might sell papers and magazines; might enliven the thrice-daily newscasts on the radio; might possibly even have some substance despite rampant scepticism.

In 1947 Mackenzie King was still Prime Minister of Canada, the Dead Sea Scrolls had just been discovered, and the transistor was invented. The United Nations was off and running and peace had cause to make news, but still fresh in peoples' memories was the dropping of The Bomb on Hiroshima and Nagasaki, bringing a sudden end to World War II. UFOs made a nice diversion from the more solid news stories.

Suddenly, UFOs were being seen everywhere, mostly as strange lights in the night sky, but occasionally daylight sightings were reported, and these descriptions led to the term, Flying Saucers. I am sure that 98 percent of the population were either reading about UFOs or talking about them.

I became a firm believer on August 7, 1969, twenty-four years after the first reported sightings. I had no choice. On that cloudless, summer morning, with the sun high, I had a remarkably clear and sharp, if distant, view of not one, but two UFOs. They were the classic flying-saucer shape, with a bright crimson red dome atop a saucer that seemed to be chrome, that reflected the light by which they were first spotted by my teenage nephew, Allan. They were moving together, moving fast, and were in range of my seven-power binoculars for an estimated thirty seconds after spotting.

It may have been later that summer that I experienced a second encounter. I was travelling on the highway between Rimbey and Forshee on a pitch-black, heavily overcast night. At 60 mph my lights went out, a dicey situation, I can tell you. I got stopped safely and the lights came on again, but I drove a hundred miles very apprehensively that night, and more miles before I learned the cause of the failure a few days later. I had seen nothing that night, but many others had. One person not only had the lights on the car doused, but the engine stopped as well. When she got out of the car, she saw the UFO beneath the overcast. When it disappeared into the murk a few seconds later, she, too, was able to proceed.

A large number of other people observed what was probably the same object as it followed a train between Lacombe and Stettler that night. The only description of it that I can remember was a circle of lights that could travel as slowly as a train, or be gone up into the cloud in a twinkling. Since that time UFOs have had nothing to do with me, or I with them, to the best of my knowledge.

Sightings are still being reported in 1996, and this year most of them are coming out of the Northwest Territories.

MORE UFO STORIES
March 5, 1996

I have heard several firsthand accounts of UFOs since I published my own sightings back in 1969. I think some of these people told me their stories because they knew that I would be an interested and sympathetic listener. I would not be asking them what they had been drinking that night, or try to come up with some ridiculous explanation of what they had really seen. Believe me, some scientists, meteorologists and Air Force brass back in the 1950s did their best to explain away the UFO phenomena with some pretty fancy theories and interpretations of eye-witness accounts. Like anyone in denial, they had some pretty weak arguments, too. Some of the common justifications for their scepticism were weather balloons, helicopters, Venus, whether an evening or morning star, meteors, lenticular clouds, and—a favourite with optometrists and doctors—floaters, or spots before your eyes.

One day some years ago, in the Red Deer Museum, I heard a couple of firsthand accounts that would tax the ingenuity of any sceptic to try to explain. I had joined a group of old-timers who had been invited there to reminisce and tell their stories of pioneer days in central Alberta. There were about eleven of us, and that is what we did for some time. We were all rural people, and I was one of the younger ones.

Eventually, the conversation strayed from the pioneer tales and quite accidentally got onto UFOs. Most of that small group had seen a UFO with their own eyes, and most had a story to tell. I had no means of recording them at the time, but I remember two of the stories well, except perhaps for minor details. Both occurred in central Alberta.

Two farmers had been to town for repairs, and were on their way home. "Where did that granary come from?" asked one of them, as what seemed to be the top of a round, bright, metal structure could be seen in a field beside the road where no building had been when they were going in to town. It was about a quarter-mile ahead and just over a rise. As they approached closer, the structure took off at a tremendous speed, and was out of sight in seconds.

The second story is even more bizarre. The two witnesses, an elderly married couple, retirees from the farm, told the story together. They had been fishing and were driving home on a warm, sunny afternoon. The vehicle's windows were down. Suddenly, an airborne vehicle appeared beside them over the ditch that paralleled the road. It stayed beside them, easily adjusting its speed to theirs. I can't remember dimensions but I have a mental memory of their description: a disc about ten feet across, and four feet deep at the centre. No sign of ports or any occupants. The wife, on the passenger side, grabbed her fishing rod and began to thrust it out the open window in an attempt to touch the strange craft. "Put that down!" yelled her husband, who was driving. She did as she was told. "No telling what might have happened," he said to the group of us. The craft followed them for some miles, then, like the granary, left at high speed, without discernible acceleration time.

It is the unknown aspect of UFOs that is a bit scary. *Homo sapiens* has always been wary, sometimes terrified of the unknown. What are these things? Where are they from? Why are they here? Why is so little reliable information about them available to interested persons? Who is suppressing it? If you hear or read a UFO story, how do you tell a hoax from a true account? Questions to ponder.

EPILOGUE

One is struck by the many skills and fascinations of Fred Schutz. At one moment, he is an historian, capturing the essence of a century, of the settlement of the Blindman River Valley, the coming of the railway, and the growth of Rimbey, Hoadley, and Bluffton. In the next moment, he is a naturalist observing the false nests of marsh wrens in the cattails, or a cowbird laying eggs in another bird's nest, or magpies dying strangely in the wet and cold. Or he might witness the booming of lakes at freeze-up in November, or the sudden settling of snow by an inch or more over a field of thirty acres. Perhaps he marvels at the night flares over Turner Valley during the Depression, or at a fogbow over Edmonton in winter. Or maybe he *smells* the ozone of an electrical storm, the freshness of newly-turned earth, the perfume of a chokecherry bloom, or the lingering stench below a buffalo jump.

Always there is a gentle humanity in Schutz. He delights in a lifelong relationship with niece Lorraine, and weeps when her life ends too soon. He sees a solitary girl ruminating by a river, and communicates with her across their generations. He hears of a young moose hung by the leg on a barbed wire fence, and he cheers its release. He watches a porcupine ravaging his trees, but he won't shoot it. And he decries wolf poison that kills everything in sight, not just wolves.

Appropriately, there is an easy sense of humour in Schutz. He chortles at drunken bumblebees and at calves learning to drink from a pail. He smiles at himself when he falls through the ice and reports the embarrassment, despite a friend's chiding that he would not. And he reinvents a mythical animal whose left legs are shorter than the right, with a cousin with legs of *four different lengths*—the preposterous side hill gouger.

Because his father had an English accent, Fred once said, "I had to learn to read to find out that the word 'Russia' did not end with an r."[1]

For Schutz there is a richness of experience in the simplest of things—a train, a tamarack, a bog orchid, an iron cooking vessel, even a slop bucket. He observes unusually well, and he describes the unusual well—a barbed wire phone, for example, or artist's fungi, or spruce gum, or birch tree syrup. He talks to a pet rock Oscar, and he listens to the strange sounds of night. He lives through hail storms and tornadoes, and he knows the weather history of each month.

He revels in visits beyond home, to other parts of Alberta and the world. He embraces what he sees, he expects joy, and he finds it. His therapy is hilltop sitting, and there he communes with all that is, accepting it, welcoming it. In that relationship he finds the highest conception of himself, the grandest vision of himself. And he finds his own peace.

Elbert Hubbard once pronounced a blessing on his friends, known and unknown, for he did not have to meet a person to be friendly: "Drink in the ozone, bathe in the sunshine, and out in the silent night under the stars, say to yourself again and yet again, 'I am part of all that my eyes behold,' and the feeling will surely come to you that you are no mere interloper between earth and sky, but that you are a necessary particle of the whole."[2]

The message comes naturally from the life of Fred Schutz, too.

David C. Jones
University of Calgary

Fred and Maxine at the Taj Mahal, 1999.

---

[1] Fred Schutz, *The Life and Times of Charlie Schutz* (Rimbey: The Printed Form, 2000), 1.

[2] Elbert Hubbard, *1001 Epigrams* (East Aurora, N.Y.: Roycroft, 1911), 33.

Myrna Pearman

Myrna Pearman was raised on a farm east of the Blindman. She graduated with a BSc in Geography from the University of Alberta in 1979, and has since worked as a house painter, chimney sweep, photographer, writer, naturalist and biologist. She lives on the south shore of Sylvan Lake and has held the biologist's position at Ellis Bird Farm, near Lacombe, since 1987.

In addition to her many outdoor pursuits, Myrna is actively involved with the Red Deer River Naturalists and the North American Bluebird Society.

Myrna received the Loran L. Goulden Memorial Award from the Federation of Alberta Naturalists, and a Nature Educator of the Year Award from the Roger Tory Peterson Institute of Natural History in 1992. She also received an award in 1996 from the North American Bluebird Society, in recognition of her work in bluebird conservation. She has written several books: *Winter Bird Feeding: An Alberta Guide; Nestboxes for Prairie Birds; NatureScape Alberta: Creating and Caring for Wildlife Habitat at Home;* and *Mountain Bluebird Trail Monitoring Guide.*

David C. Jones

David C. Jones is a Professor of History in the Faculty of Education at the University of Calgary. After seven years as a high school Social Studies and English teacher (1966-1974), he was appointed to the University of Calgary in 1977. He has written or edited twenty-six books, including the award-winning *Empire of Dust: Settling and Abandoning the Prairie Dry Belt* (1987, 2002) and *Feasting on Misfortune: Journeys of the Human Spirit in Alberta's Past* (1998). Concerning teaching, he has edited *The Spirit of Teaching Excellence* (1995), *Sayings for Teachers* (1997) and *Sayings for Mentors and Tutors* (2001). His writing, speaking and leadership skills have been singled out for recognition many times. In 2000, he received the President's Circle Award for Teaching Excellence at the University of Calgary.

William Peter Baergen

William Peter Baergen was raised on farms at Irma and Vauxhall, Alberta. After graduate degrees in education and history at the University of Alberta, Bill earned a PhD at the University of Oregon in 1982. He has taught history and English at the high school and college levels, and has administrative experience as a principal in Whitecourt, superintendent in Stettler, board chairman of the Clearview School Division, and president of the Central Alberta Historical Society. In addition to many letters to editors, Bill has written curriculum for Alberta Education, and one book, *The Ku Klux Klan in Central Alberta* (2000). In 2003, he received an Annual Award from the Historical Society of Alberta for his outstanding contribution to Alberta history. He is one of seven commissioners for the Alberta Human Rights and Citizenship Commission.

Index

Abandoned house 121 (photo)
Abies balsamea 176
Abies lasiocarpa 176-7
Abilene, Texas 107
Abominable Snowman 265
Adams, Mr. and Mrs. Peat 29-30
Adams, Dave 29-30
Adamson, Miss Bertha 43
Adamson, J. 43
Aden 150
Africa 242, 278, 319-20
AGT 92
Air Force, and UFOs 328
Alaska 203, 221, Brown Bear 204-6,
  snow 279
Alberta, archaeology 35, artifacts
  137, bird protection 217, black
  widow 189, Cadomin cave 145,
  caribou 258, chinook arch 285,
  cuckoo 188, dinosaurs 146-7, 207,
  dried-out south 63, elk 259, ferries
  104, flying squirrel 253, first look
  at 25, frost 300, fungi 169,
  geological sites 150, Gypsies 134,
  homestead 8, Indians 323, jumping spiders 190, magpies 226,
  1924 map 153, mild Christmas
  274, monarch butterfly 186,
  mushrooms 160, mustang 228,
  official gemstone 295-6, oil capital
  157, oldest living thing 166,

parkland 321, porcupine 236, pre-
  history 45, 154, provincial tree 165,
  rabbits 262, seniors' care 3, Stone
  Age 138, tent caterpillars 187,
  tree frogs 262, UFOs 328, visited
  by Fred 331, whoopers 223, 225,
  wild roses 161-2, wild sweet
  clover, 308, wolverine 203-4,
  wooded sections 72
Alberta Archaeological Society 153
Alberta Farm Journal 67
Alberta Federation of Rock Clubs
  294
Alberta Fish and Wildlife 241
Alberta Forestry Association 179
Alberta government 103
Alberta Pacific Grain Elevator 102
Alberta Pacific Pulp Mill 325
Alberta Place Names 124
Alberta, Province of, Golden Jubilee
  29
Alberta Provincial Museum 207
Alberta Provincial Police 180
Alberta Trees of Renown—*An*
  Honour Roll of Alberta Trees 179
Alder Flats 42, 307, name 126
Aldrich, Audrey 50
Aldrich, Elton 50
Aldrich, Lee 50
Aleutian Islands 50
Alhambra 307

337

338

341

343

Ponoka County 140
Porcupine Hills 151, 179, 206, 306
    (photo), 326
Porcupine-Hilton 239
Portland 68
Potts, Jerry 326
Powell, Henry 42-4
Prairies 15
Pre-mechanized farming 75
Premier Bennett 106
Presbyterian 52
Prime Minister of Canada 327
Prince Albert 25
Prince Albert Museum 206
Prince George 152
Prince of Wales Hotel 326
Prince Rupert 3, 16
Proctor and Gamble 228
Proved up 58
Provost 179
Psikla, Ernie 248
Puffer, W.F. 30
Pukak 280

Qali 279
Qamaniq 279
Quebec 59
Queen's University 52

Rapid City, Manitoba 4, 6
RCMP 22, 24, 43
Reading, England 319
Reber, Mrs. 25
Red Deer xix, 92, 152, 173, 202, 262,
    284, 289
Red Deer author 217
Red Deer Museum 328
Red Deer River 103, 146, 207, 296
    315
Red Deer River Badlands 146, 293, 296
Red Deer River Naturalists xx, 207,
    311, 319
Red Deer River valley 262, 295

Red River carts 76, 265
Red Rock Canyon 294, 326
Red Rock Coulee 149
Red Rock Park 150 (photo)
"Redwing" 107
Reynolds, Jim 25-6
Richardson, Clark 128
Richardson's ground squirrel 253-4
Ricinus, name 126, 204
Riel Rebellion 25
Riley, life of 233
Rimbey xvii-xviii, xxi, 12-13, 18, 29,
    39, 43, 45, 54, 59-60, 90-1, 96-9,
    107,129, 131, 134-5, 137, 142,
    149, 157, 176, 188-9, 204, 208,
    224-6, 258, 284, 289-90, 307, 320,
    327, 330
Rimbey Anglican Church xix
Rimbey Auxiliary Hospital 3-4
Rimbey Cemetery 42
Rimbey district xxi
Rimbey elevators 133
Rimbey Fire Department 17
Rimbey Gas Plant 307
Rimbey Historical Society xix, 35
Rimbey museum xix
Rimbey Record, The ix, xviii-xix, 29,
    46, 91, 149
Rimbey Review, The xxi, Jubilee 124
Rimbey Rockhounds xxi, 269
Rimbey, Sam, Ben, Jim, nephew
    Oscar, name 124
Rio Grande 107
Riverside S.D. #1735 129
Rocky Canoe Club 311
Rocky Mountain Chain 152
Rocky Mountain Gouger 266
Rockies xx, 285, 325
Rocky Mountain House 24, 49, 106,
    137, 139, 173, 204, 206, 274,
    311,312
Rocky Mountain House Mountaineer,
    The xix, 24

347

Six-hundred-dollar men 63
Ski Hill 323
Slate Mountain, Ontario 1
Smallboy's camp 320
Smith, Bill 15
Smith, Charlie 38
Smith, Hon. Vernor Winfield 126
Snake Lake 126
Snyder, Alton 43
Soldier Settlement Board 19
Sons of the Pioneers 107
Soper, Dr. Dewey 253
South American 237
Southampton 7
South Dakota 145
South Saskatchewan 103
Spalding, Dave 207
Spanish-American War 43, 89
Spanish Missions 139
Spike pitcher 117
Spitzbergen, Norway 301
Springdale, name 125
Spruham, George 20
Stampede Grounds, Calgary 52
Stankewich, Lyn 324
Starr, Ringo 54
Steele, Sam, of the Mounted 105
Steeves, Alvin 128
Steeves, David 140
Steeves, Ila 50
Stephanie 190
Stettler 152, 327
Steveville 103
St. John's Boys' School 268
Stockdale maple 179
Stockholm cream separator 77
Stock market crash 61
Stone Age 293
Stoney Indians 126, 289, reserve 294
St. Patrick's Day 285-6
St. Paul-Minneapolis Winter
  Carnival 9
St. Paul, Nebraska 28

Strain, Cheryl 47
Strain, Harry 44-8, 75-6, 128, 140,
  179, 185, 254-5
Strain, Marge 186
Strawberry, John 138
Strawberry Lake 250 (photo)
"The Strawberry Roan" 108
Stuart, Daisy 149
Stuart, Darrel 149
Suffield 151-2
"Sundance River" 125
Sunday, work 117
Sundre 106, 108
Sunset Hill 323
Swan Lake 126, 320
Swede saw 176
Sweden 77
Swedish axes 71
Sweetgrass, Montana 150
Sweetgrass Hills 149-151
Sylvan Lake, name 126, 219, 322-3
Sylvester (Syllie), the Cat 32-4
Sylvilagus nuttali 262

Taber 189
Texaco 326
Texas 107, 223, 225, Longhorns 89, -
  style storm 316
Theede, Orville 83 (photo)
"The Old Woman's Buffalo jump" 154
Thompson, David 126, 289, 312
Thoreau, Henry David 227
Three Hills 314
Toonerville Trolley, The 12, 101
Township Forty-four 20-1
Township Forty-five 289
"Tree-in-the-road" 179
"Trail of the Lonesome Pine" 107
Tributaries to the Blindman 29, 38,
  284
Trochu xvi, 1, 3, 5, 60, 186, 314
Trudeau, Pierre Elliot 106
Turner Valley 156-8, 326, 330